MY HERO ACADEMIA TEAM-UP MISSIONS 3

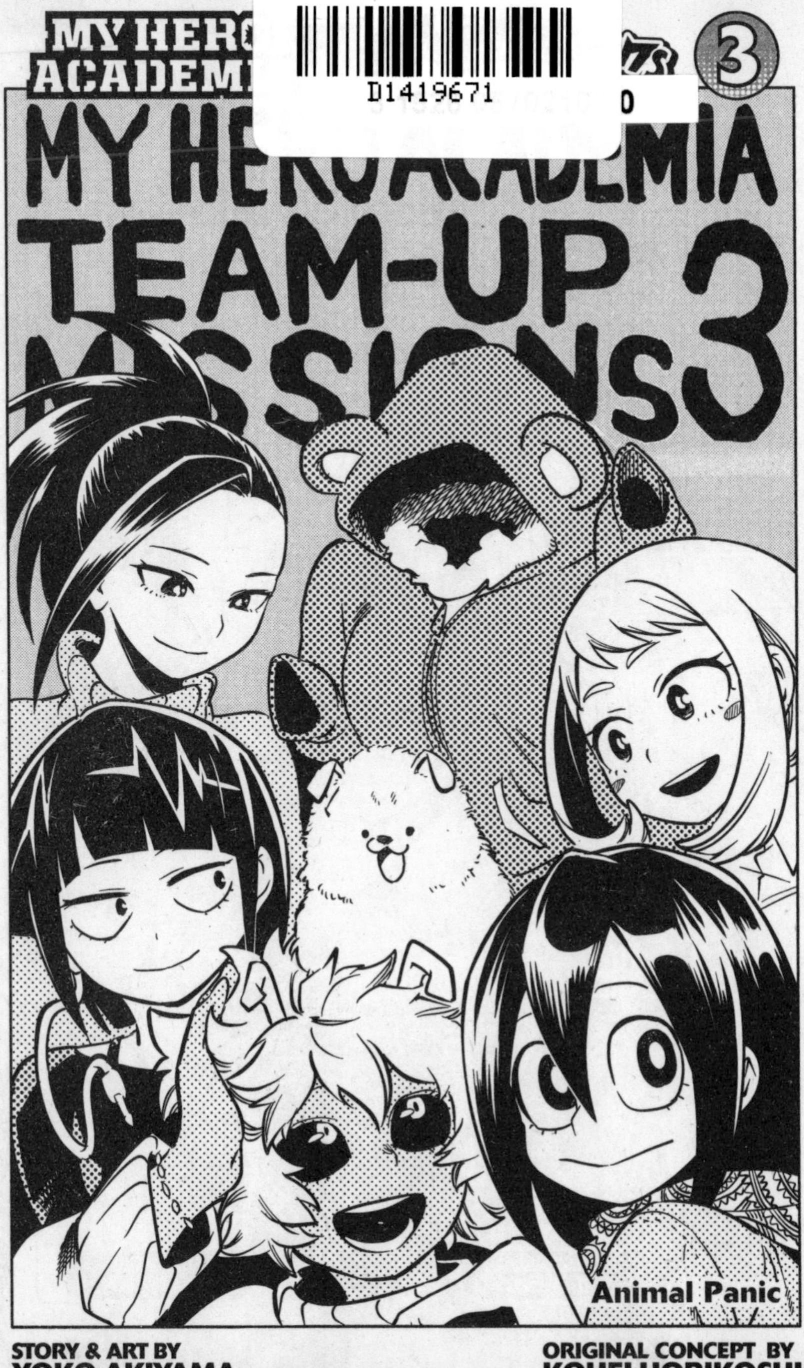

Animal Panic

STORY & ART BY
YOKO AKIYAMA

ORIGINAL CONCEPT BY
KOHEI HORIKOSHI

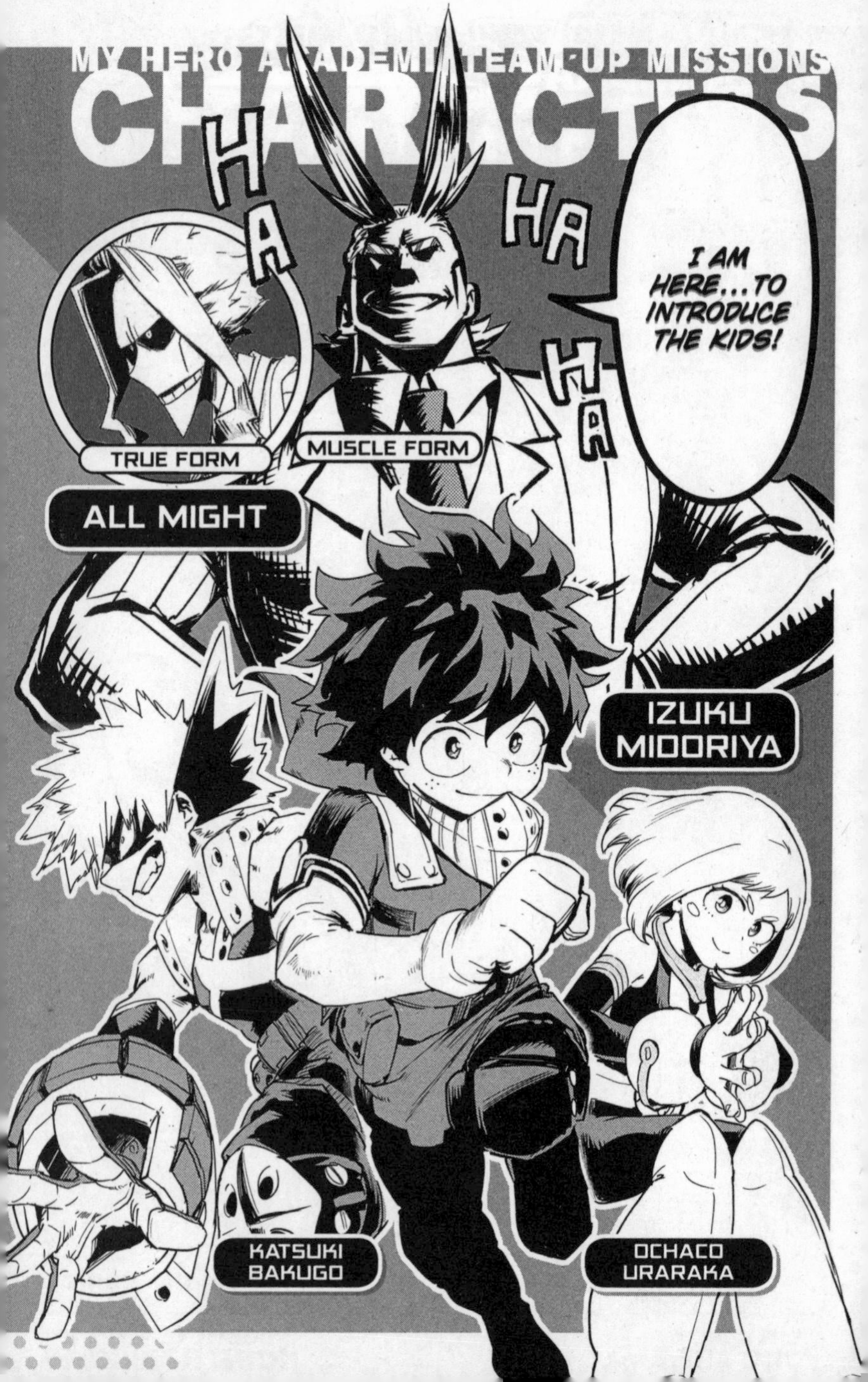
MY HERO ACADEMIA TEAM-UP MISSIONS
CHARACTERS
I AM HERE...TO INTRODUCE THE KIDS!
HA HA HA HA HA
MUSCLE FORM
TRUE FORM
ALL MIGHT
IZUKU MIDORIYA
OCHACO URARAKA
KATSUKI BAKUGO

STORY

MY HERO ACADEMIA

One day, people began manifesting special abilities that came to be known as "Quirks," and before long, the world was full of superpowered humans. The world then saw an uptick in crime, perpetrated by villains armed with new abilities. Heroes emerged to protect society and are now officially authorized to fight crime in the name of peace.

WHAT'S A TEAM-UP MISSION?

For many years, All Might was known as "the Symbol of Peace," and his mere presence was enough to deter crime. With his retirement from public duty, people are clamoring for the next generation of heroes to rise up, which has led to the creation of a new program—centered around hero students—called Team-Up Missions. By pairing schools all over the country with pro heroes, these heroes in training get a chance to improve their teamwork!

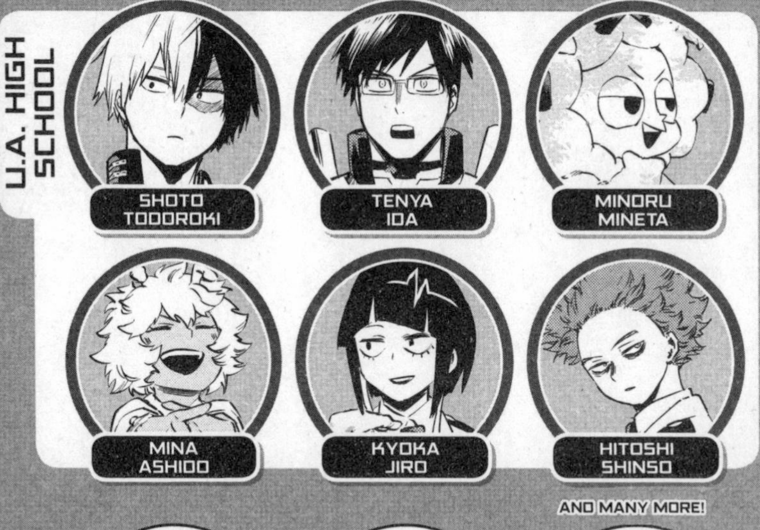
U.A. HIGH SCHOOL
SHOTO TODOROKI
TENYA IDA
MINORU MINETA
MINA ASHIDO
KYOKA JIRO
HITOSHI SHINSO

AND MANY MORE!

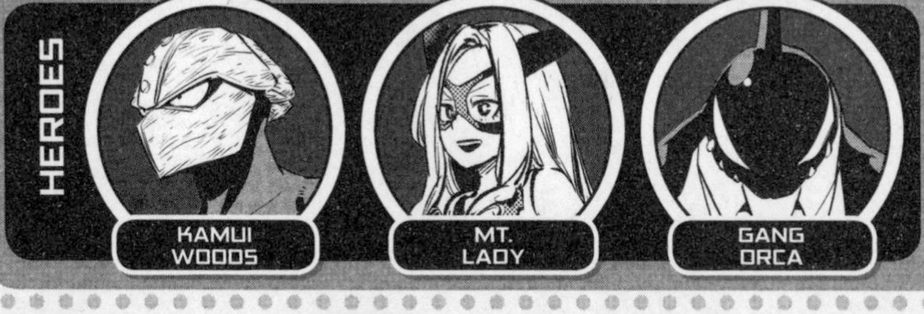
HEROES
KAMUI WOODS
MT. LADY
GANG ORCA

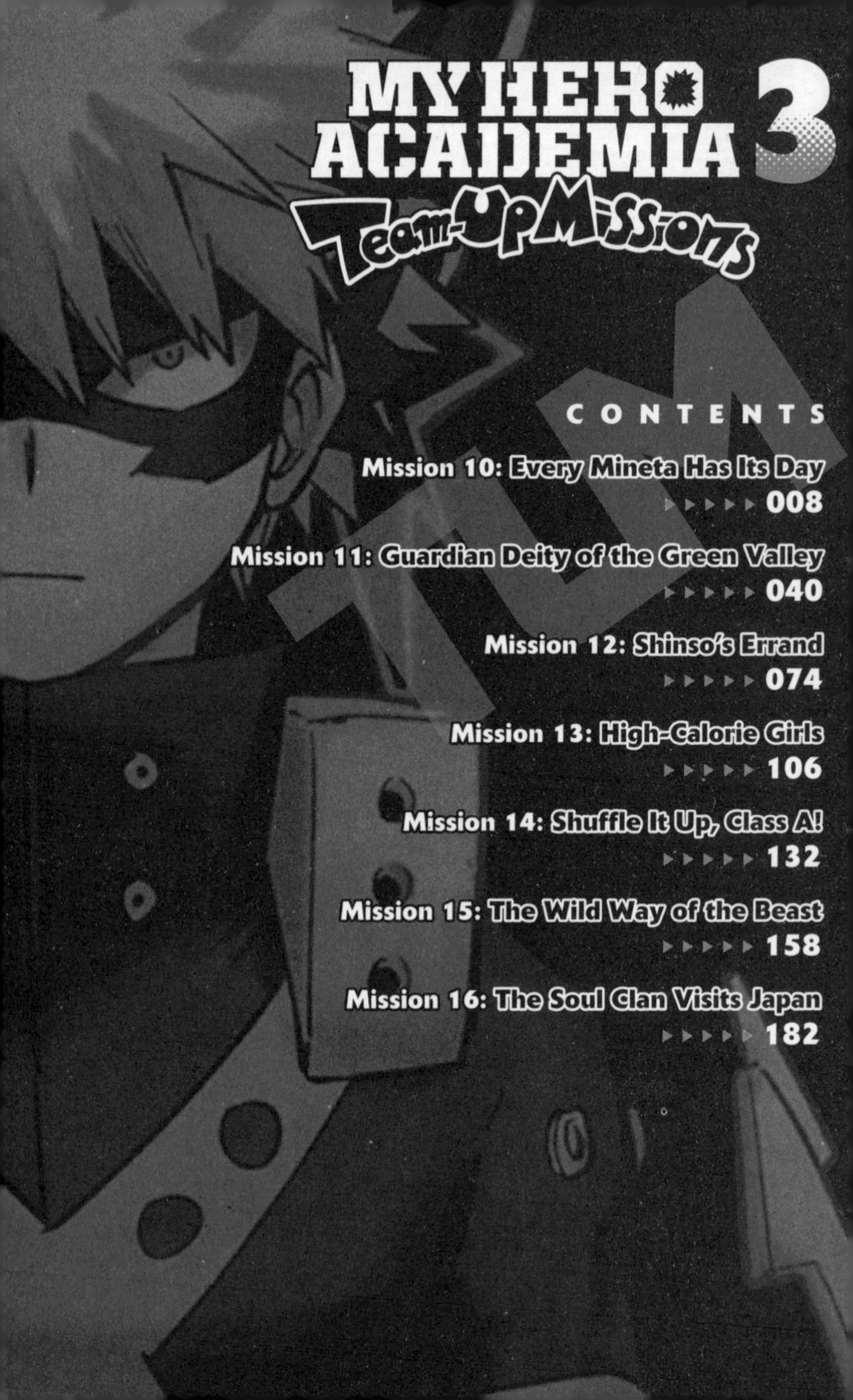

MY HERO ACADEMIA 3
Team-Up Missions

CONTENTS

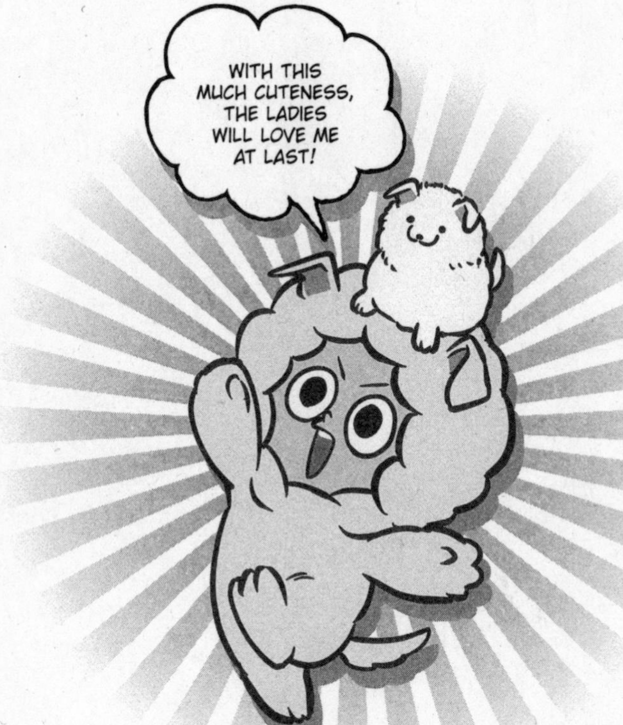
WITH THIS MUCH CUTENESS, THE LADIES WILL LOVE ME AT LAST!

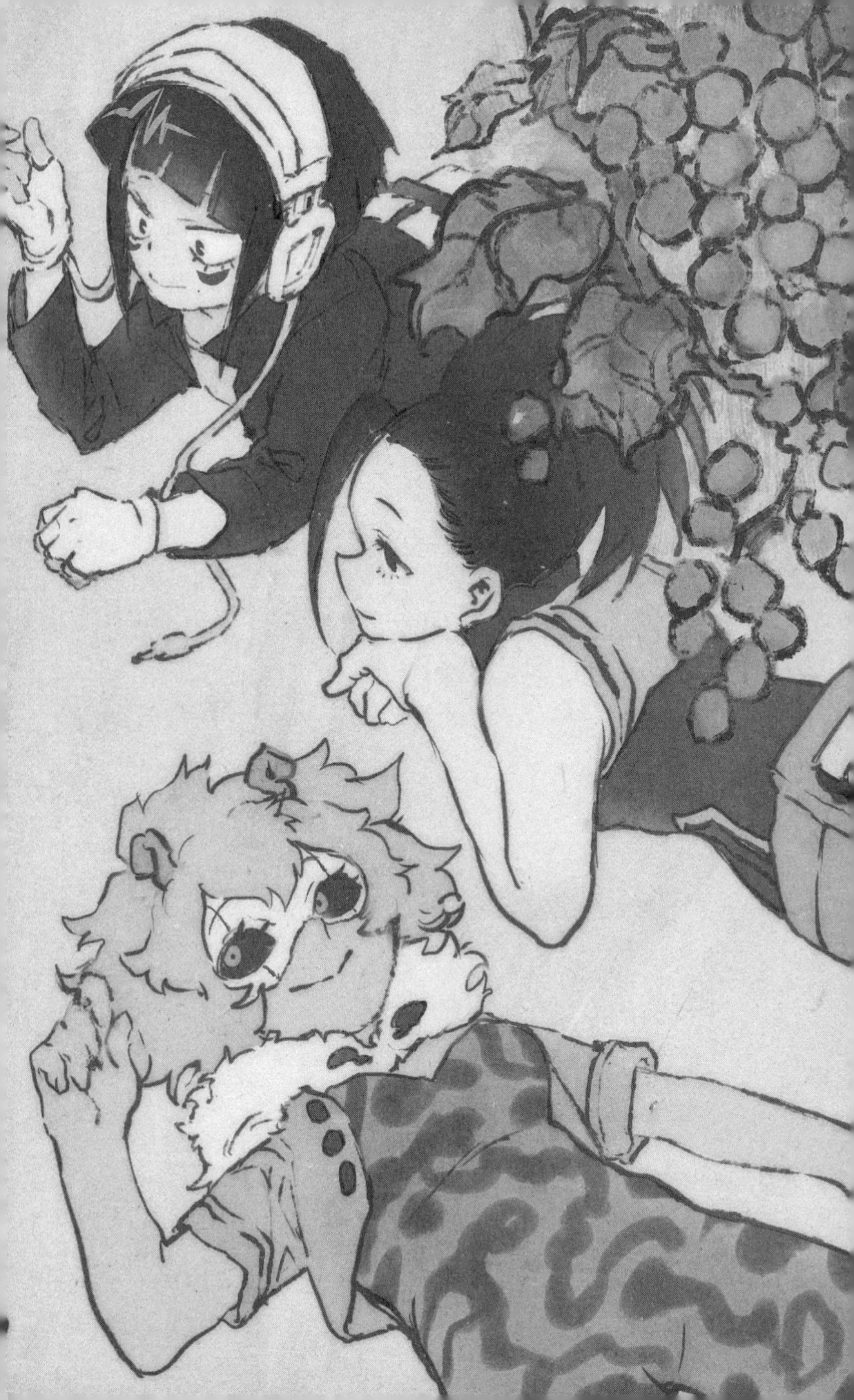

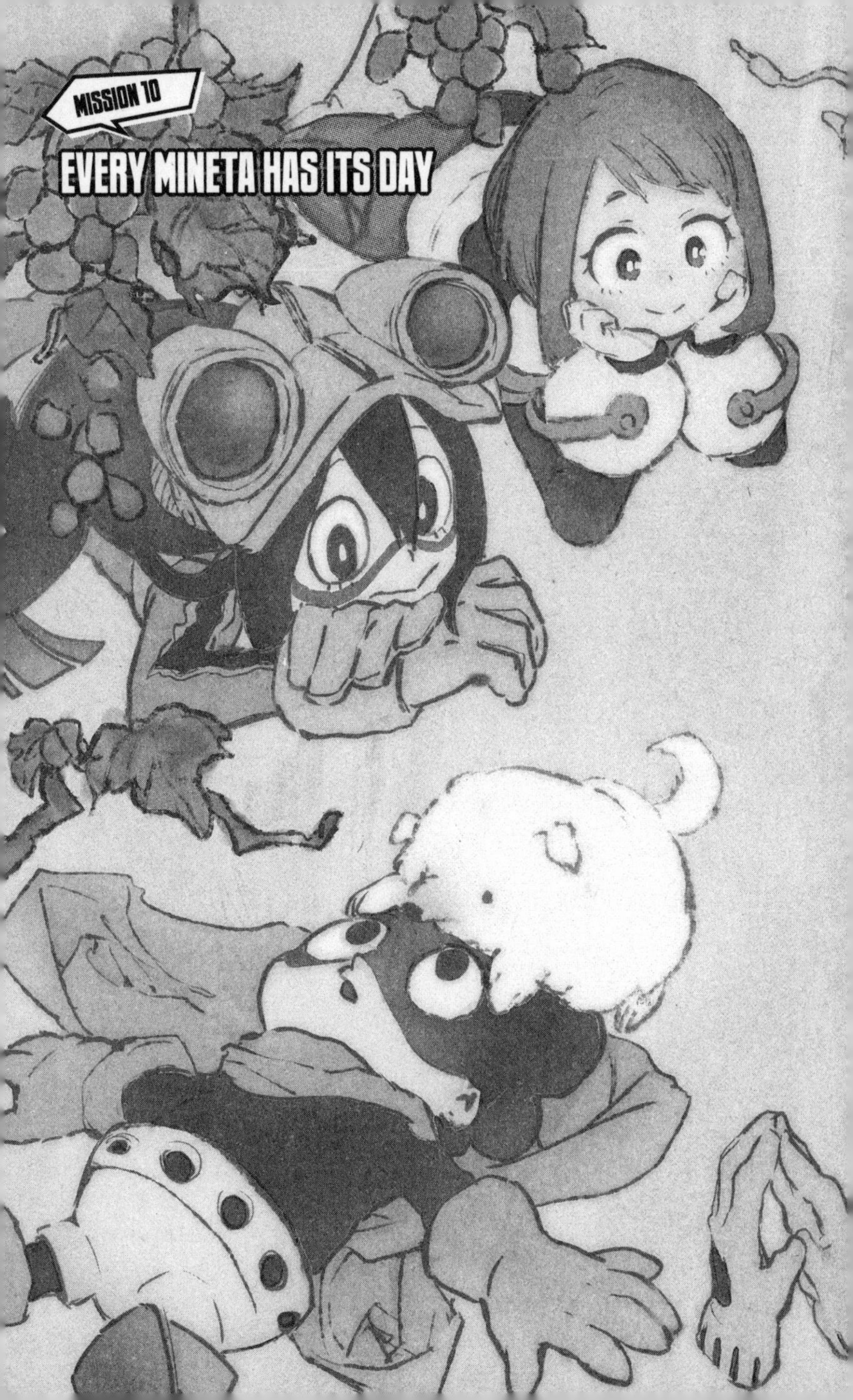
MISSION 10
EVERY MINETA HAS ITS DAY

MY HERO ACADEMIA
Team-Up Missions

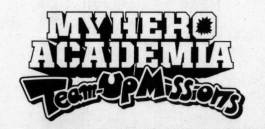

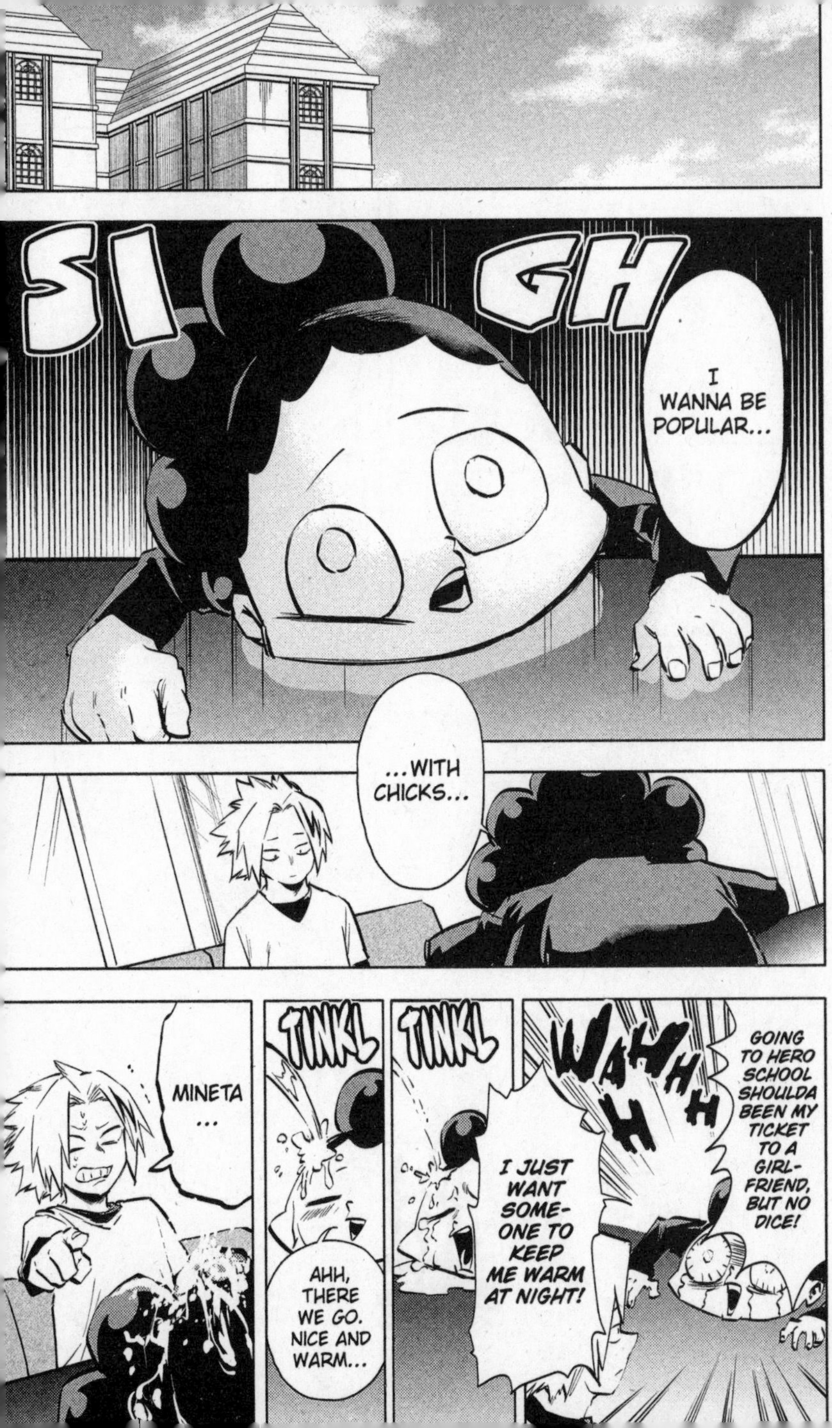
SIGH
I WANNA BE POPULAR...
...WITH CHICKS...
WAHHHH
GOING TO HERO SCHOOL SHOULDA BEEN MY TICKET TO A GIRLFRIEND, BUT NO DICE!
I JUST WANT SOMEONE TO KEEP ME WARM AT NIGHT!
TINKL
TINKL
AHH, THERE WE GO. NICE AND WARM...
MINETA...

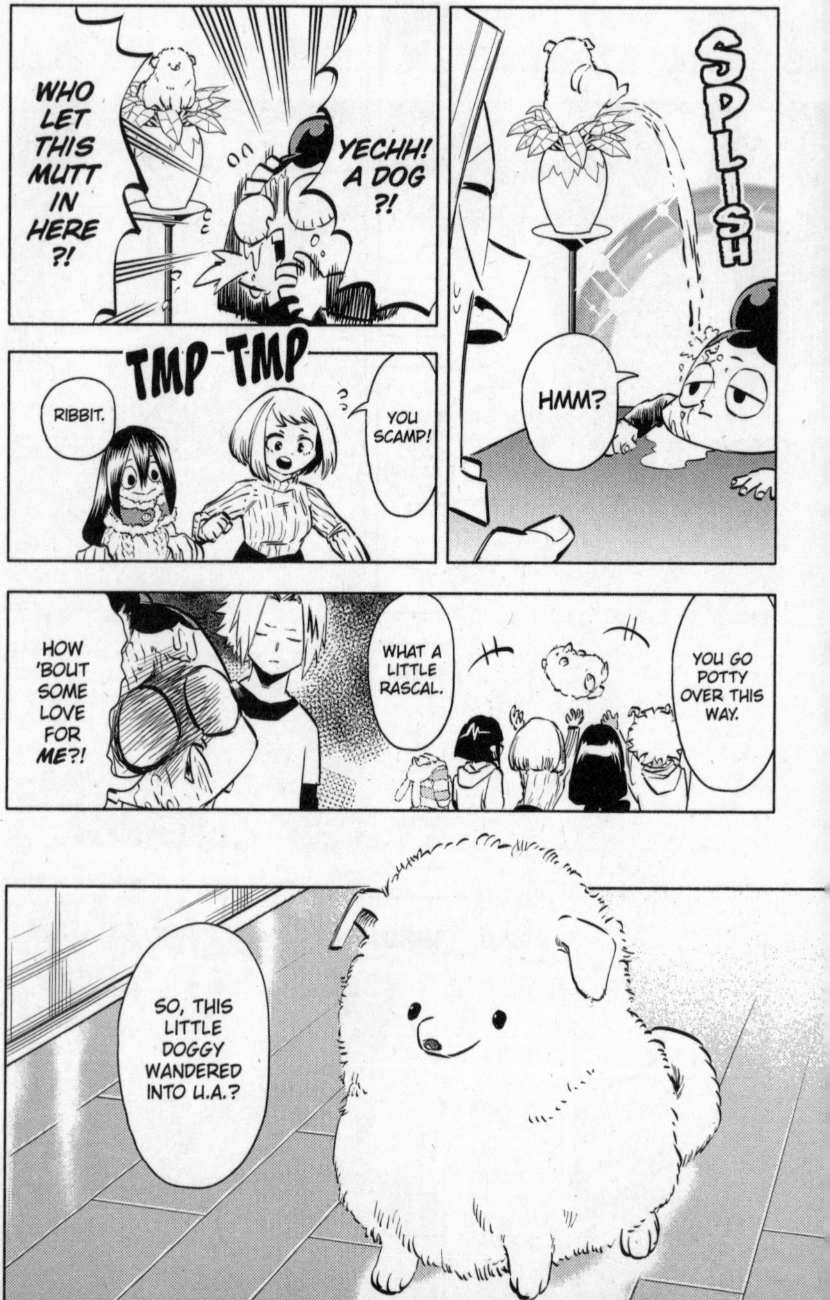
SPLISH
HMM?
YECHH! A DOG?!
WHO LET THIS MUTT IN HERE?!
TMP TMP
YOU SCAMP!
RIBBIT.
YOU GO POTTY OVER THIS WAY.
WHAT A LITTLE RASCAL.
HOW 'BOUT SOME LOVE FOR ME?!
SO, THIS LITTLE DOGGY WANDERED INTO U.A.?

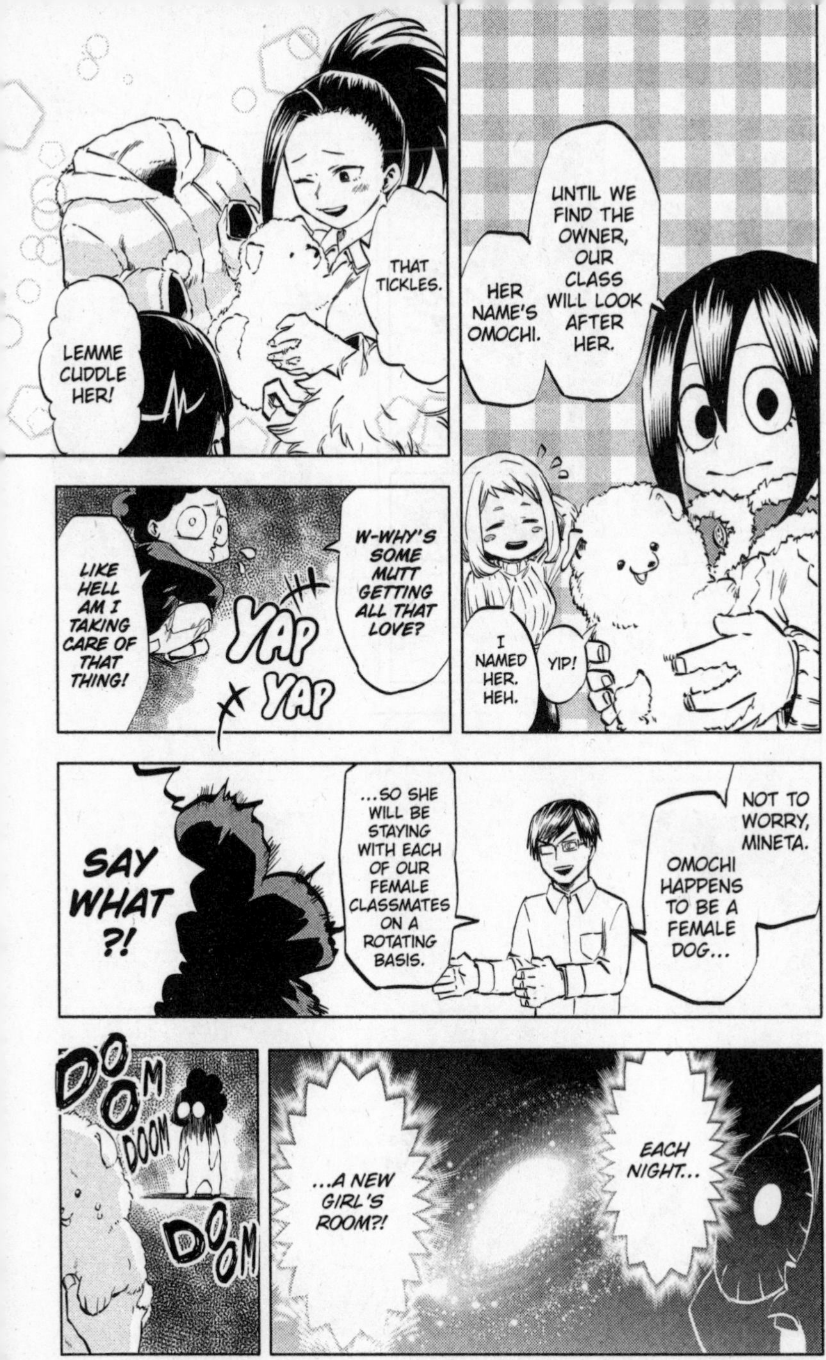
UNTIL WE FIND THE OWNER, OUR CLASS WILL LOOK AFTER HER.
HER NAME'S OMOCHI.
I NAMED HER. HEH.
YIP!
THAT TICKLES.
LEMME CUDDLE HER!
W-WHY'S SOME MUTT GETTING ALL THAT LOVE?
YAP YAP
LIKE HELL AM I TAKING CARE OF THAT THING!
NOT TO WORRY, MINETA.
OMOCHI HAPPENS TO BE A FEMALE DOG…
…SO SHE WILL BE STAYING WITH EACH OF OUR FEMALE CLASSMATES ON A ROTATING BASIS.
SAY WHAT?!
EACH NIGHT…
…A NEW GIRL'S ROOM?!
DOOM DOOM DOOM DOOM

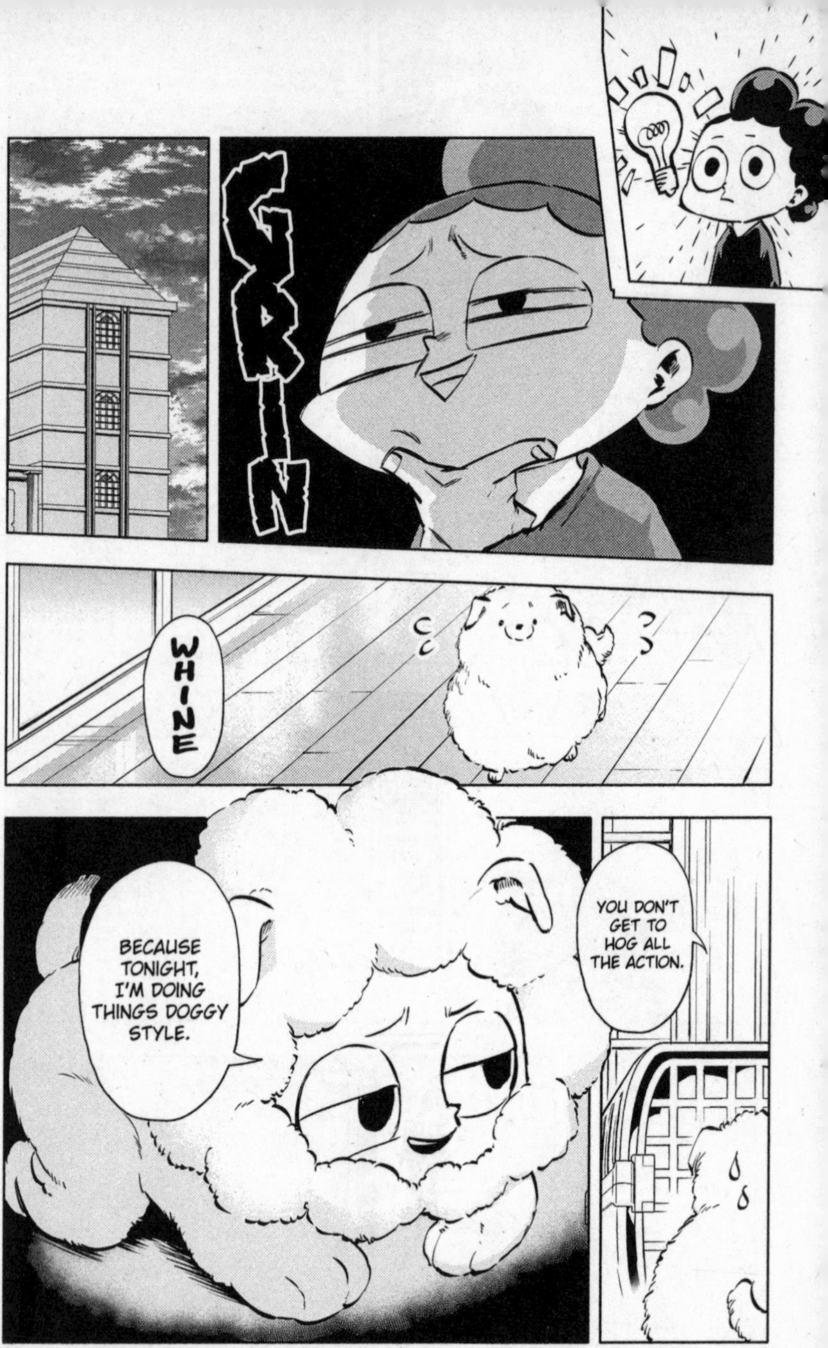
GRIN
WHINE
YOU DON'T GET TO HOG ALL THE ACTION.
BECAUSE TONIGHT, I'M DOING THINGS DOGGY STYLE.

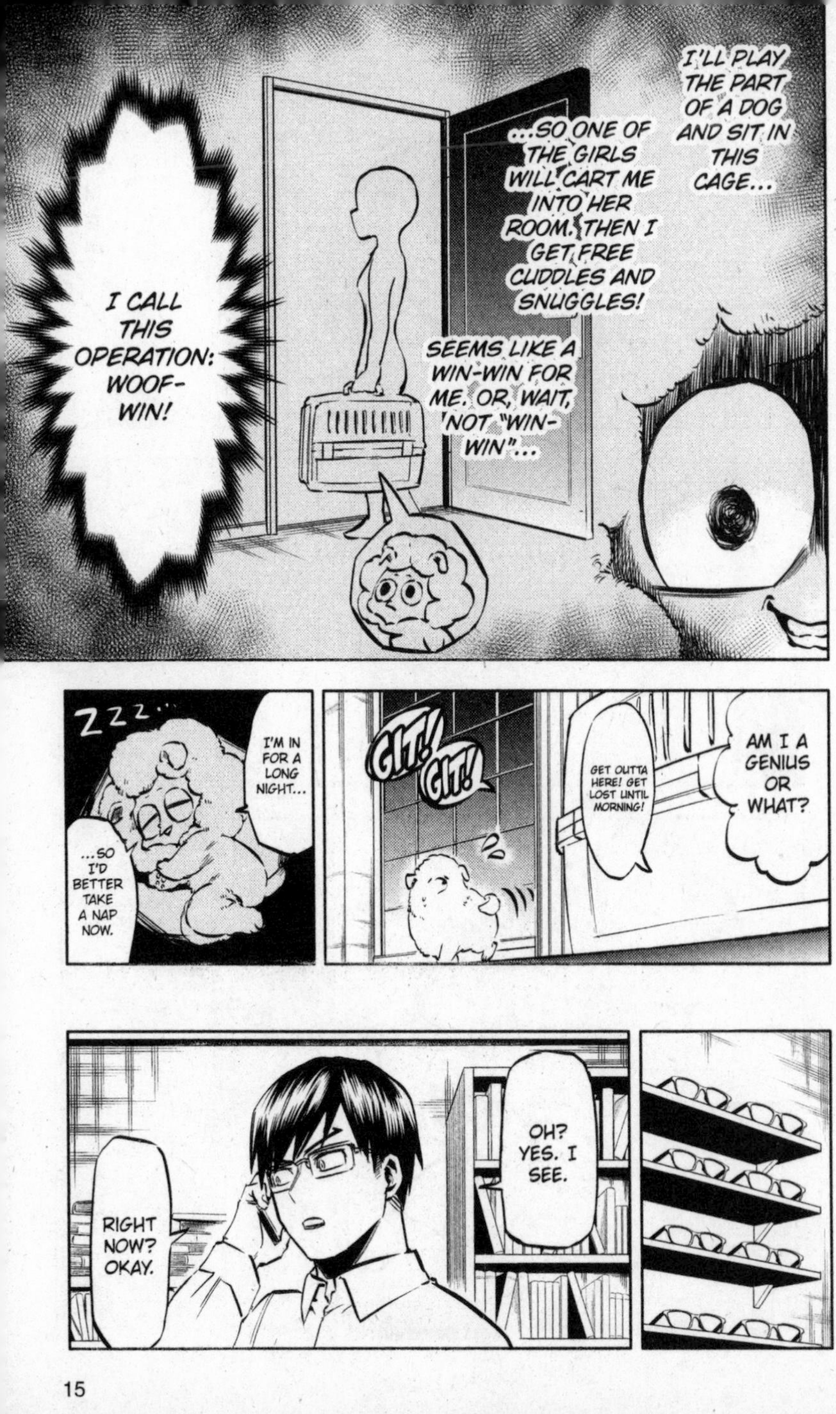
I'LL PLAY THE PART OF A DOG AND SIT IN THIS CAGE...
...SO ONE OF THE GIRLS WILL CART ME INTO HER ROOM. THEN I GET FREE CUDDLES AND SNUGGLES!
SEEMS LIKE A WIN-WIN FOR ME. OR, WAIT, NOT "WIN-WIN"...
I CALL THIS OPERATION: WOOF-WIN!
AM I A GENIUS OR WHAT?
GET OUTTA HERE! GET LOST UNTIL MORNING!
GIT! GIT!
I'M IN FOR A LONG NIGHT...
ZZZ...
...SO I'D BETTER TAKE A NAP NOW.
OH? YES. I SEE.
RIGHT NOW? OKAY.

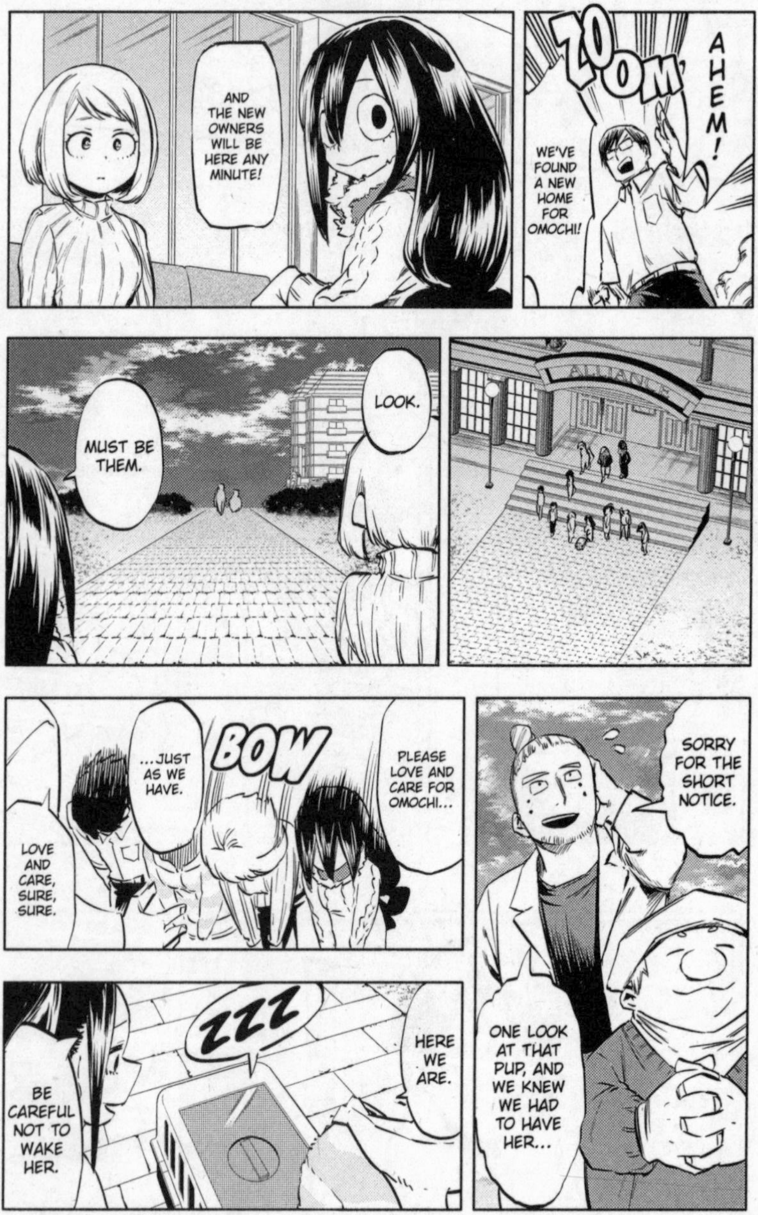
ZOOM
AHEM!
WE'VE FOUND A NEW HOME FOR OMOCHI!
AND THE NEW OWNERS WILL BE HERE ANY MINUTE!
LOOK.
MUST BE THEM.
SORRY FOR THE SHORT NOTICE.
ONE LOOK AT THAT PUP, AND WE KNEW WE HAD TO HAVE HER...
PLEASE LOVE AND CARE FOR OMOCHI...
BOW
...JUST AS WE HAVE.
LOVE AND CARE, SURE, SURE.
HERE WE ARE.
ZZZ
BE CAREFUL NOT TO WAKE HER.

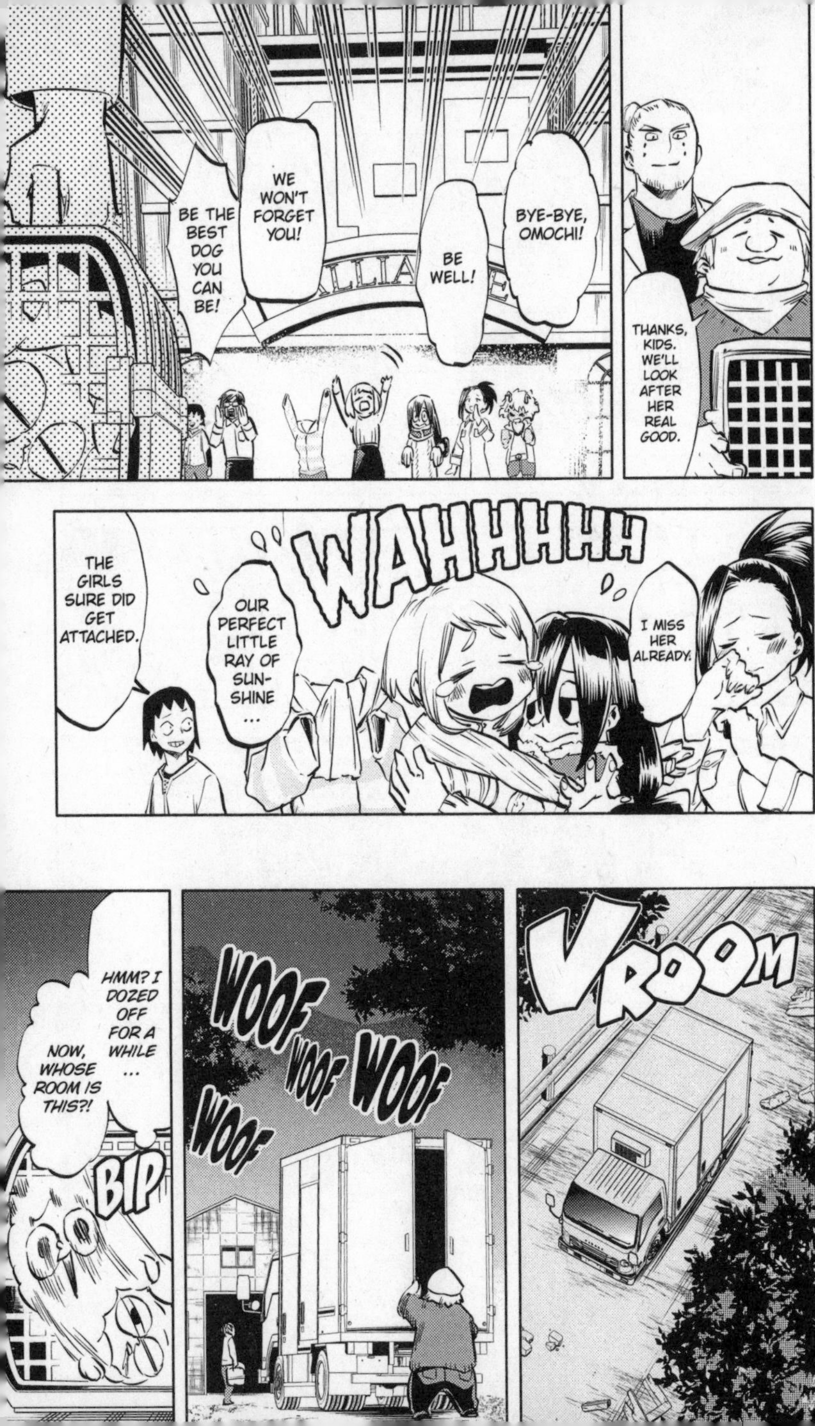
THANKS, KIDS. WE'LL LOOK AFTER HER REAL GOOD.
BYE-BYE, OMOCHI!
BE WELL!
WE WON'T FORGET YOU!
BE THE BEST DOG YOU CAN BE!
WAHHHHH
I MISS HER ALREADY.
OUR PERFECT LITTLE RAY OF SUN-SHINE ...
THE GIRLS SURE DID GET ATTACHED.
VROOM
WOOF WOOF WOOF WOOF
HMM? I DOZED OFF FOR A WHILE ...
NOW, WHOSE ROOM IS THIS?!
BIP

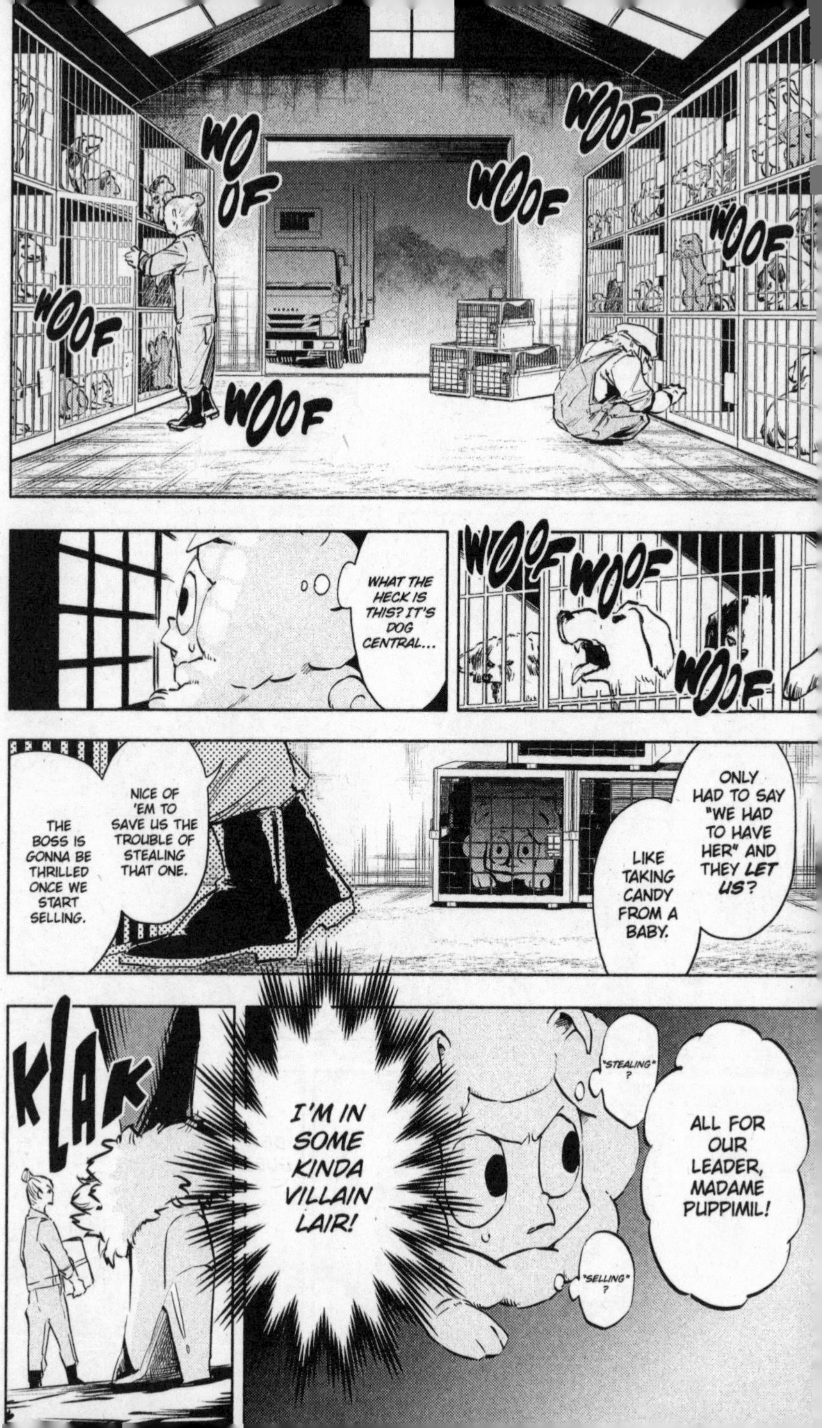
WOOF
WOOF
WOOF
WOOF
WOOF
WOOF
WOOF
WOOF
WOOF
WHAT THE HECK IS THIS? IT'S DOG CENTRAL...
ONLY HAD TO SAY "WE HAD TO HAVE HER" AND THEY *LET US*?
LIKE TAKING CANDY FROM A BABY.
NICE OF 'EM TO SAVE US THE TROUBLE OF STEALING THAT ONE.
THE BOSS IS GONNA BE THRILLED ONCE WE START SELLING.
ALL FOR OUR LEADER, MADAME PUPPIMIL!
"STEALING"?
"SELLING"?
I'M IN SOME KINDA VILLAIN LAIR!
KLAK

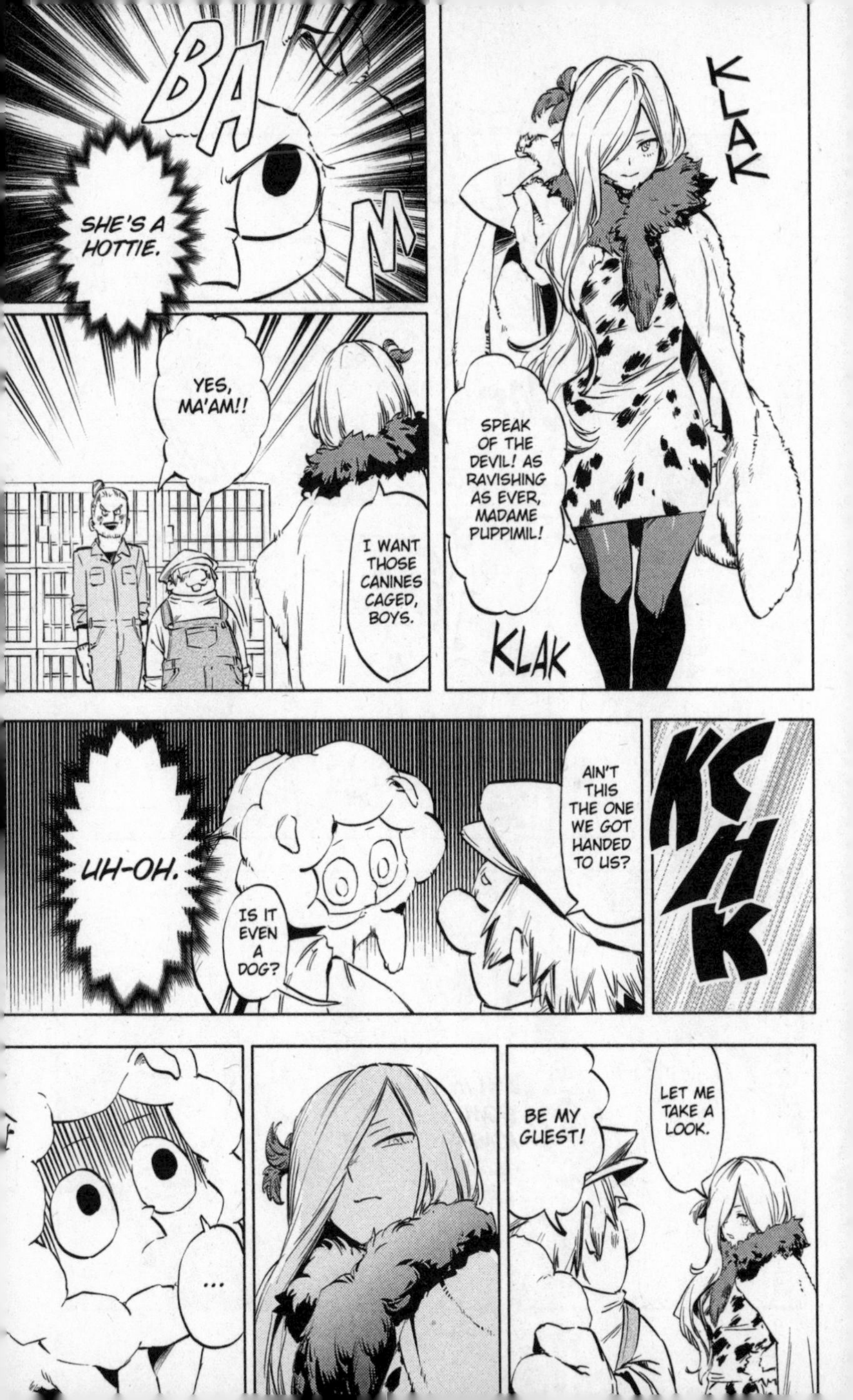
KLAK
SPEAK OF THE DEVIL! AS RAVISHING AS EVER, MADAME PUPPIMIL!
KLAK
BAM
SHE'S A HOTTIE.
I WANT THOSE CANINES CAGED, BOYS.
YES, MA'AM!!
KCHAK
AIN'T THIS THE ONE WE GOT HANDED TO US?
IS IT EVEN A DOG?
UH-OH.
LET ME TAKE A LOOK.
BE MY GUEST!
...

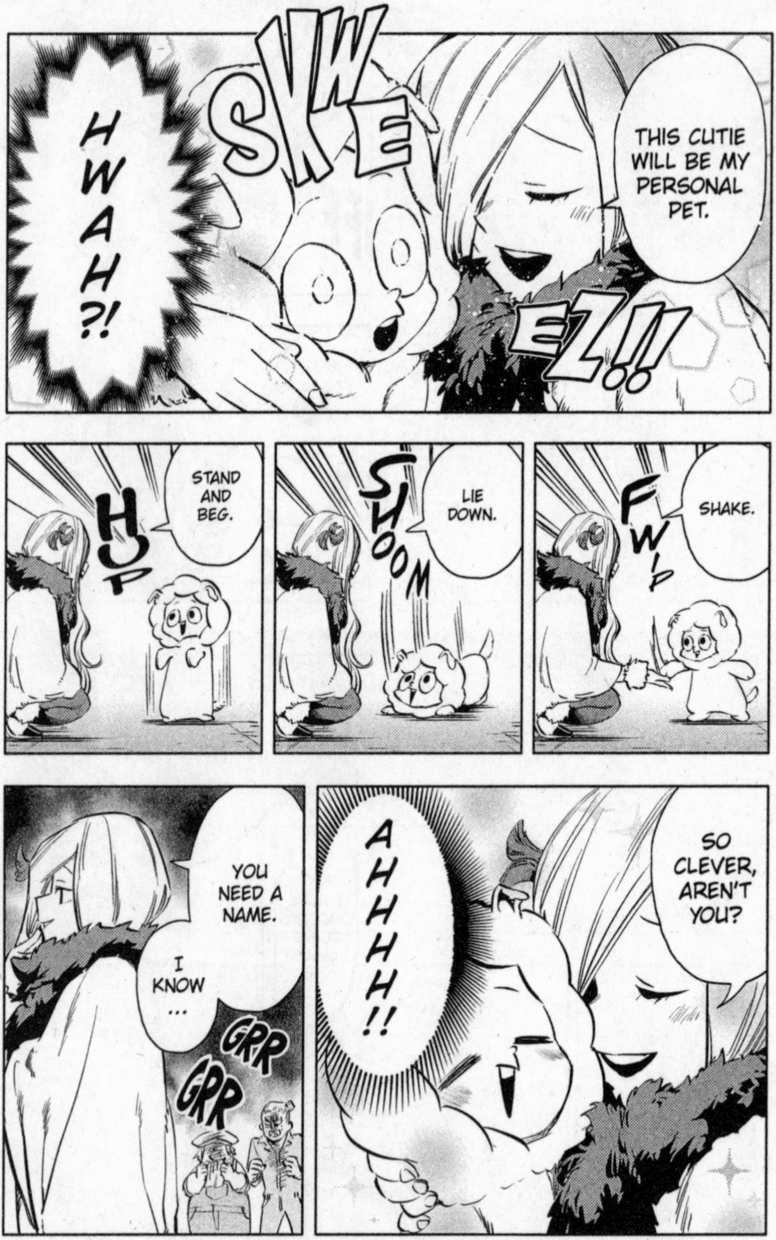
THIS CUTIE WILL BE MY PERSONAL PET.
SKWE EZ!!
HWAH?!
SHAKE.
FWIP
LIE DOWN.
SHOOM
STAND AND BEG.
HUP
SO CLEVER, AREN'T YOU?
AHHHH!!
YOU NEED A NAME.
I KNOW...
GRR
GRR

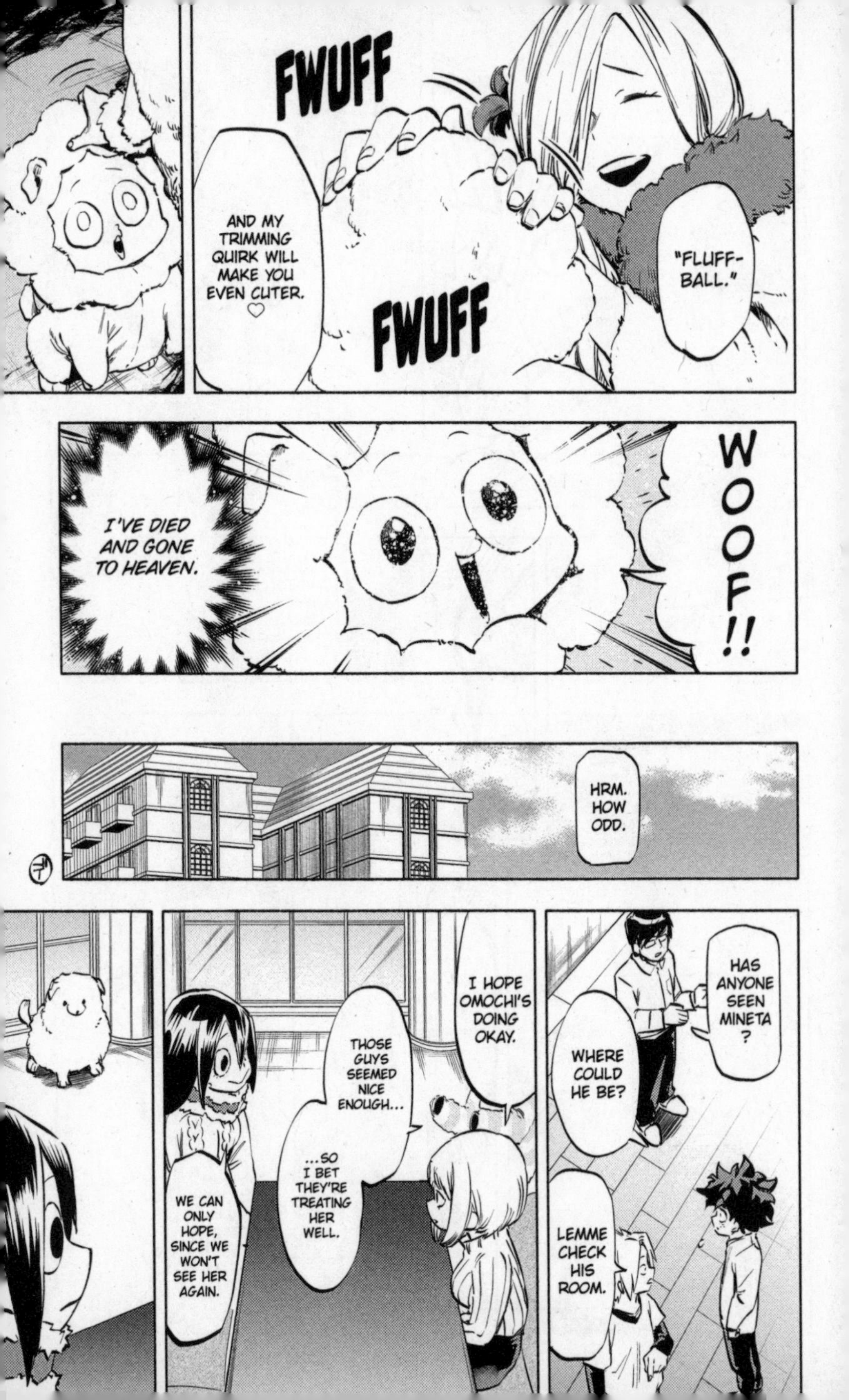
"FLUFF-BALL."
FWUFF
FWUFF
AND MY TRIMMING QUIRK WILL MAKE YOU EVEN CUTER. ♡
WOOF!!
I'VE DIED AND GONE TO HEAVEN.
HRM. HOW ODD.
HAS ANYONE SEEN MINETA?
WHERE COULD HE BE?
LEMME CHECK HIS ROOM.
I HOPE OMOCHI'S DOING OKAY.
THOSE GUYS SEEMED NICE ENOUGH...
...SO I BET THEY'RE TREATING HER WELL.
WE CAN ONLY HOPE, SINCE WE WON'T SEE HER AGAIN.

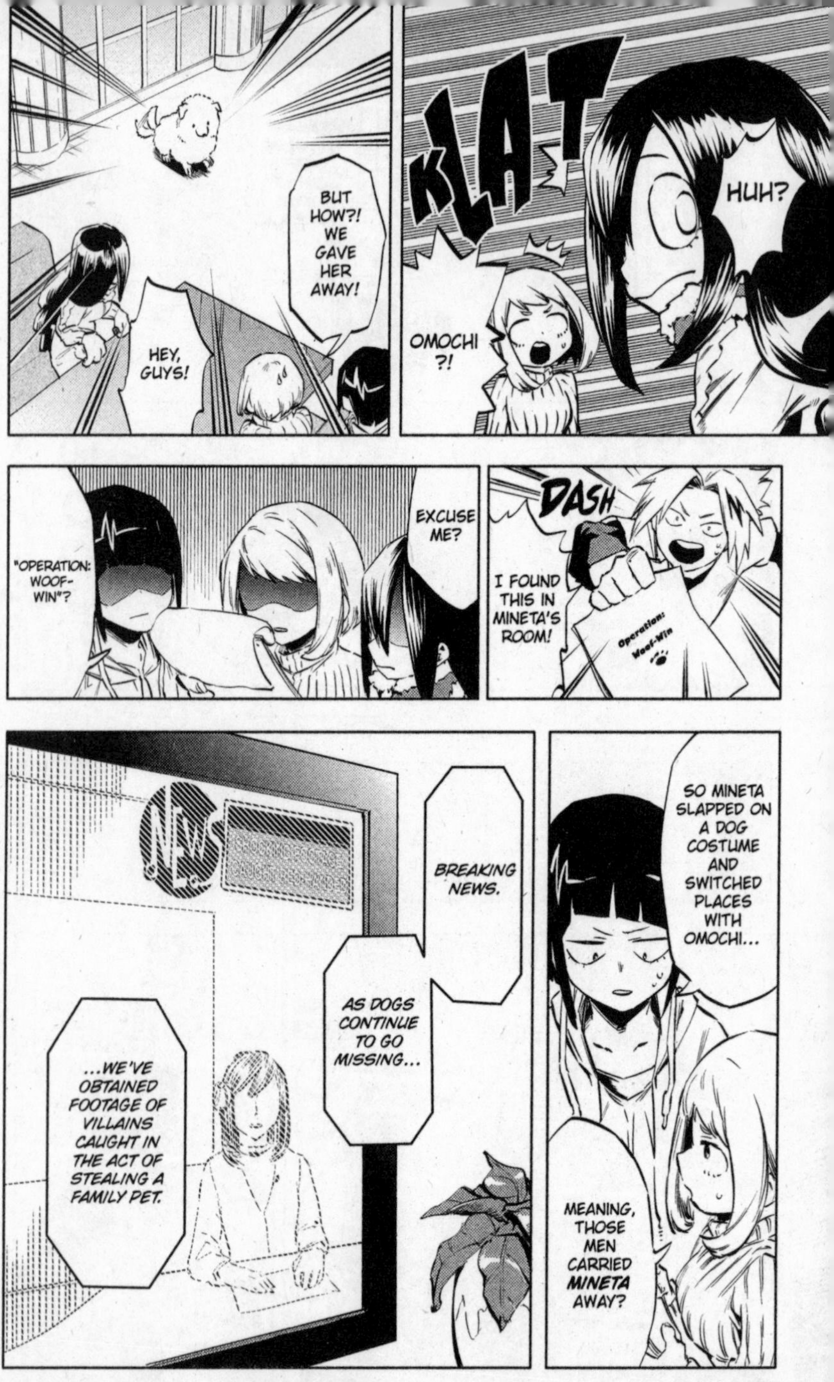
KLAT
HUH?
OMOCHI?!
BUT HOW?! WE GAVE HER AWAY!
HEY, GUYS!
DASH
I FOUND THIS IN MINETA'S ROOM!
Operation: Woof-Win
EXCUSE ME?
"OPERATION: WOOF-WIN"?
SO MINETA SLAPPED ON A DOG COSTUME AND SWITCHED PLACES WITH OMOCHI...
MEANING, THOSE MEN CARRIED MINETA AWAY?
BREAKING NEWS.
AS DOGS CONTINUE TO GO MISSING...
...WE'VE OBTAINED FOOTAGE OF VILLAINS CAUGHT IN THE ACT OF STEALING A FAMILY PET.

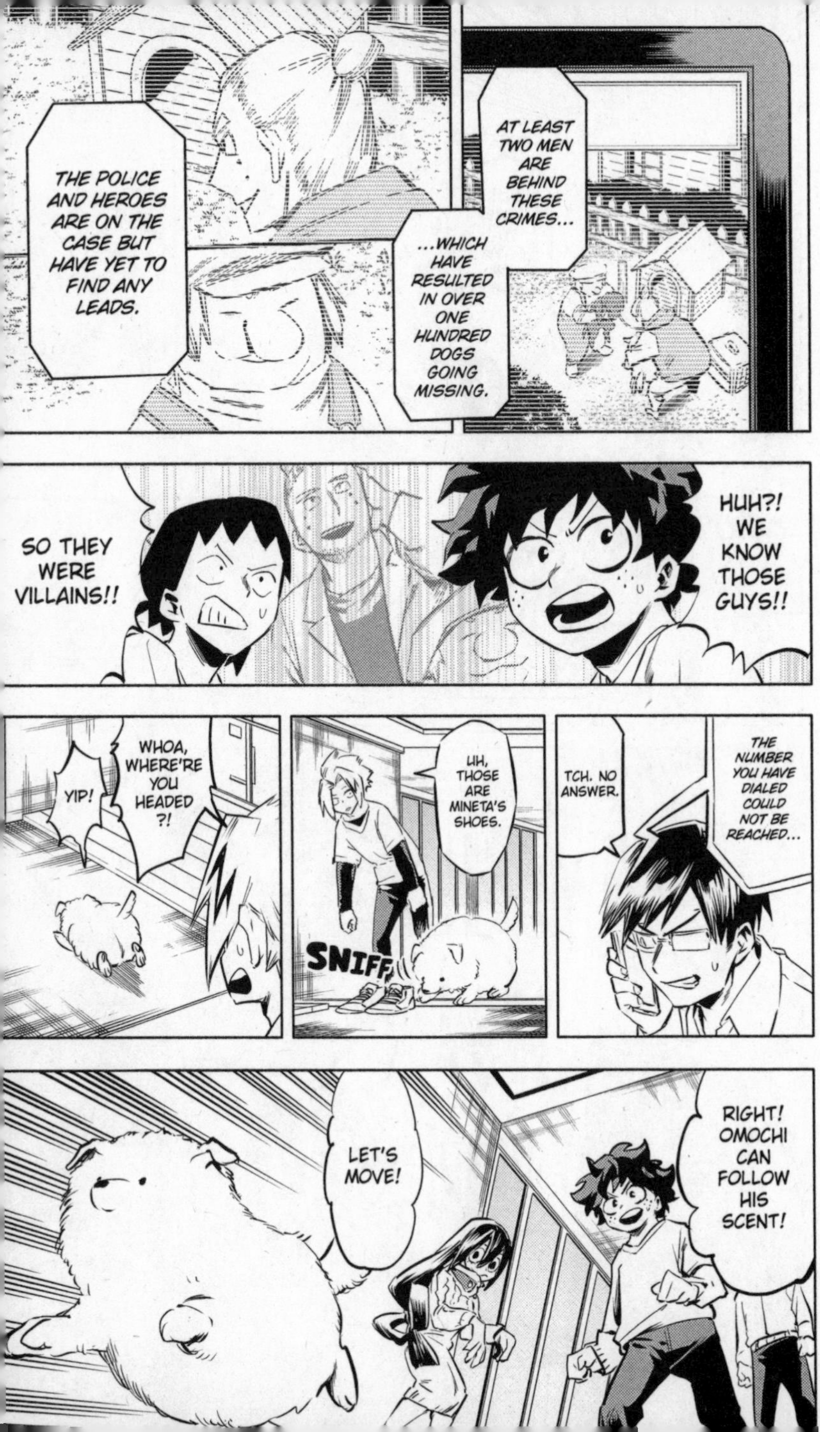
AT LEAST TWO MEN ARE BEHIND THESE CRIMES...
...WHICH HAVE RESULTED IN OVER ONE HUNDRED DOGS GOING MISSING.
THE POLICE AND HEROES ARE ON THE CASE BUT HAVE YET TO FIND ANY LEADS.
HUH?! WE KNOW THOSE GUYS!!
SO THEY WERE VILLAINS!!
THE NUMBER YOU HAVE DIALED COULD NOT BE REACHED...
TCH. NO ANSWER.
UH, THOSE ARE MINETA'S SHOES.
SNIFF
WHOA, WHERE'RE YOU HEADED ?!
YIP!
RIGHT! OMOCHI CAN FOLLOW HIS SCENT!
LET'S MOVE!

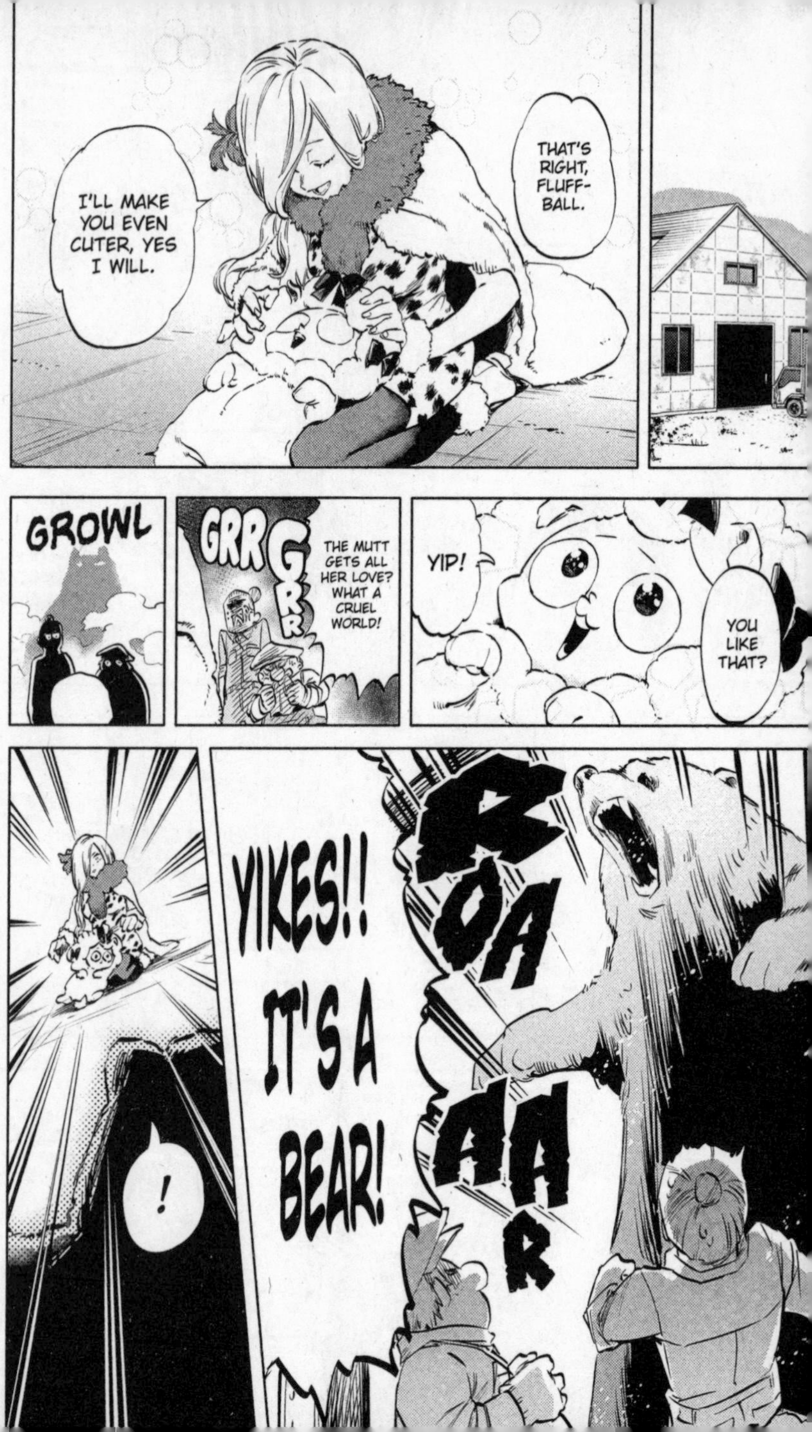
THAT'S RIGHT, FLUFF-BALL.
I'LL MAKE YOU EVEN CUTER, YES I WILL.
YOU LIKE THAT?
YIP!
GRR GRRR
THE MUTT GETS ALL HER LOVE? WHAT A CRUEL WORLD!
GROWL
ROAAAR
YIKES!! IT'S A BEAR!
!

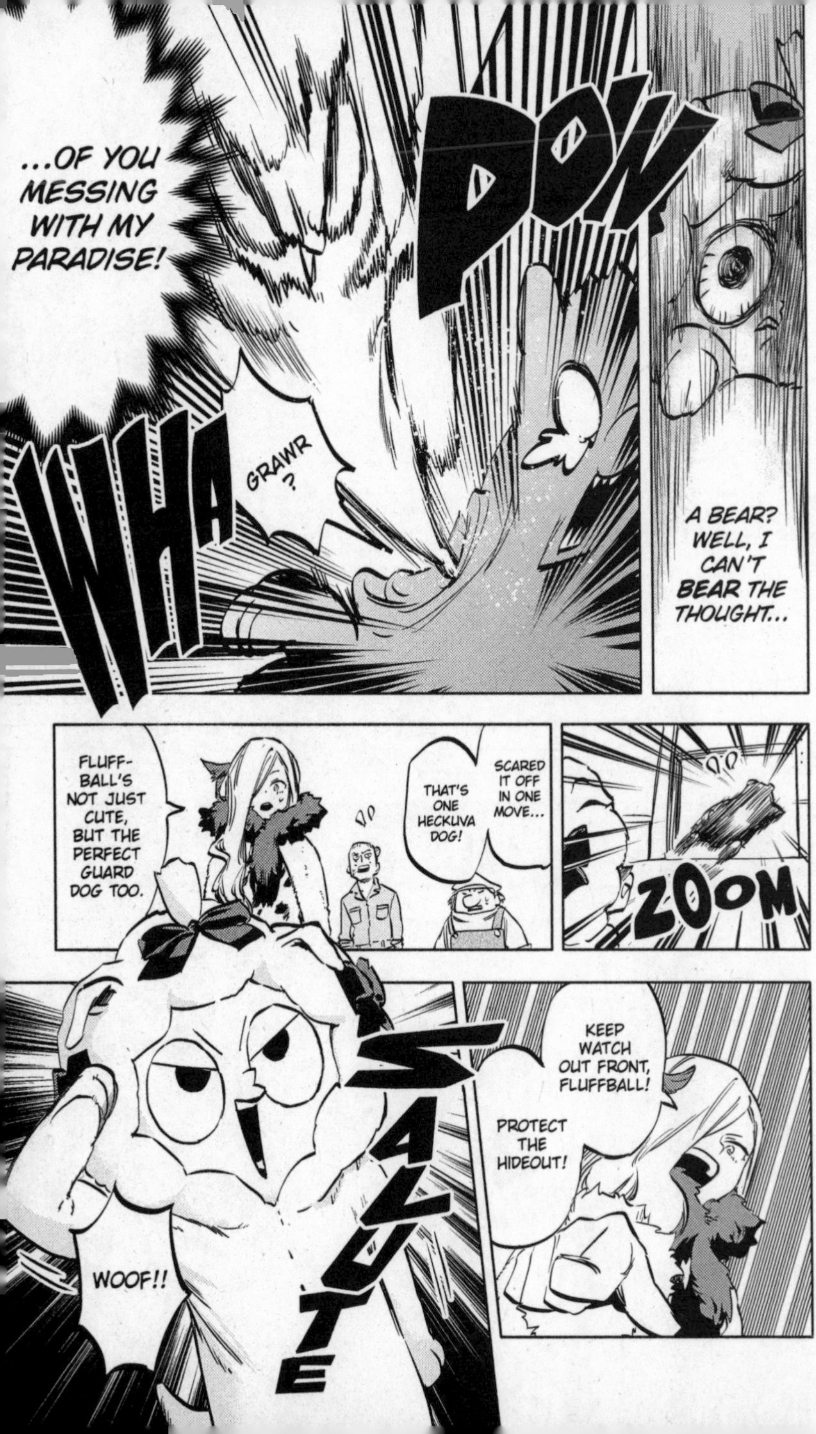
A BEAR? WELL, I CAN'T BEAR THE THOUGHT...
DON
...OF YOU MESSING WITH MY PARADISE!
GRAWR ?
WHA
ZOOM
SCARED IT OFF IN ONE MOVE...
THAT'S ONE HECKUVA DOG!
FLUFF-BALL'S NOT JUST CUTE, BUT THE PERFECT GUARD DOG TOO.
KEEP WATCH OUT FRONT, FLUFFBALL!
PROTECT THE HIDEOUT!
SALUTE
WOOF!!

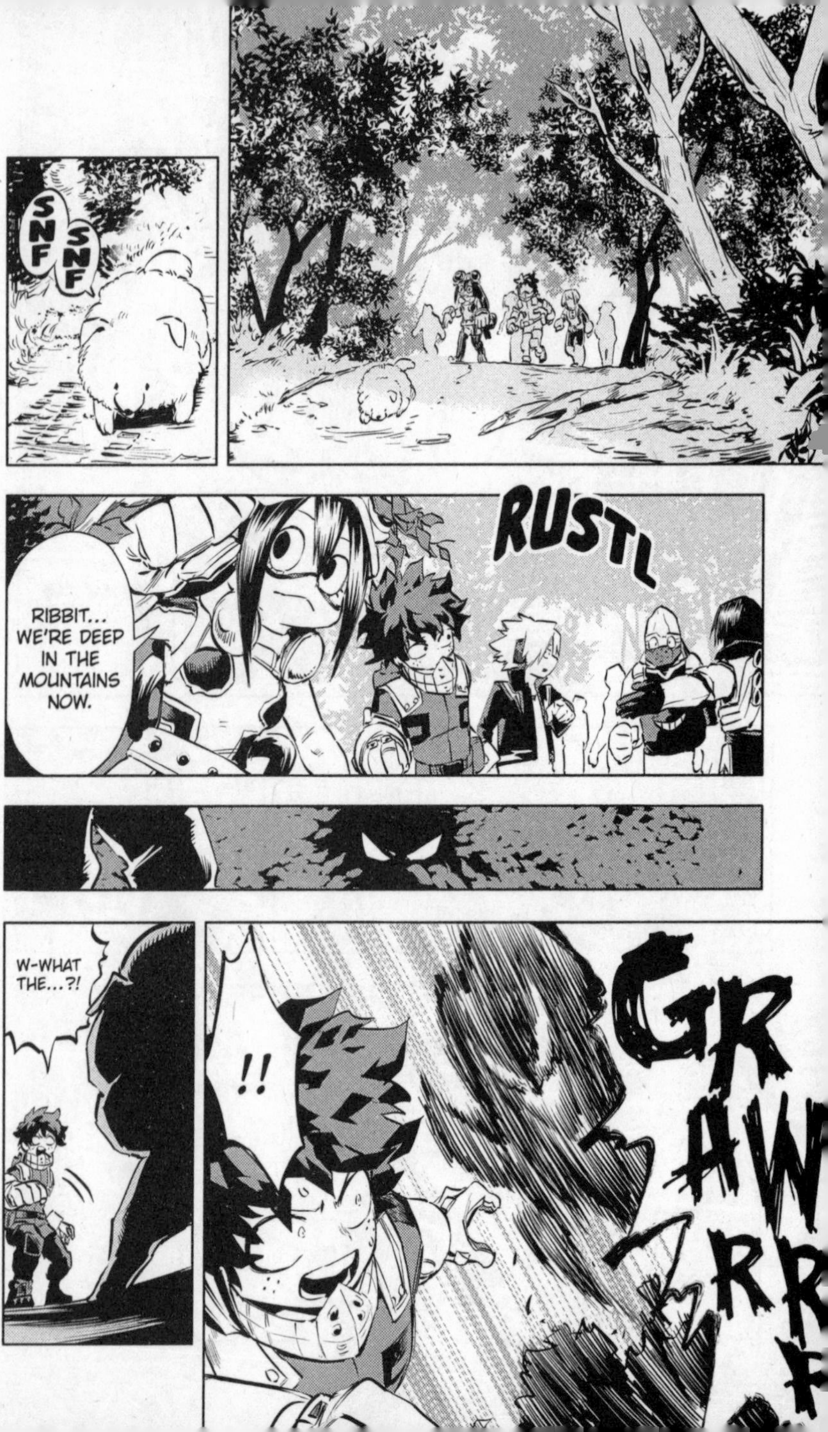
SNF SNF
RUSTL
RIBBIT... WE'RE DEEP IN THE MOUNTAINS NOW.
GR AW RR R F
!!
W-WHAT THE...?!

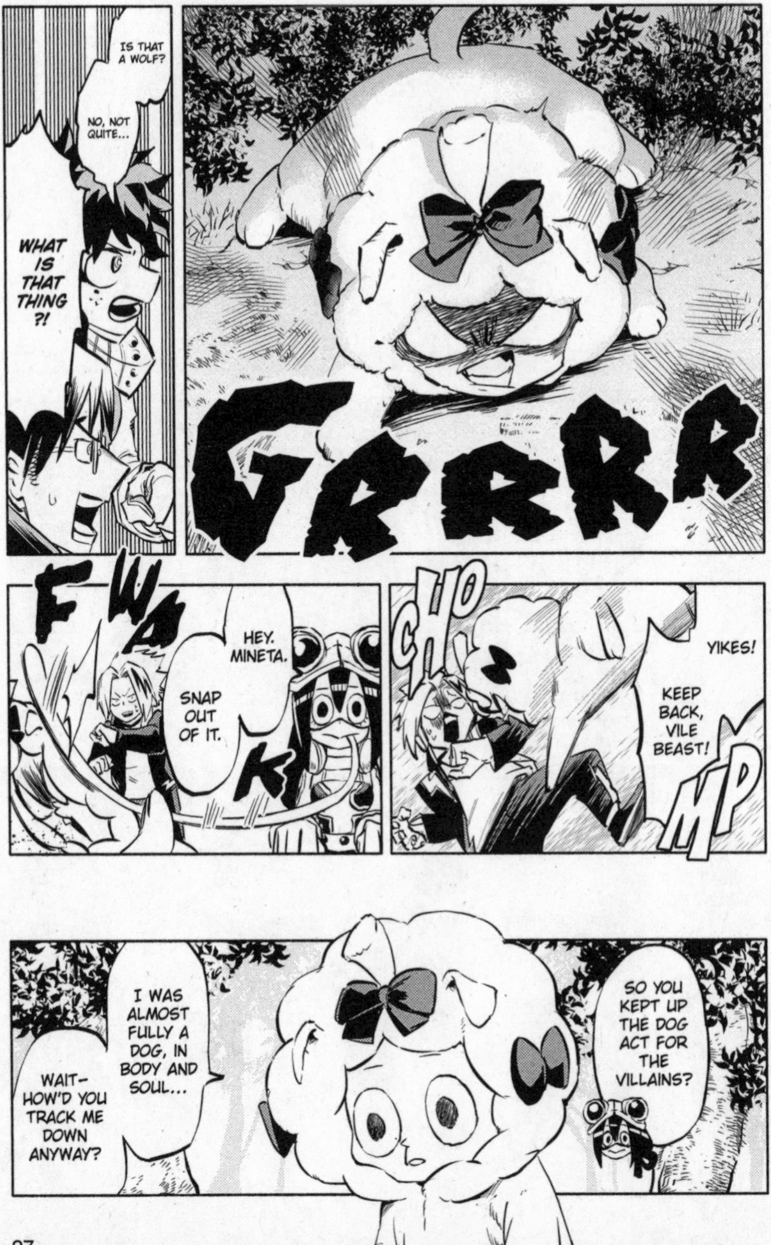
GRRRR
IS THAT A WOLF?
NO, NOT QUITE...
WHAT IS THAT THING?!
CHOMP
YIKES!
KEEP BACK, VILE BEAST!
FWAK
HEY. MINETA.
SNAP OUT OF IT.
SO YOU KEPT UP THE DOG ACT FOR THE VILLAINS?
I WAS ALMOST FULLY A DOG, IN BODY AND SOUL...
WAIT—HOW'D YOU TRACK ME DOWN ANYWAY?

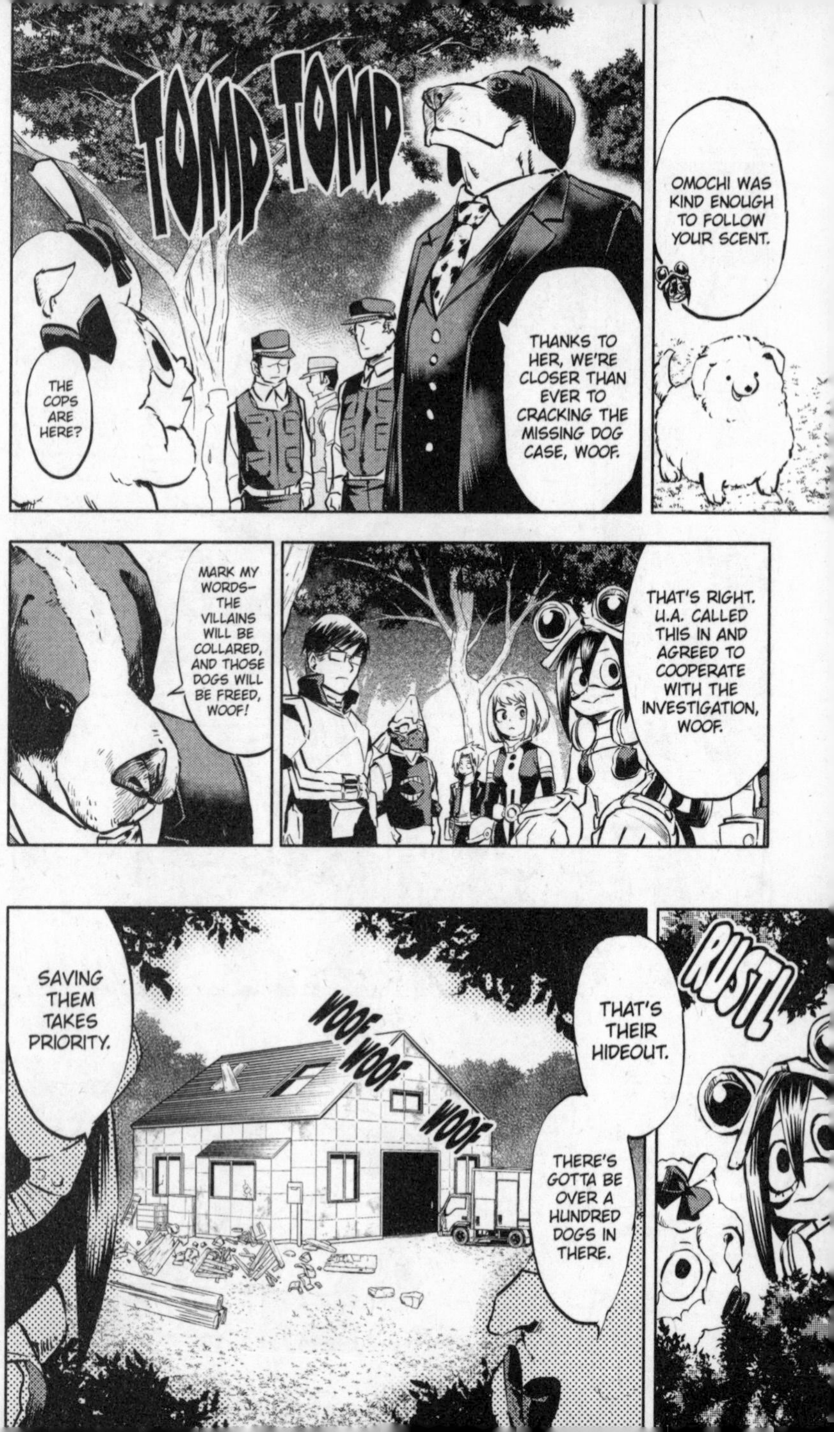
OMOCHI WAS KIND ENOUGH TO FOLLOW YOUR SCENT.
TOMP TOMP
THANKS TO HER, WE'RE CLOSER THAN EVER TO CRACKING THE MISSING DOG CASE, WOOF.
THE COPS ARE HERE?
THAT'S RIGHT. U.A. CALLED THIS IN AND AGREED TO COOPERATE WITH THE INVESTIGATION, WOOF.
MARK MY WORDS—THE VILLAINS WILL BE COLLARED, AND THOSE DOGS WILL BE FREED, WOOF!
RUSTL
THAT'S THEIR HIDEOUT.
THERE'S GOTTA BE OVER A HUNDRED DOGS IN THERE.
WOOF WOOF WOOF
SAVING THEM TAKES PRIORITY.

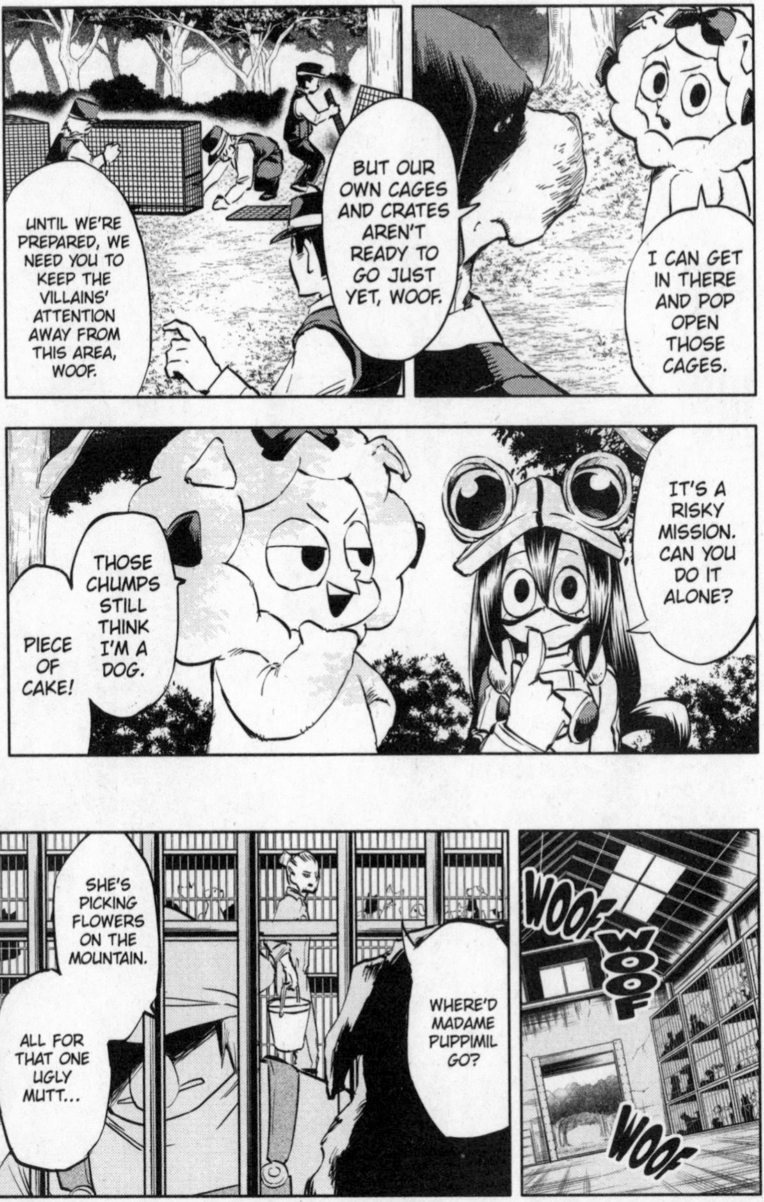
I CAN GET IN THERE AND POP OPEN THOSE CAGES.
BUT OUR OWN CAGES AND CRATES AREN'T READY TO GO JUST YET, WOOF.
UNTIL WE'RE PREPARED, WE NEED YOU TO KEEP THE VILLAINS' ATTENTION AWAY FROM THIS AREA, WOOF.
IT'S A RISKY MISSION. CAN YOU DO IT ALONE?
THOSE CHUMPS STILL THINK I'M A DOG.
PIECE OF CAKE!
WOOF
WOOF
WOOF
WHERE'D MADAME PUPPIMIL GO?
SHE'S PICKING FLOWERS ON THE MOUNTAIN.
ALL FOR THAT ONE UGLY MUTT...

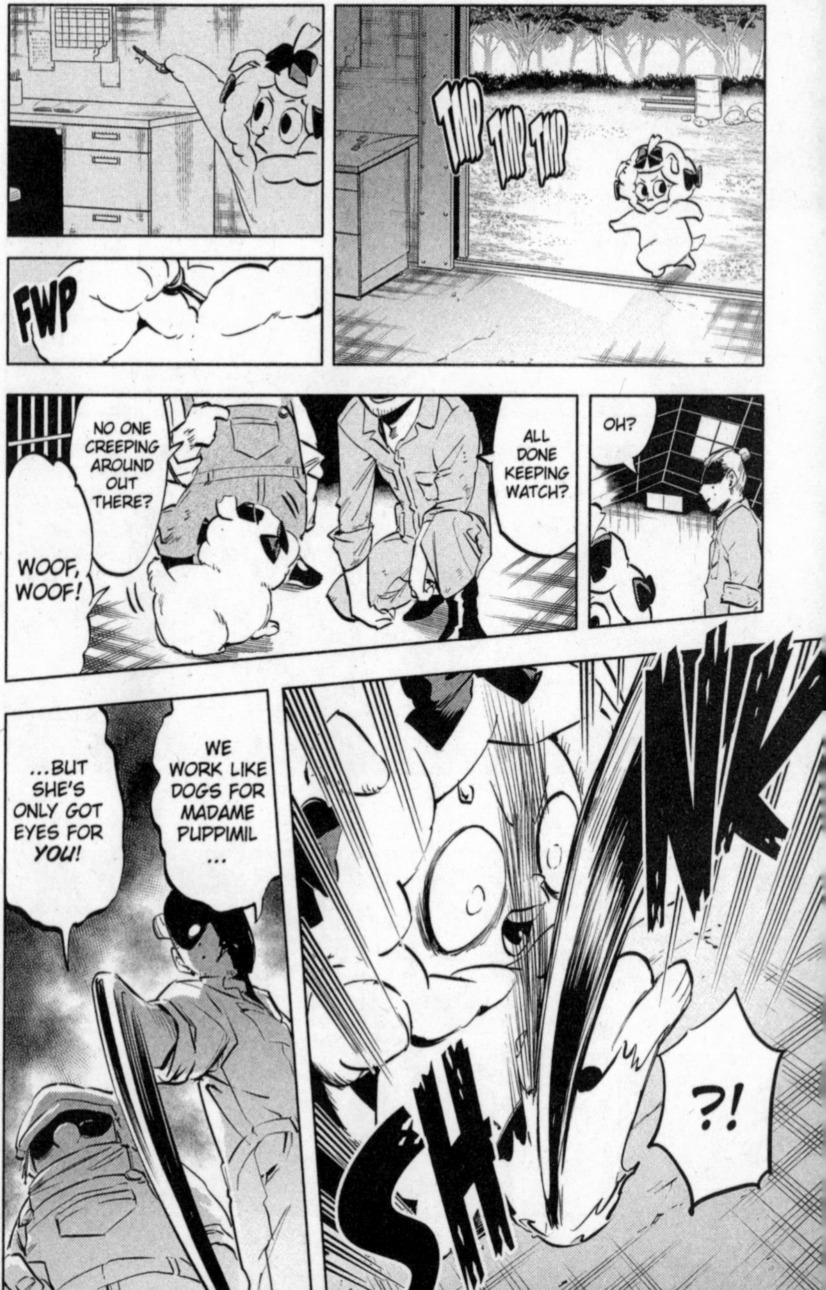
TMP TMP TMP
FWP
OH?
ALL DONE KEEPING WATCH?
NO ONE CREEPING AROUND OUT THERE?
WOOF, WOOF!
SHNK
?!
WE WORK LIKE DOGS FOR MADAME PUPPIMIL ...
...BUT SHE'S ONLY GOT EYES FOR YOU!

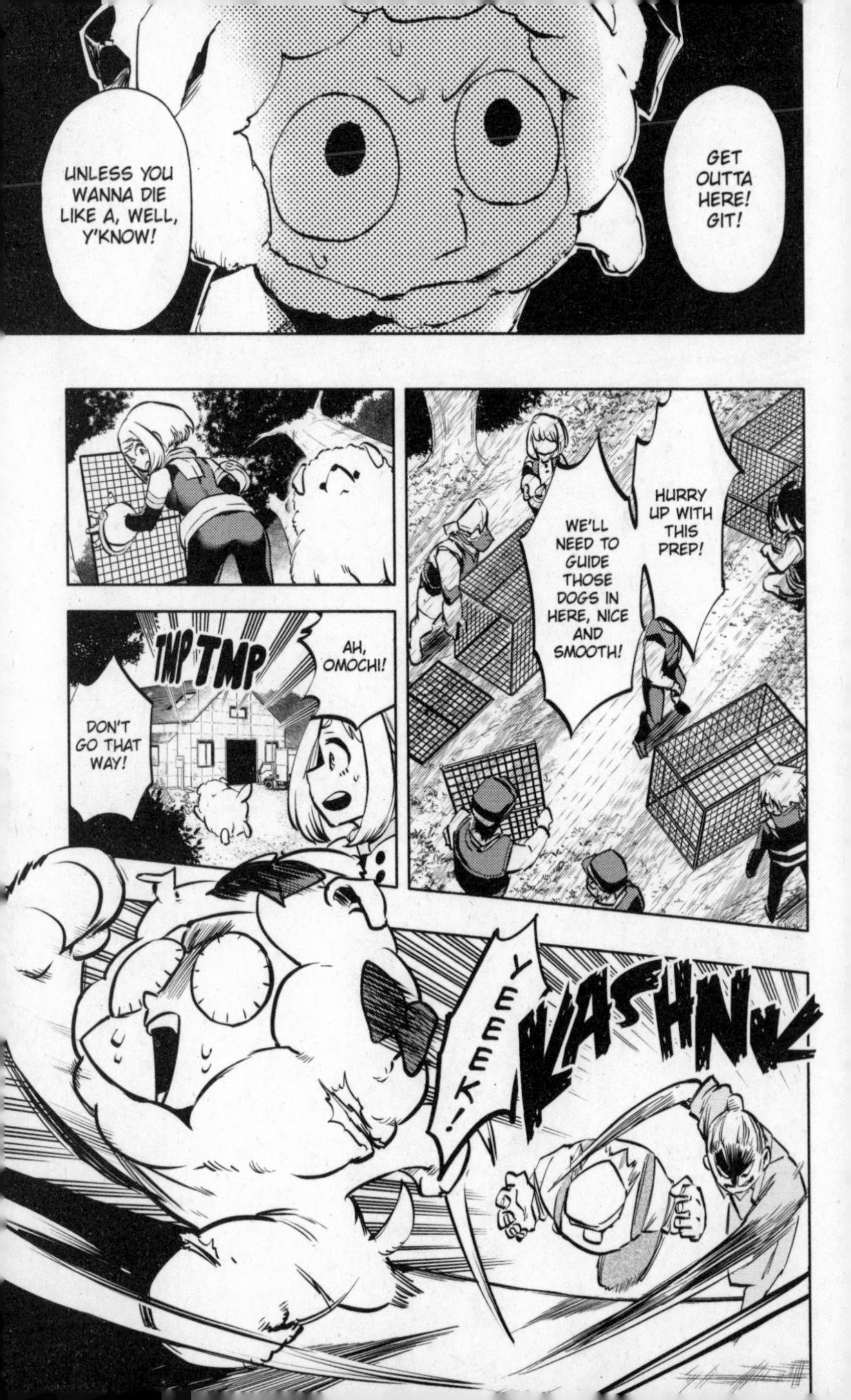
GET OUTTA HERE! GIT!
UNLESS YOU WANNA DIE LIKE A, WELL, Y'KNOW!
HURRY UP WITH THIS PREP!
WE'LL NEED TO GUIDE THOSE DOGS IN HERE, NICE AND SMOOTH!
TMP TMP
AH, OMOCHI!
DON'T GO THAT WAY!
KASHNK
YEEEEK!

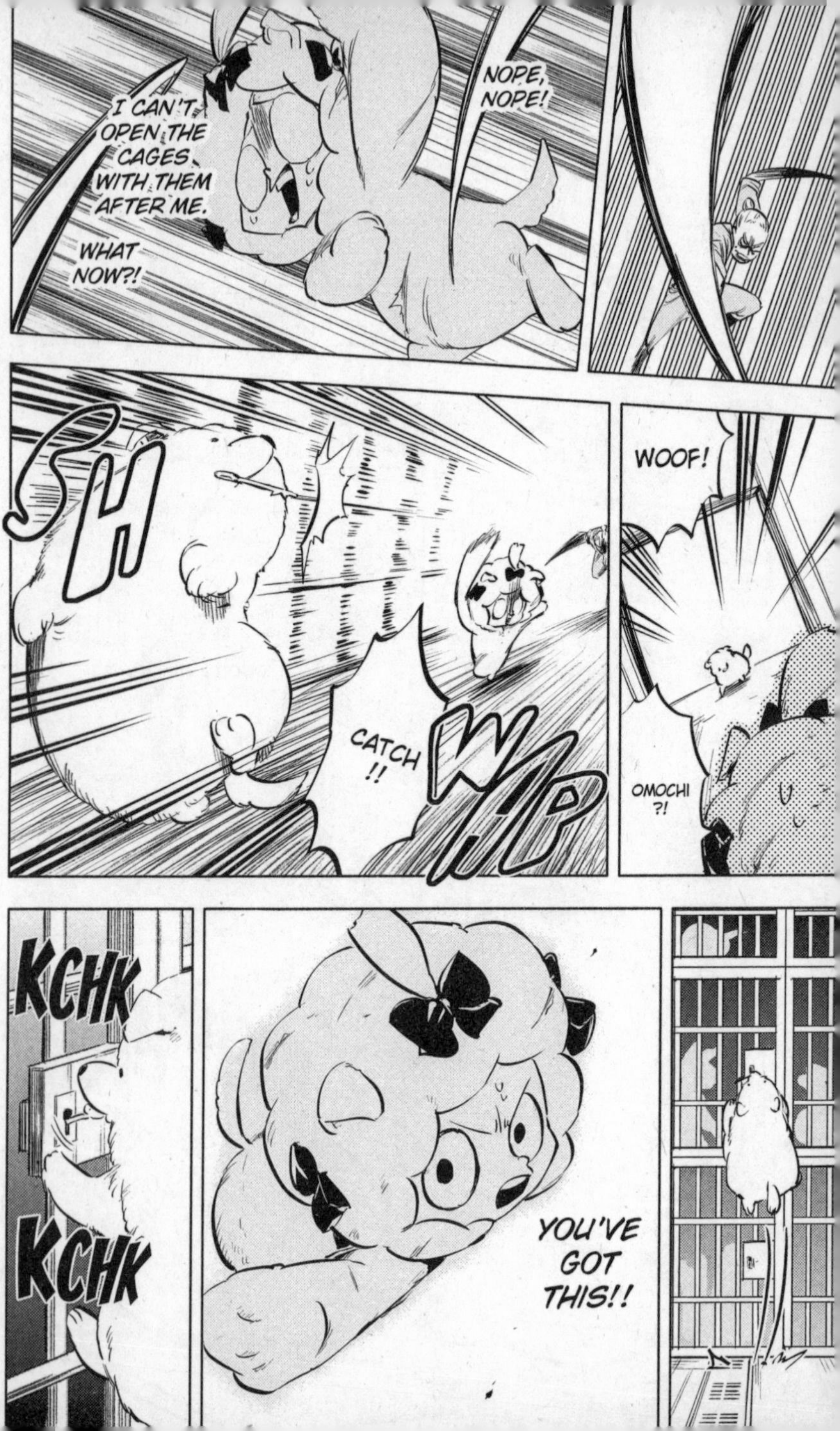
NOPE, NOPE!
I CAN'T OPEN THE CAGES WITH THEM AFTER ME.
WHAT NOW?!
WOOF!
OMOCHI ?!
SH
CATCH !!
WHIP
YOU'VE GOT THIS!!
KCHK
KCHK

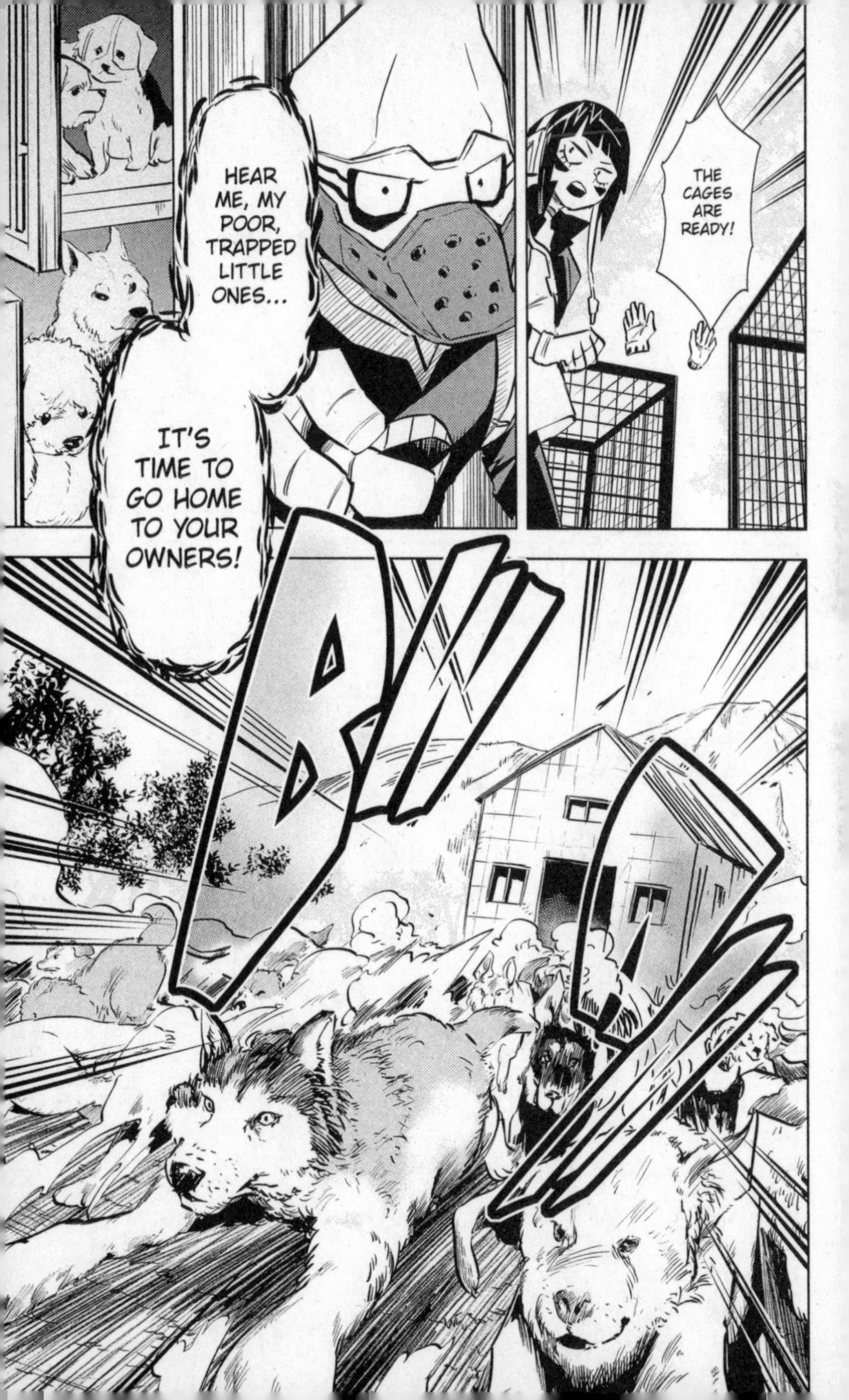
THE CAGES ARE READY!
HEAR ME, MY POOR, TRAPPED LITTLE ONES...
IT'S TIME TO GO HOME TO YOUR OWNERS!

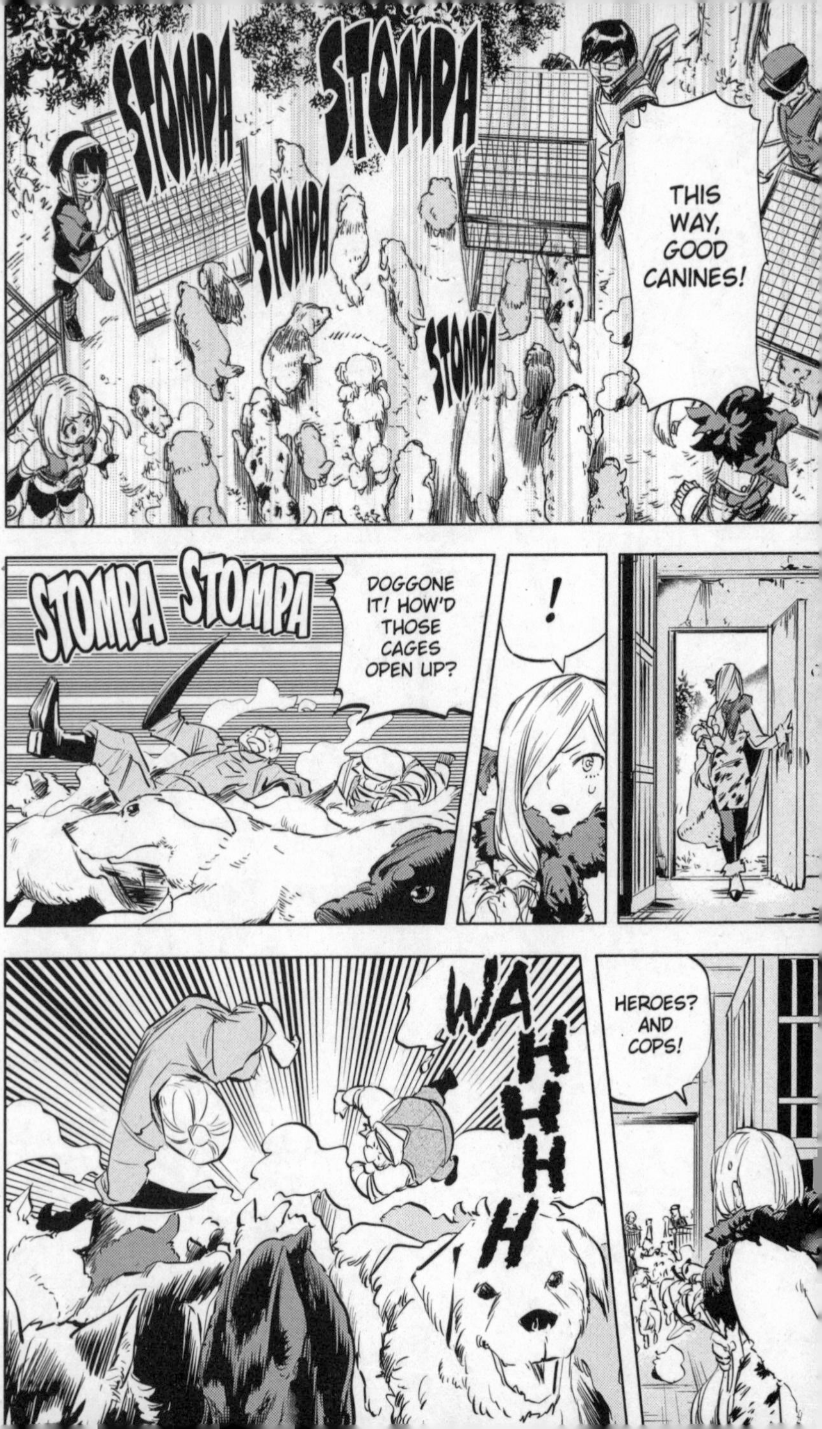
THIS WAY, GOOD CANINES!
STOMPA
STOMPA
STOMPA
STOMPA
!
DOGGONE IT! HOW'D THOSE CAGES OPEN UP?
STOMPA STOMPA
HEROES? AND COPS!
WAHHHHHH

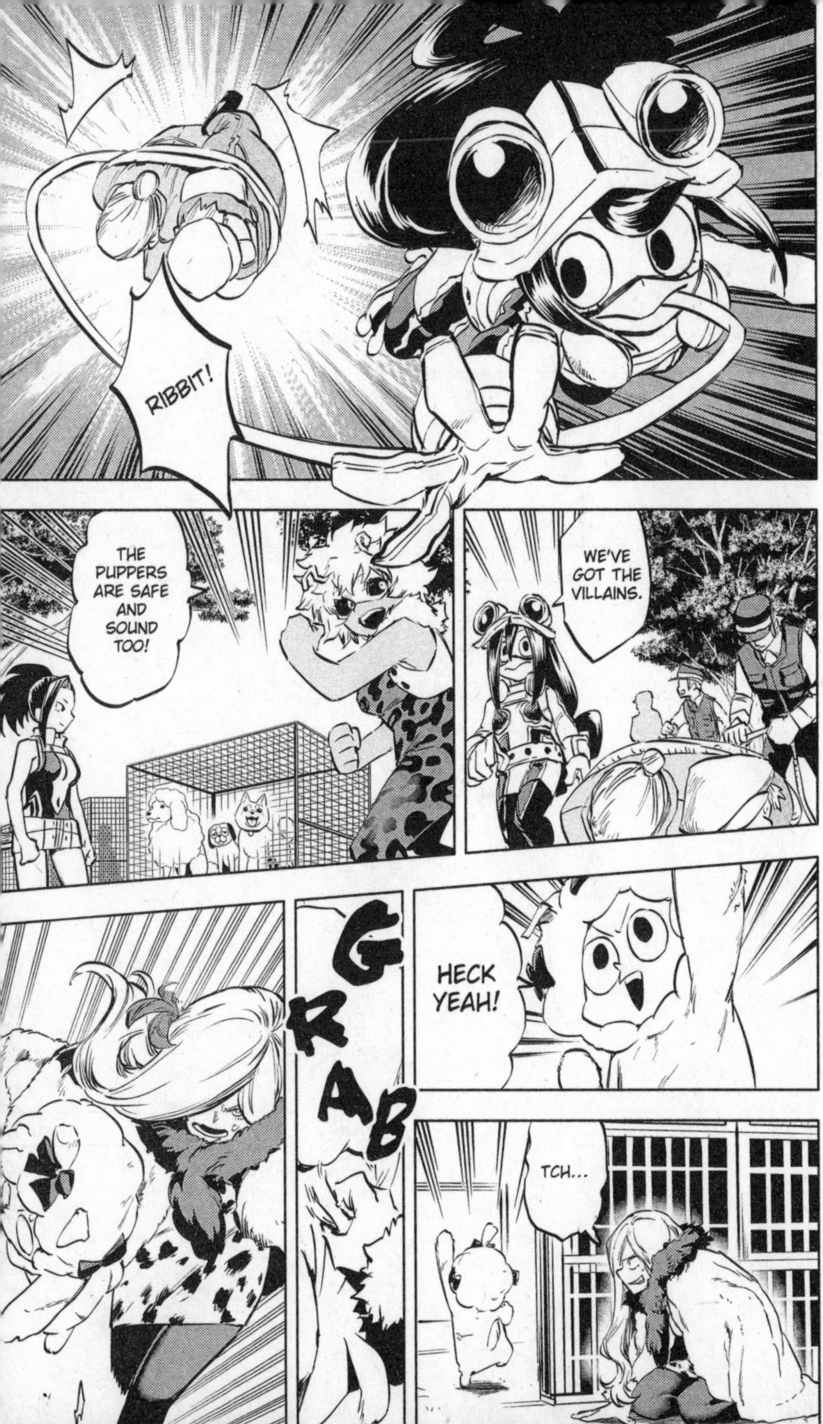
RIBBIT!
WE'VE GOT THE VILLAINS.
THE PUPPERS ARE SAFE AND SOUND TOO!
HECK YEAH!
TCH...
GRAB

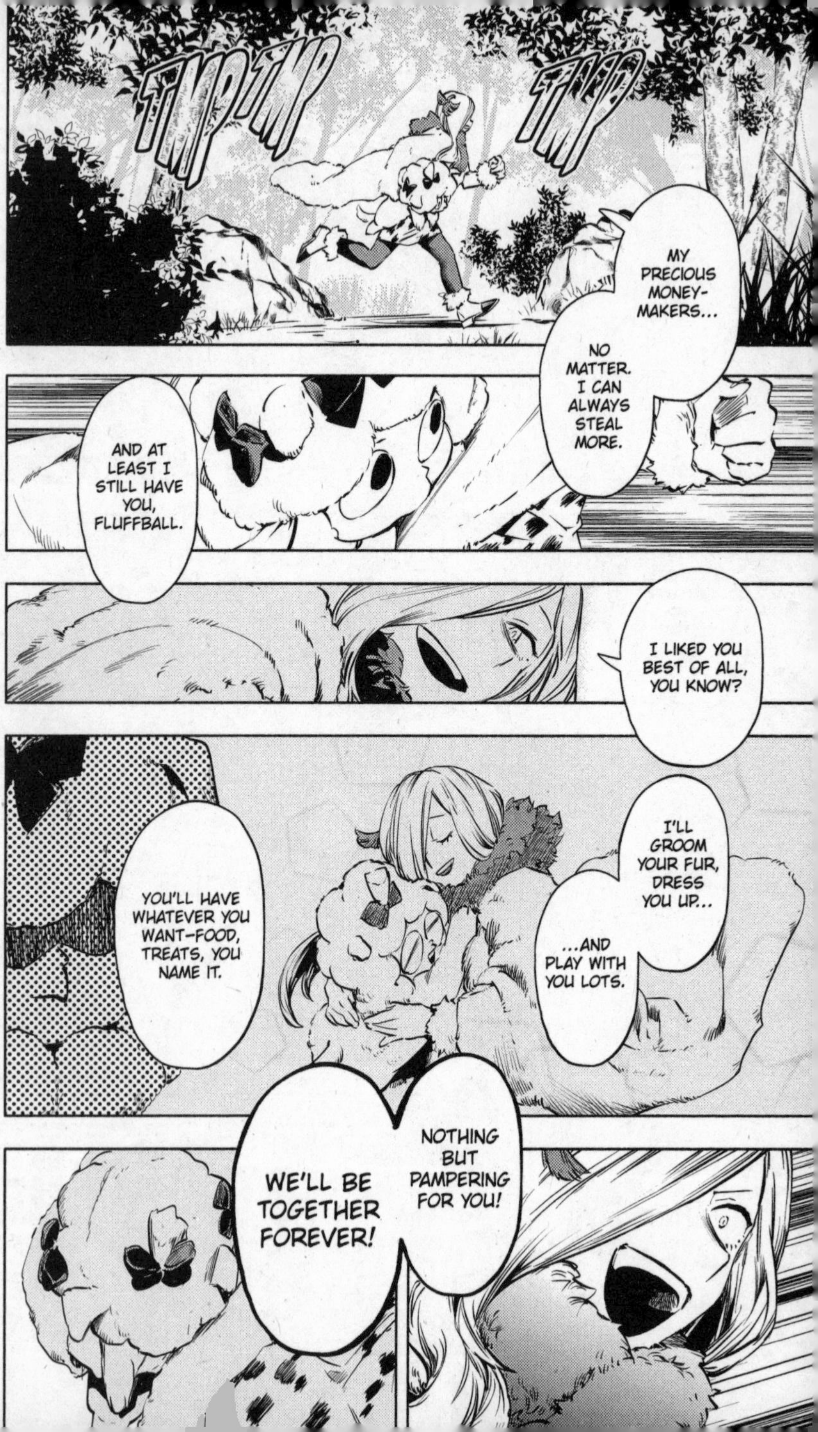
TMP
TMP TMP
MY PRECIOUS MONEY-MAKERS...
NO MATTER. I CAN ALWAYS STEAL MORE.
AND AT LEAST I STILL HAVE YOU, FLUFFBALL.
I LIKED YOU BEST OF ALL, YOU KNOW?
I'LL GROOM YOUR FUR, DRESS YOU UP...
...AND PLAY WITH YOU LOTS.
YOU'LL HAVE WHATEVER YOU WANT—FOOD, TREATS, YOU NAME IT.
NOTHING BUT PAMPERING FOR YOU!
WE'LL BE TOGETHER FOREVER!

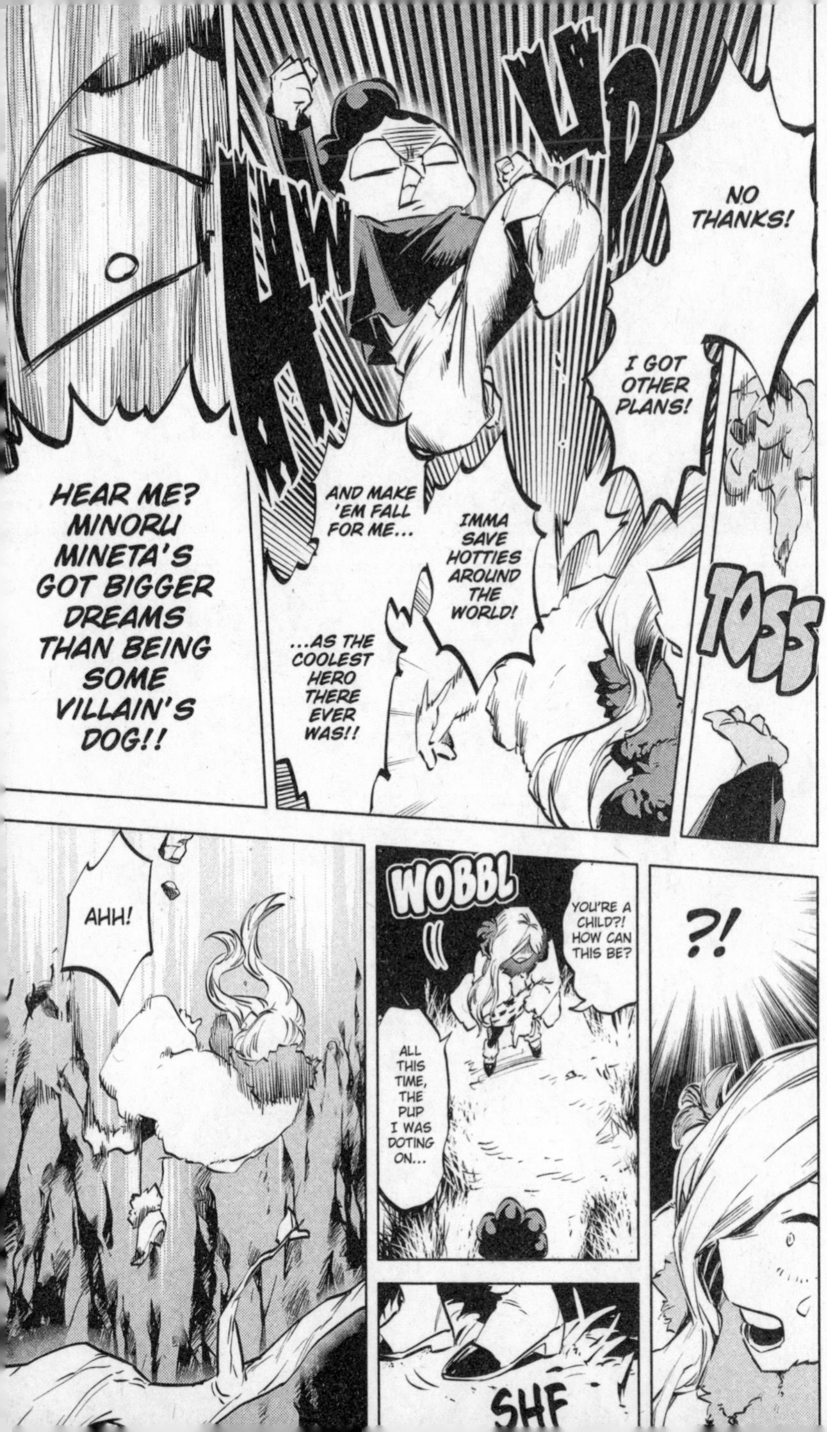
NO THANKS!
I GOT OTHER PLANS!
TOSS
IMMA SAVE HOTTIES AROUND THE WORLD!
AND MAKE 'EM FALL FOR ME...
...AS THE COOLEST HERO THERE EVER WAS!!
HEAR ME? MINORU MINETA'S GOT BIGGER DREAMS THAN BEING SOME VILLAIN'S DOG!!
?!
WOBBL
YOU'RE A CHILD?! HOW CAN THIS BE?
ALL THIS TIME, THE PUP I WAS DOTING ON...
SHF
AHH!

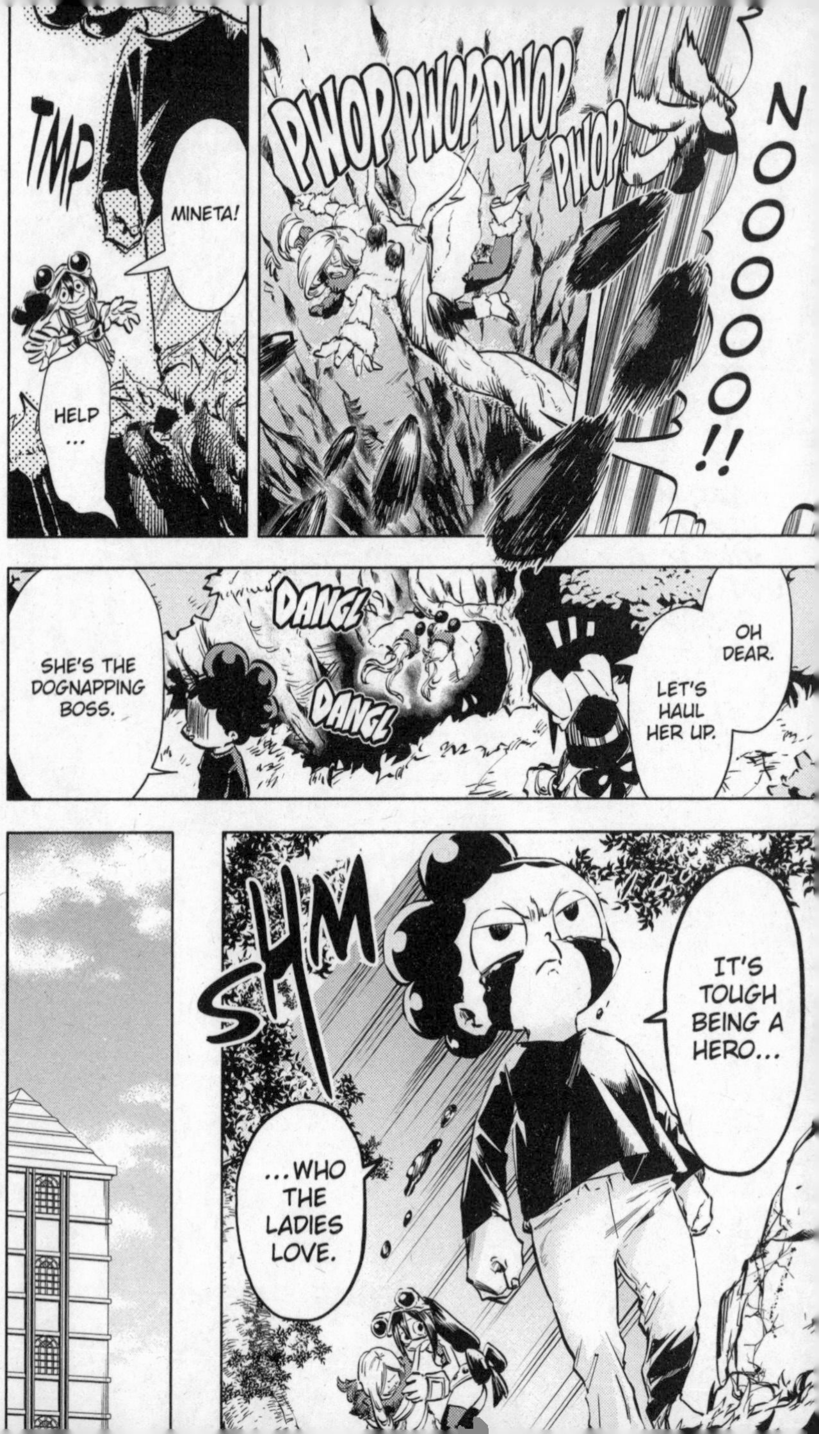
NOOOOOO!!
PWOP PWOP PWOP PWOP
TMP
MINETA!
HELP ...
OH DEAR. LET'S HAUL HER UP.
DANGL
DANGL
SHE'S THE DOGNAPPING BOSS.
IT'S TOUGH BEING A HERO...
SHM
...WHO THE LADIES LOVE.

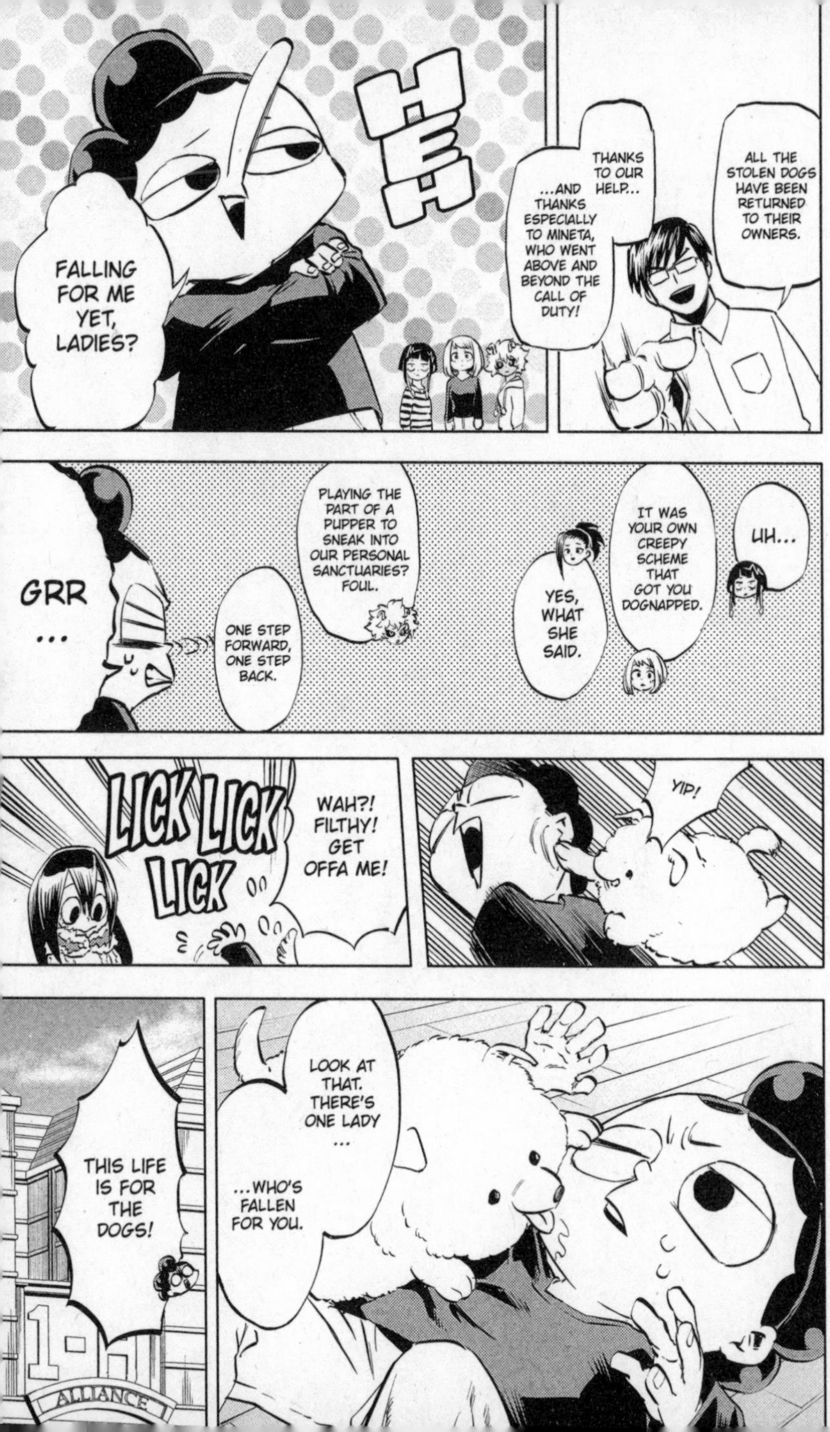
ALL THE STOLEN DOGS HAVE BEEN RETURNED TO THEIR OWNERS.
THANKS TO OUR HELP...
...AND THANKS ESPECIALLY TO MINETA, WHO WENT ABOVE AND BEYOND THE CALL OF DUTY!
HEH
FALLING FOR ME YET, LADIES?
UH...
IT WAS YOUR OWN CREEPY SCHEME THAT GOT YOU DOGNAPPED.
YES, WHAT SHE SAID.
PLAYING THE PART OF A PUPPER TO SNEAK INTO OUR PERSONAL SANCTUARIES? FOUL.
ONE STEP FORWARD, ONE STEP BACK.
GRR...
YIP!
WAH?! FILTHY! GET OFFA ME!
LICK LICK LICK
LOOK AT THAT. THERE'S ONE LADY...
...WHO'S FALLEN FOR YOU.
THIS LIFE IS FOR THE DOGS!
ALLIANCE

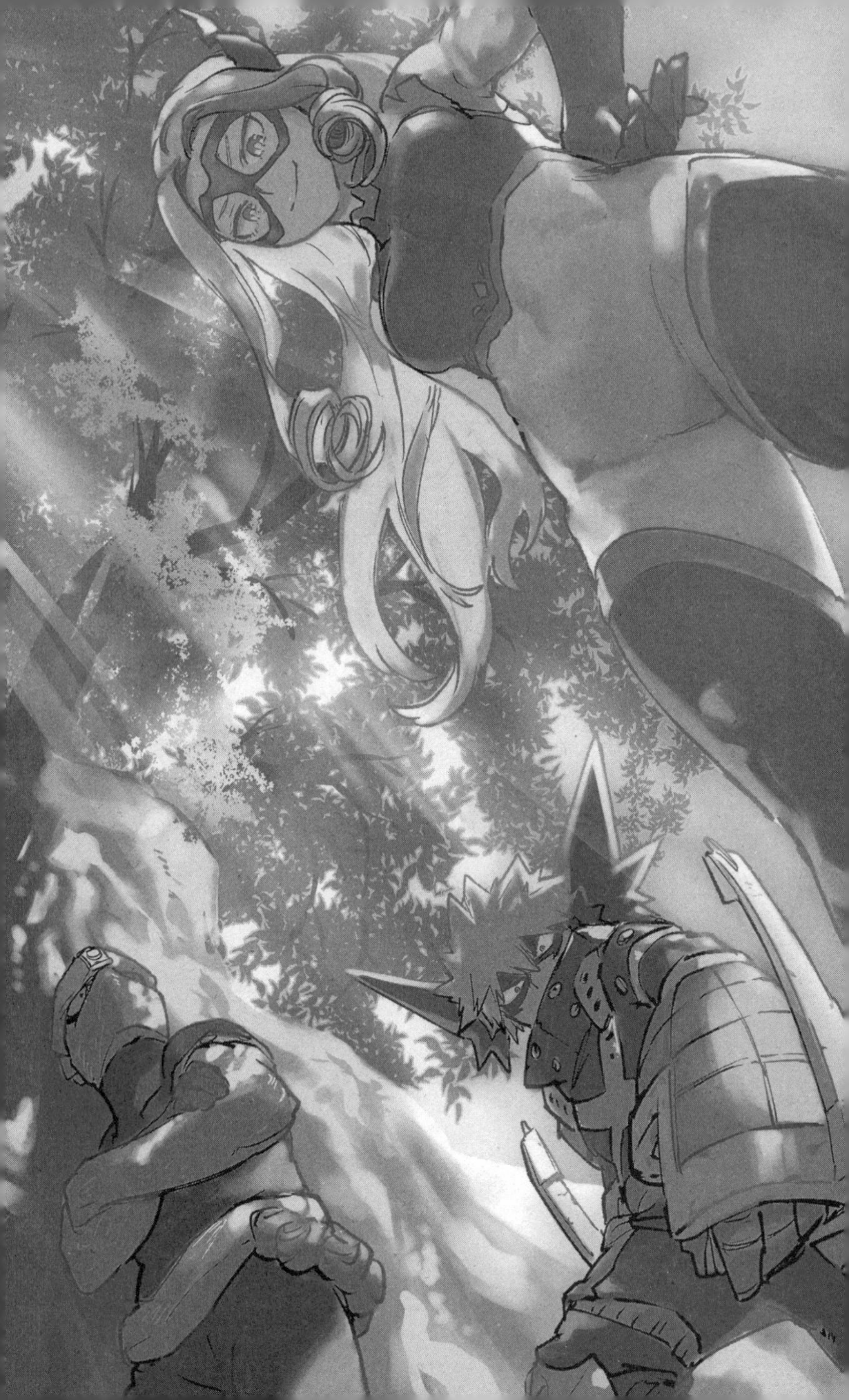

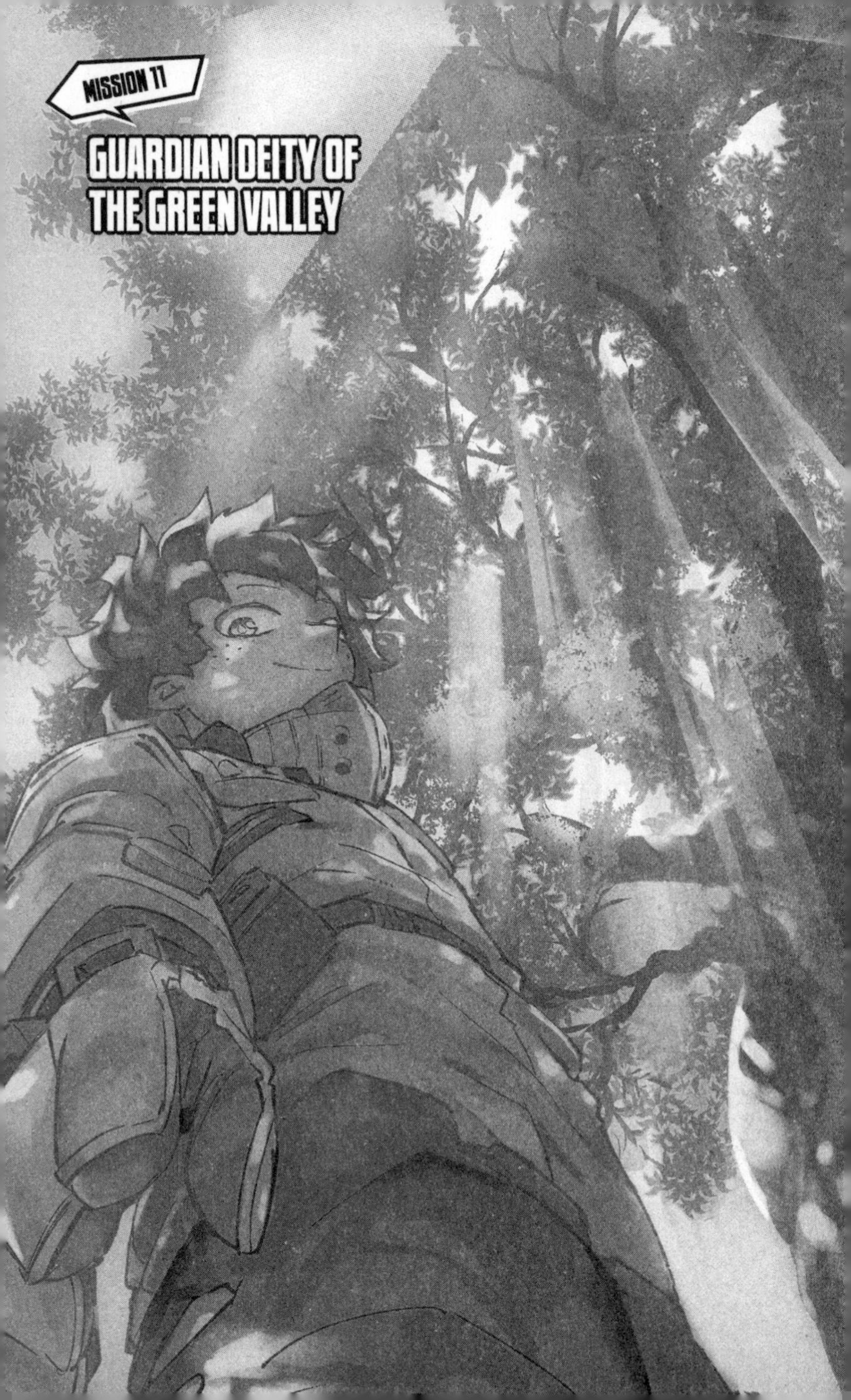
MISSION 11
GUARDIAN DEITY OF
THE GREEN VALLEY

Ripe grapes on the vine
Entwined, entangled, engaged
The dragonfly gawks
But uninvolved as it is
Love is a forbidden fruit

MINORU
MINETA

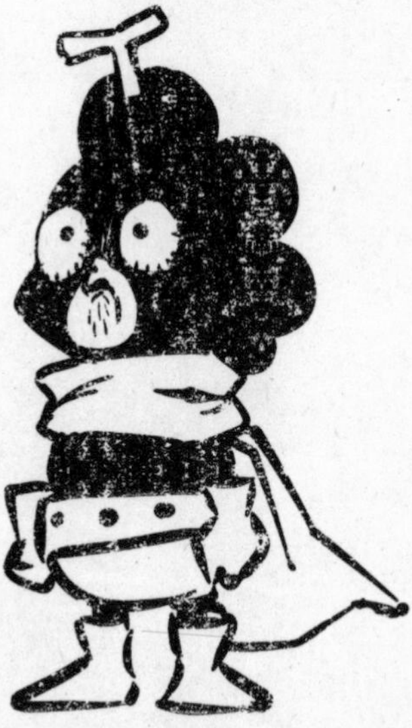

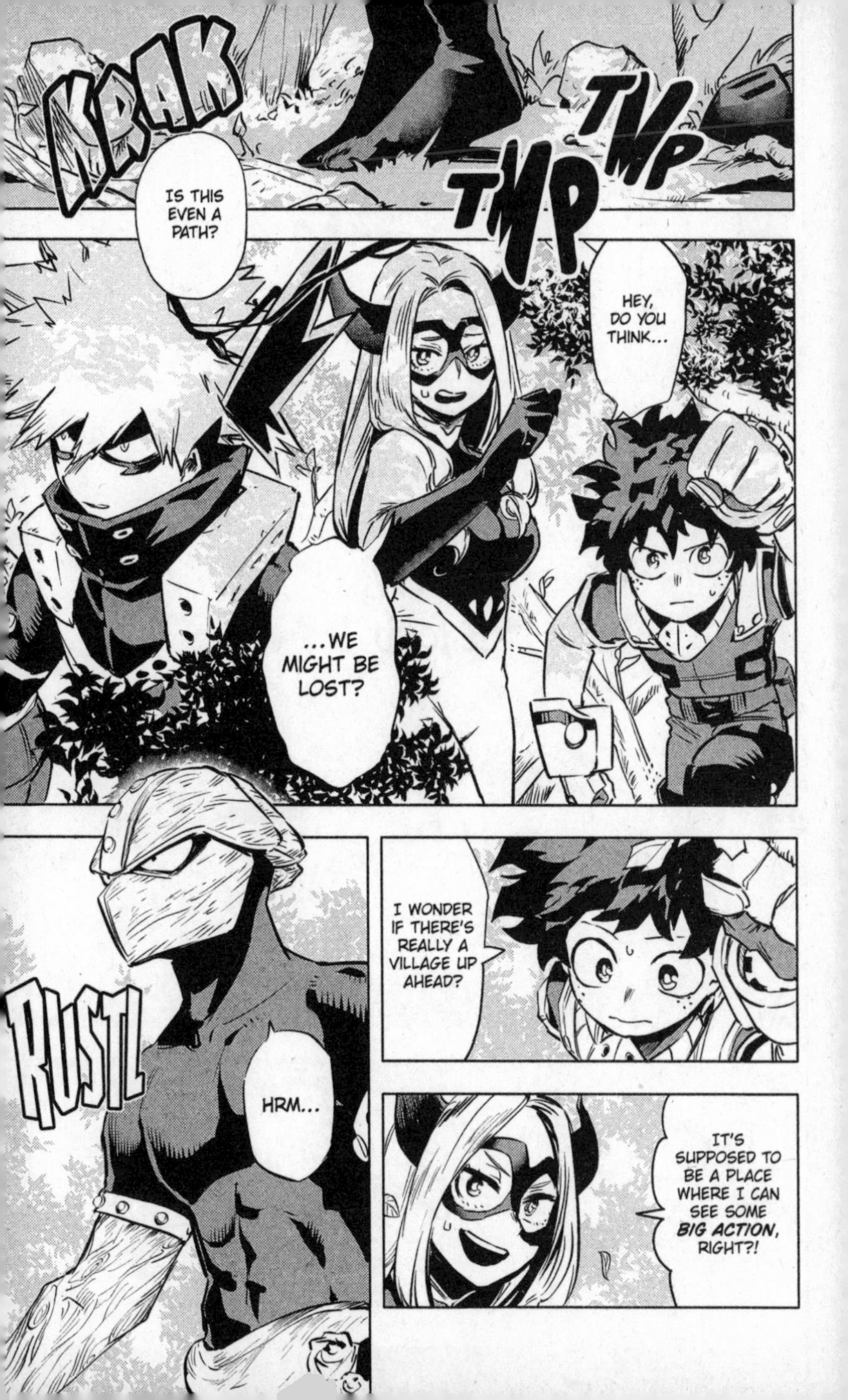
TMP TMP
IS THIS EVEN A PATH?
KRAK
HEY, DO YOU THINK...
...WE MIGHT BE LOST?
I WONDER IF THERE'S REALLY A VILLAGE UP AHEAD?
IT'S SUPPOSED TO BE A PLACE WHERE I CAN SEE SOME ***BIG ACTION***, RIGHT?!
RUSTL
HRM...

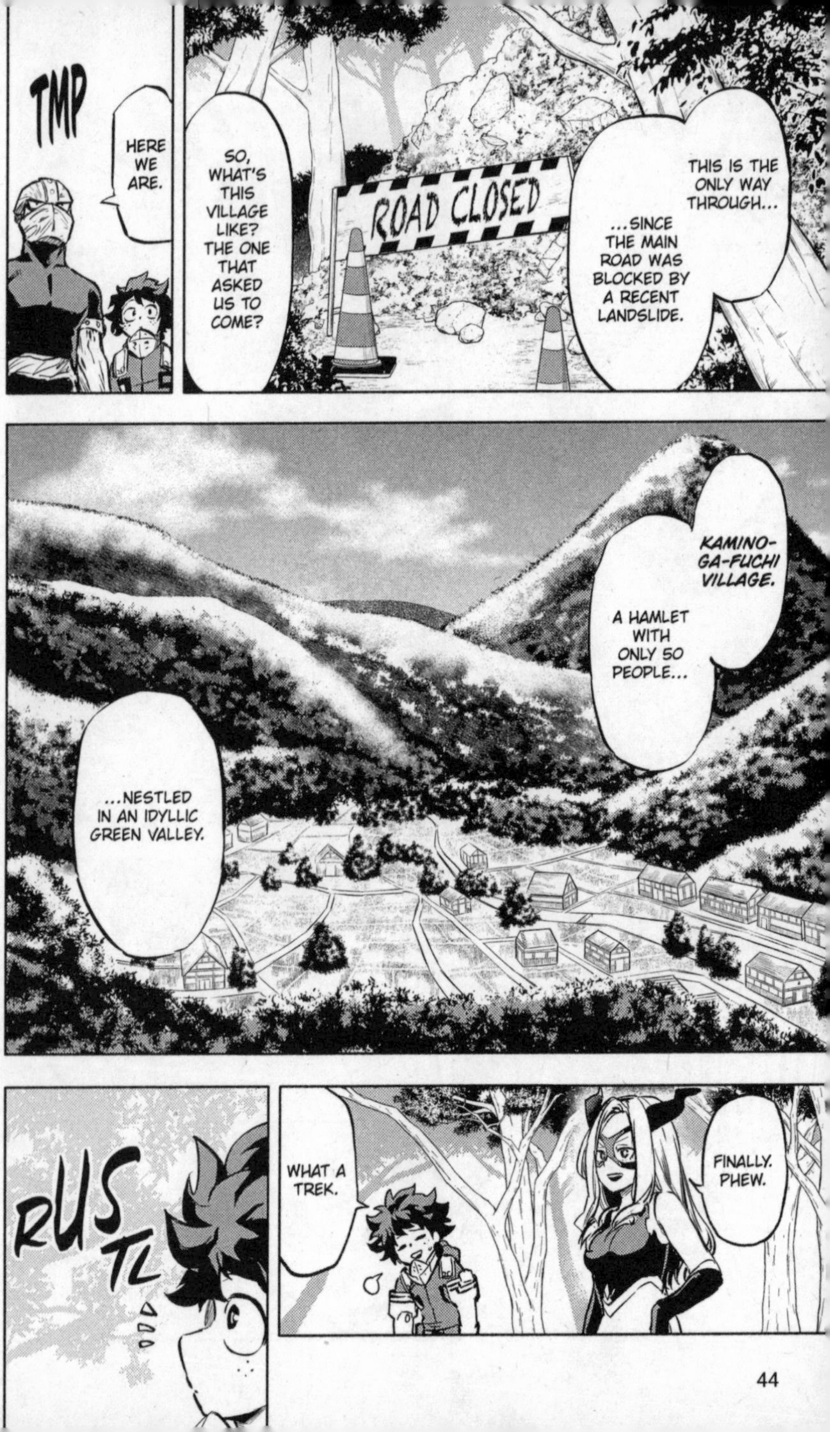
ROAD CLOSED
THIS IS THE ONLY WAY THROUGH...
...SINCE THE MAIN ROAD WAS BLOCKED BY A RECENT LANDSLIDE.
SO, WHAT'S THIS VILLAGE LIKE? THE ONE THAT ASKED US TO COME?
HERE WE ARE.
TMP
KAMINO-GA-FUCHI VILLAGE.
A HAMLET WITH ONLY 50 PEOPLE...
...NESTLED IN AN IDYLLIC GREEN VALLEY.
FINALLY. PHEW.
WHAT A TREK.
RUSTL

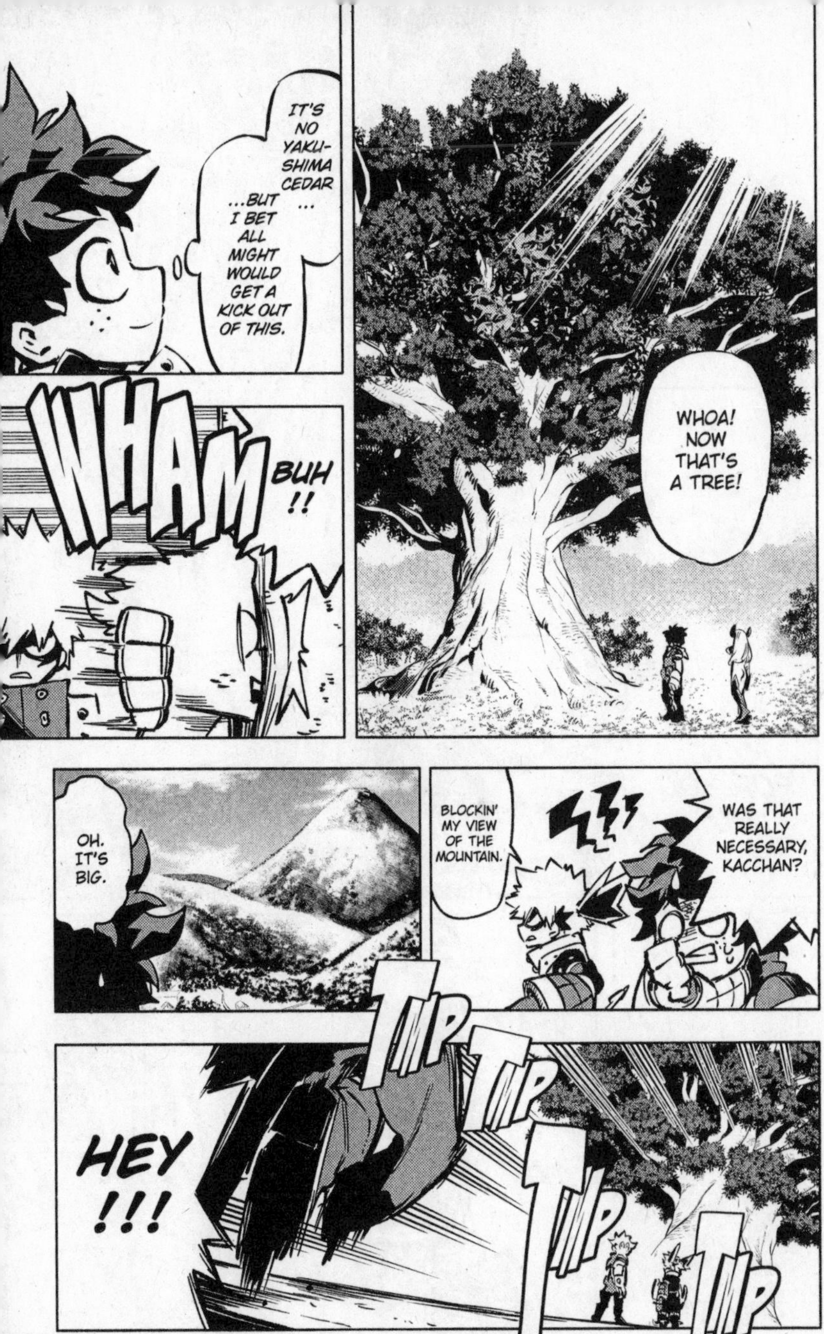
WHOA! NOW THAT'S A TREE!
IT'S NO YAKUSHIMA CEDAR...
...BUT I BET ALL MIGHT WOULD GET A KICK OUT OF THIS.
WHAM
BUH!!
WAS THAT REALLY NECESSARY, KACCHAN?
BLOCKIN' MY VIEW OF THE MOUNTAIN.
OH. IT'S BIG.
TMP
TMP
TMP
TMP
HEY!!!

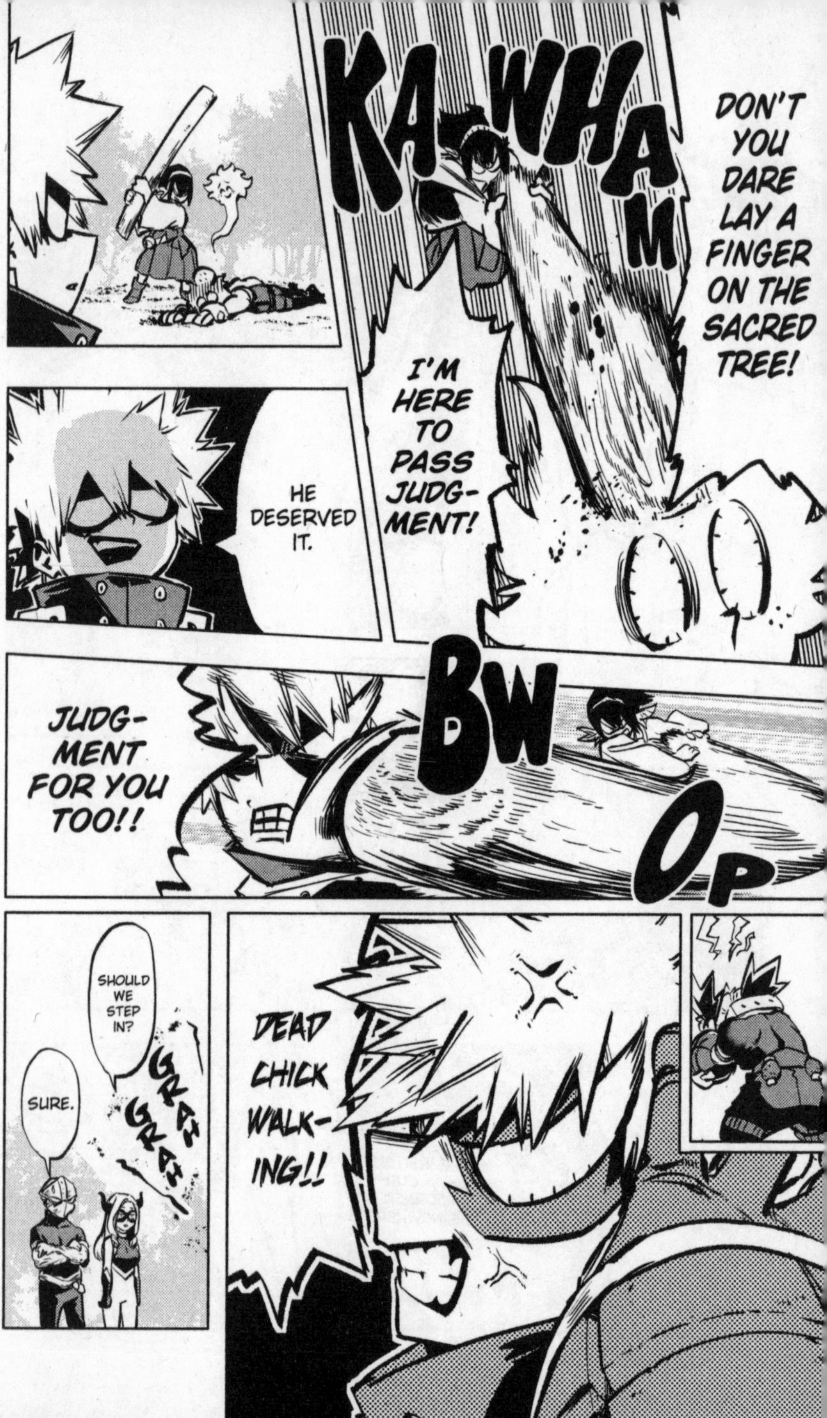
KA-WHAM
DON'T YOU DARE LAY A FINGER ON THE SACRED TREE!
I'M HERE TO PASS JUDG-MENT!
HE DESERVED IT.
BWOOP
JUDG-MENT FOR YOU TOO!!
DEAD CHICK WALK-ING!!
SHOULD WE STEP IN?
SURE.
GRAH GRAH

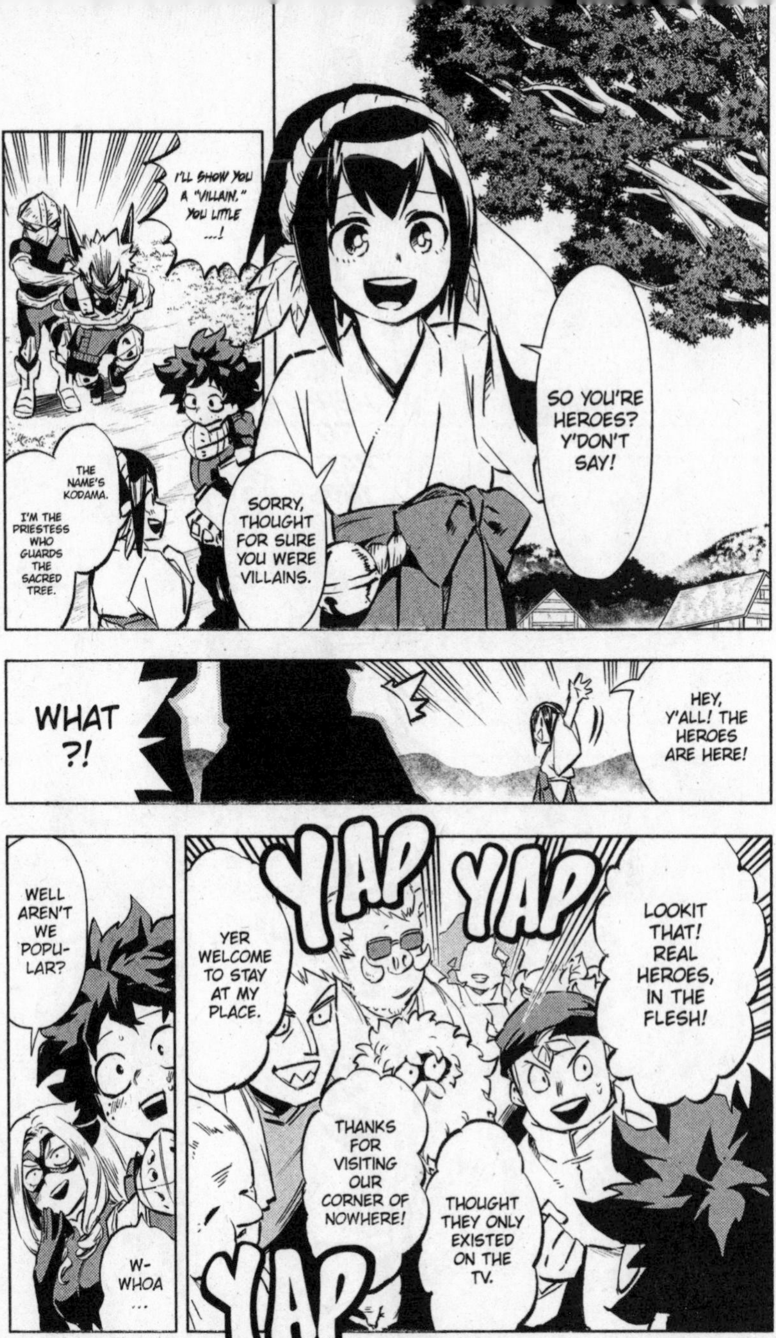
SO YOU'RE HEROES? Y'DON'T SAY!
SORRY, THOUGHT FOR SURE YOU WERE VILLAINS.
I'LL SHOW YOU A "VILLAIN," YOU LITTLE ...!
THE NAME'S KODAMA.
I'M THE PRIESTESS WHO GUARDS THE SACRED TREE.
HEY, Y'ALL! THE HEROES ARE HERE!
WHAT ?!
YAP YAP
LOOKIT THAT! REAL HEROES, IN THE FLESH!
YER WELCOME TO STAY AT MY PLACE.
THOUGHT THEY ONLY EXISTED ON THE TV.
THANKS FOR VISITING OUR CORNER OF NOWHERE!
YAP
WELL AREN'T WE POPU-LAR?
W-WHOA ...

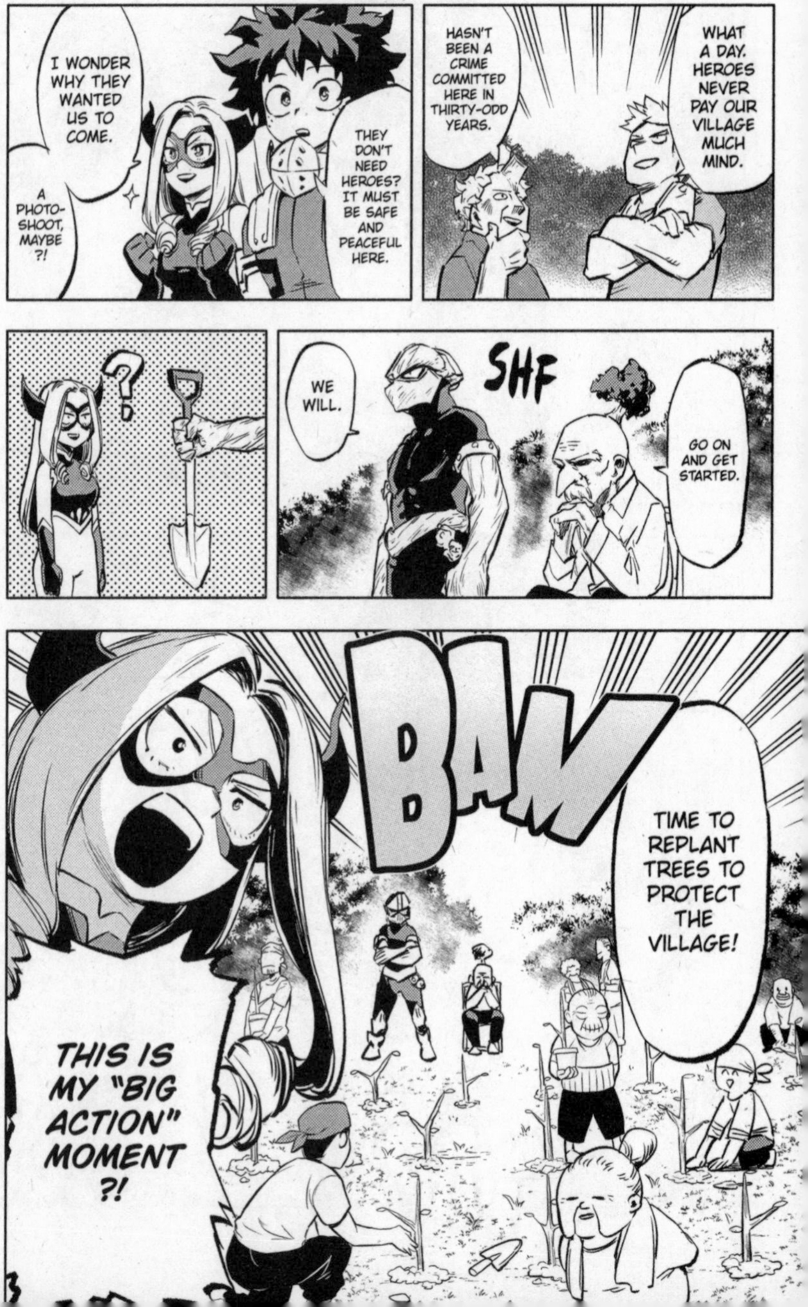
WHAT A DAY. HEROES NEVER PAY OUR VILLAGE MUCH MIND.
HASN'T BEEN A CRIME COMMITTED HERE IN THIRTY-ODD YEARS.
THEY DON'T NEED HEROES? IT MUST BE SAFE AND PEACEFUL HERE.
I WONDER WHY THEY WANTED US TO COME.
A PHOTO-SHOOT, MAYBE ?!
GO ON AND GET STARTED.
SHF
WE WILL.
?
BAM
TIME TO REPLANT TREES TO PROTECT THE VILLAGE!
THIS IS MY "BIG ACTION" MOMENT ?!

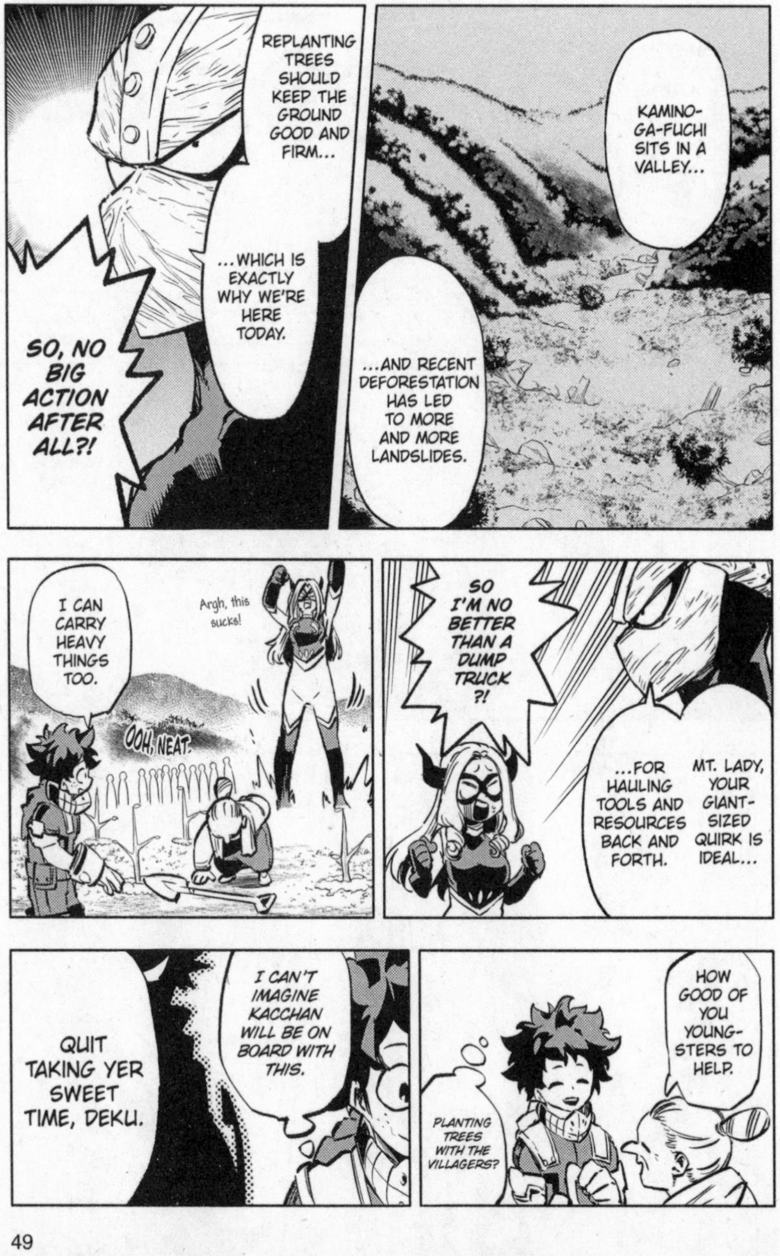
KAMINO-GA-FUCHI SITS IN A VALLEY...
...AND RECENT DEFORESTATION HAS LED TO MORE AND MORE LANDSLIDES.
REPLANTING TREES SHOULD KEEP THE GROUND GOOD AND FIRM...
...WHICH IS EXACTLY WHY WE'RE HERE TODAY.
SO, NO BIG ACTION AFTER ALL?!
MT. LADY, YOUR GIANT-SIZED QUIRK IS IDEAL...
...FOR HAULING TOOLS AND RESOURCES BACK AND FORTH.
SO I'M NO BETTER THAN A DUMP TRUCK?!
Argh, this sucks!
I CAN CARRY HEAVY THINGS TOO.
OOH, NEAT.
HOW GOOD OF YOU YOUNGSTERS TO HELP.
PLANTING TREES WITH THE VILLAGERS?
I CAN'T IMAGINE KACCHAN WILL BE ON BOARD WITH THIS.
QUIT TAKING YER SWEET TIME, DEKU.

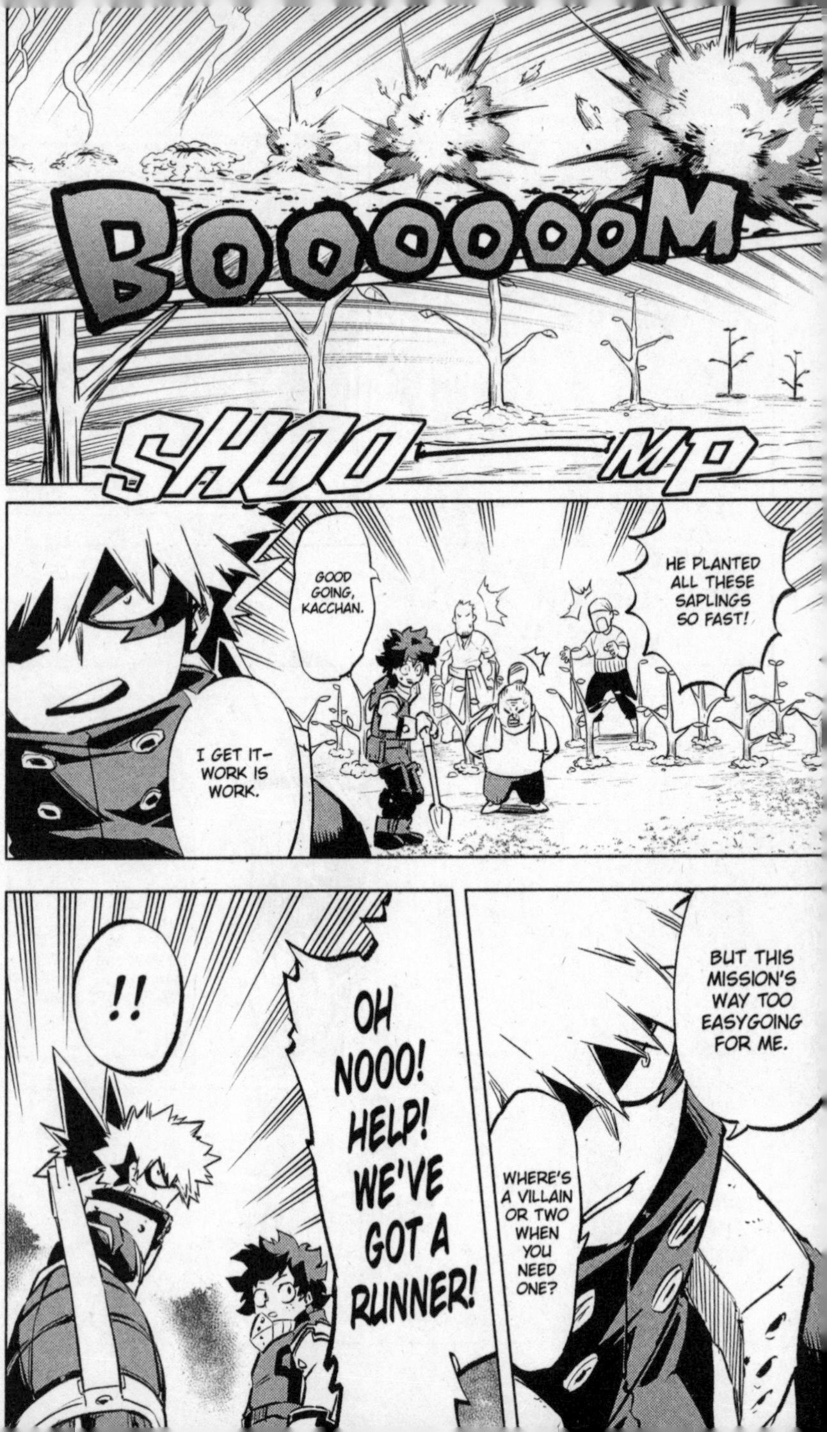
BOOOOOOM
SHOO—MP
HE PLANTED ALL THESE SAPLINGS SO FAST!
GOOD GOING, KACCHAN.
I GET IT—WORK IS WORK.
BUT THIS MISSION'S WAY TOO EASYGOING FOR ME.
WHERE'S A VILLAIN OR TWO WHEN YOU NEED ONE?
OH NOOO! HELP! WE'VE GOT A RUNNER!
!!

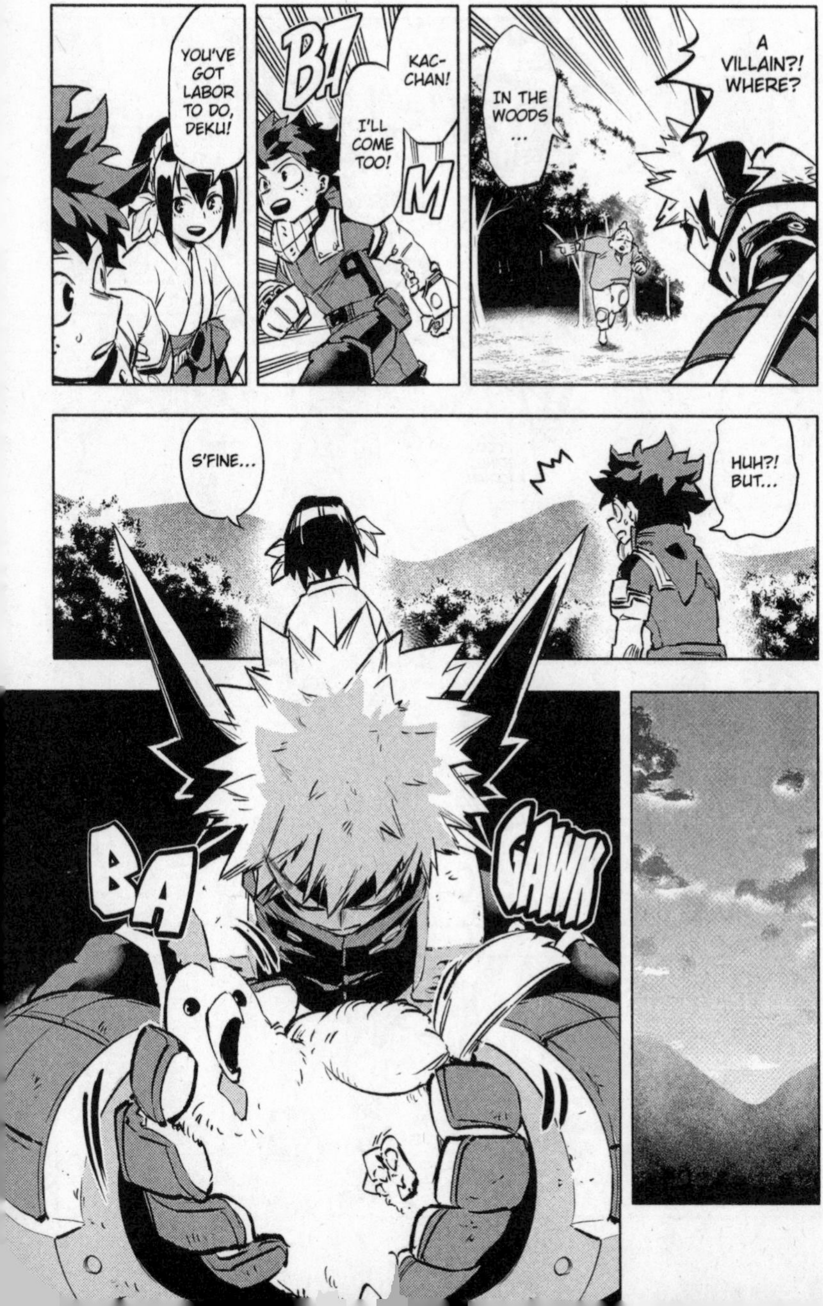
A VILLAIN?! WHERE?
IN THE WOODS...
KAC-CHAN!
BA
I'LL COME TOO!
M
YOU'VE GOT LABOR TO DO, DEKU!
HUH?! BUT...
S'FINE...
GAWK
BA

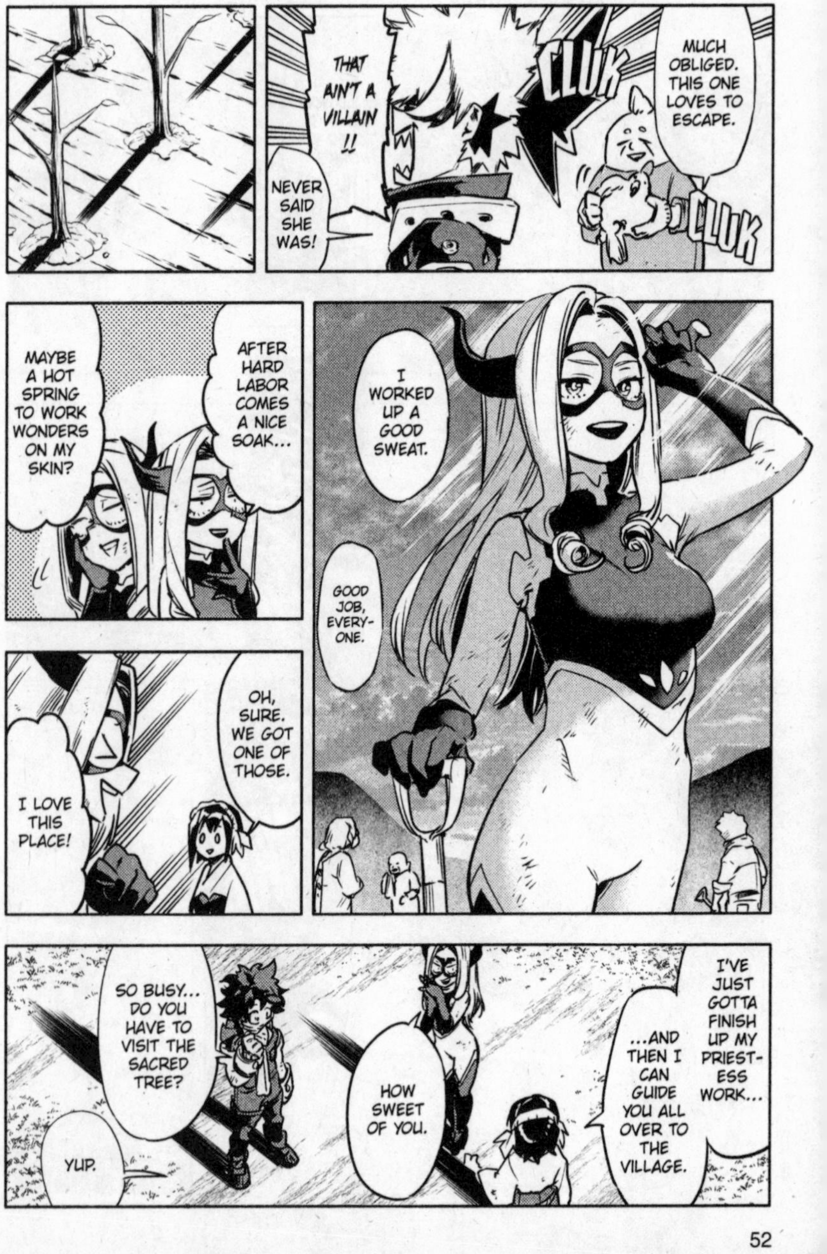
MUCH OBLIGED. THIS ONE LOVES TO ESCAPE.
CLUK
CLUK
THAT AIN'T A VILLAIN !!
NEVER SAID SHE WAS!
I WORKED UP A GOOD SWEAT.
GOOD JOB, EVERY-ONE.
AFTER HARD LABOR COMES A NICE SOAK...
MAYBE A HOT SPRING TO WORK WONDERS ON MY SKIN?
OH, SURE. WE GOT ONE OF THOSE.
I LOVE THIS PLACE!
I'VE JUST GOTTA FINISH UP MY PRIEST-ESS WORK...
...AND THEN I CAN GUIDE YOU ALL OVER TO THE VILLAGE.
HOW SWEET OF YOU.
SO BUSY... DO YOU HAVE TO VISIT THE SACRED TREE?
YUP.

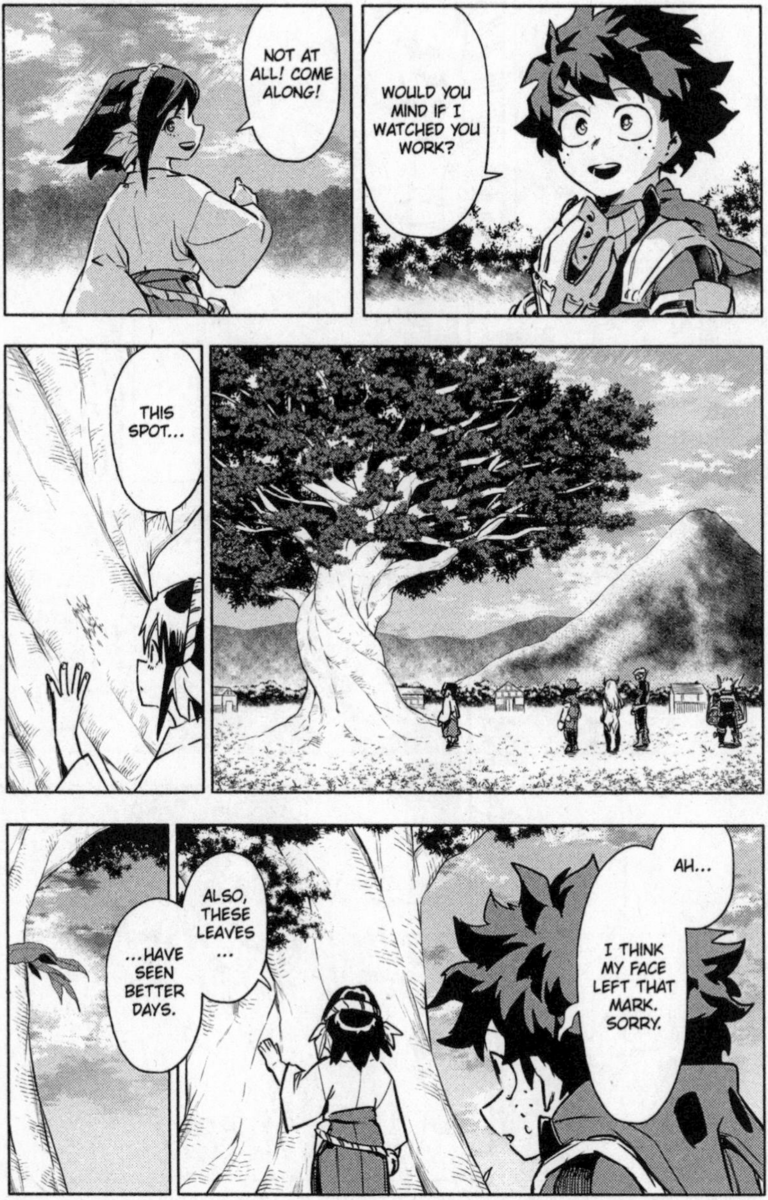
WOULD YOU MIND IF I WATCHED YOU WORK?
NOT AT ALL! COME ALONG!
THIS SPOT...
AH...
I THINK MY FACE LEFT THAT MARK. SORRY.
ALSO, THESE LEAVES ...
...HAVE SEEN BETTER DAYS.

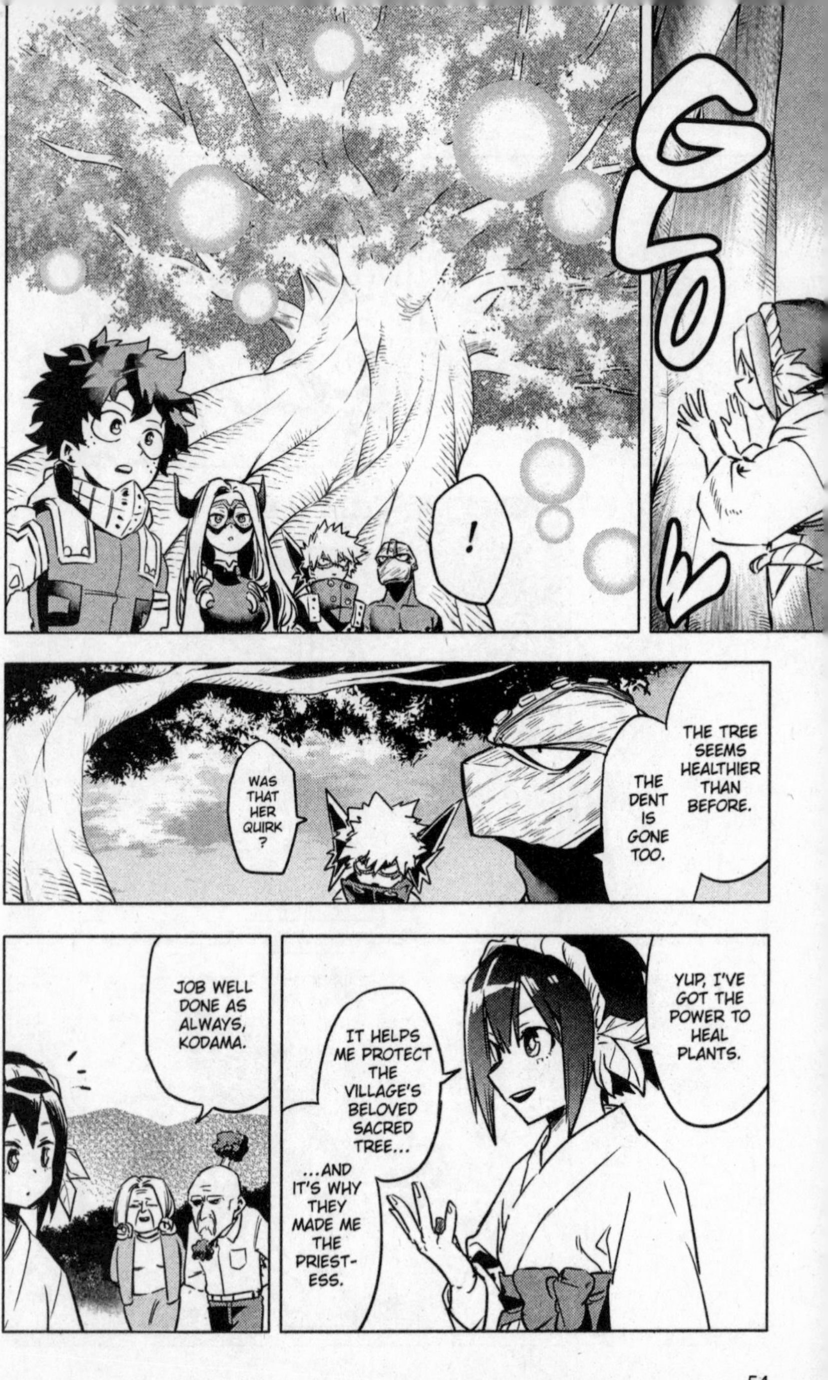
GLOW
!
THE TREE SEEMS HEALTHIER THAN BEFORE.
THE DENT IS GONE TOO.
WAS THAT HER QUIRK?
YUP, I'VE GOT THE POWER TO HEAL PLANTS.
IT HELPS ME PROTECT THE VILLAGE'S BELOVED SACRED TREE...
...AND IT'S WHY THEY MADE ME THE PRIEST-ESS.
JOB WELL DONE AS ALWAYS, KODAMA.

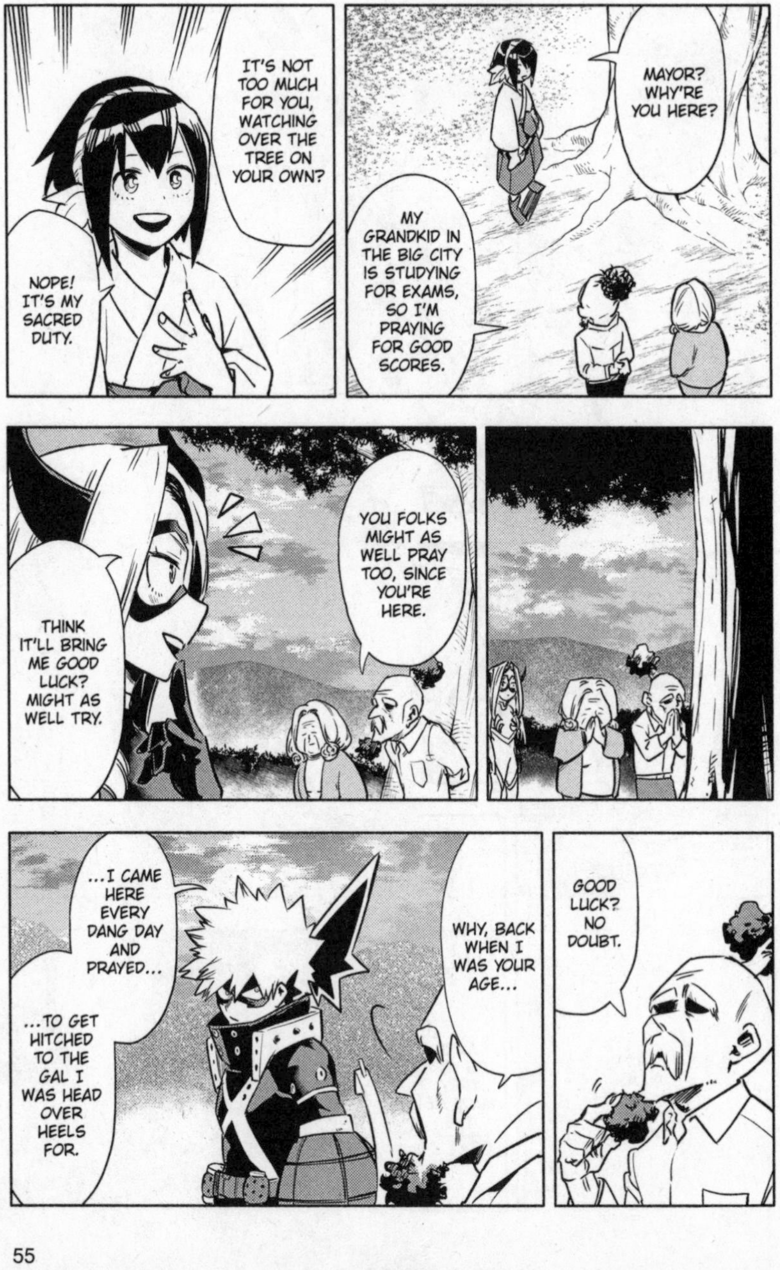
MAYOR? WHY'RE YOU HERE?
MY GRANDKID IN THE BIG CITY IS STUDYING FOR EXAMS, SO I'M PRAYING FOR GOOD SCORES.
IT'S NOT TOO MUCH FOR YOU, WATCHING OVER THE TREE ON YOUR OWN?
NOPE! IT'S MY SACRED DUTY.
YOU FOLKS MIGHT AS WELL PRAY TOO, SINCE YOU'RE HERE.
THINK IT'LL BRING ME GOOD LUCK? MIGHT AS WELL TRY.
GOOD LUCK? NO DOUBT.
WHY, BACK WHEN I WAS YOUR AGE...
...I CAME HERE EVERY DANG DAY AND PRAYED...
...TO GET HITCHED TO THE GAL I WAS HEAD OVER HEELS FOR.

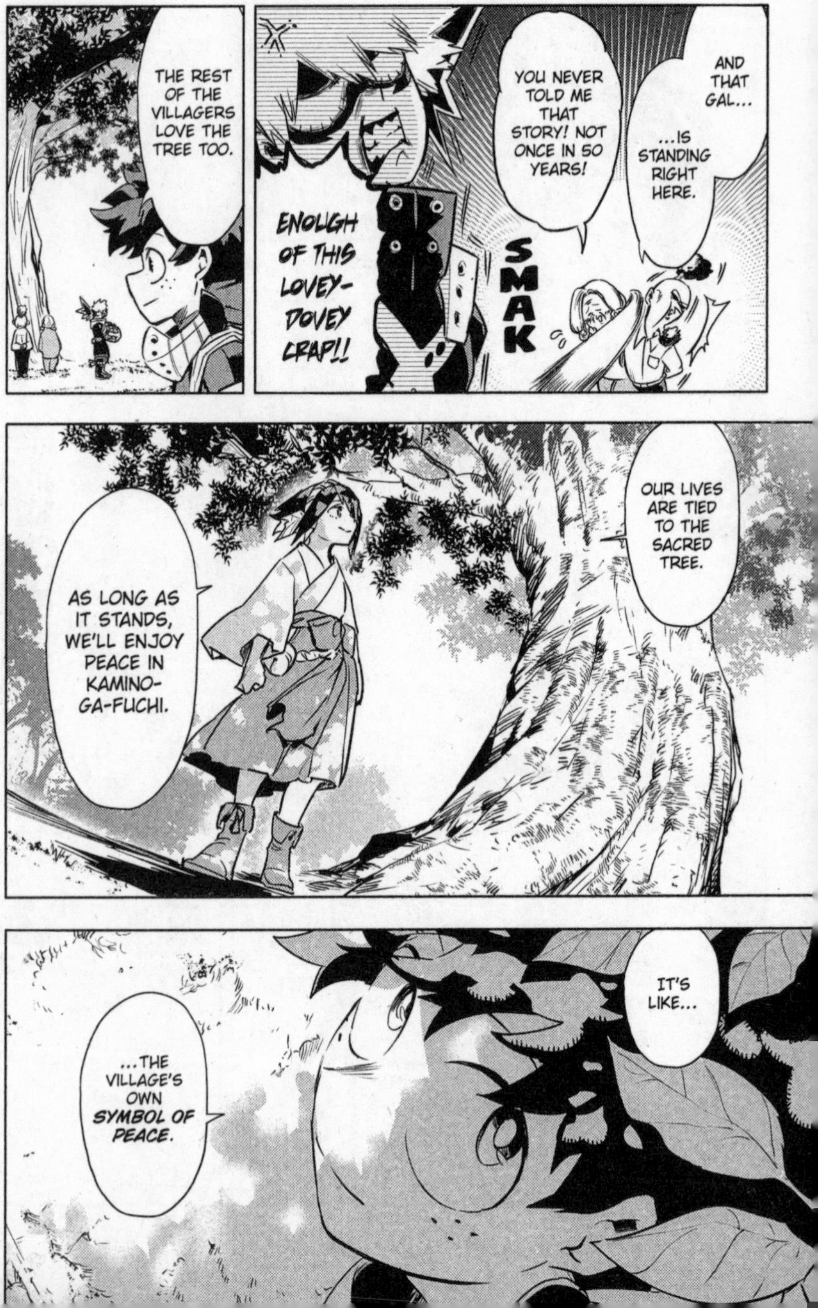
AND THAT GAL...
...IS STANDING RIGHT HERE.
YOU NEVER TOLD ME THAT STORY! NOT ONCE IN 50 YEARS!
SMAK
ENOUGH OF THIS LOVEY-DOVEY CRAP!!
THE REST OF THE VILLAGERS LOVE THE TREE TOO.
OUR LIVES ARE TIED TO THE SACRED TREE.
AS LONG AS IT STANDS, WE'LL ENJOY PEACE IN KAMINO-GA-FUCHI.
IT'S LIKE...
...THE VILLAGE'S OWN SYMBOL OF PEACE.

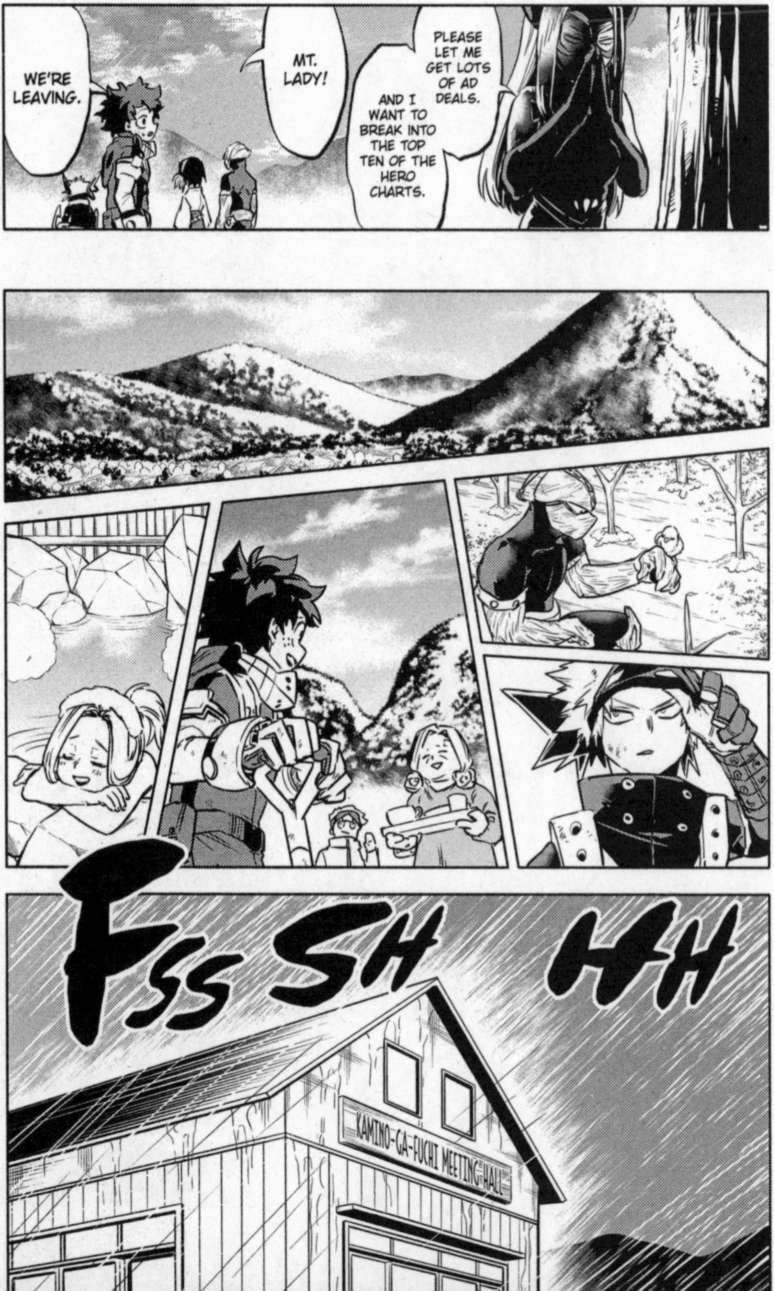
PLEASE LET ME GET LOTS OF AD DEALS.
AND I WANT TO BREAK INTO THE TOP TEN OF THE HERO CHARTS.
MT. LADY!
WE'RE LEAVING.
FSS SH HH
KAMINO-GA-FUCHI MEETING HALL

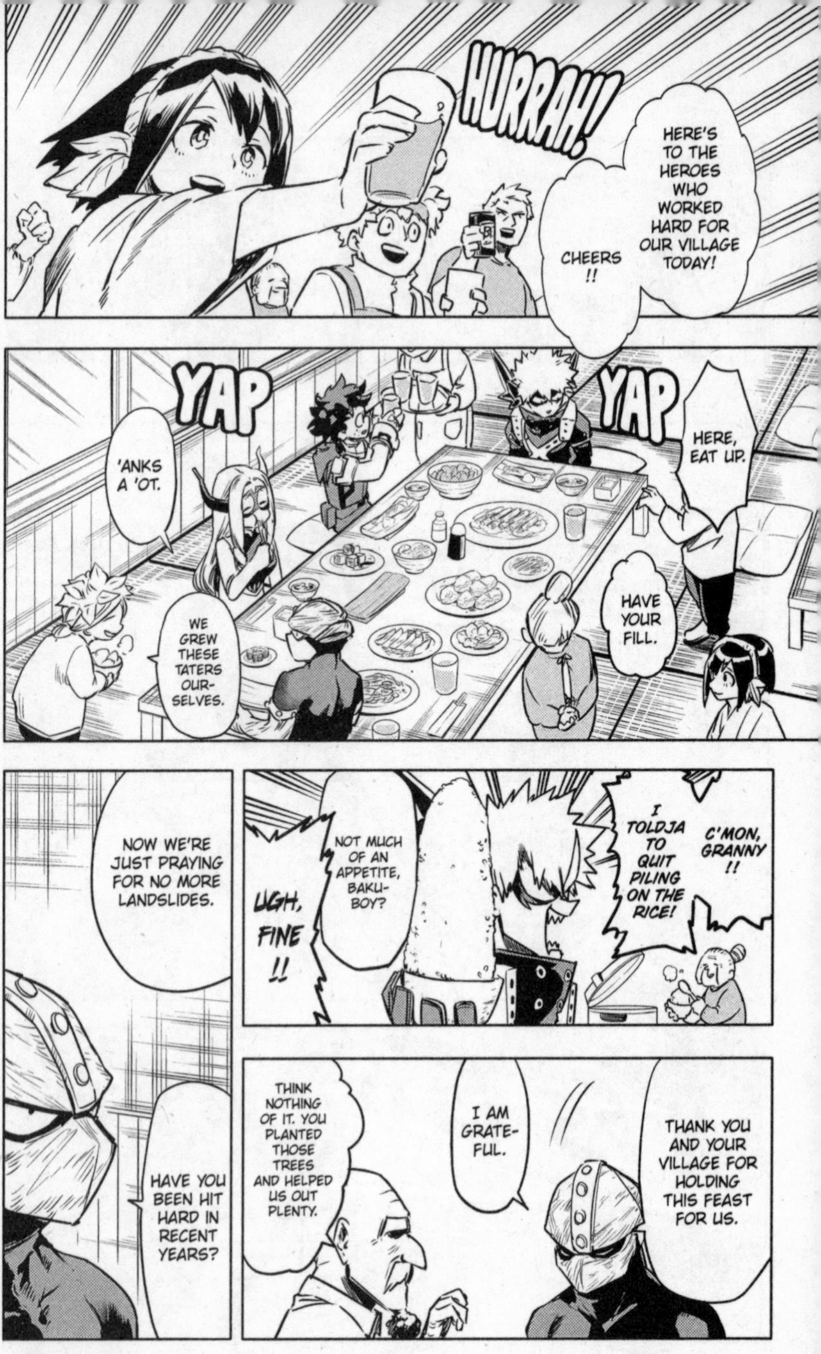
HERE'S TO THE HEROES WHO WORKED HARD FOR OUR VILLAGE TODAY!
CHEERS !!
HURRAH!!
HERE, EAT UP.
YAP
HAVE YOUR FILL.
YAP
'ANKS A 'OT.
WE GREW THESE TATERS OUR-SELVES.
C'MON, GRANNY !!
I TOLDJA TO QUIT PILING ON THE RICE!
NOT MUCH OF AN APPETITE, BAKU-BOY?
UGH, FINE !!
THANK YOU AND YOUR VILLAGE FOR HOLDING THIS FEAST FOR US.
I AM GRATE-FUL.
THINK NOTHING OF IT. YOU PLANTED THOSE TREES AND HELPED US OUT PLENTY.
HAVE YOU BEEN HIT HARD IN RECENT YEARS?
NOW WE'RE JUST PRAYING FOR NO MORE LANDSLIDES.

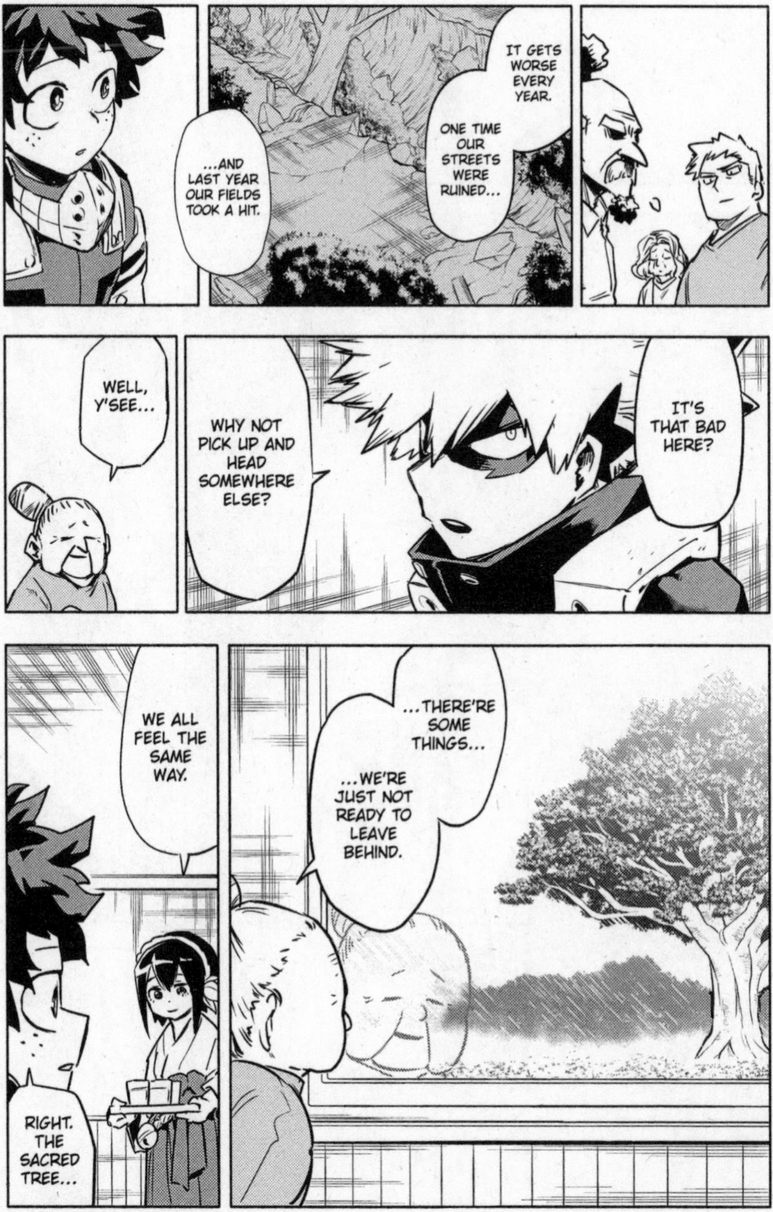
IT GETS WORSE EVERY YEAR.
ONE TIME OUR STREETS WERE RUINED...
...AND LAST YEAR OUR FIELDS TOOK A HIT.
IT'S THAT BAD HERE?
WHY NOT PICK UP AND HEAD SOMEWHERE ELSE?
WELL, Y'SEE...
...THERE'RE SOME THINGS...
...WE'RE JUST NOT READY TO LEAVE BEHIND.
WE ALL FEEL THE SAME WAY.
RIGHT. THE SACRED TREE...

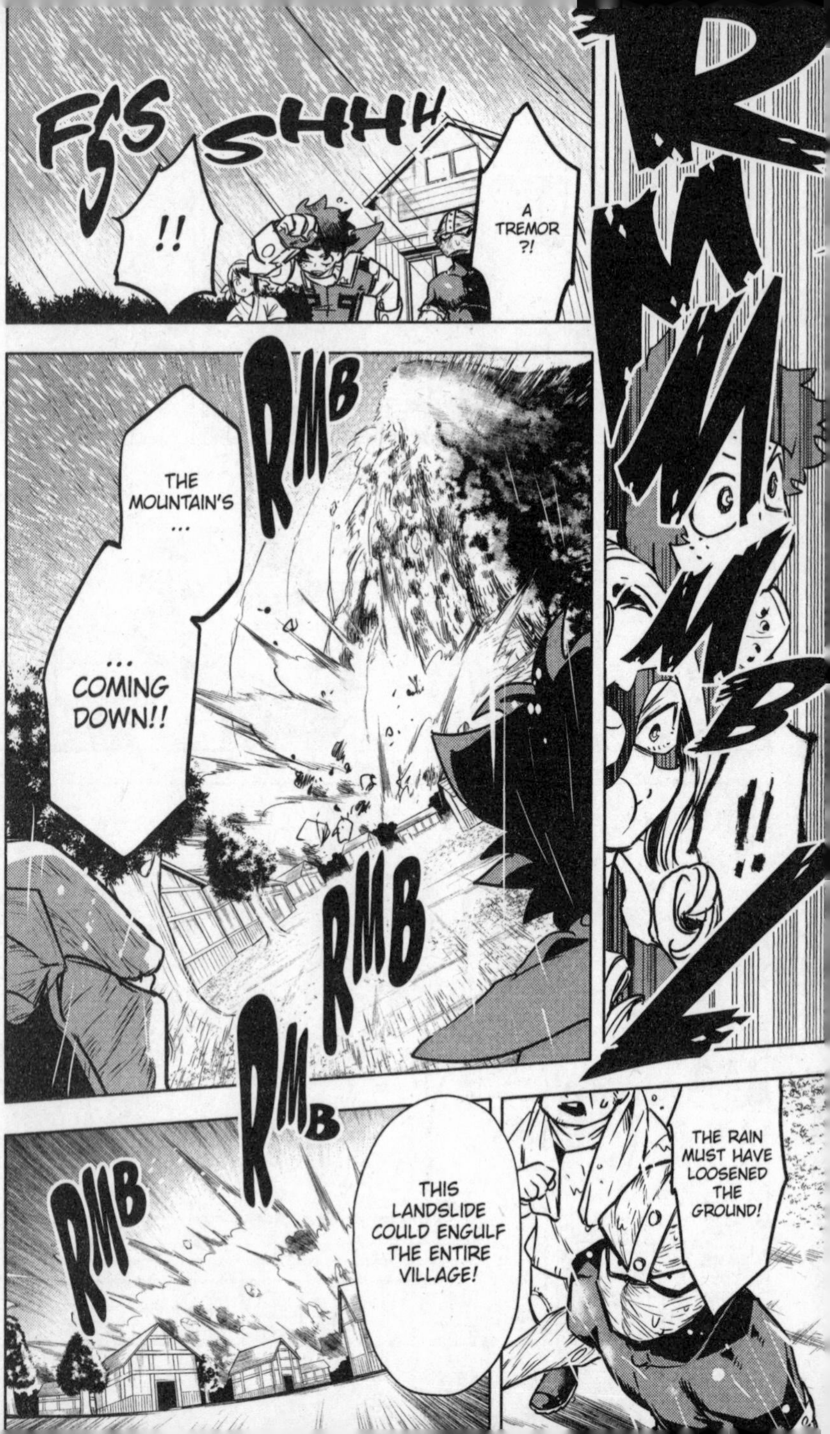
RMMMB
!!
A TREMOR ?!
FSSHHH
!!
RMB
THE MOUNTAIN'S ...
... COMING DOWN!!
RMB
RMB
THE RAIN MUST HAVE LOOSENED THE GROUND!
RMB
THIS LANDSLIDE COULD ENGULF THE ENTIRE VILLAGE!

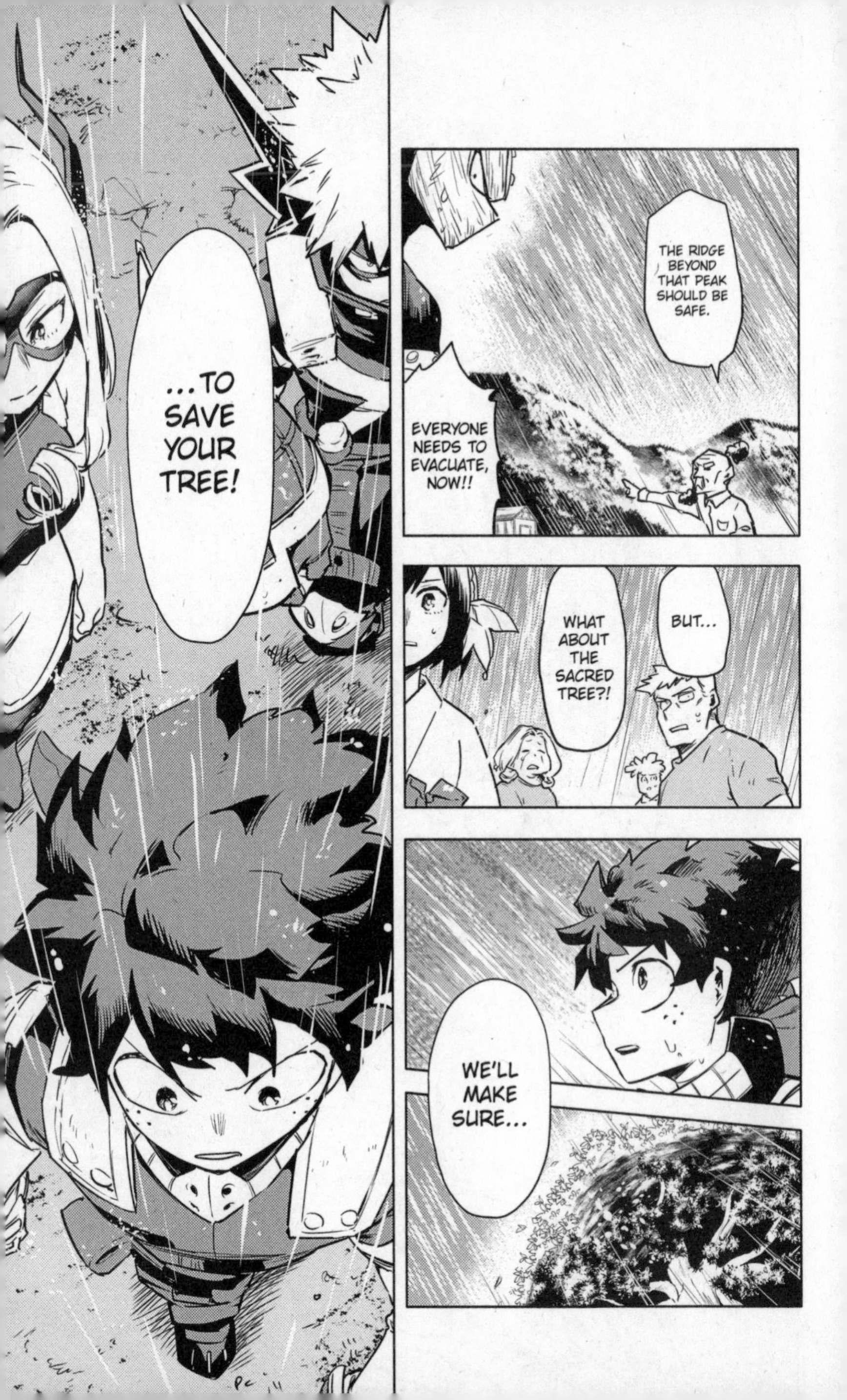

THE RIDGE BEYOND THAT PEAK SHOULD BE SAFE.
EVERYONE NEEDS TO EVACUATE, NOW!!
BUT...
WHAT ABOUT THE SACRED TREE?!
WE'LL MAKE SURE...
...TO SAVE YOUR TREE!

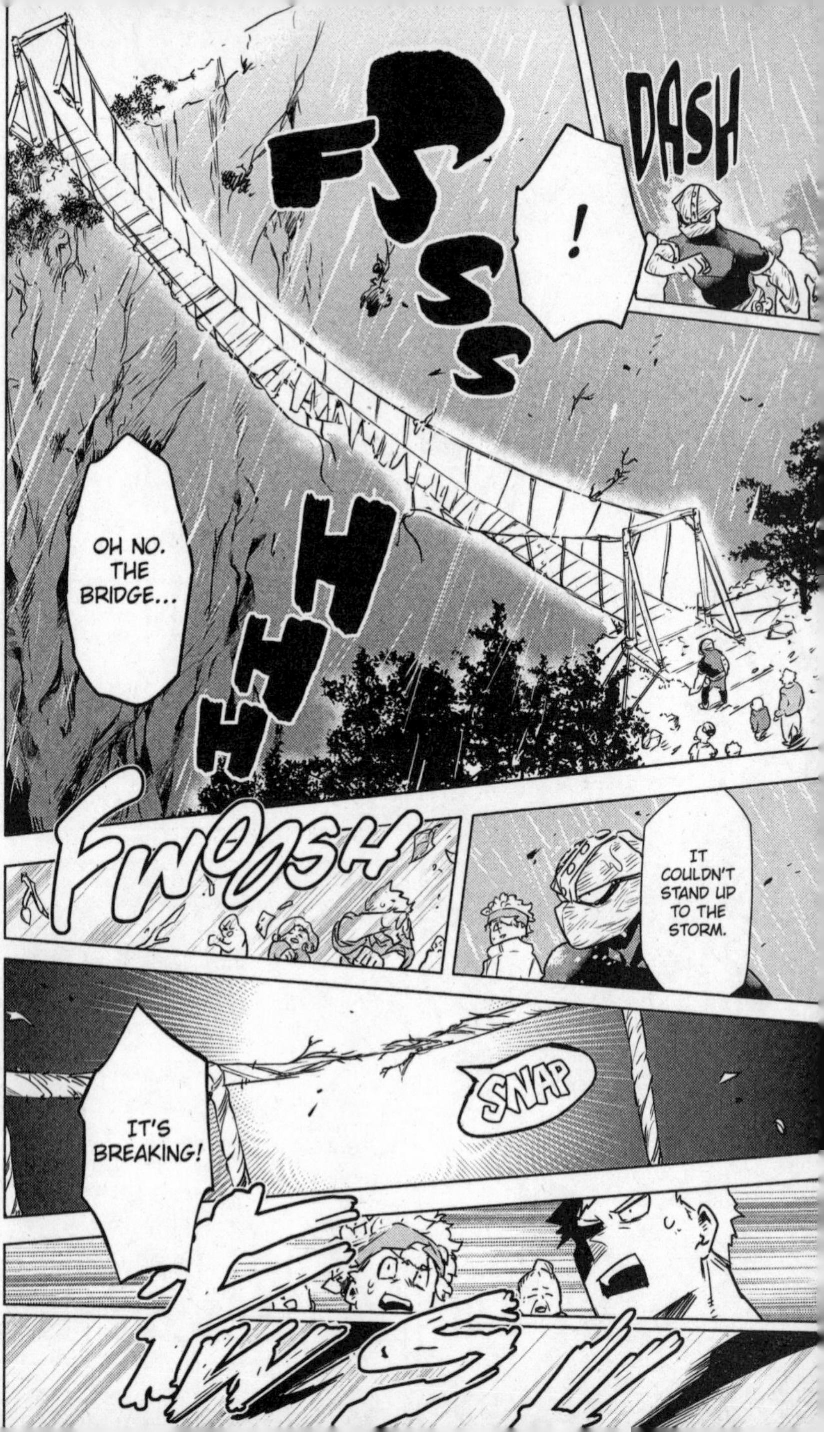
DASH
!
FSSSHHHH
OH NO. THE BRIDGE...
IT COULDN'T STAND UP TO THE STORM.
FWOOSH
SNAP
IT'S BREAKING!

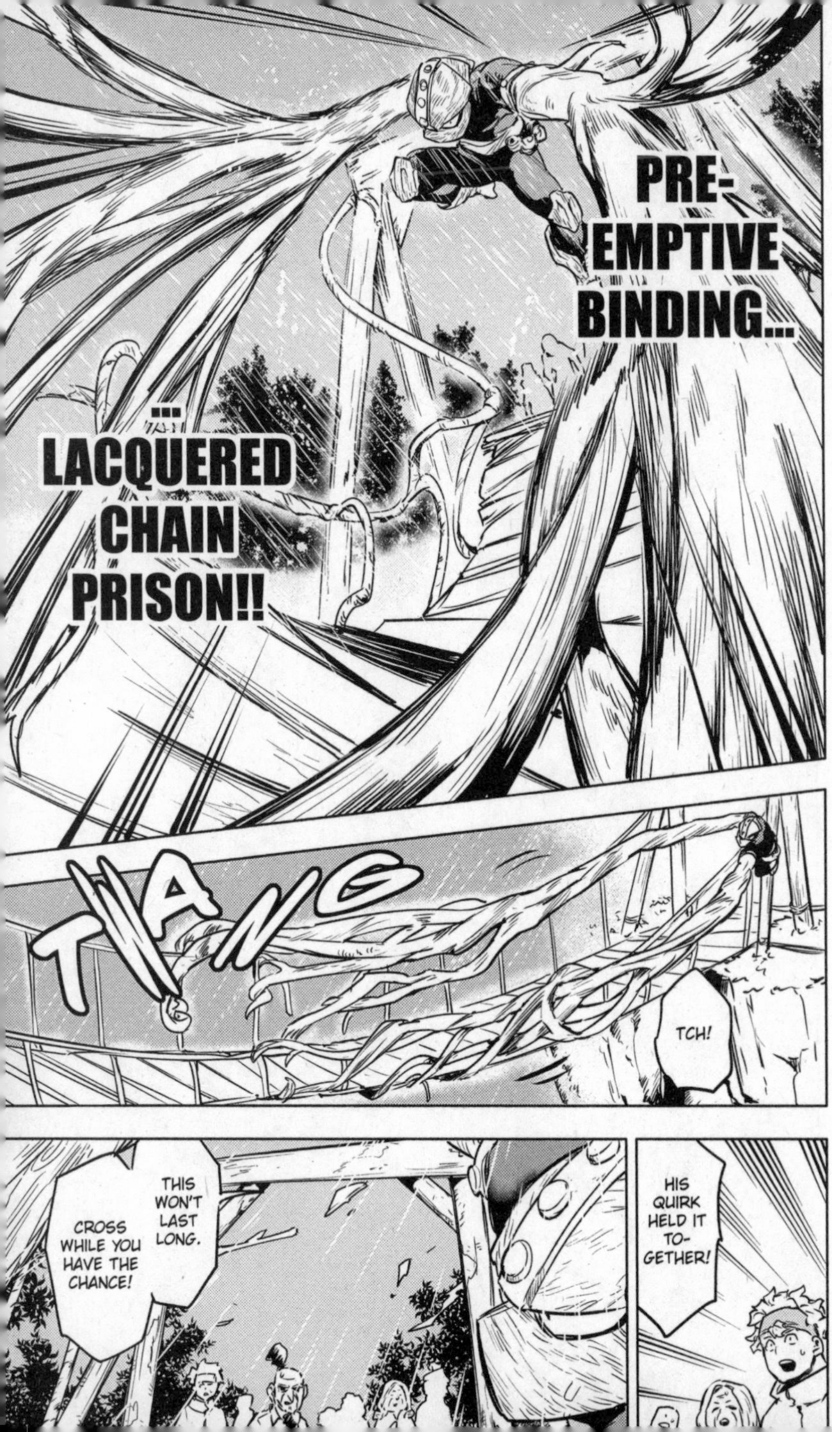
PRE-EMPTIVE BINDING...
...LACQUERED CHAIN PRISON!!
TWANG
TCH!
HIS QUIRK HELD IT TO-GETHER!
THIS WON'T LAST LONG.
CROSS WHILE YOU HAVE THE CHANCE!

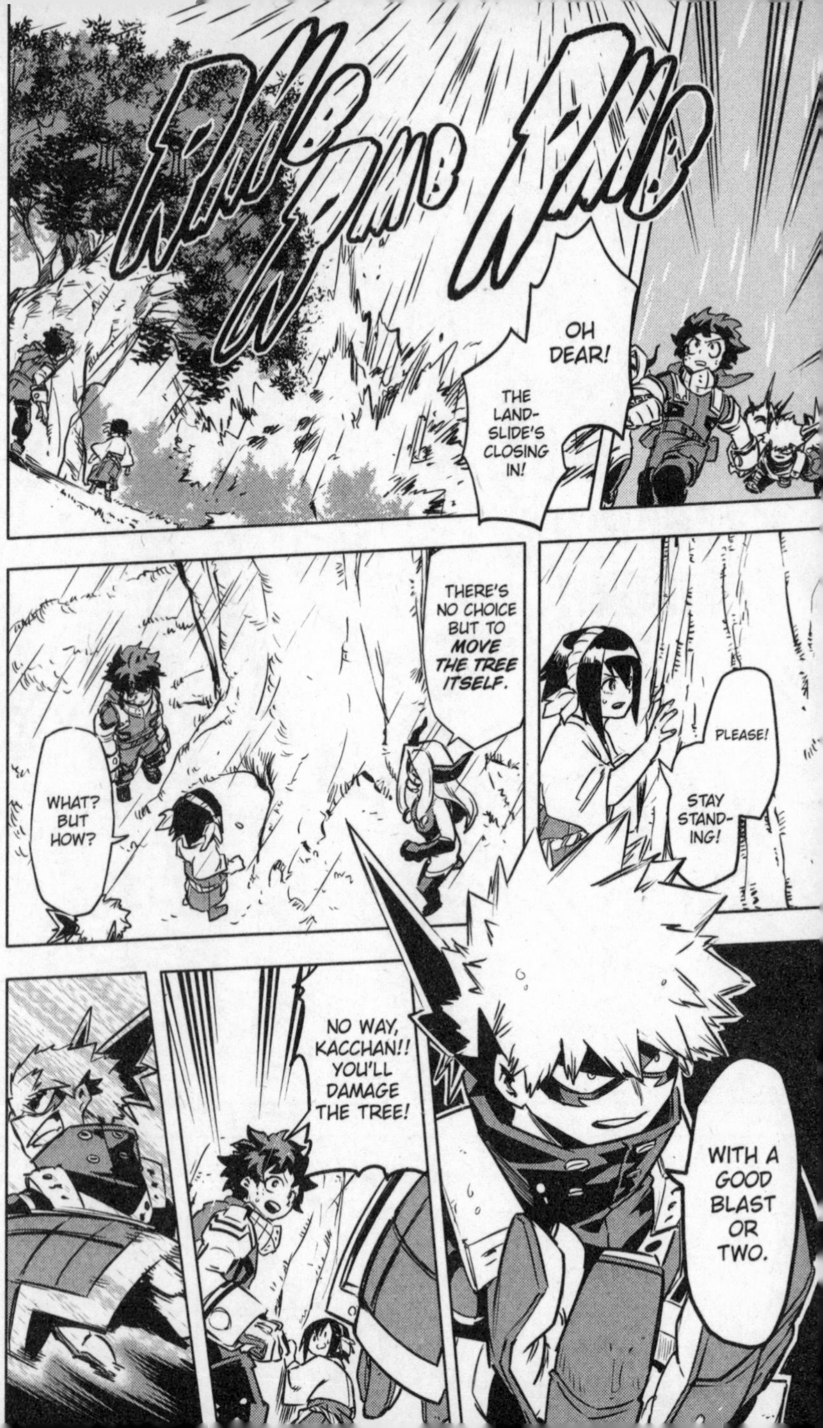
OH DEAR!
THE LAND-SLIDE'S CLOSING IN!
PLEASE!
STAY STAND-ING!
THERE'S NO CHOICE BUT TO *MOVE THE TREE ITSELF*.
WHAT? BUT HOW?
WITH A GOOD BLAST OR TWO.
NO WAY, KACCHAN!! YOU'LL DAMAGE THE TREE!

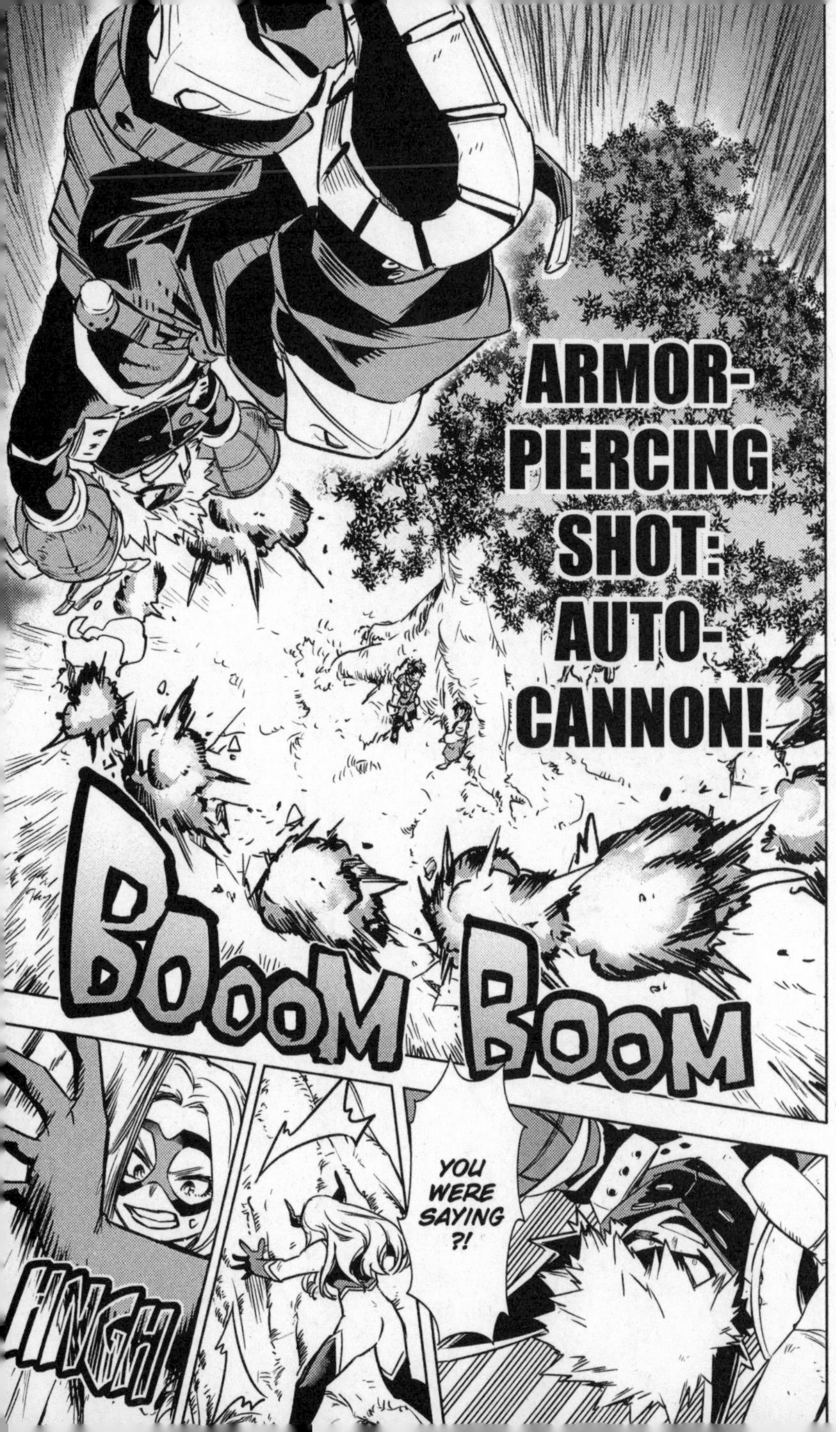
ARMOR-PIERCING SHOT: AUTO-CANNON!
BOOOM BOOM
YOU WERE SAYING?!
HNGH

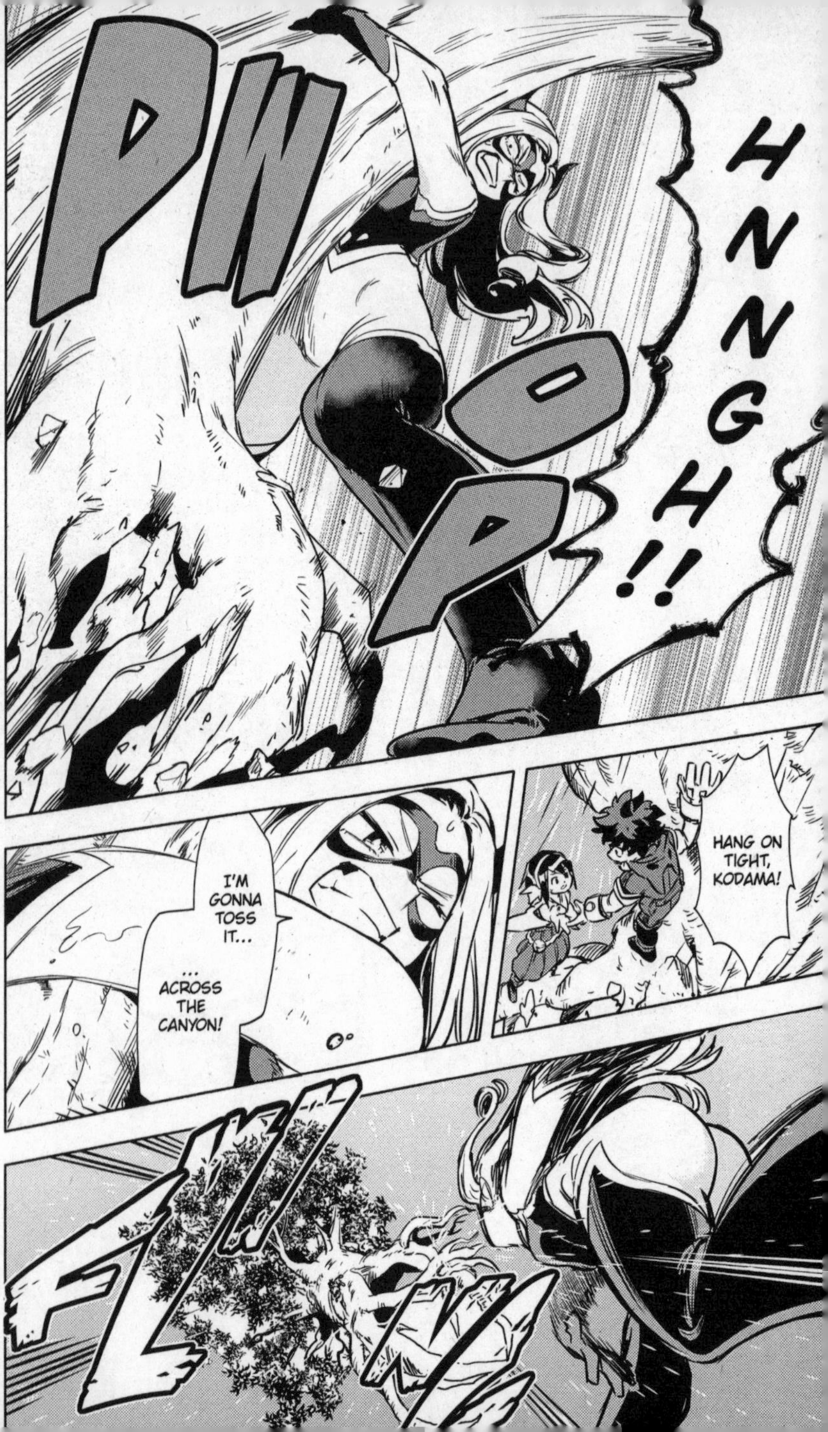
HNNGH!!
DWOP
HANG ON TIGHT, KODAMA!
I'M GONNA TOSS IT...
...ACROSS THE CANYON!

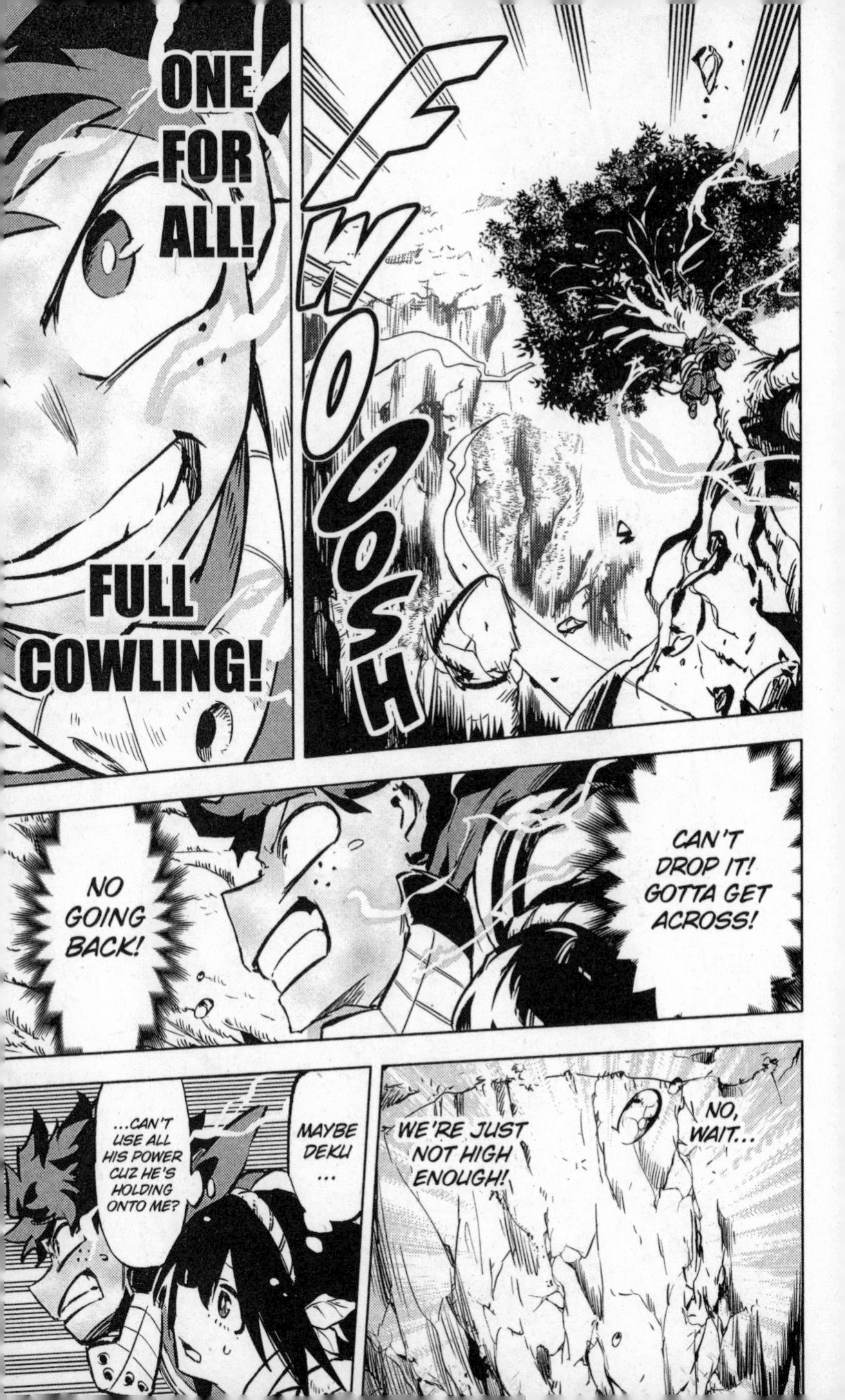
FWOOOOSH
ONE FOR ALL!
FULL COWLING!
CAN'T DROP IT! GOTTA GET ACROSS!
NO GOING BACK!
NO, WAIT...
WE'RE JUST NOT HIGH ENOUGH!
MAYBE DEKU ...
...CAN'T USE ALL HIS POWER CUZ HE'S HOLDING ONTO ME?

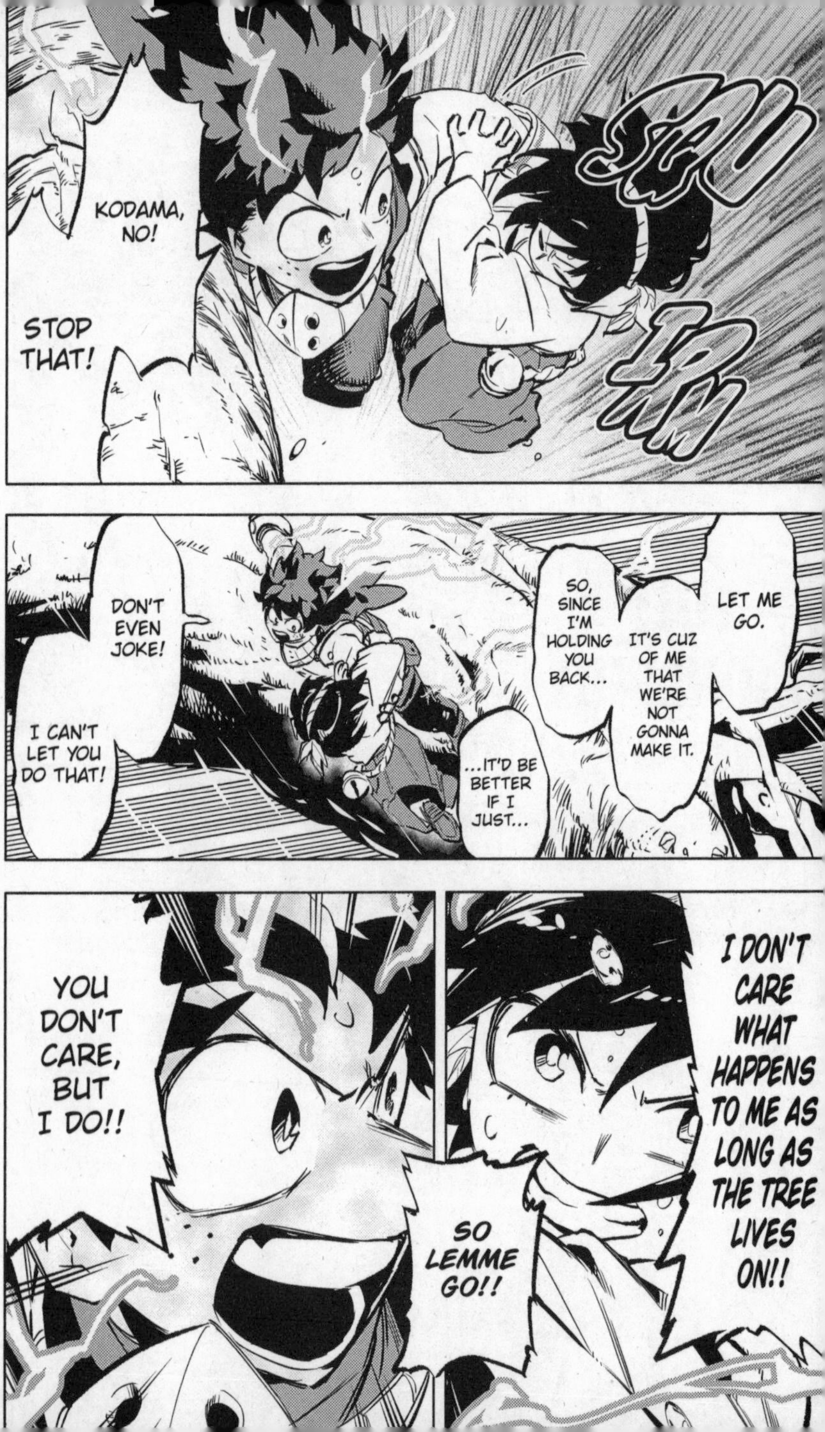
KODAMA, NO!
STOP THAT!
LET ME GO.
IT'S CUZ OF ME THAT WE'RE NOT GONNA MAKE IT.
SO, SINCE I'M HOLDING YOU BACK...
...IT'D BE BETTER IF I JUST...
DON'T EVEN JOKE!
I CAN'T LET YOU DO THAT!
I DON'T CARE WHAT HAPPENS TO ME AS LONG AS THE TREE LIVES ON!!
SO LEMME GO!!
YOU DON'T CARE, BUT I DO!!

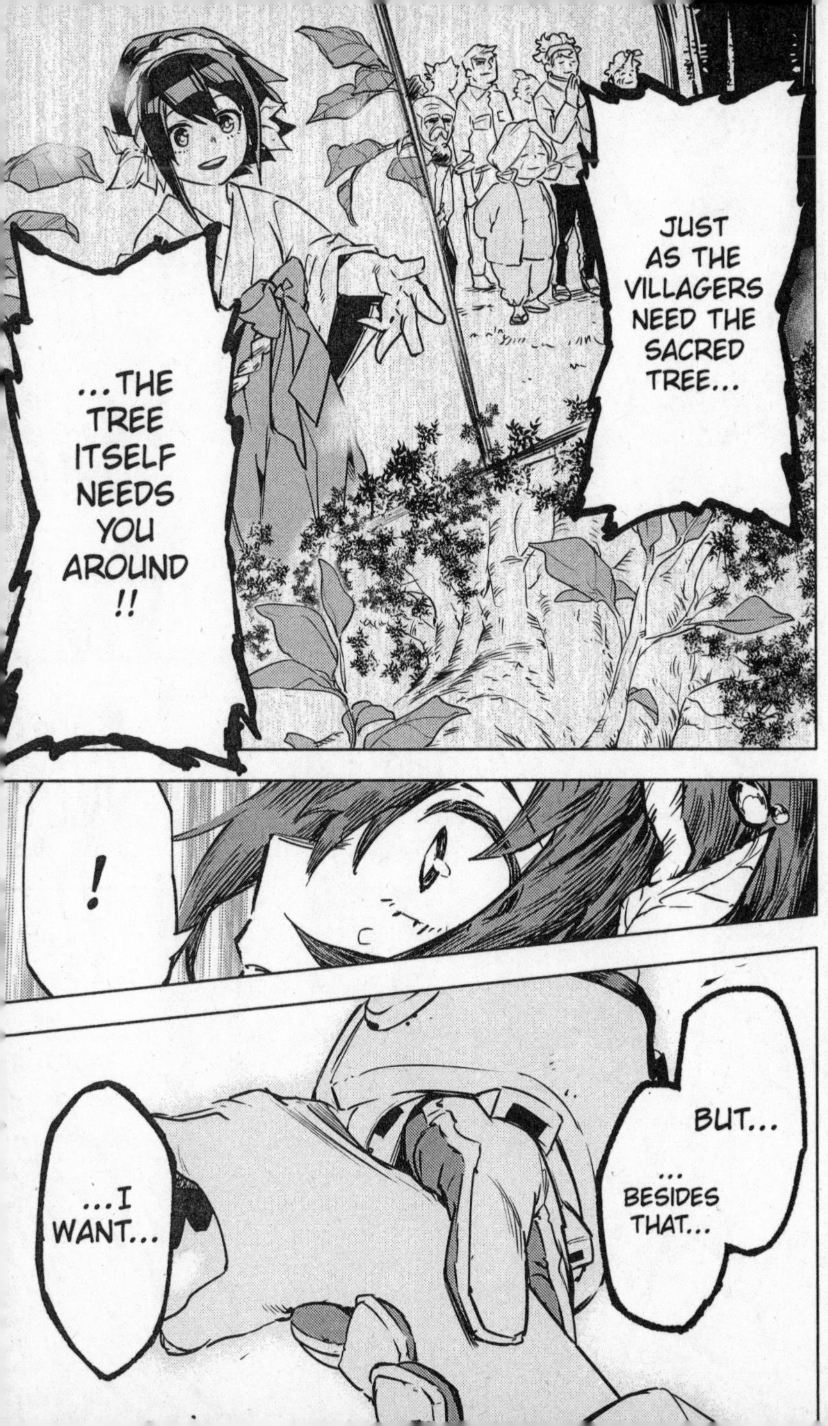
JUST AS THE VILLAGERS NEED THE SACRED TREE...
...THE TREE ITSELF NEEDS YOU AROUND!!
!
BUT...
...BESIDES THAT...
...I WANT...

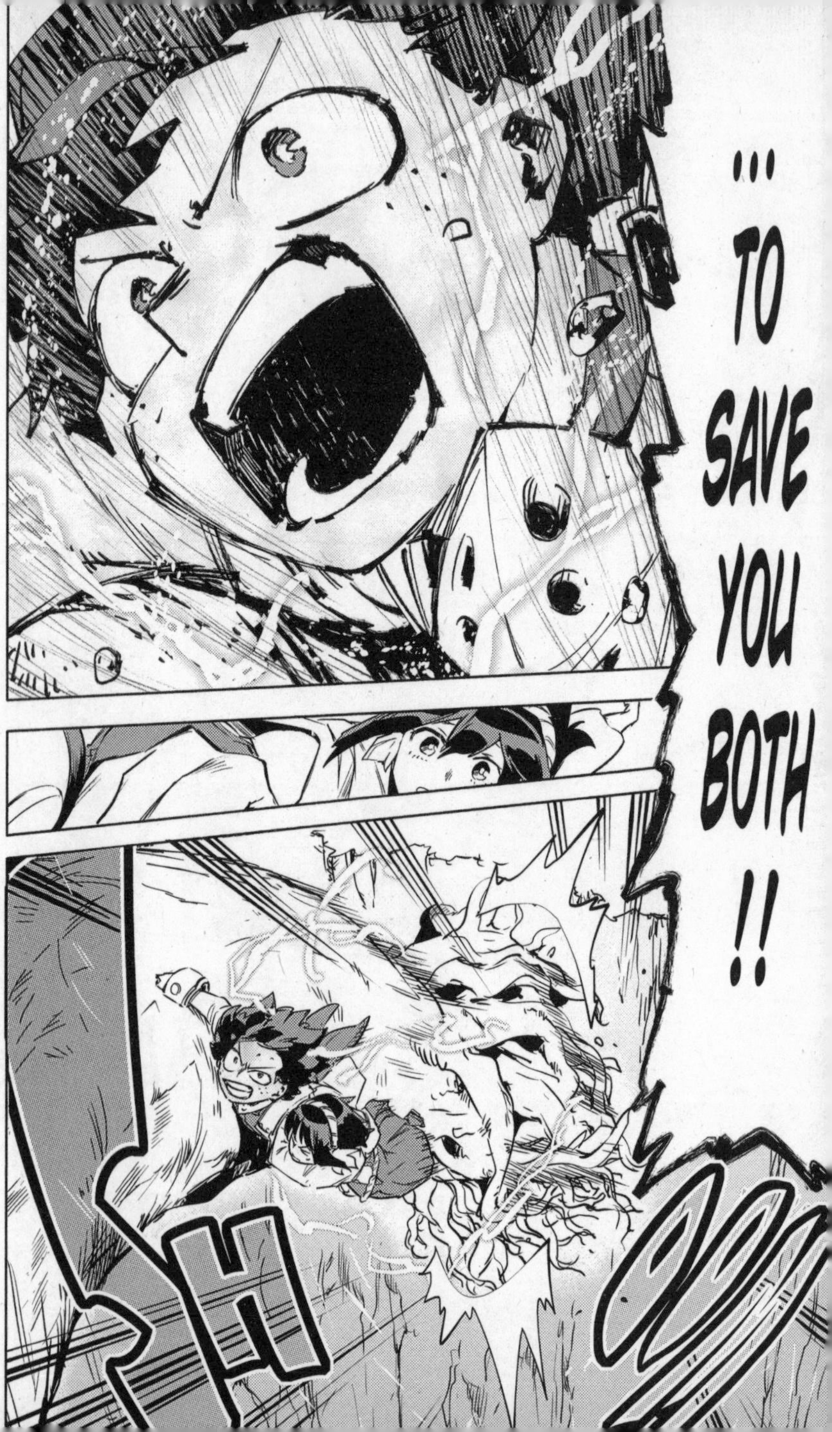
...TO SAVE YOU BOTH!!

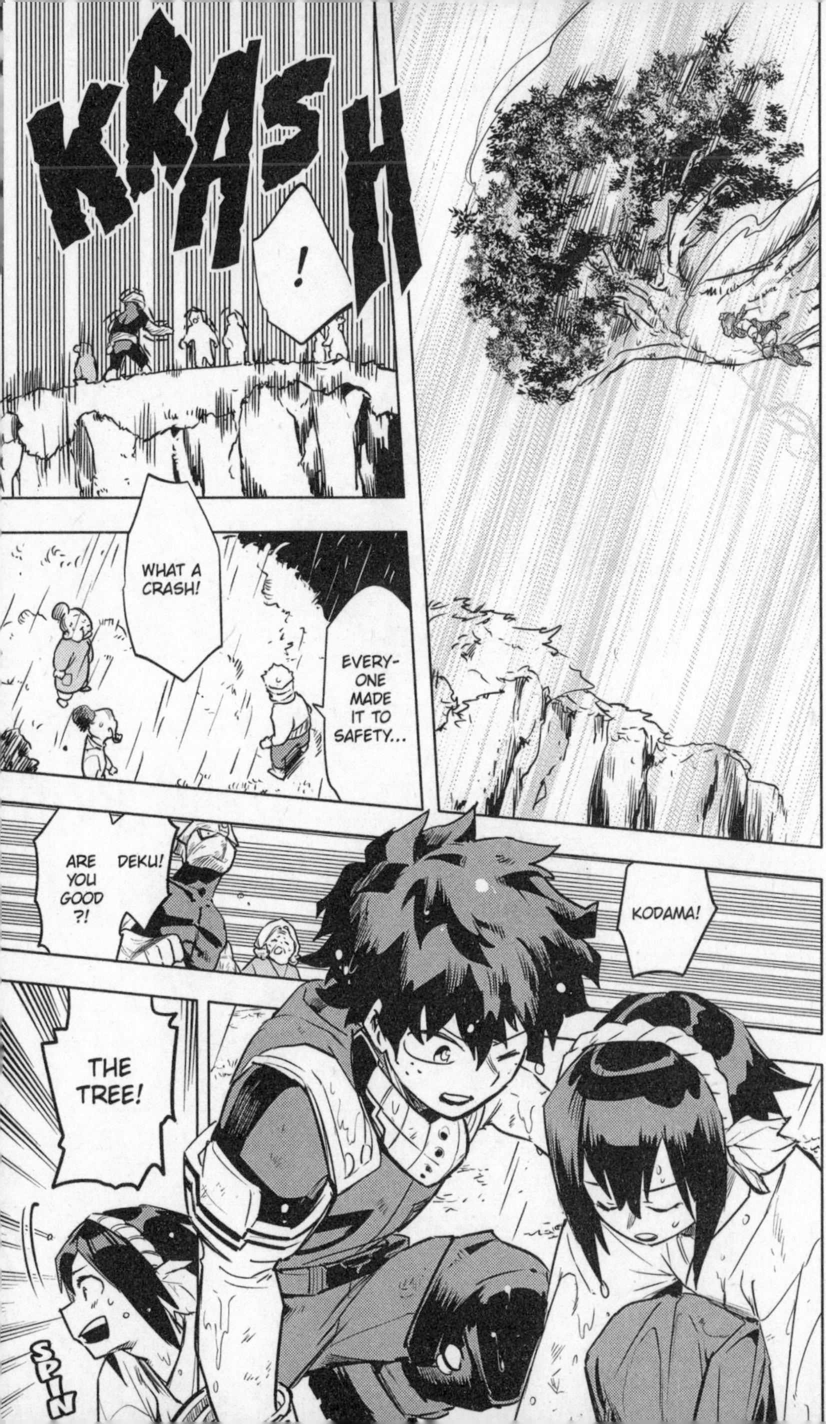

KRASH
!
EVERY-ONE MADE IT TO SAFETY...
WHAT A CRASH!
KODAMA!
DEKU!
ARE YOU GOOD?!
THE TREE!
SPIN

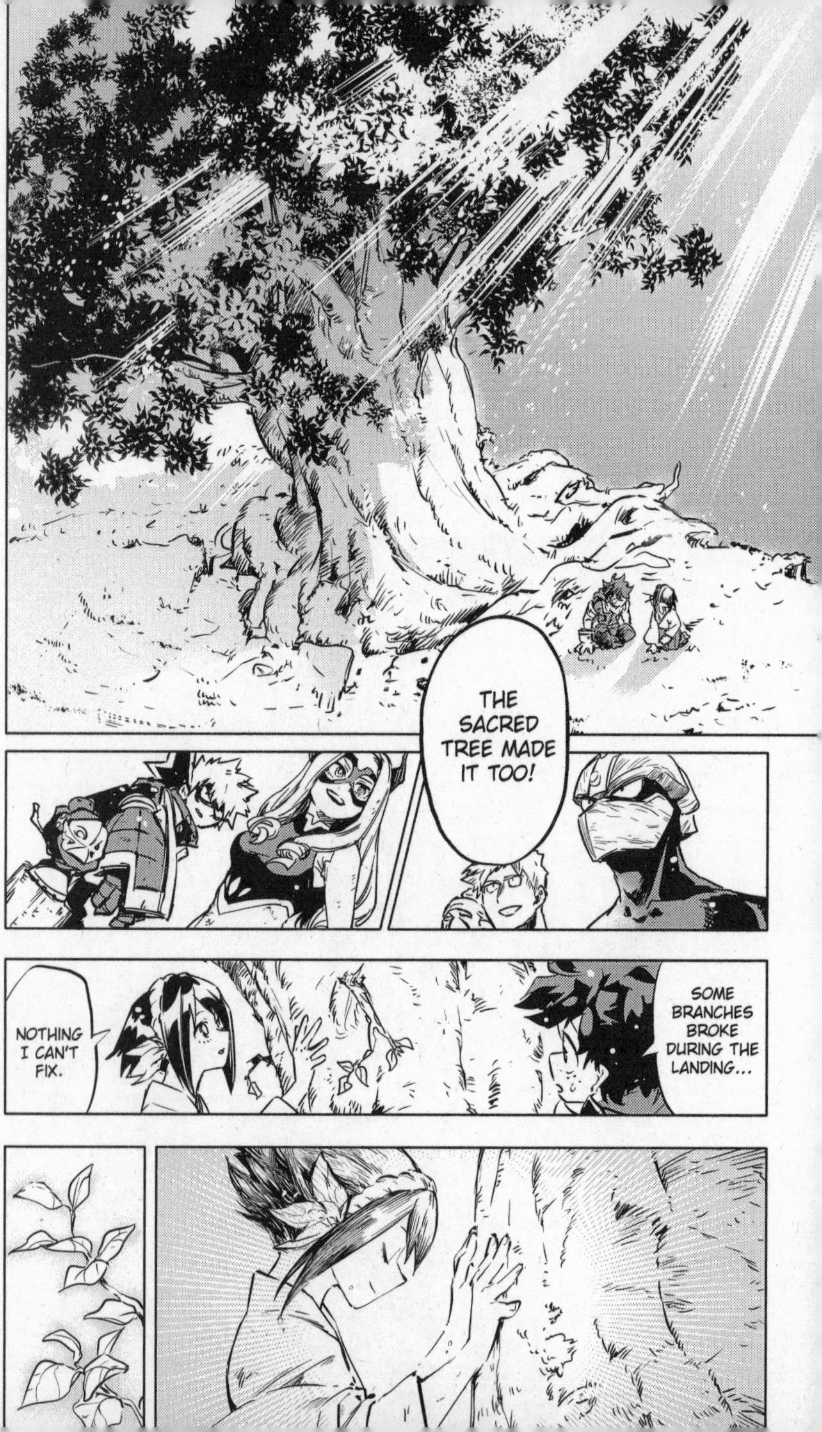
THE SACRED TREE MADE IT TOO!
SOME BRANCHES BROKE DURING THE LANDING...
NOTHING I CAN'T FIX.

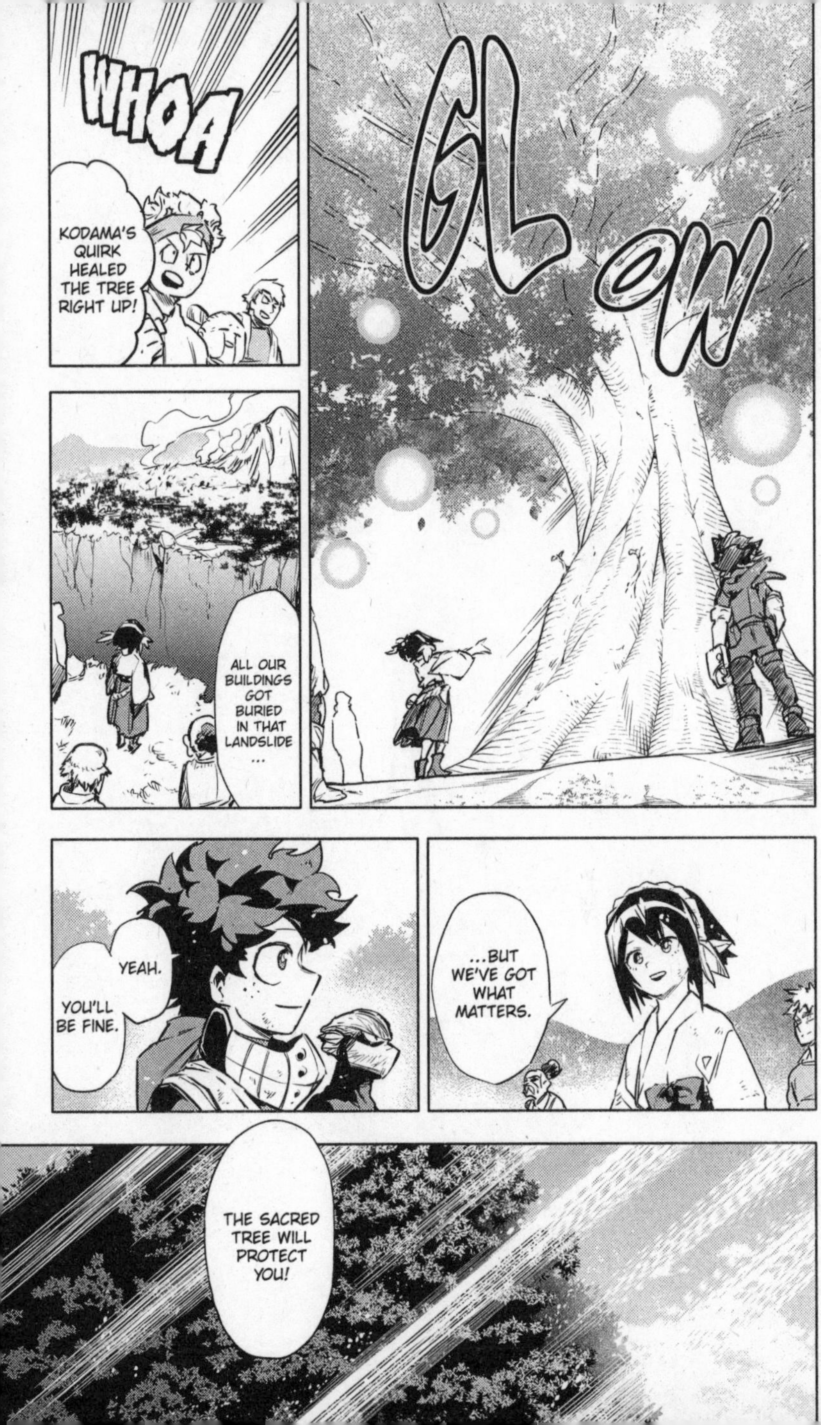
GLOW
WHOA
KODAMA'S QUIRK HEALED THE TREE RIGHT UP!
ALL OUR BUILDINGS GOT BURIED IN THAT LANDSLIDE ...
...BUT WE'VE GOT WHAT MATTERS.
YEAH.
YOU'LL BE FINE.
THE SACRED TREE WILL PROTECT YOU!

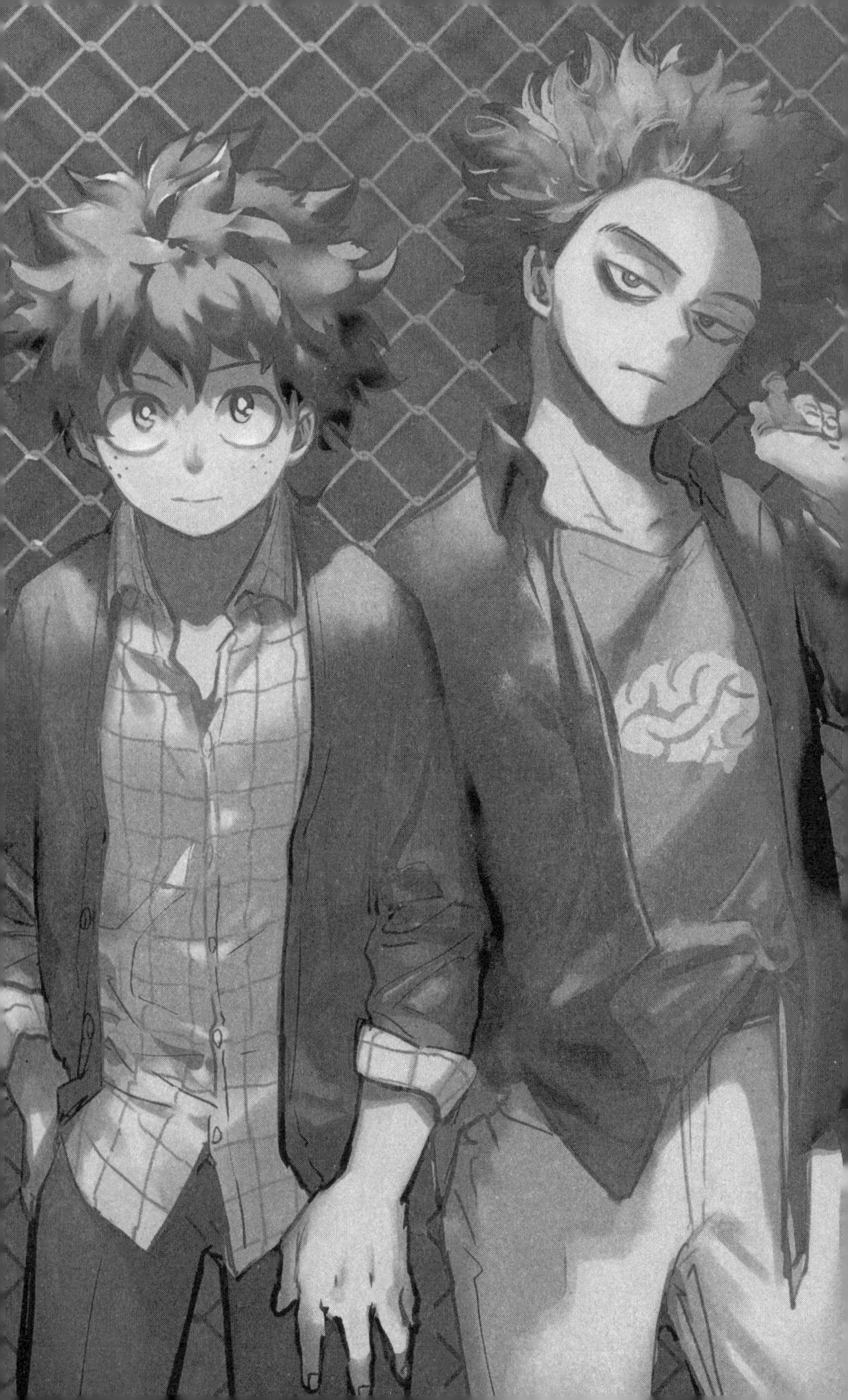

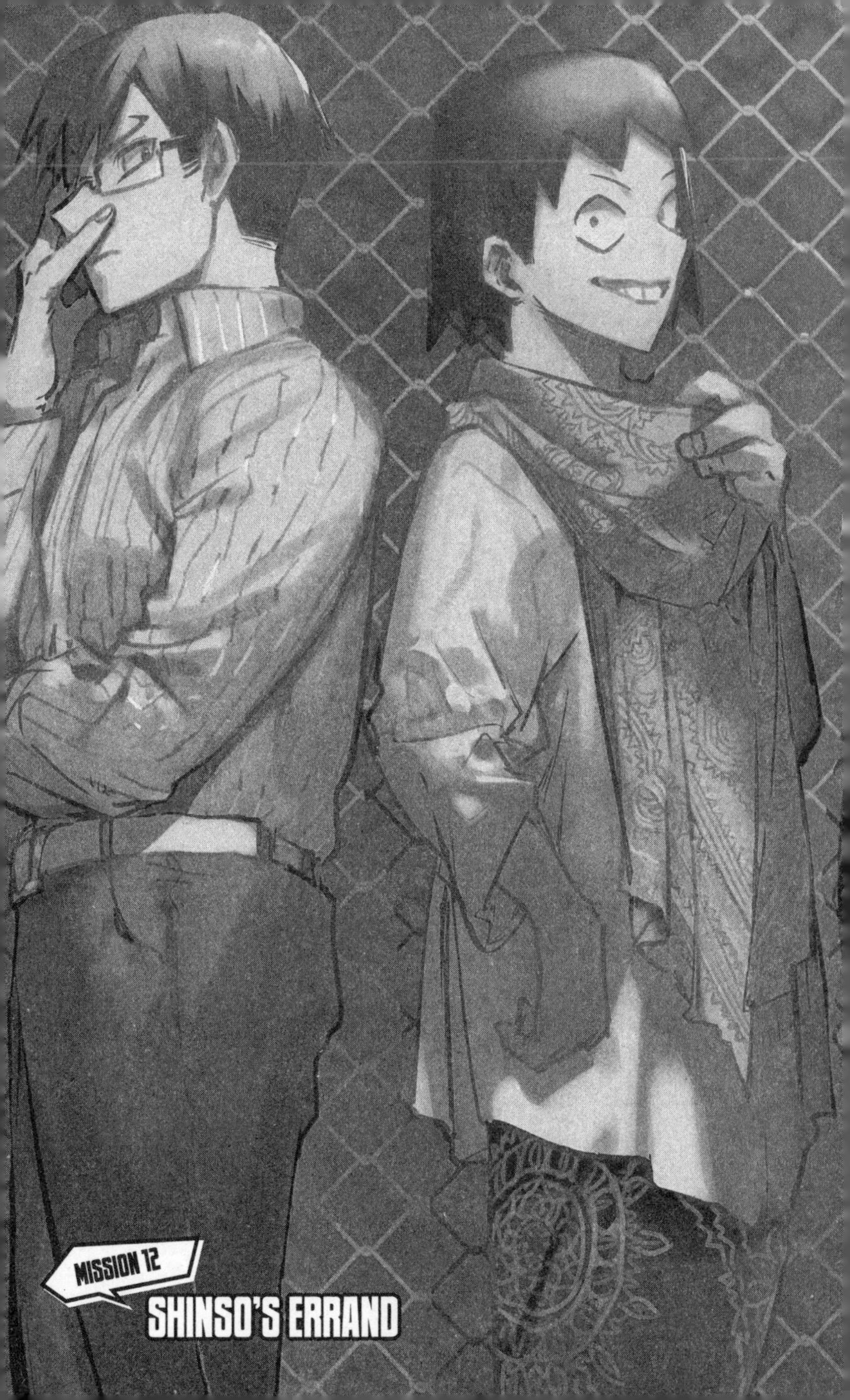
MISSION 12
SHINSO'S ERRAND

MY HERO ACADEMIA
Team-Up Missions

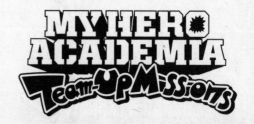

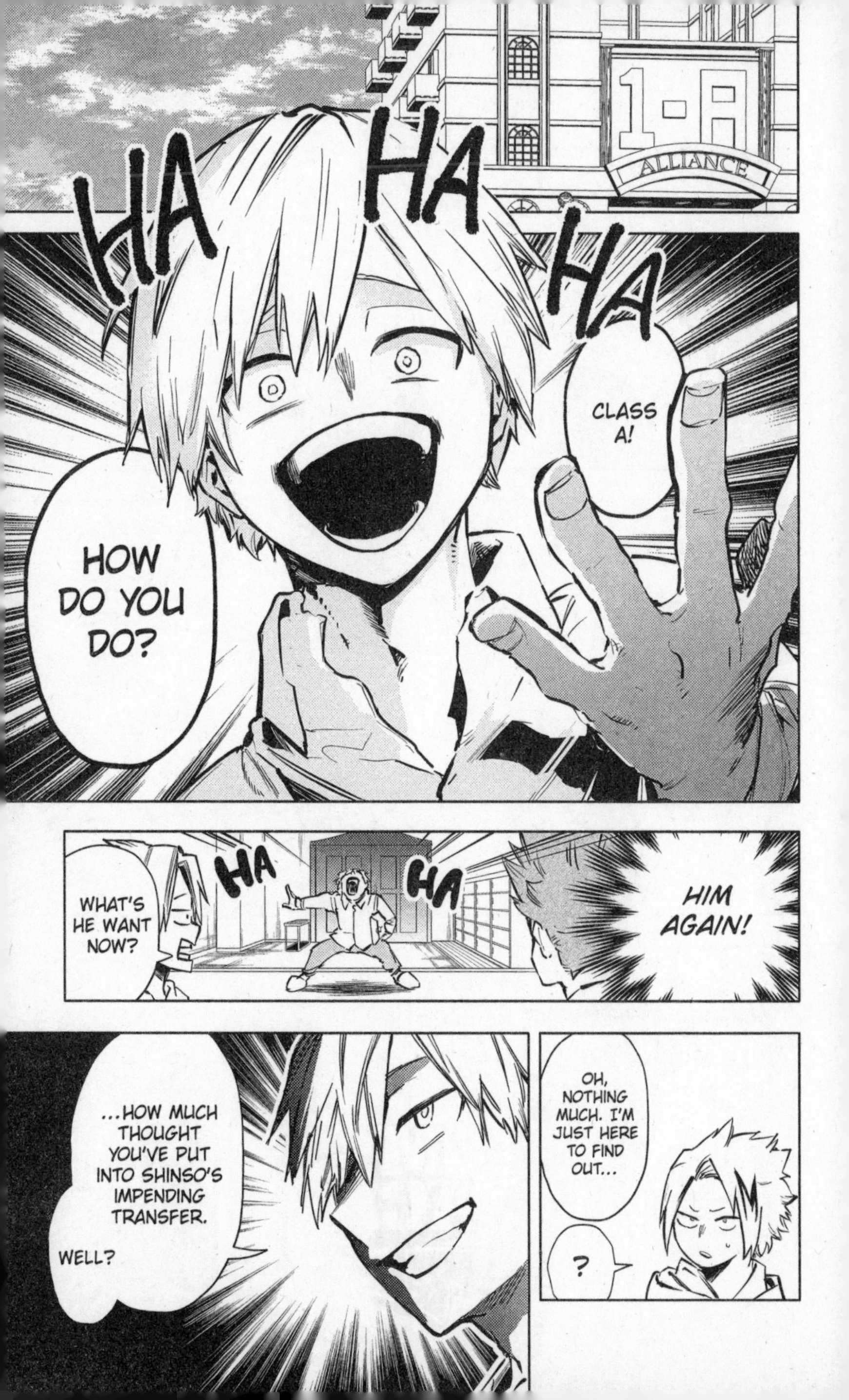
1-A
ALLIANCE
HA HA HA HA
CLASS A!
HOW DO YOU DO?
HIM AGAIN!
HA HA
WHAT'S HE WANT NOW?
OH, NOTHING MUCH. I'M JUST HERE TO FIND OUT...
?
...HOW MUCH THOUGHT YOU'VE PUT INTO SHINSO'S IMPENDING TRANSFER.
WELL?

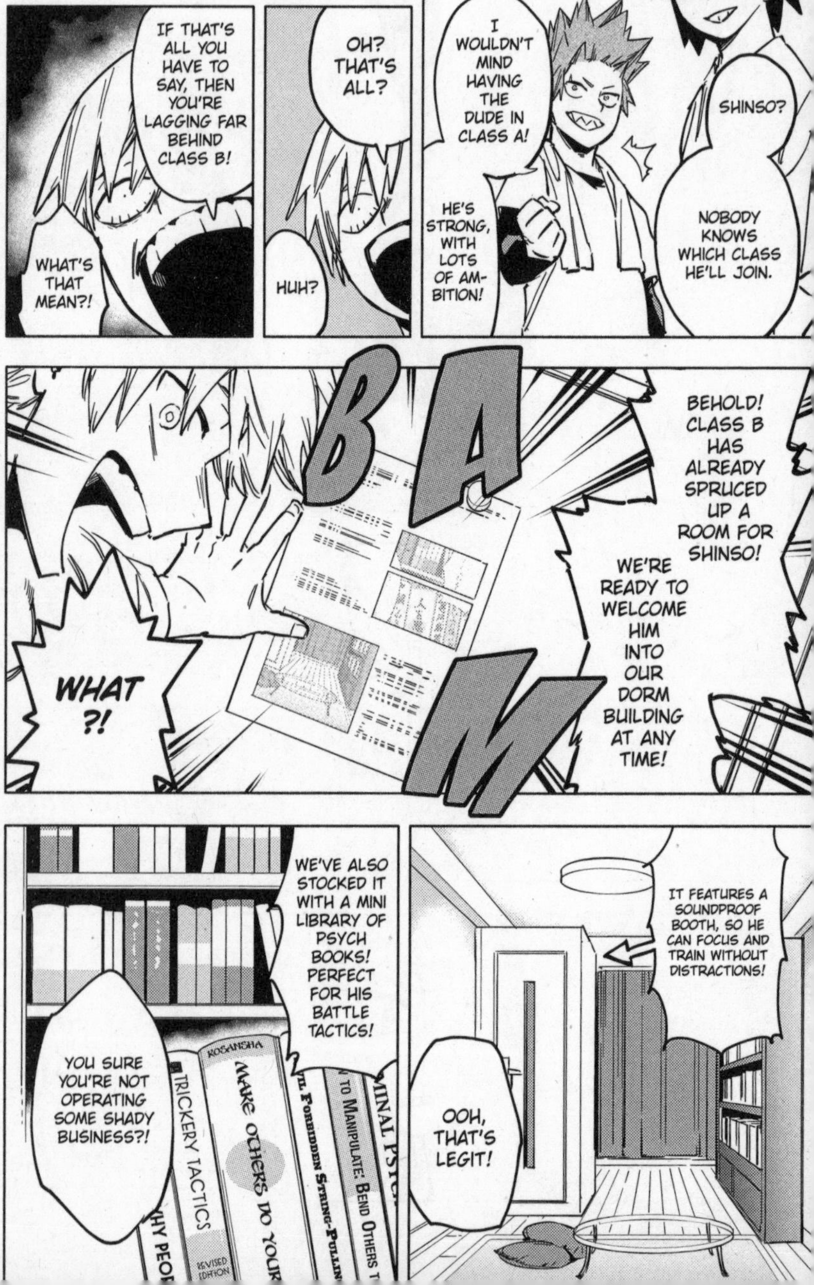
SHINSO?
NOBODY KNOWS WHICH CLASS HE'LL JOIN.
I WOULDN'T MIND HAVING THE DUDE IN CLASS A!
HE'S STRONG, WITH LOTS OF AM-BITION!
OH? THAT'S ALL?
HUH?
IF THAT'S ALL YOU HAVE TO SAY, THEN YOU'RE LAGGING FAR BEHIND CLASS B!
WHAT'S THAT MEAN?!
BAM
BEHOLD! CLASS B HAS ALREADY SPRUCED UP A ROOM FOR SHINSO!
WE'RE READY TO WELCOME HIM INTO OUR DORM BUILDING AT ANY TIME!
WHAT?!
IT FEATURES A SOUNDPROOF BOOTH, SO HE CAN FOCUS AND TRAIN WITHOUT DISTRACTIONS!
OOH, THAT'S LEGIT!
WE'VE ALSO STOCKED IT WITH A MINI LIBRARY OF PSYCH BOOKS! PERFECT FOR HIS BATTLE TACTICS!
YOU SURE YOU'RE NOT OPERATING SOME SHADY BUSINESS?!
TRICKERY TACTICS
KOSANSHA
MAKE OTHERS DO YOUR
REVISED EDITION
TO MANIPULATE: BEND OTHERS
FORBIDDEN STRING-PULLIN

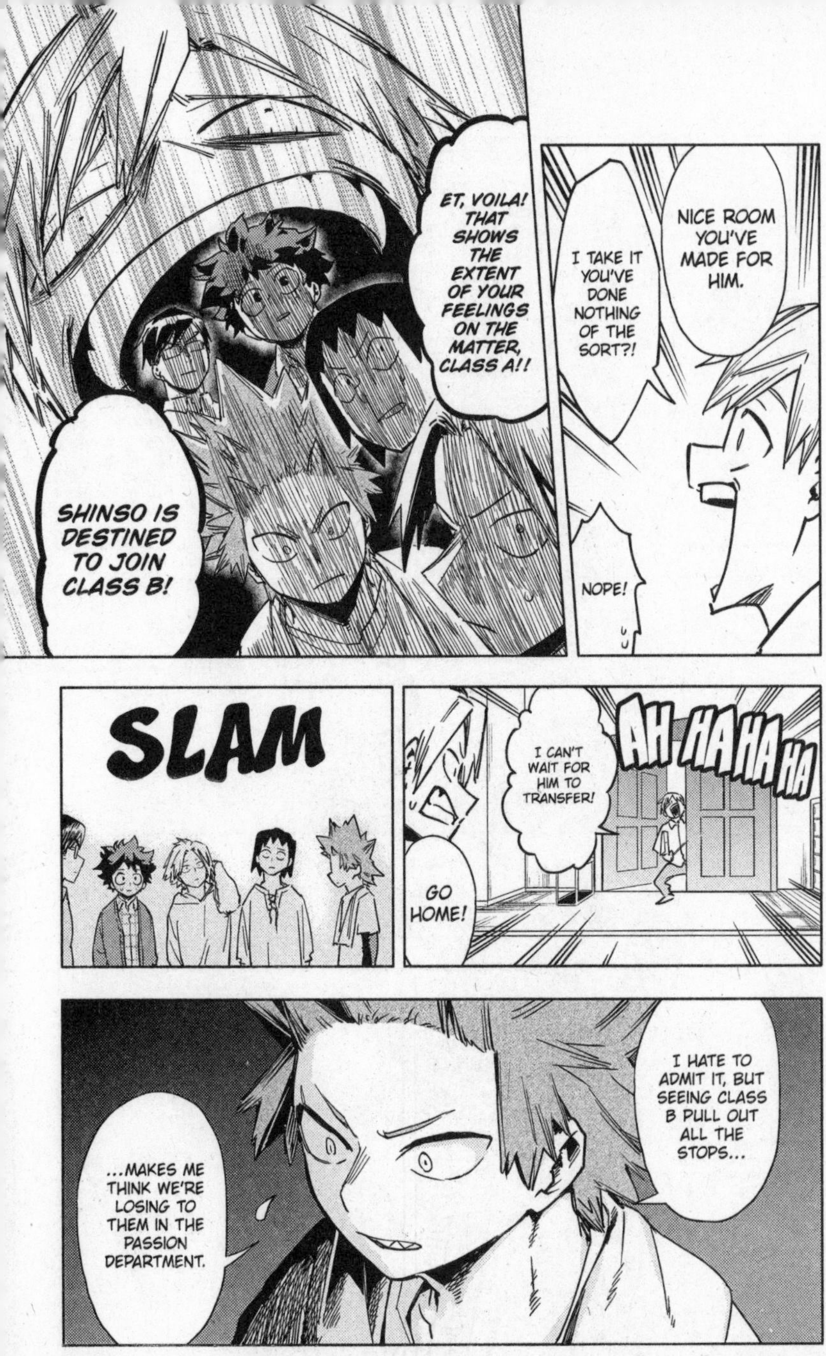
NICE ROOM YOU'VE MADE FOR HIM.
I TAKE IT YOU'VE DONE NOTHING OF THE SORT?!
NOPE!
ET, VOILA! THAT SHOWS THE EXTENT OF YOUR FEELINGS ON THE MATTER, CLASS A!!
SHINSO IS DESTINED TO JOIN CLASS B!
AH HA HA HA HA
I CAN'T WAIT FOR HIM TO TRANSFER!
GO HOME!
SLAM
I HATE TO ADMIT IT, BUT SEEING CLASS B PULL OUT ALL THE STOPS...
...MAKES ME THINK WE'RE LOSING TO THEM IN THE PASSION DEPARTMENT.

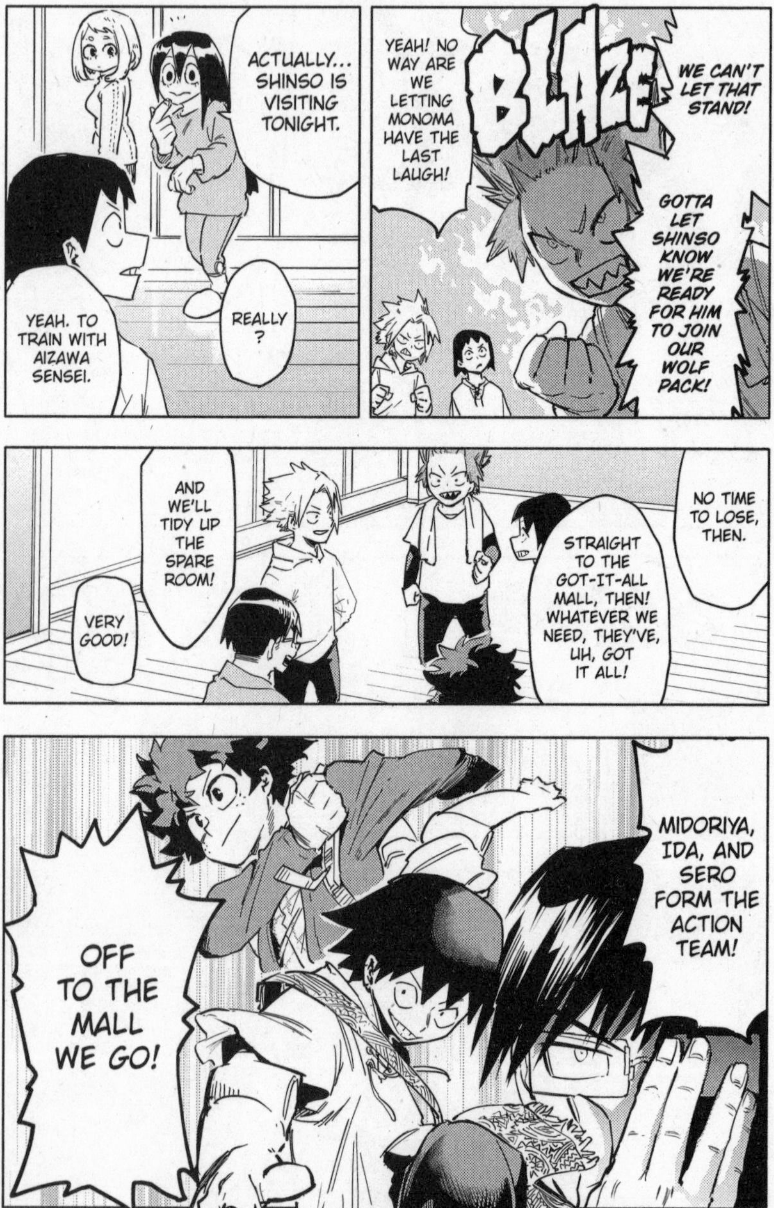
WE CAN'T LET THAT STAND!
BLAZE
YEAH! NO WAY ARE WE LETTING MONOMA HAVE THE LAST LAUGH!
GOTTA LET SHINSO KNOW WE'RE READY FOR HIM TO JOIN OUR WOLF PACK!
ACTUALLY... SHINSO IS VISITING TONIGHT.
REALLY?
YEAH. TO TRAIN WITH AIZAWA SENSEI.
NO TIME TO LOSE, THEN.
STRAIGHT TO THE GOT-IT-ALL MALL, THEN! WHATEVER WE NEED, THEY'VE, UH, GOT IT ALL!
AND WE'LL TIDY UP THE SPARE ROOM!
VERY GOOD!
MIDORIYA, IDA, AND SERO FORM THE ACTION TEAM!
OFF TO THE MALL WE GO!

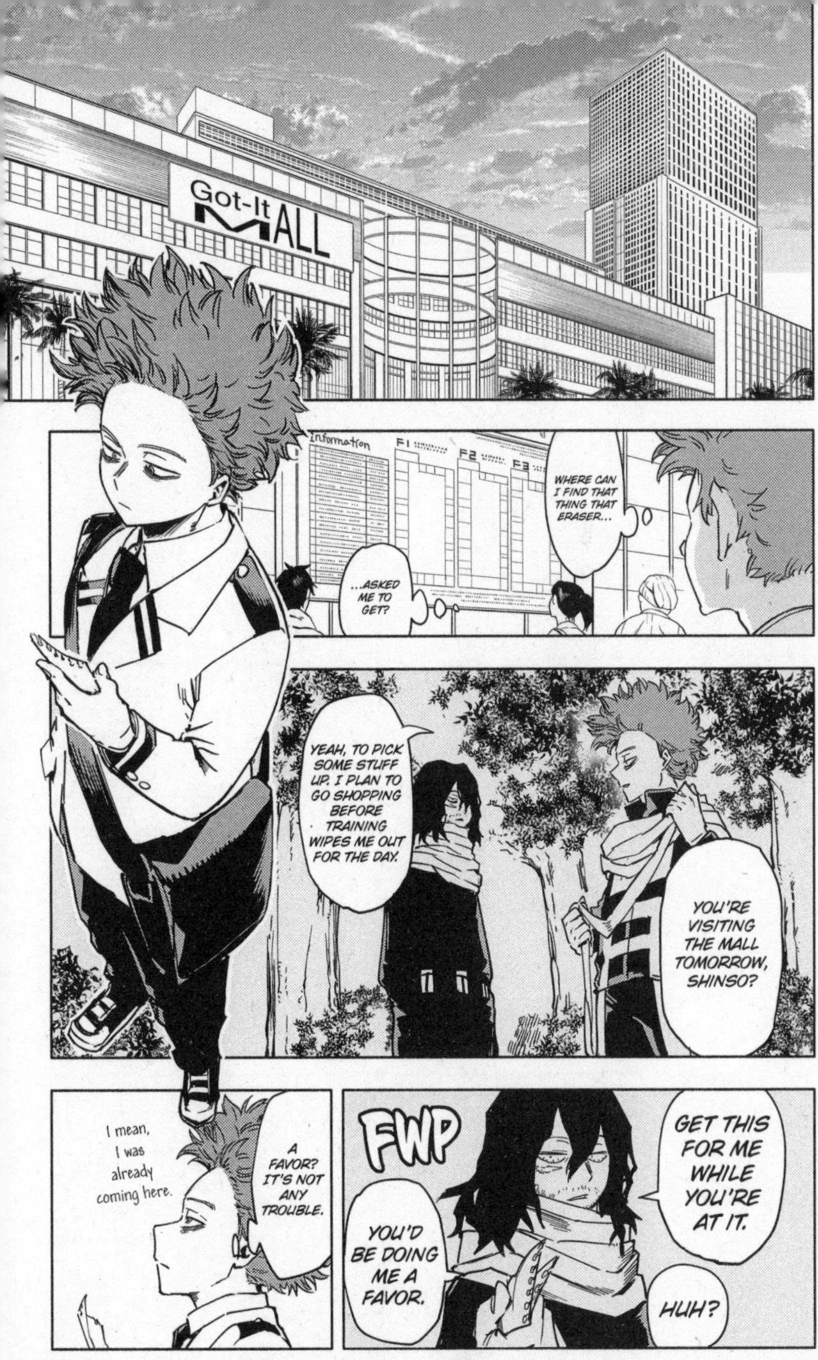
Got-It MALL
Information
WHERE CAN I FIND THAT THING THAT ERASER...
...ASKED ME TO GET?
YOU'RE VISITING THE MALL TOMORROW, SHINSO?
YEAH, TO PICK SOME STUFF UP. I PLAN TO GO SHOPPING BEFORE TRAINING WIPES ME OUT FOR THE DAY.
GET THIS FOR ME WHILE YOU'RE AT IT.
FWP
HUH?
YOU'D BE DOING ME A FAVOR.
A FAVOR? IT'S NOT ANY TROUBLE.
I mean, I was already coming here.

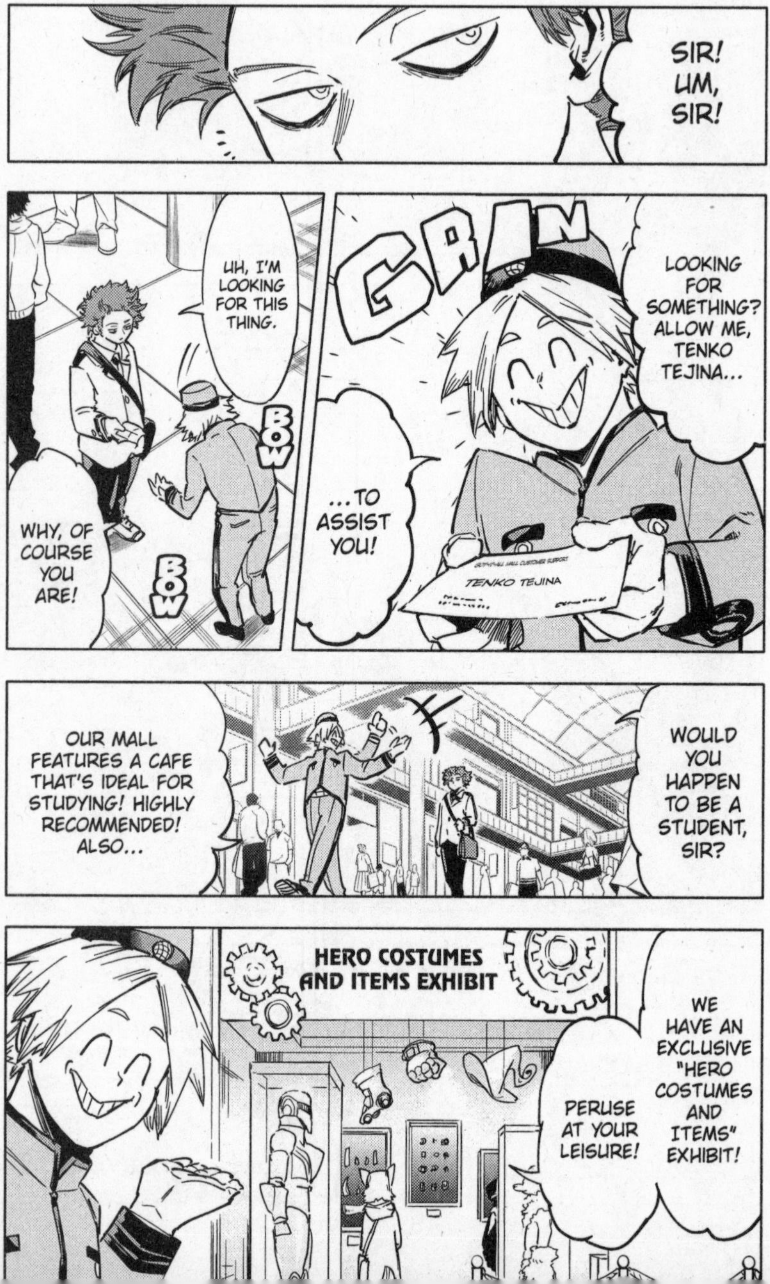
SIR! UM, SIR!
GRIN
LOOKING FOR SOMETHING? ALLOW ME, TENKO TEJINA...
...TO ASSIST YOU!
TENKO TEJINA
UH, I'M LOOKING FOR THIS THING.
BOW
BOW
WHY, OF COURSE YOU ARE!
WOULD YOU HAPPEN TO BE A STUDENT, SIR?
OUR MALL FEATURES A CAFE THAT'S IDEAL FOR STUDYING! HIGHLY RECOMMENDED! ALSO...
HERO COSTUMES AND ITEMS EXHIBIT
WE HAVE AN EXCLUSIVE "HERO COSTUMES AND ITEMS" EXHIBIT!
PERUSE AT YOUR LEISURE!

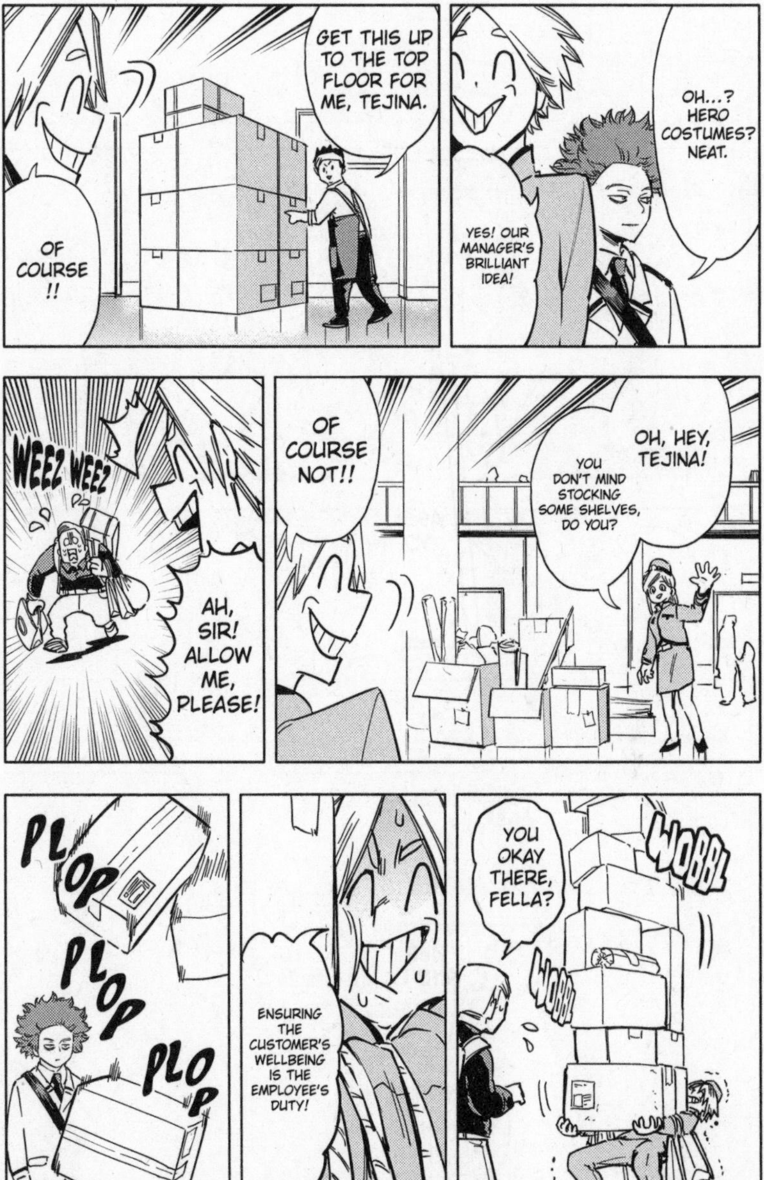
OH...? HERO COSTUMES? NEAT.
YES! OUR MANAGER'S BRILLIANT IDEA!
GET THIS UP TO THE TOP FLOOR FOR ME, TEJINA.
OF COURSE !!
OH, HEY, TEJINA!
YOU DON'T MIND STOCKING SOME SHELVES, DO YOU?
OF COURSE NOT!!
WEEZ WEEZ
AH, SIR! ALLOW ME, PLEASE!
WOBBL
YOU OKAY THERE, FELLA?
WOBBL
ENSURING THE CUSTOMER'S WELLBEING IS THE EMPLOYEE'S DUTY!
PLOP
PLOP
PLOP

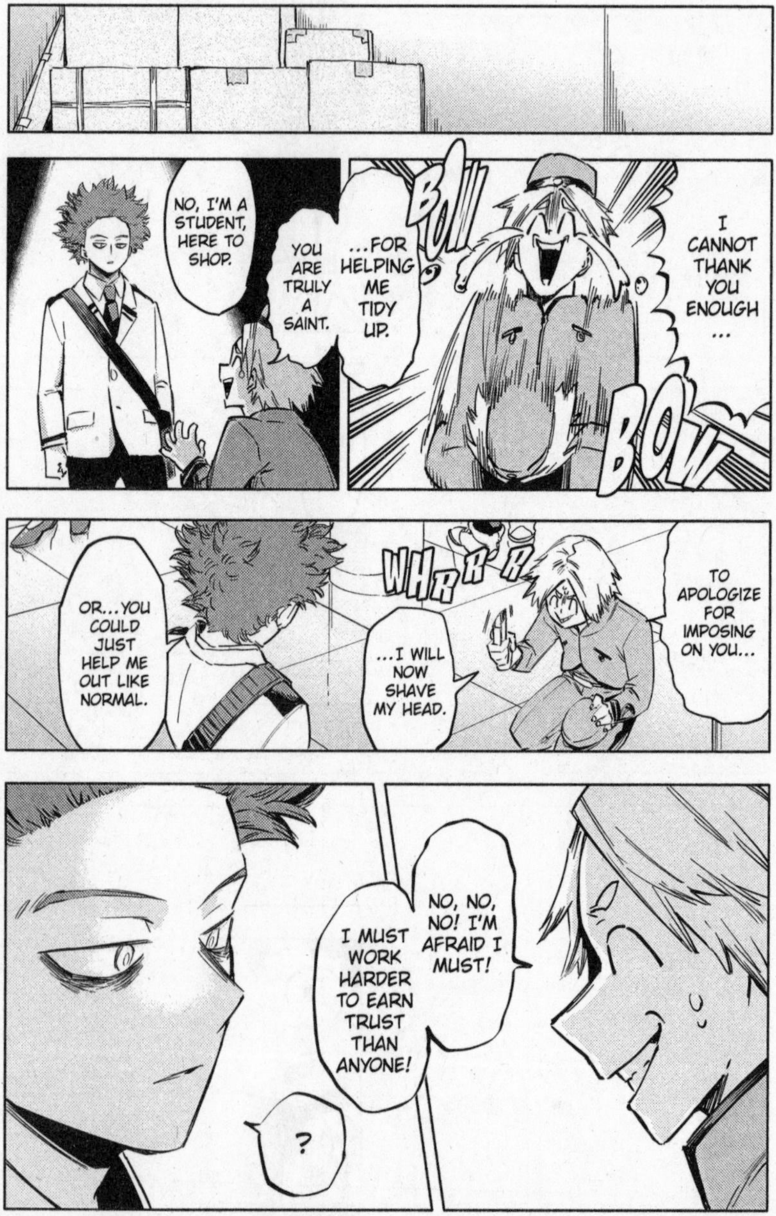
I CANNOT THANK YOU ENOUGH...
BOW
...FOR HELPING ME TIDY UP.
YOU ARE TRULY A SAINT.
NO, I'M A STUDENT, HERE TO SHOP.
TO APOLOGIZE FOR IMPOSING ON YOU...
WHRRR
...I WILL NOW SHAVE MY HEAD.
OR...YOU COULD JUST HELP ME OUT LIKE NORMAL.
NO, NO, NO! I'M AFRAID I MUST!
I MUST WORK HARDER TO EARN TRUST THAN ANYONE!
?

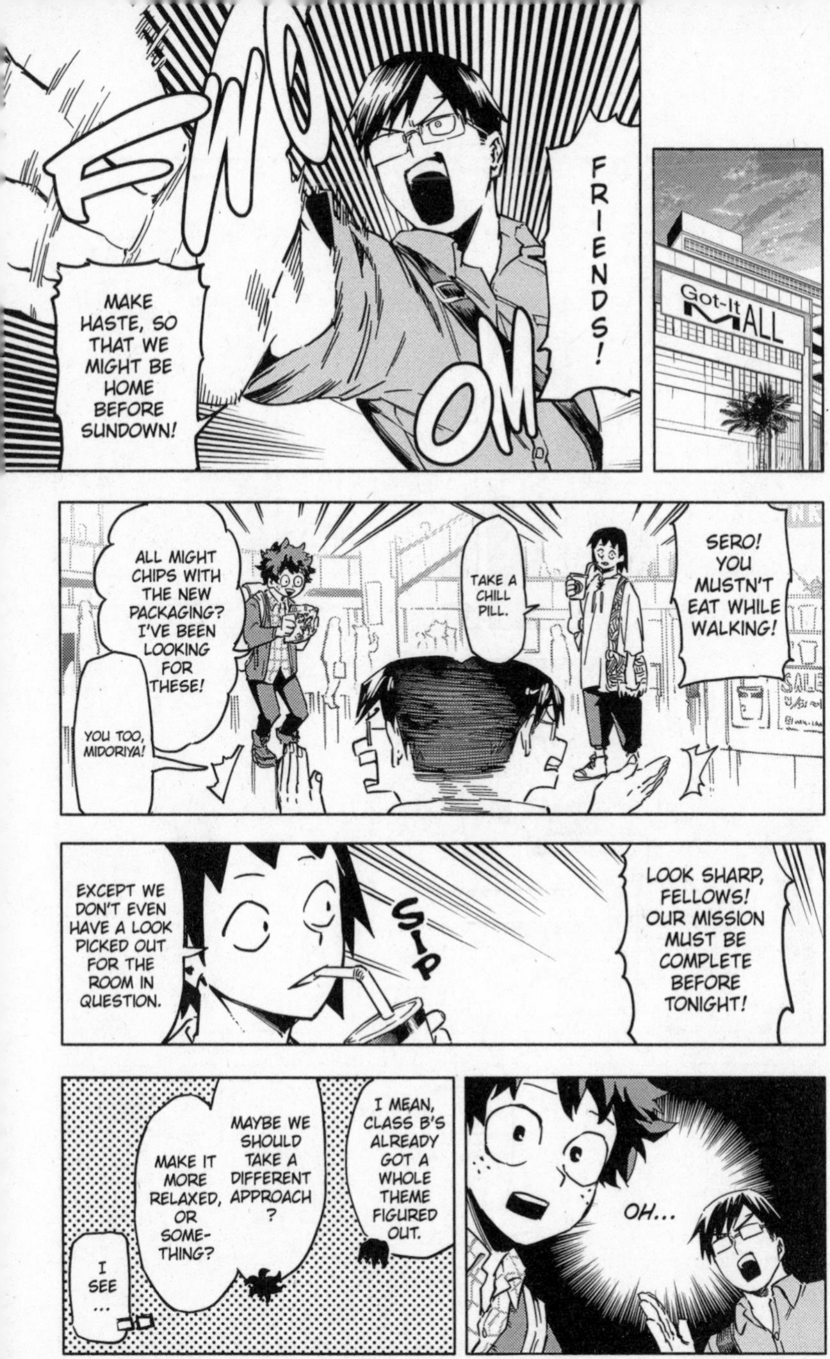
Got-It MALL
FRIENDS!
MAKE HASTE, SO THAT WE MIGHT BE HOME BEFORE SUNDOWN!
SERO! YOU MUSTN'T EAT WHILE WALKING!
TAKE A CHILL PILL.
ALL MIGHT CHIPS WITH THE NEW PACKAGING? I'VE BEEN LOOKING FOR THESE!
YOU TOO, MIDORIYA!
LOOK SHARP, FELLOWS! OUR MISSION MUST BE COMPLETE BEFORE TONIGHT!
SIP
EXCEPT WE DON'T EVEN HAVE A LOOK PICKED OUT FOR THE ROOM IN QUESTION.
OH...
I MEAN, CLASS B'S ALREADY GOT A WHOLE THEME FIGURED OUT.
MAYBE WE SHOULD TAKE A DIFFERENT APPROACH?
MAKE IT MORE RELAXED, OR SOME-THING?
I SEE...

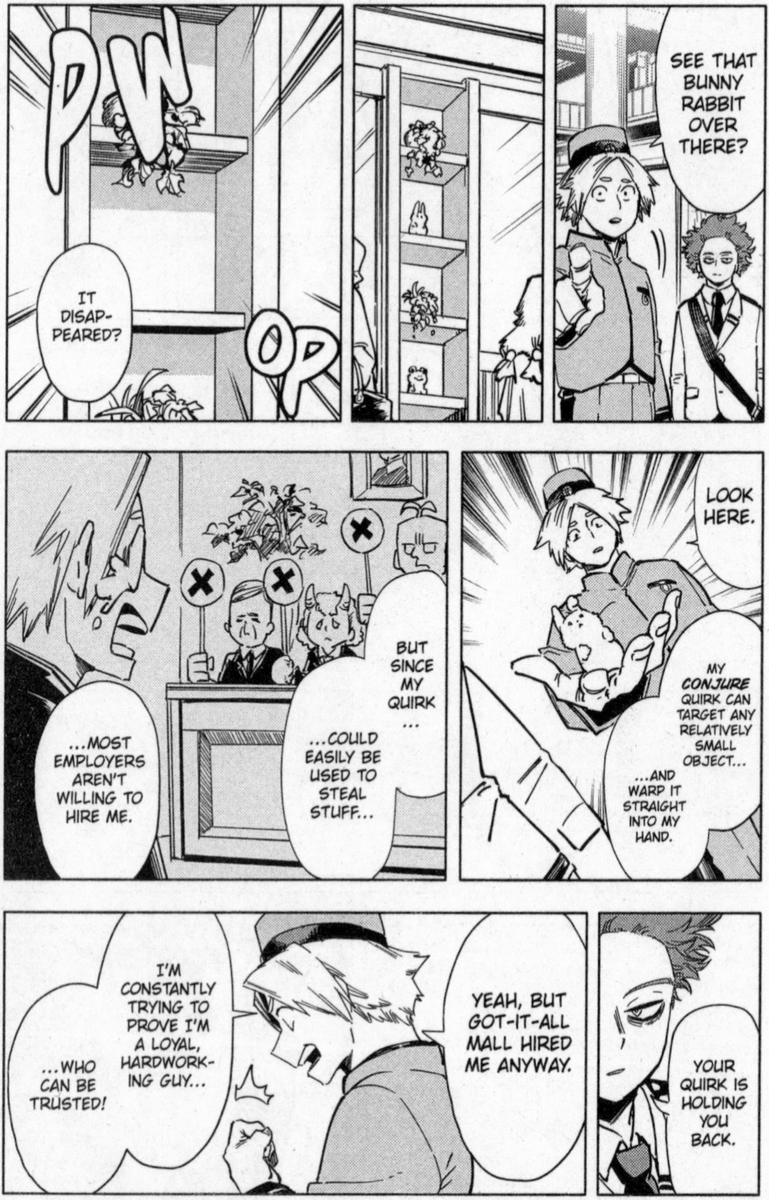
SEE THAT BUNNY RABBIT OVER THERE?
PWOOP
IT DISAPPEARED?
LOOK HERE.
MY CONJURE QUIRK CAN TARGET ANY RELATIVELY SMALL OBJECT...
...AND WARP IT STRAIGHT INTO MY HAND.
BUT SINCE MY QUIRK ...
...COULD EASILY BE USED TO STEAL STUFF...
...MOST EMPLOYERS AREN'T WILLING TO HIRE ME.
YOUR QUIRK IS HOLDING YOU BACK.
YEAH, BUT GOT-IT-ALL MALL HIRED ME ANYWAY.
I'M CONSTANTLY TRYING TO PROVE I'M A LOYAL, HARDWORKING GUY...
...WHO CAN BE TRUSTED!

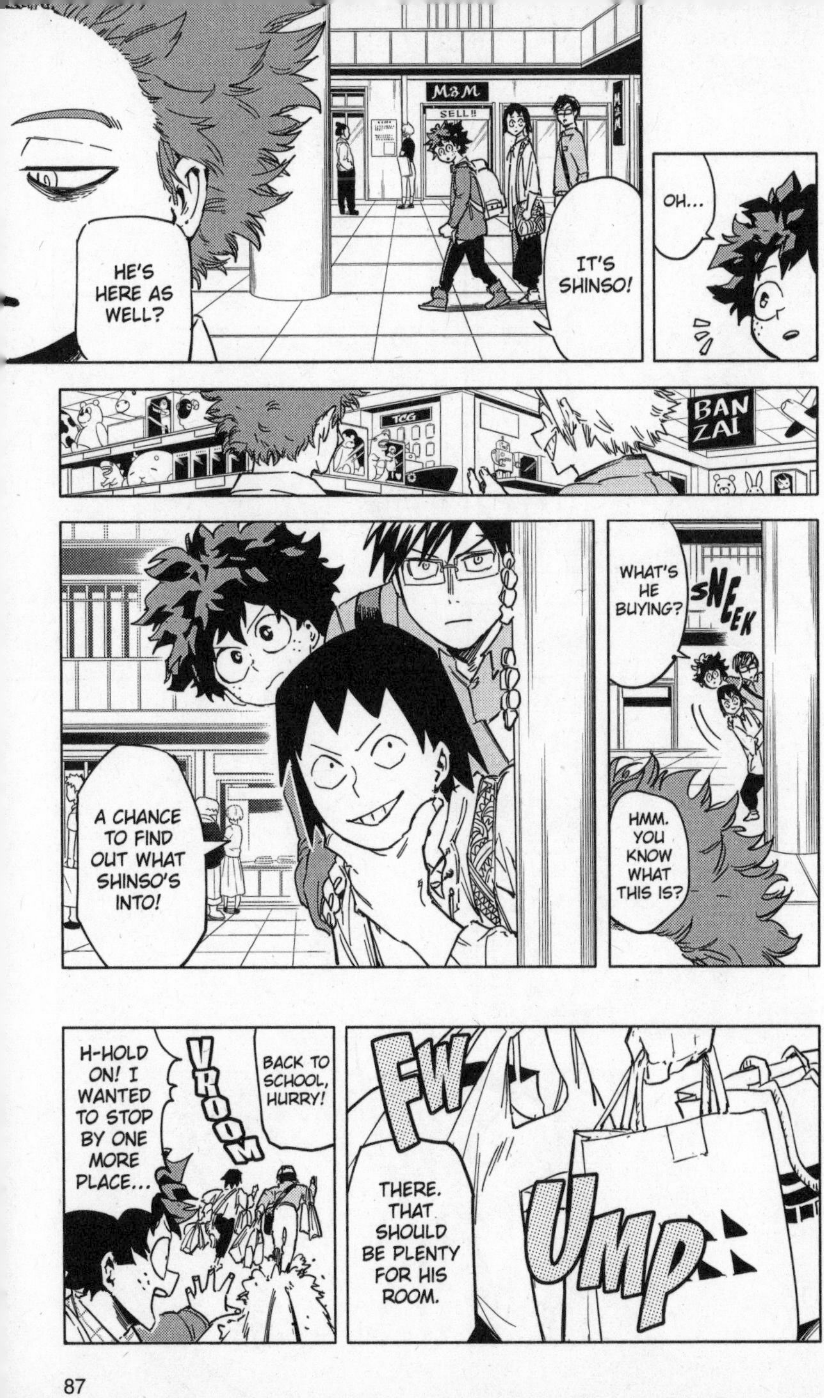
OH...
M&M
SELL!!
IT'S SHINSO!
HE'S HERE AS WELL?
BANZAI
TCG
WHAT'S HE BUYING?
SNEEK
HMM. YOU KNOW WHAT THIS IS?
A CHANCE TO FIND OUT WHAT SHINSO'S INTO!
FWUMP
THERE. THAT SHOULD BE PLENTY FOR HIS ROOM.
BACK TO SCHOOL, HURRY!
VROOM
H-HOLD ON! I WANTED TO STOP BY ONE MORE PLACE...

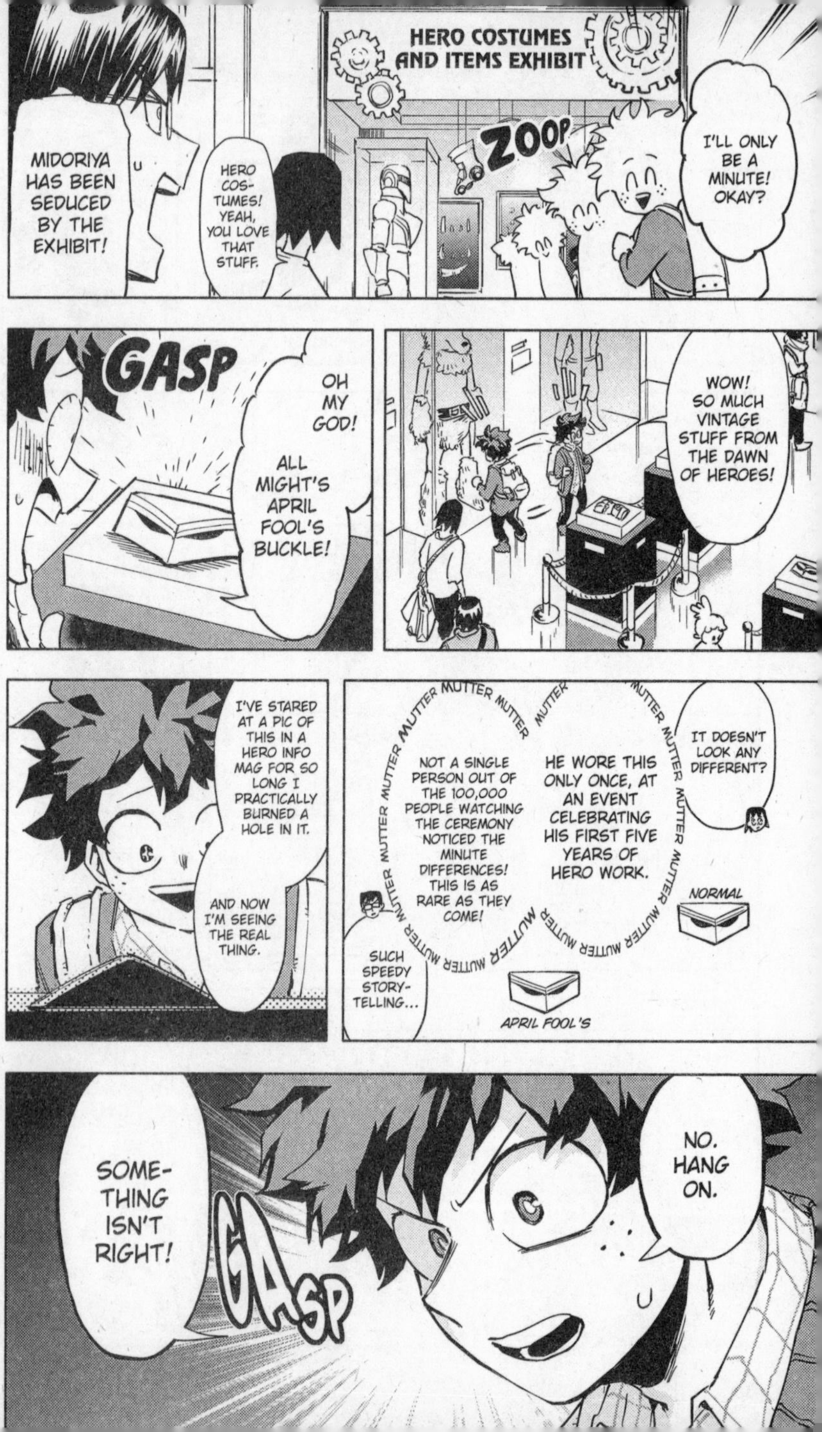
HERO COSTUMES AND ITEMS EXHIBIT
I'LL ONLY BE A MINUTE! OKAY?
ZOOP
HERO COSTUMES! YEAH, YOU LOVE THAT STUFF.
MIDORIYA HAS BEEN SEDUCED BY THE EXHIBIT!
WOW! SO MUCH VINTAGE STUFF FROM THE DAWN OF HEROES!
GASP
OH MY GOD!
ALL MIGHT'S APRIL FOOL'S BUCKLE!
IT DOESN'T LOOK ANY DIFFERENT?
HE WORE THIS ONLY ONCE, AT AN EVENT CELEBRATING HIS FIRST FIVE YEARS OF HERO WORK.
NOT A SINGLE PERSON OUT OF THE 100,000 PEOPLE WATCHING THE CEREMONY NOTICED THE MINUTE DIFFERENCES! THIS IS AS RARE AS THEY COME!
MUTTER MUTTER MUTTER MUTTER MUTTER MUTTER MUTTER MUTTER MUTTER MUTTER MUTTER MUTTER MUTTER MUTTER
NORMAL
APRIL FOOL'S
SUCH SPEEDY STORYTELLING...
I'VE STARED AT A PIC OF THIS IN A HERO INFO MAG FOR SO LONG I PRACTICALLY BURNED A HOLE IN IT.
AND NOW I'M SEEING THE REAL THING.
NO. HANG ON.
GASP
SOMETHING ISN'T RIGHT!

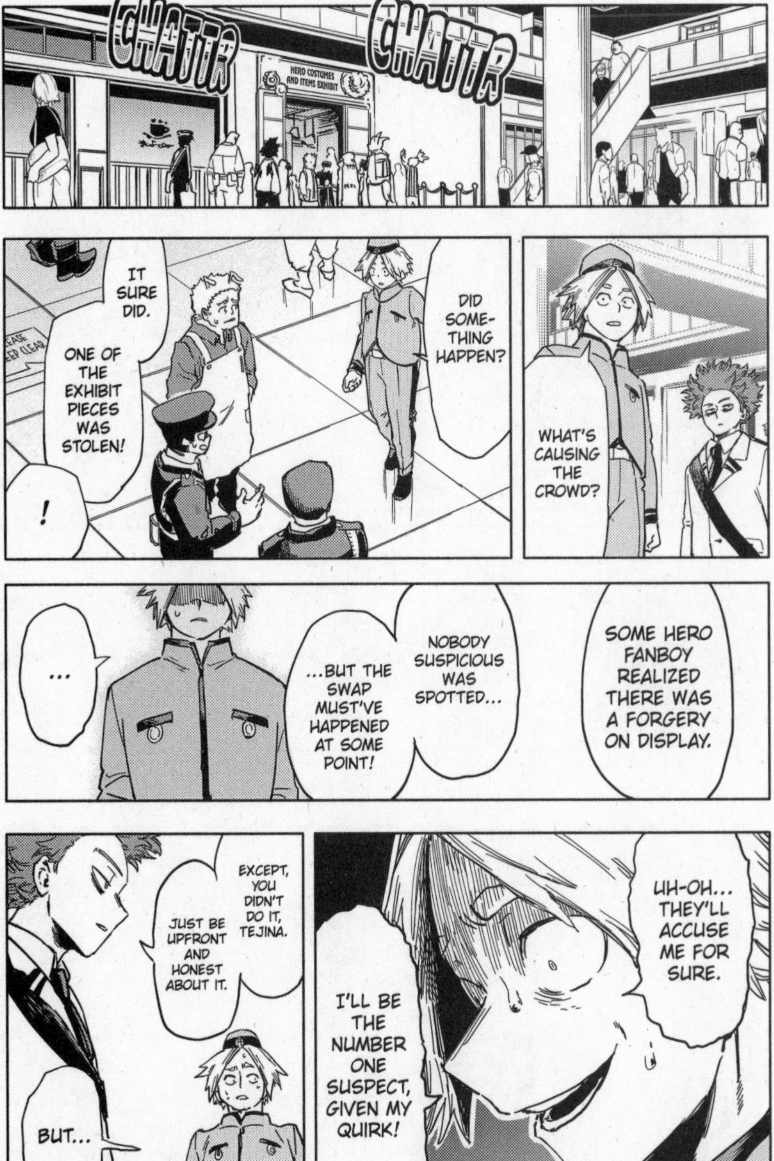
CHATTR
CHATTR
HERO COSTUMES AND ITEMS EXHIBIT
WHAT'S CAUSING THE CROWD?
DID SOMETHING HAPPEN?
IT SURE DID.
ONE OF THE EXHIBIT PIECES WAS STOLEN!
!
SOME HERO FANBOY REALIZED THERE WAS A FORGERY ON DISPLAY.
NOBODY SUSPICIOUS WAS SPOTTED...
...BUT THE SWAP MUST'VE HAPPENED AT SOME POINT!
...
UH-OH... THEY'LL ACCUSE ME FOR SURE.
I'LL BE THE NUMBER ONE SUSPECT, GIVEN MY QUIRK!
EXCEPT, YOU DIDN'T DO IT, TEJINA.
JUST BE UPFRONT AND HONEST ABOUT IT.
BUT...

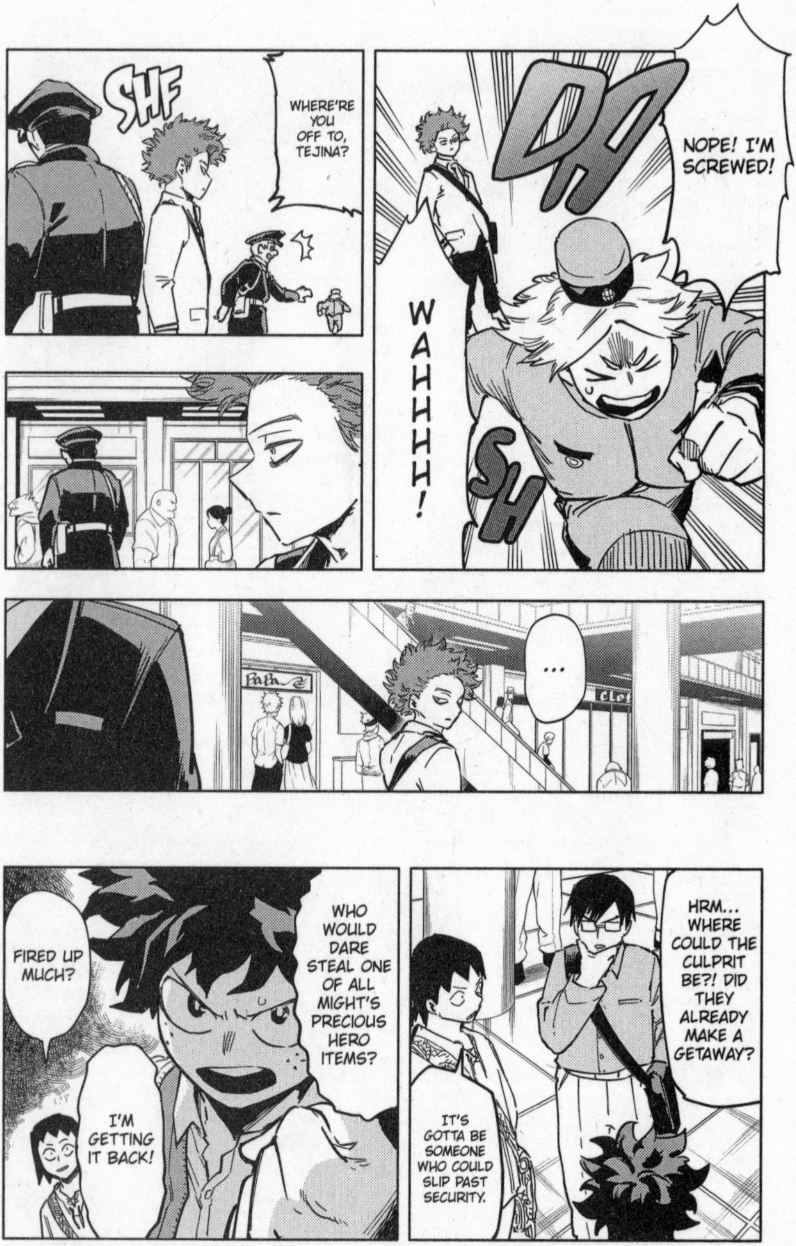
DA
NOPE! I'M SCREWED!
WAHHHHH!
SH
SHF
WHERE'RE YOU OFF TO, TEJINA?
...
HRM... WHERE COULD THE CULPRIT BE?! DID THEY ALREADY MAKE A GETAWAY?
IT'S GOTTA BE SOMEONE WHO COULD SLIP PAST SECURITY.
WHO WOULD DARE STEAL ONE OF ALL MIGHT'S PRECIOUS HERO ITEMS?
I'M GETTING IT BACK!
FIRED UP MUCH?

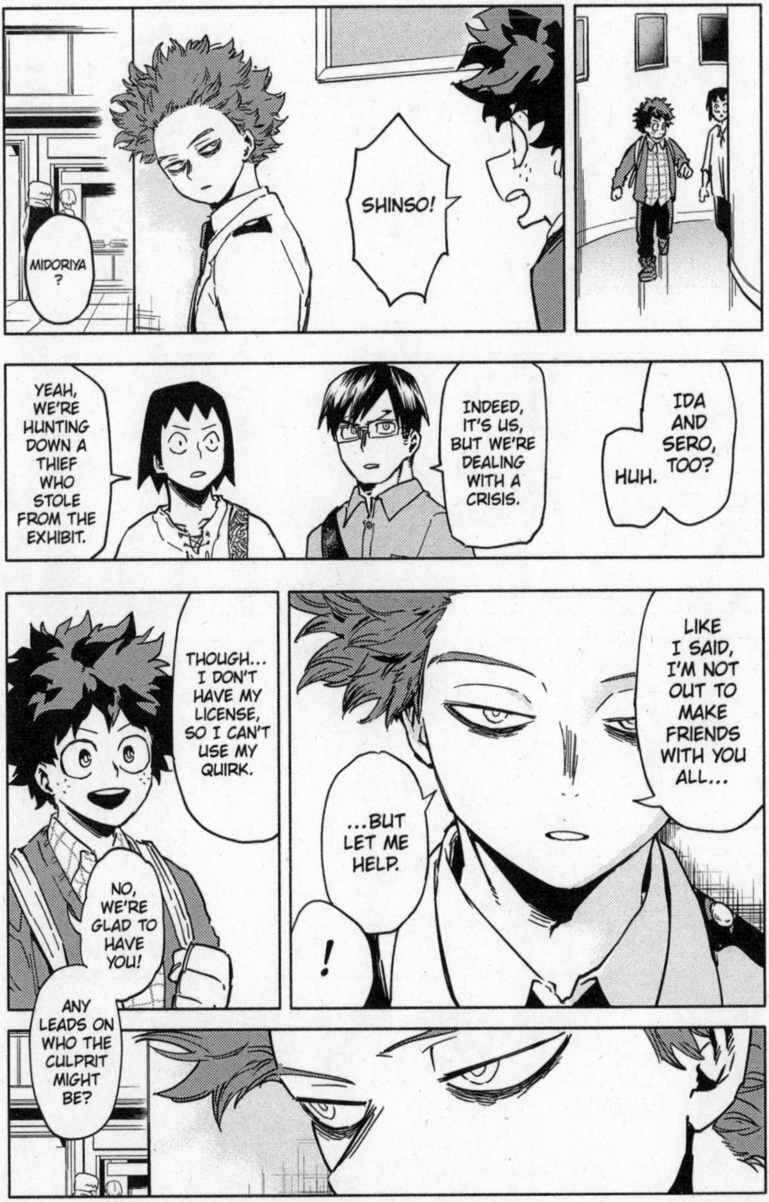
SHINSO!
MIDORIYA?
IDA AND SERO, TOO?
HUH.
INDEED, IT'S US, BUT WE'RE DEALING WITH A CRISIS.
YEAH, WE'RE HUNTING DOWN A THIEF WHO STOLE FROM THE EXHIBIT.
LIKE I SAID, I'M NOT OUT TO MAKE FRIENDS WITH YOU ALL...
...BUT LET ME HELP.
!
THOUGH... I DON'T HAVE MY LICENSE, SO I CAN'T USE MY QUIRK.
NO, WE'RE GLAD TO HAVE YOU!
ANY LEADS ON WHO THE CULPRIT MIGHT BE?

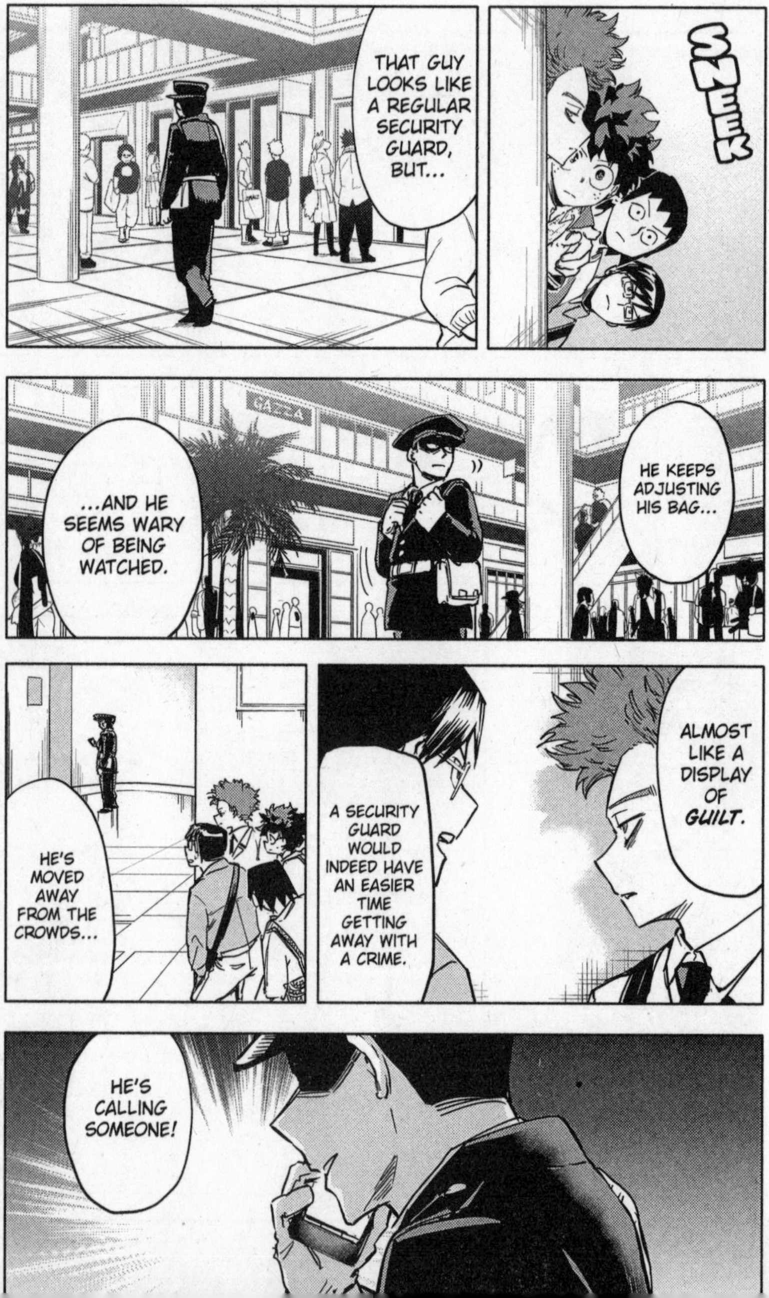
SNEEK
THAT GUY LOOKS LIKE A REGULAR SECURITY GUARD, BUT...
HE KEEPS ADJUSTING HIS BAG...
...AND HE SEEMS WARY OF BEING WATCHED.
ALMOST LIKE A DISPLAY OF *GUILT*.
A SECURITY GUARD WOULD INDEED HAVE AN EASIER TIME GETTING AWAY WITH A CRIME.
HE'S MOVED AWAY FROM THE CROWDS...
HE'S CALLING SOMEONE!

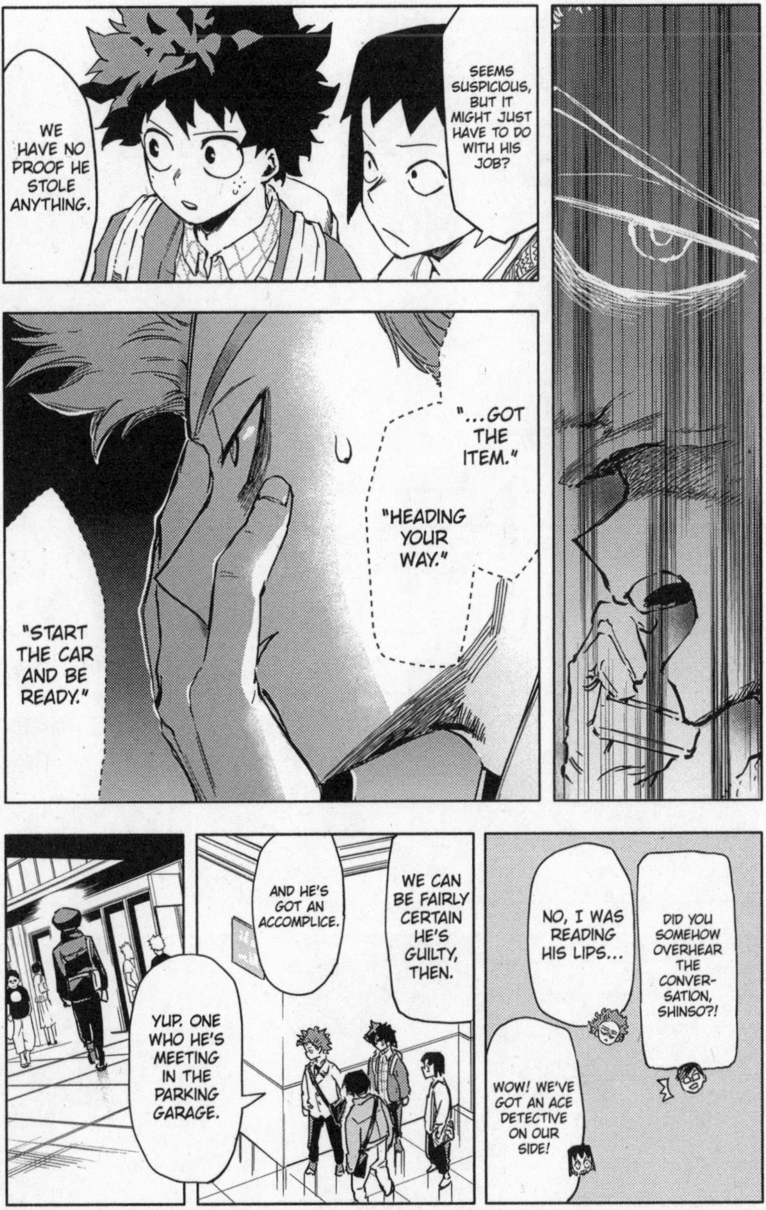
SEEMS SUSPICIOUS, BUT IT MIGHT JUST HAVE TO DO WITH HIS JOB?
WE HAVE NO PROOF HE STOLE ANYTHING.
"...GOT THE ITEM."
"HEADING YOUR WAY."
"START THE CAR AND BE READY."
DID YOU SOMEHOW OVERHEAR THE CONVER-SATION, SHINSO?!
NO, I WAS READING HIS LIPS...
WOW! WE'VE GOT AN ACE DETECTIVE ON OUR SIDE!
WE CAN BE FAIRLY CERTAIN HE'S GUILTY, THEN.
AND HE'S GOT AN ACCOMPLICE.
YUP. ONE WHO HE'S MEETING IN THE PARKING GARAGE.

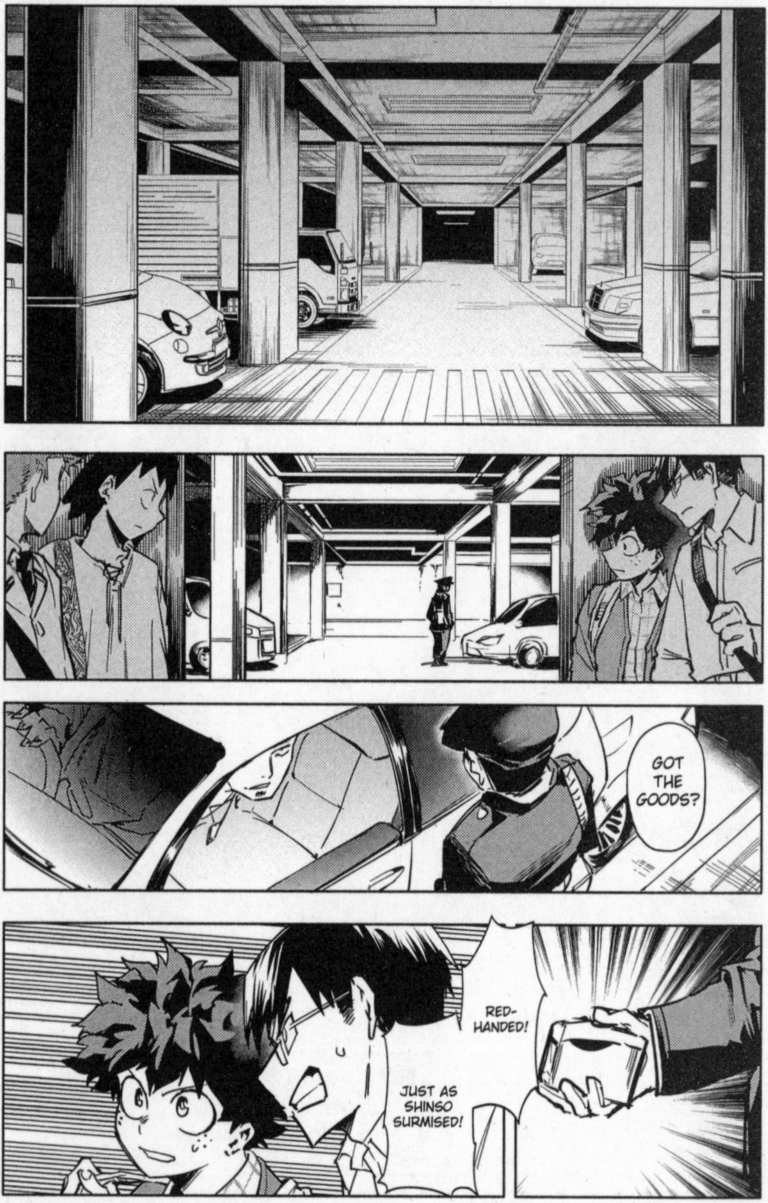
GOT THE GOODS?
RED-HANDED!
JUST AS SHINSO SURMISED!

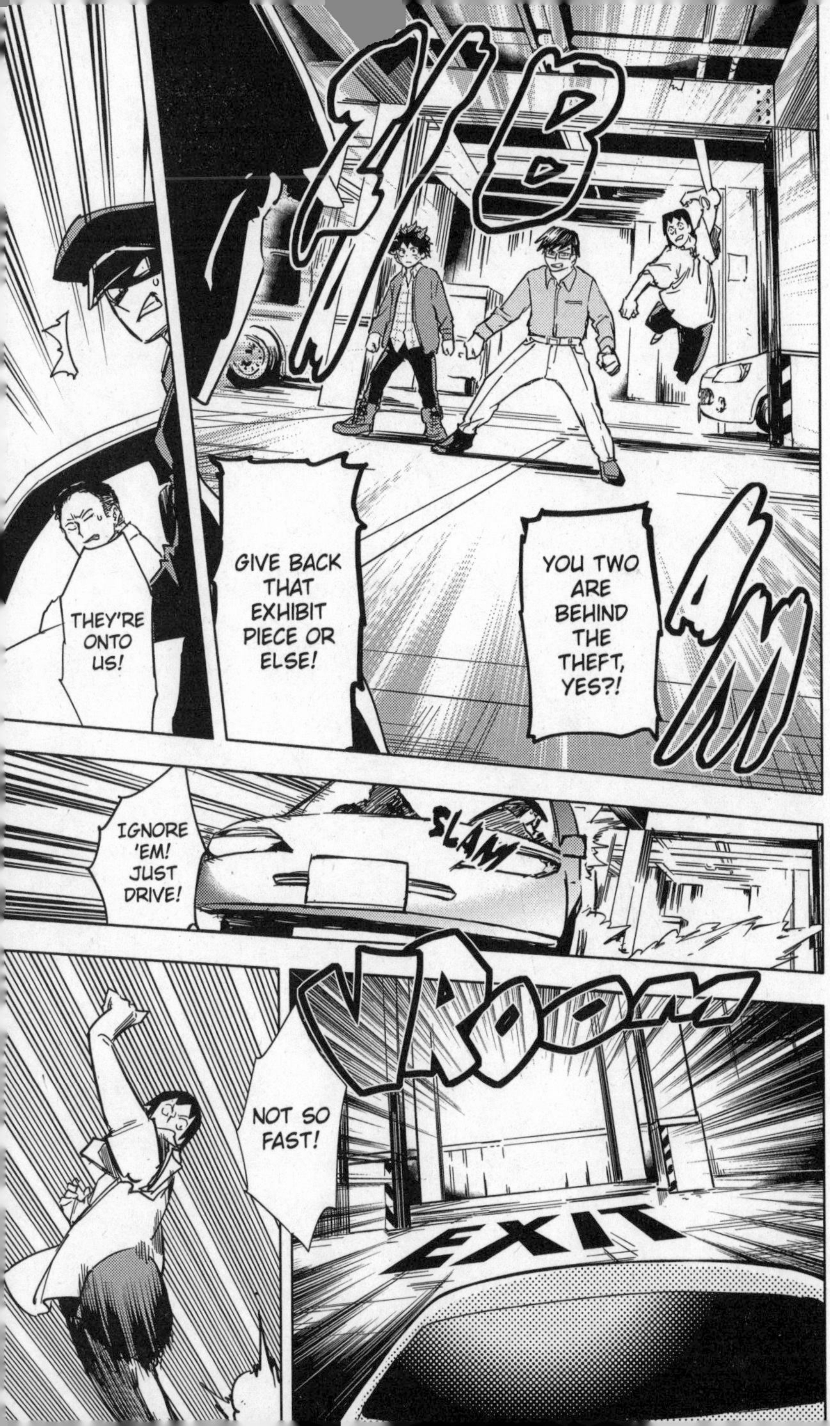
YOU TWO ARE BEHIND THE THEFT, YES?!
GIVE BACK THAT EXHIBIT PIECE OR ELSE!
THEY'RE ONTO US!
SLAM
IGNORE 'EM! JUST DRIVE!
VROOM
EXIT
NOT SO FAST!

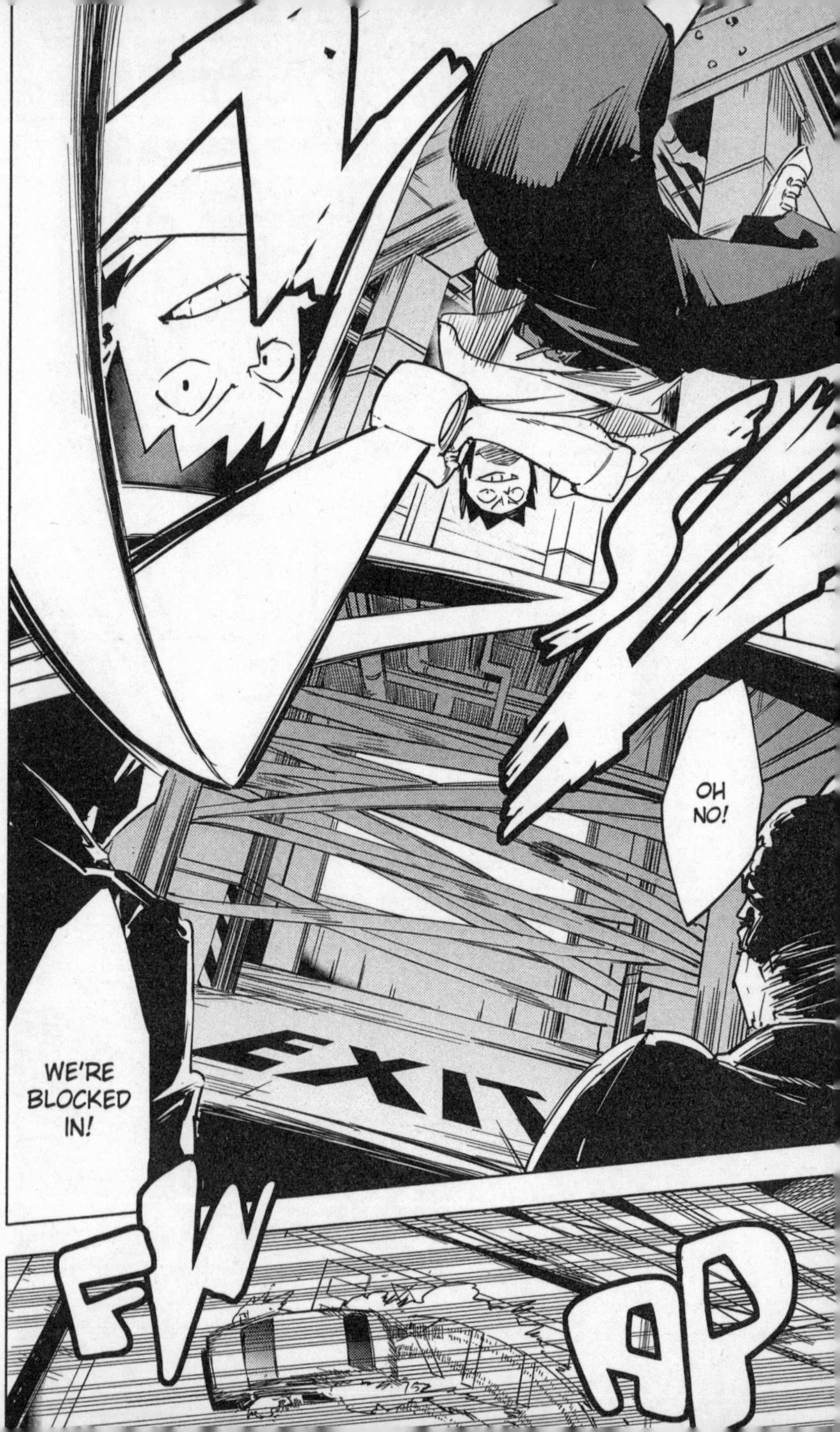
OH NO!
WE'RE BLOCKED IN!
FWAP

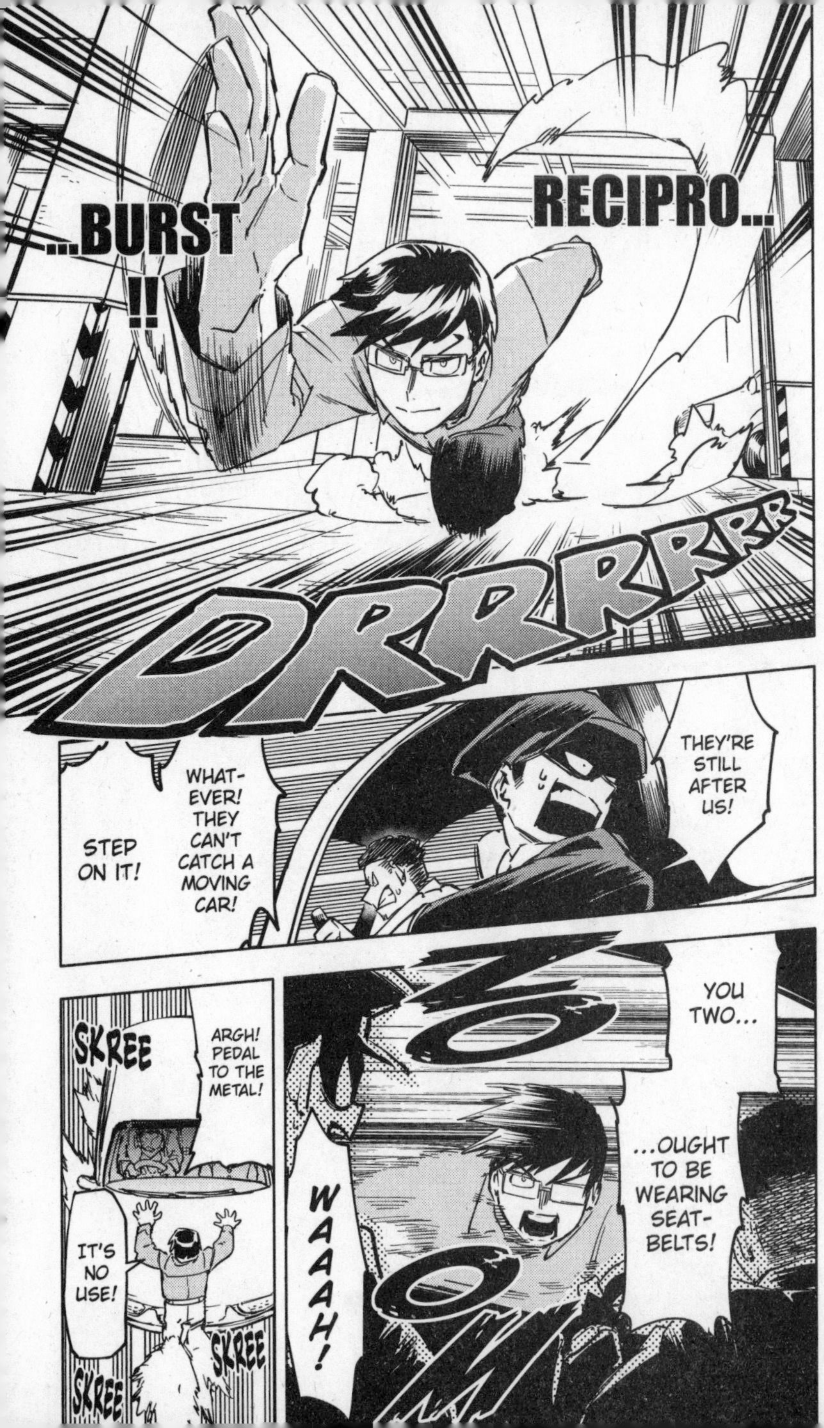
RECIPRO...
...BURST !!
DRRRRRR
THEY'RE STILL AFTER US!
WHAT-EVER! THEY CAN'T CATCH A MOVING CAR!
STEP ON IT!
YOU TWO...
...OUGHT TO BE WEARING SEAT-BELTS!
WAAAAH!
SKREE
ARGH! PEDAL TO THE METAL!
IT'S NO USE!
SKREE
SKREE

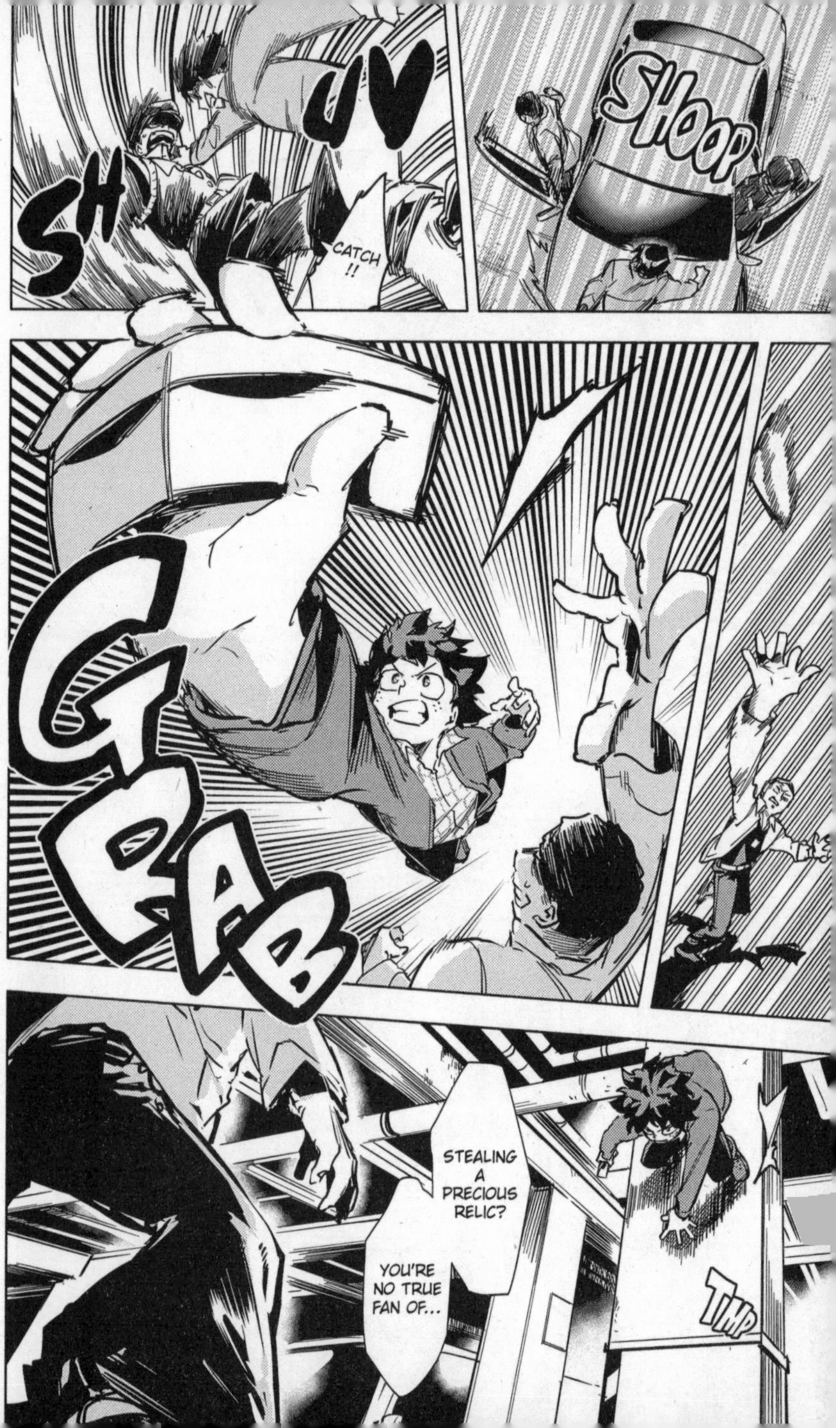
SHOOP
SHUV
CATCH !!
GRAB
TMP
STEALING A PRECIOUS RELIC?
YOU'RE NO TRUE FAN OF...

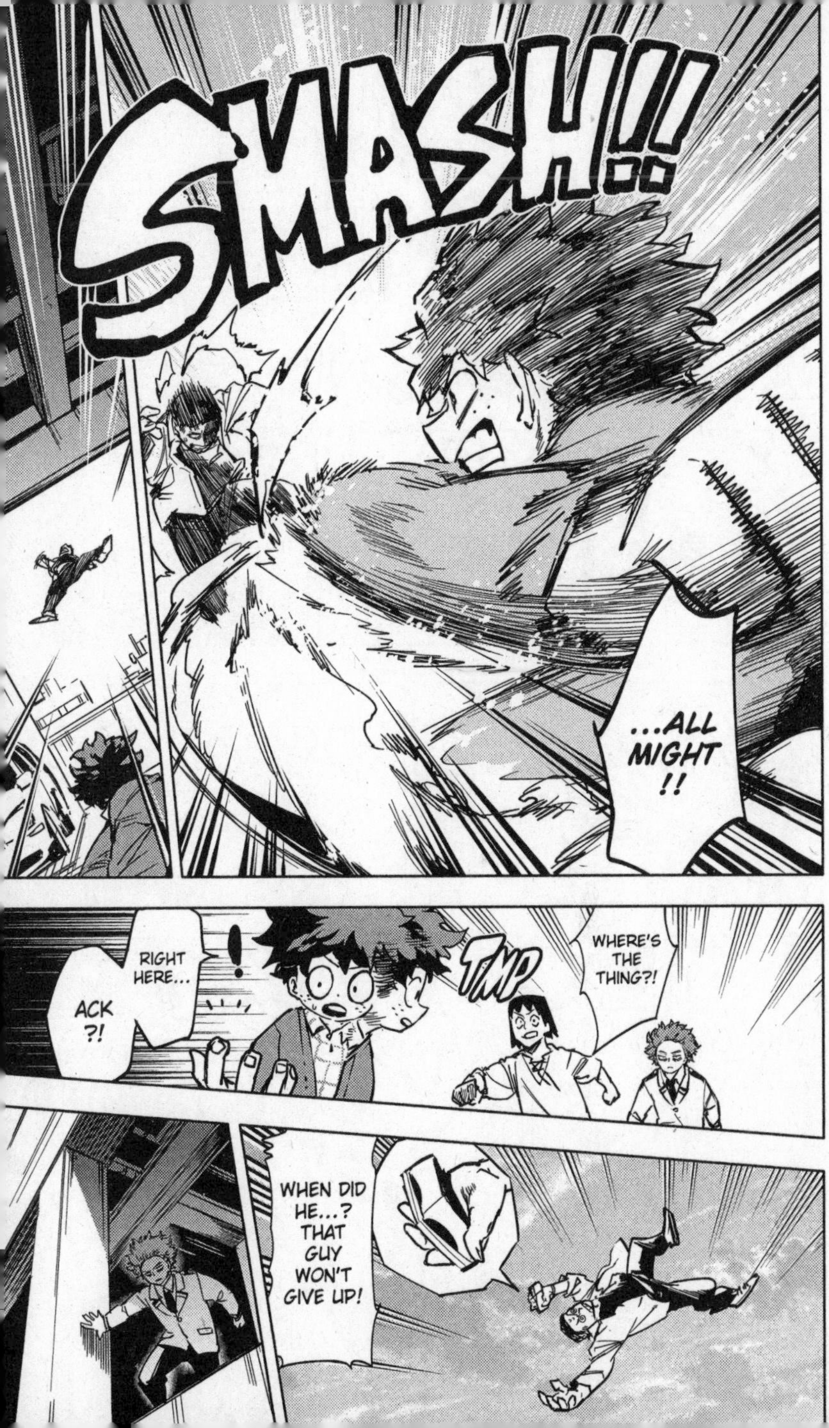
SMASH!!
...ALL MIGHT !!
WHERE'S THE THING?!
TMP
!
RIGHT HERE...
ACK ?!
WHEN DID HE...? THAT GUY WON'T GIVE UP!

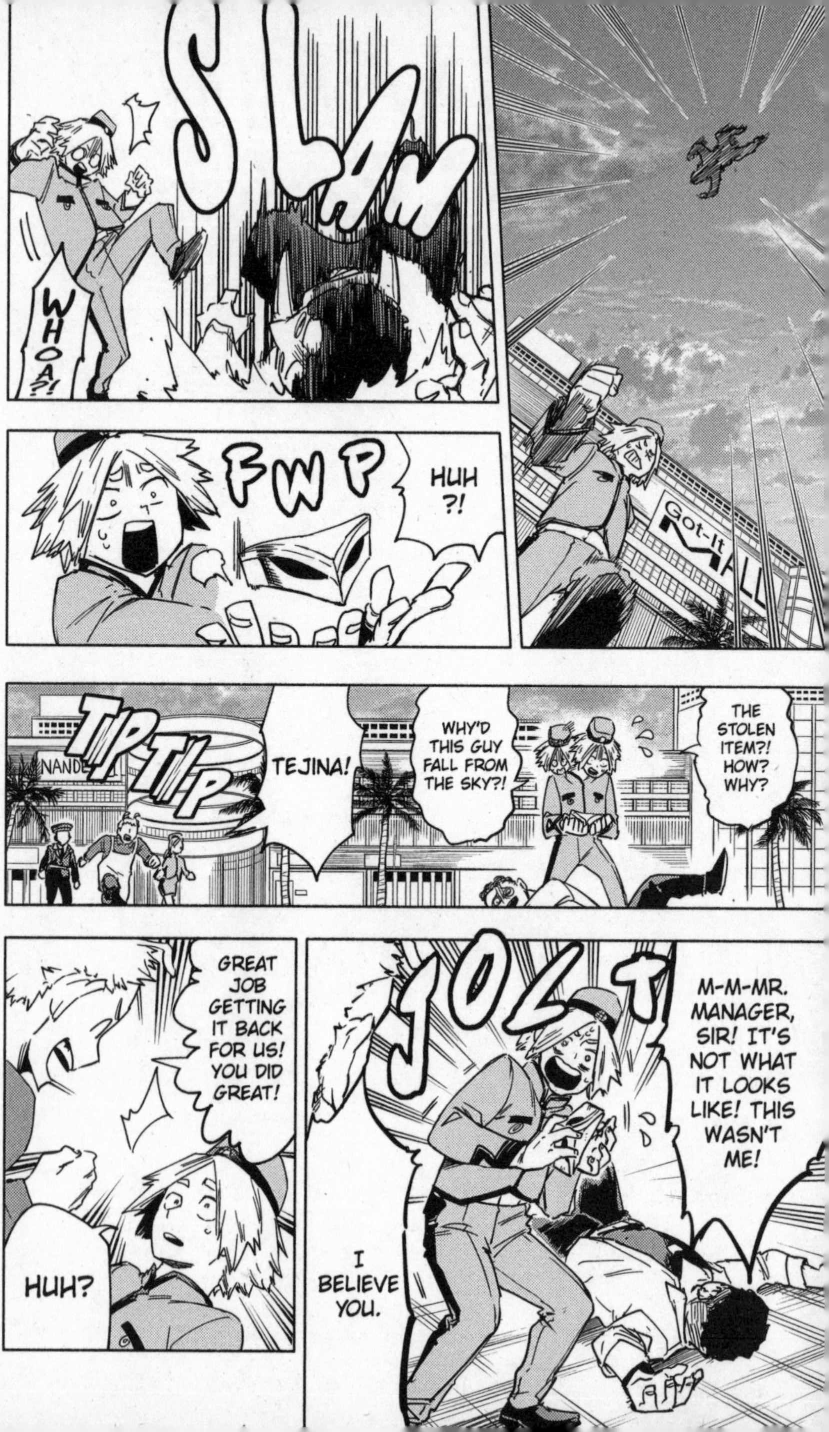
Got-It MALL
SLAM
WHOA?!
FWP
HUH ?!
THE STOLEN ITEM?! HOW? WHY?
WHY'D THIS GUY FALL FROM THE SKY?!
TEJINA!
TIP TIP
NANDE
JOLT
M-M-MR. MANAGER, SIR! IT'S NOT WHAT IT LOOKS LIKE! THIS WASN'T ME!
I BELIEVE YOU.
GREAT JOB GETTING IT BACK FOR US! YOU DID GREAT!
HUH?

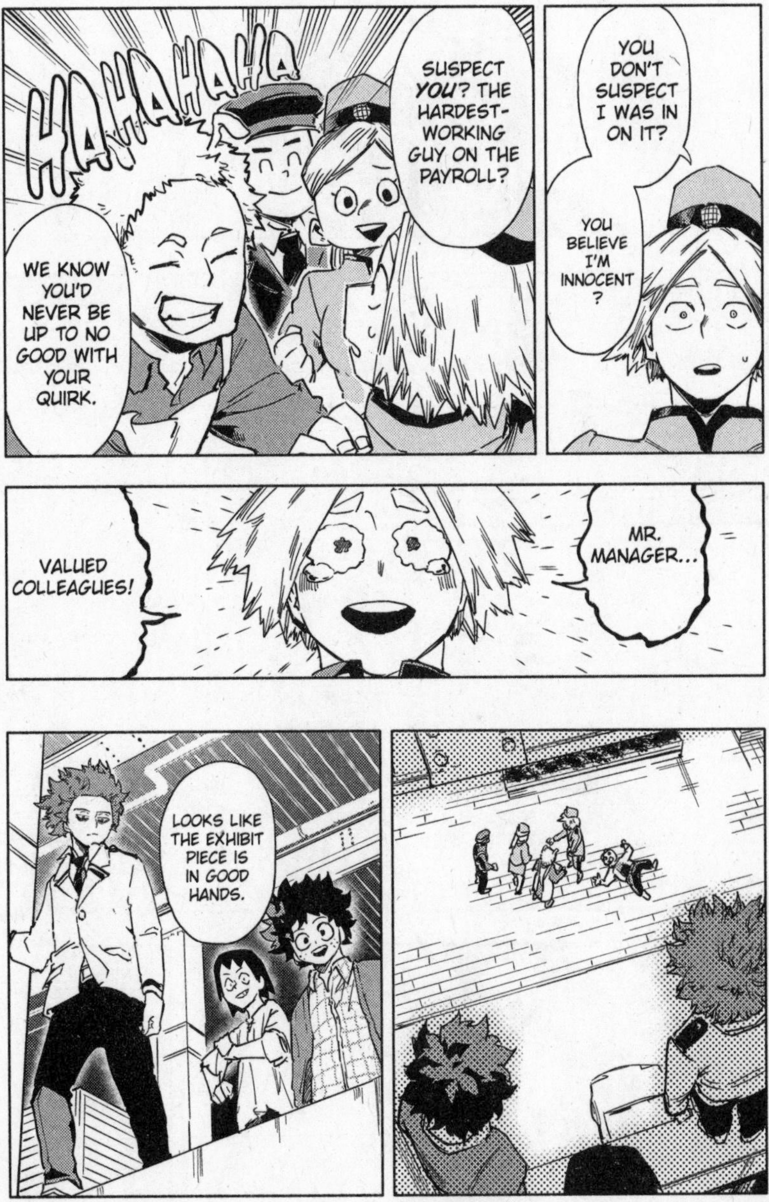
YOU DON'T SUSPECT I WAS IN ON IT?
YOU BELIEVE I'M INNOCENT?
SUSPECT *YOU*? THE HARDEST-WORKING GUY ON THE PAYROLL?
HAHAHAHAHA
WE KNOW YOU'D NEVER BE UP TO NO GOOD WITH YOUR QUIRK.
MR. MANAGER...
VALUED COLLEAGUES!
LOOKS LIKE THE EXHIBIT PIECE IS IN GOOD HANDS.

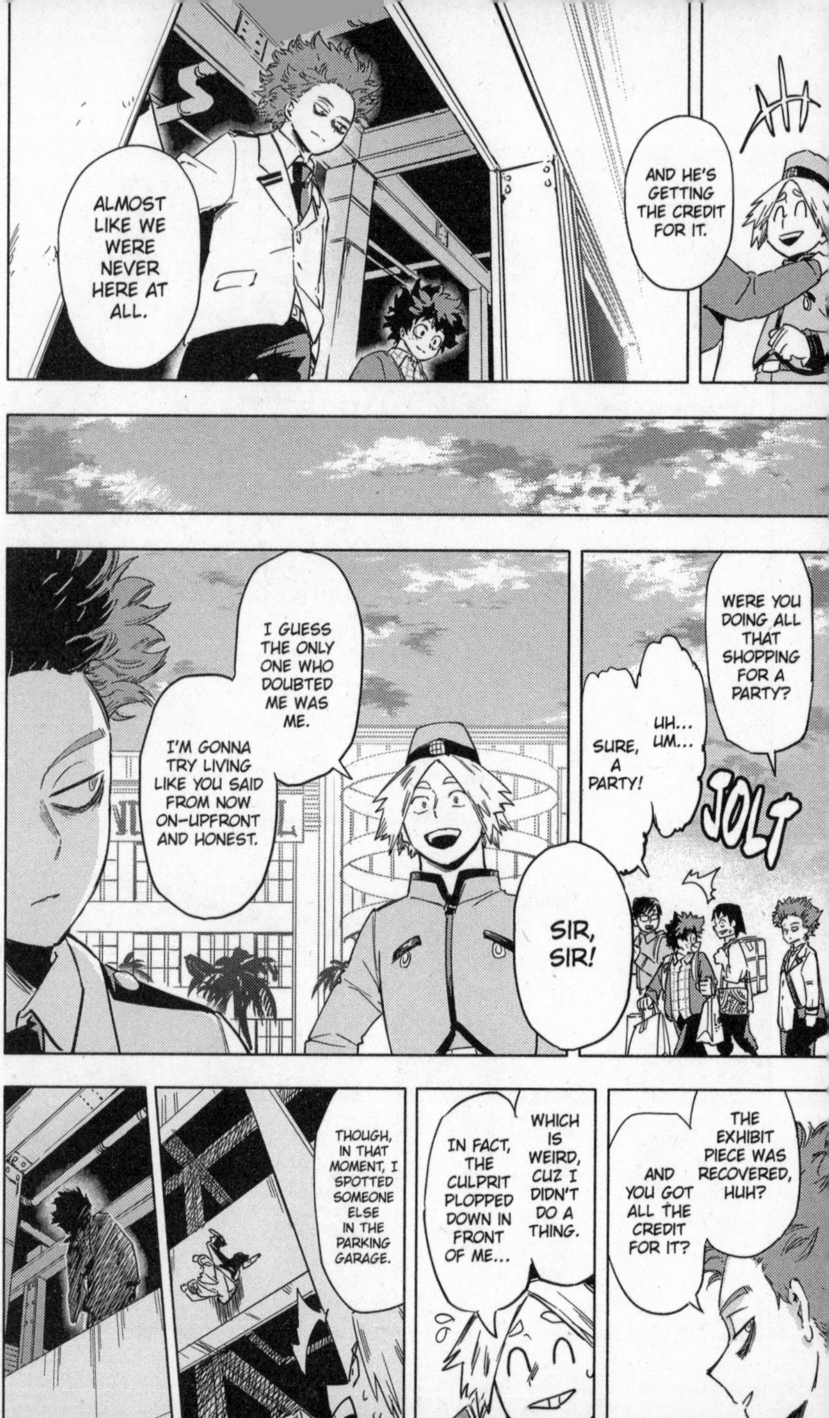
AND HE'S GETTING THE CREDIT FOR IT.
ALMOST LIKE WE WERE NEVER HERE AT ALL.
WERE YOU DOING ALL THAT SHOPPING FOR A PARTY?
JOLT
UH... UM...
SURE, A PARTY!
SIR, SIR!
I GUESS THE ONLY ONE WHO DOUBTED ME WAS ME.
I'M GONNA TRY LIVING LIKE YOU SAID FROM NOW ON—UPFRONT AND HONEST.
THE EXHIBIT PIECE WAS RECOVERED, HUH?
AND YOU GOT ALL THE CREDIT FOR IT?
WHICH IS WEIRD, CUZ I DIDN'T DO A THING.
IN FACT, THE CULPRIT PLOPPED DOWN IN FRONT OF ME...
THOUGH, IN THAT MOMENT, I SPOTTED SOMEONE ELSE IN THE PARKING GARAGE.

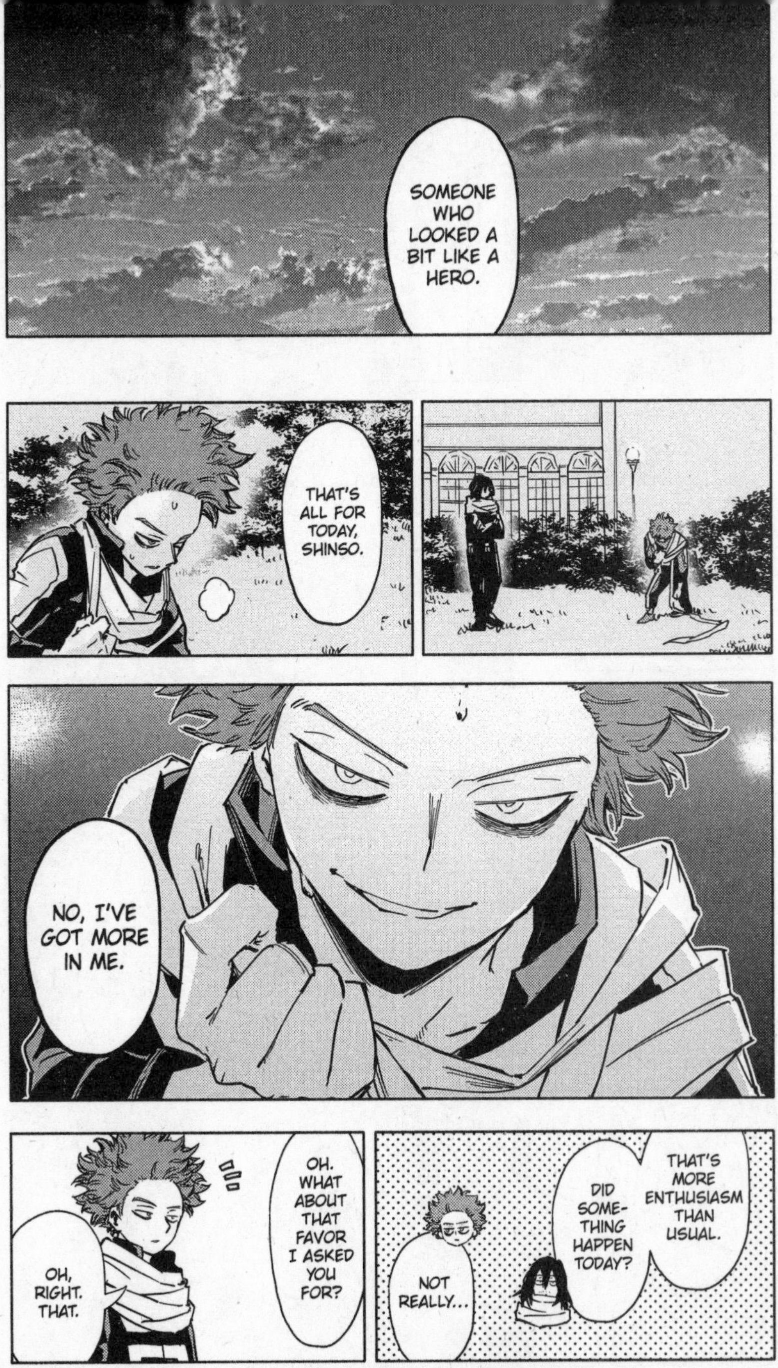
SOMEONE WHO LOOKED A BIT LIKE A HERO.
THAT'S ALL FOR TODAY, SHINSO.
NO, I'VE GOT MORE IN ME.
THAT'S MORE ENTHUSIASM THAN USUAL.
DID SOME-THING HAPPEN TODAY?
NOT REALLY...
OH. WHAT ABOUT THAT FAVOR I ASKED YOU FOR?
OH, RIGHT. THAT.

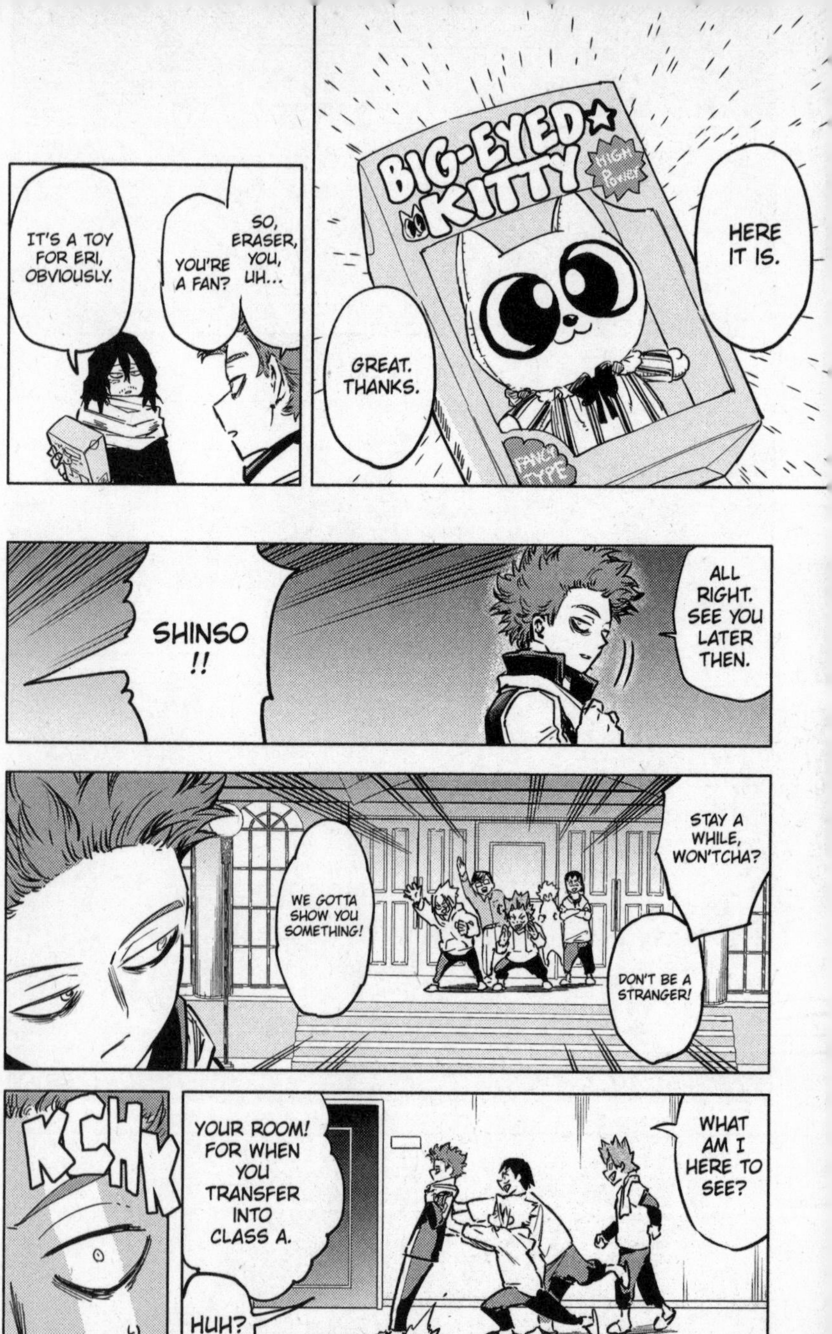
BIG-EYED☆KITTY
HIGH Power
HERE IT IS.
GREAT. THANKS.
SO, ERASER, YOU, UH...
YOU'RE A FAN?
IT'S A TOY FOR ERI, OBVIOUSLY.
ALL RIGHT. SEE YOU LATER THEN.
SHINSO !!
STAY A WHILE, WON'TCHA?
DON'T BE A STRANGER!
WE GOTTA SHOW YOU SOMETHING!
WHAT AM I HERE TO SEE?
YOUR ROOM! FOR WHEN YOU TRANSFER INTO CLASS A.
HUH?
KCHK

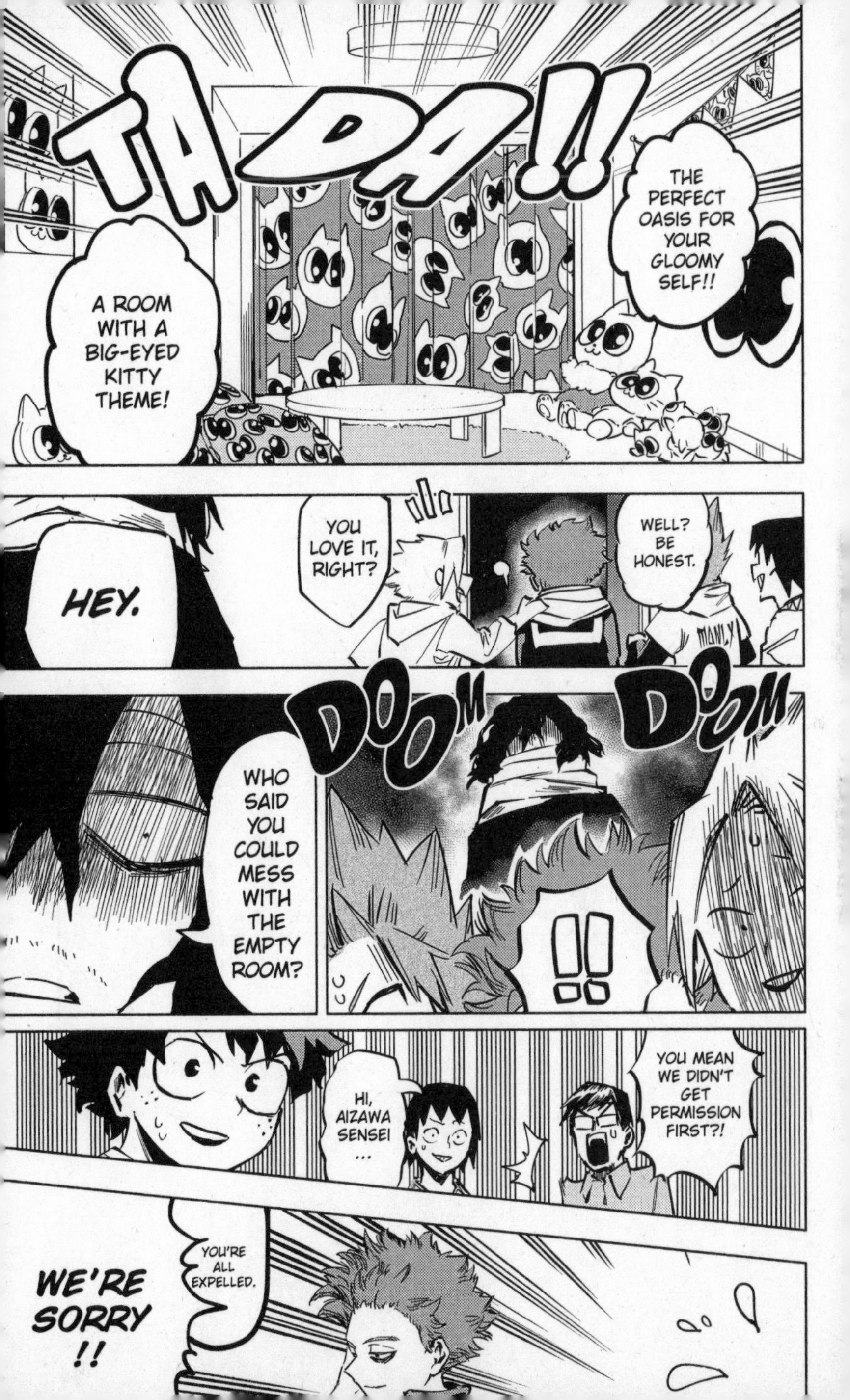
TA DA!!
THE PERFECT OASIS FOR YOUR GLOOMY SELF!!
A ROOM WITH A BIG-EYED KITTY THEME!
WELL? BE HONEST.
YOU LOVE IT, RIGHT?
HEY.
DOOM DOOM
WHO SAID YOU COULD MESS WITH THE EMPTY ROOM?
!!
YOU MEAN WE DIDN'T GET PERMISSION FIRST?!
HI, AIZAWA SENSEI ...
YOU'RE ALL EXPELLED.
WE'RE SORRY!!

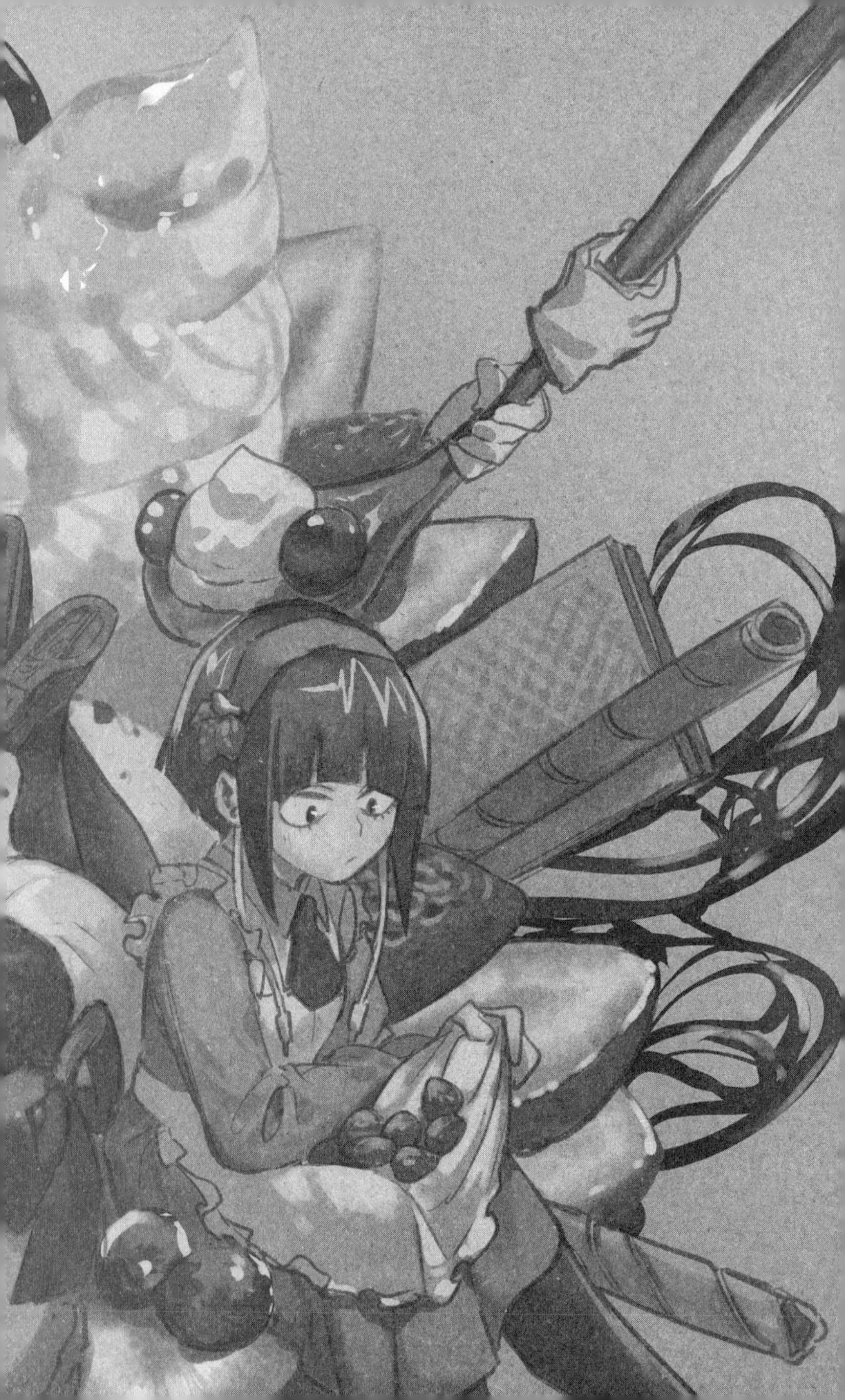

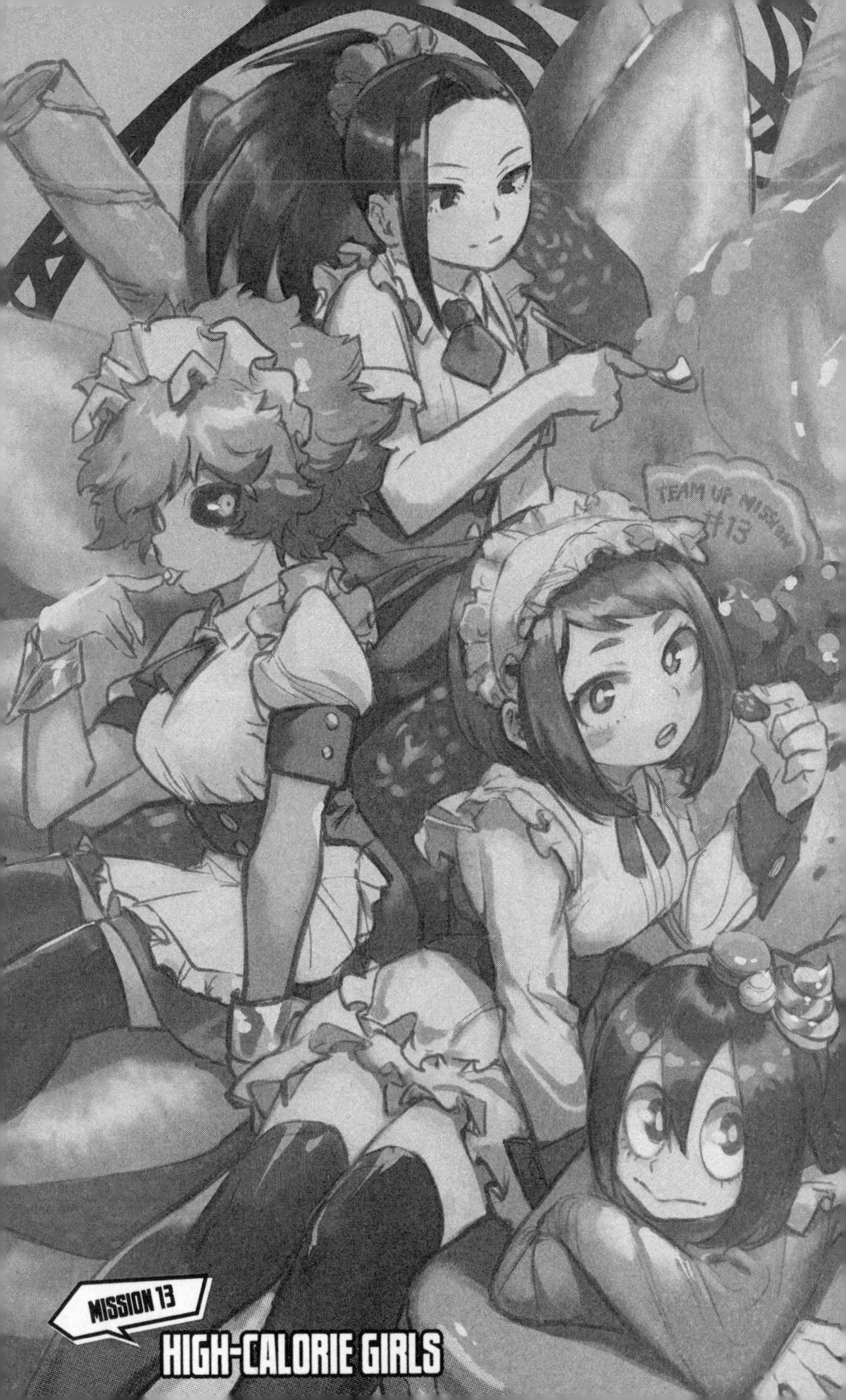
TEAM UP MISSION #13
MISSION 13
HIGH-CALORIE GIRLS

MY HERO ACADEMIA
Team-Up Missions

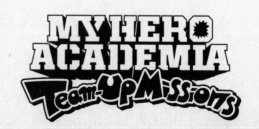

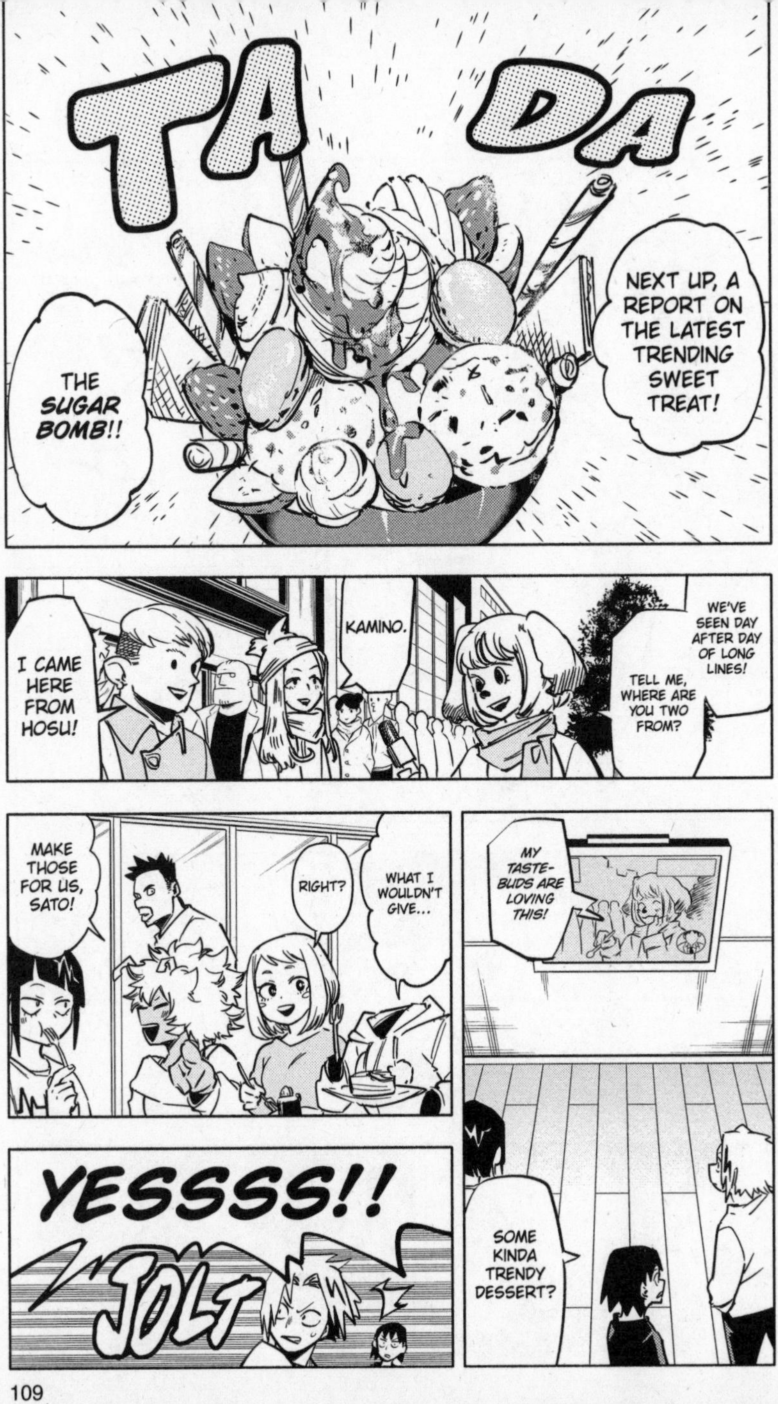
TA DA
NEXT UP, A REPORT ON THE LATEST TRENDING SWEET TREAT!
THE *SUGAR BOMB!!*
WE'VE SEEN DAY AFTER DAY OF LONG LINES!
TELL ME, WHERE ARE YOU TWO FROM?
KAMINO.
I CAME HERE FROM HOSU!
MY TASTE-BUDS ARE LOVING THIS!
SOME KINDA TRENDY DESSERT?
WHAT I WOULDN'T GIVE...
RIGHT?
MAKE THOSE FOR US, SATO!
YESSSS!!
JOLT

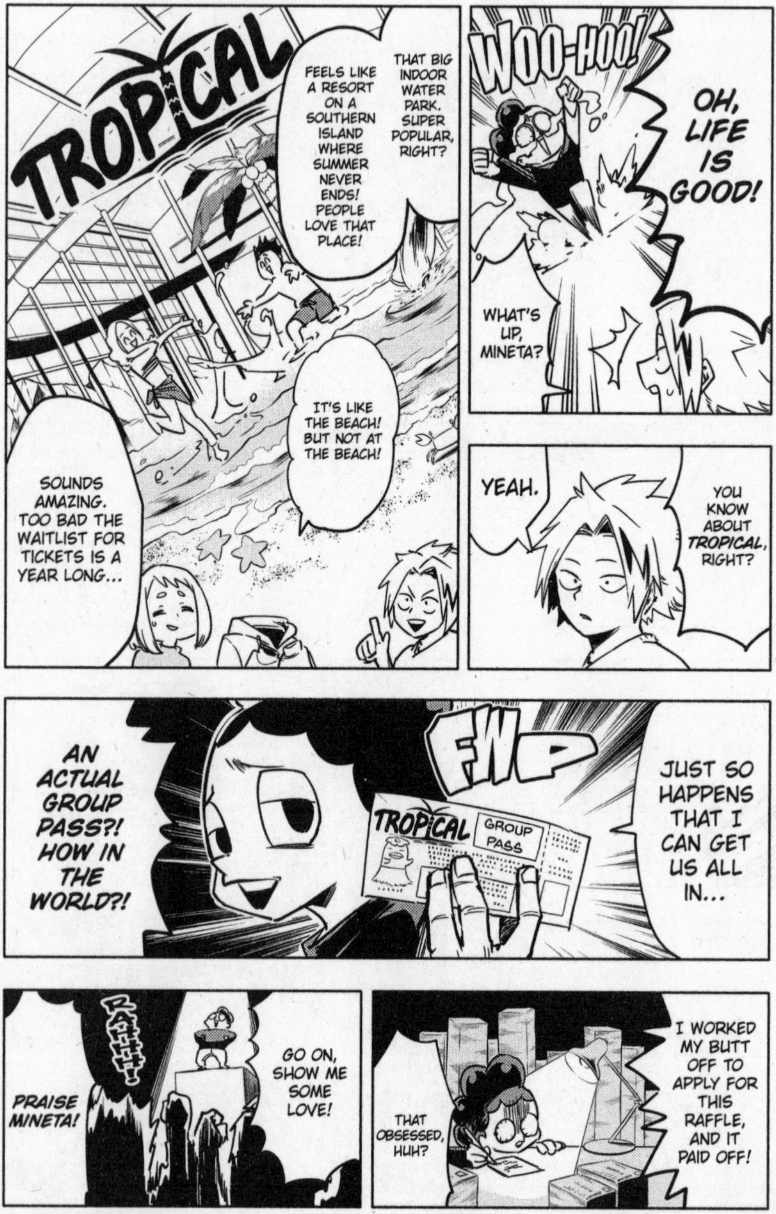
WOO-HOO!
OH, LIFE IS GOOD!
WHAT'S UP, MINETA?
YOU KNOW ABOUT TROPICAL, RIGHT?
YEAH.
TROPICAL
THAT BIG INDOOR WATER PARK. SUPER POPULAR, RIGHT?
FEELS LIKE A RESORT ON A SOUTHERN ISLAND WHERE SUMMER NEVER ENDS! PEOPLE LOVE THAT PLACE!
IT'S LIKE THE BEACH! BUT NOT AT THE BEACH!
SOUNDS AMAZING. TOO BAD THE WAITLIST FOR TICKETS IS A YEAR LONG...
JUST SO HAPPENS THAT I CAN GET US ALL IN...
FWP
TROPICAL GROUP PASS
AN ACTUAL GROUP PASS?! HOW IN THE WORLD?!
I WORKED MY BUTT OFF TO APPLY FOR THIS RAFFLE, AND IT PAID OFF!
THAT OBSESSED, HUH?
RAHHH!
GO ON, SHOW ME SOME LOVE!
PRAISE MINETA!

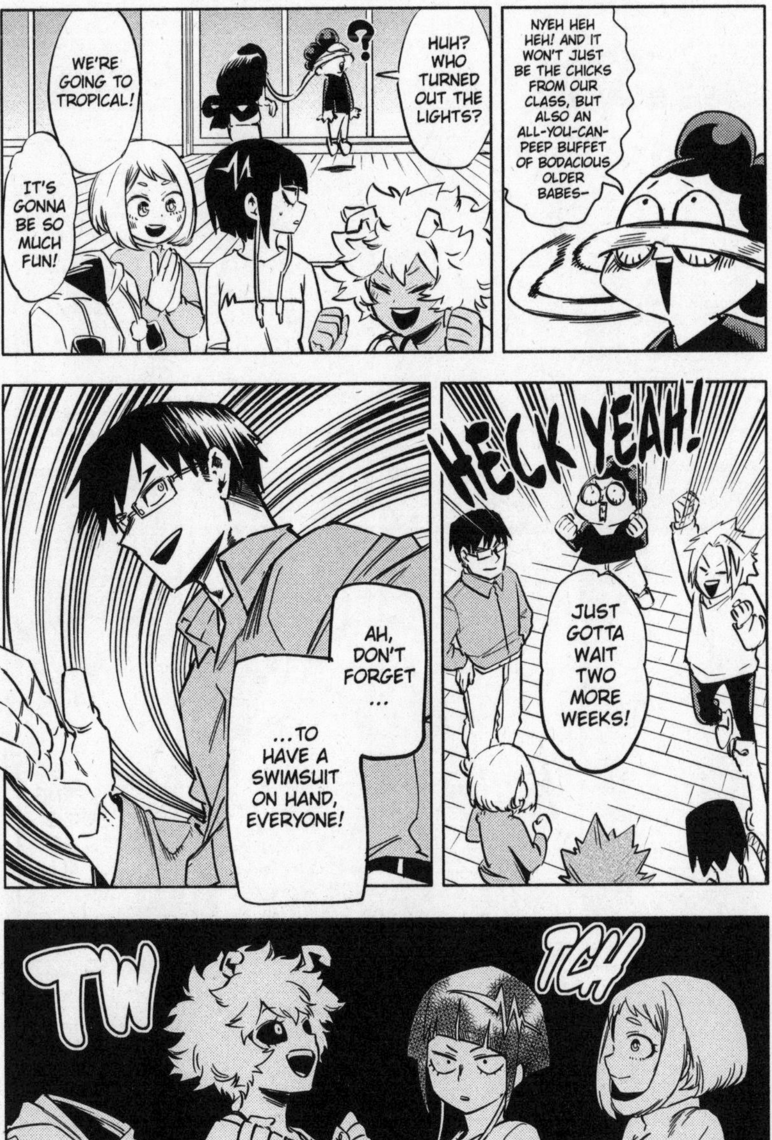
NYEH HEH HEH! AND IT WON'T JUST BE THE CHICKS FROM OUR CLASS, BUT ALSO AN ALL-YOU-CAN-PEEP BUFFET OF BODACIOUS OLDER BABES-
HUH? WHO TURNED OUT THE LIGHTS?
WE'RE GOING TO TROPICAL!
IT'S GONNA BE SO MUCH FUN!
HECK YEAH!
JUST GOTTA WAIT TWO MORE WEEKS!
AH, DON'T FORGET ...
...TO HAVE A SWIMSUIT ON HAND, EVERYONE!
TW TCH

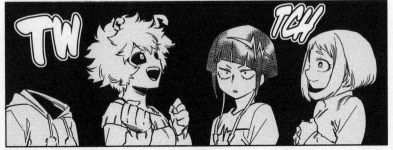

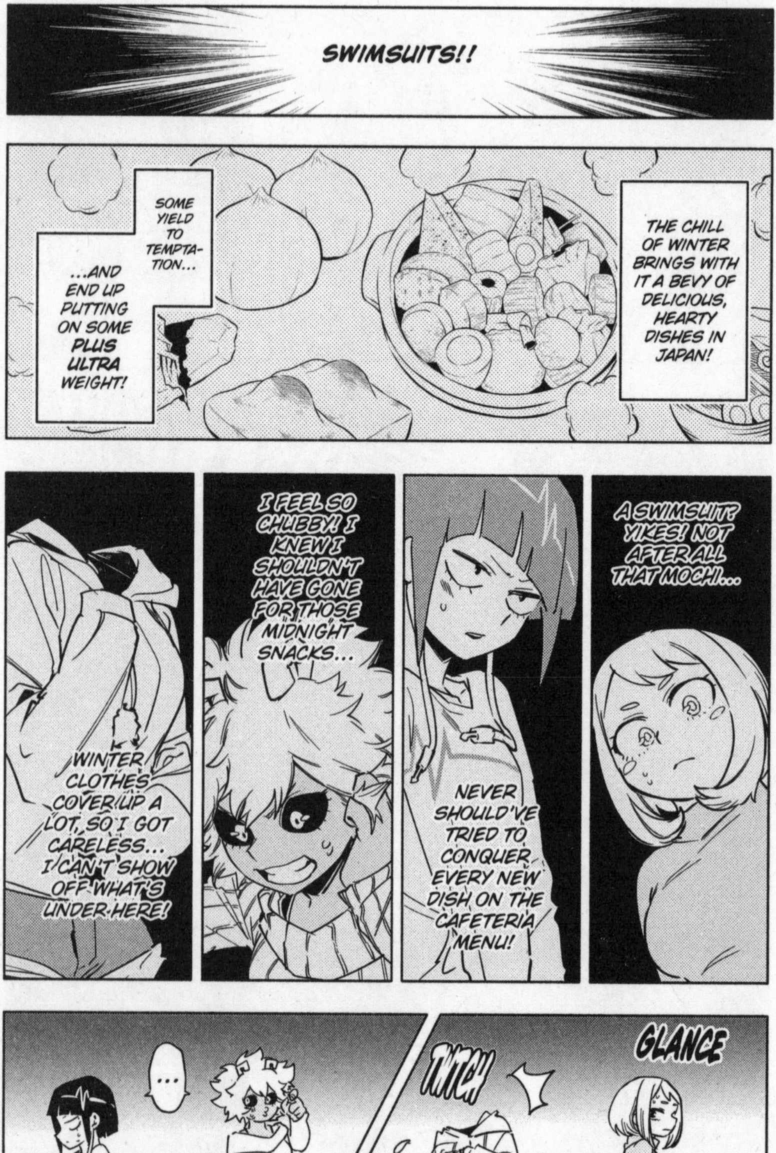
SWIMSUITS!!
THE CHILL OF WINTER BRINGS WITH IT A BEVY OF DELICIOUS, HEARTY DISHES IN JAPAN!
SOME YIELD TO TEMPTATION...
...AND END UP PUTTING ON SOME PLUS ULTRA WEIGHT!
A SWIMSUIT? YIKES! NOT AFTER ALL THAT MOCHI...
NEVER SHOULD'VE TRIED TO CONQUER EVERY NEW DISH ON THE CAFETERIA MENU!
I FEEL SO CHUBBY! I KNEW I SHOULDN'T HAVE GONE FOR THOSE MIDNIGHT SNACKS...
WINTER CLOTHES COVER UP A LOT, SO I GOT CARELESS... I CAN'T SHOW OFF WHAT'S UNDER HERE!
GLANCE
!
TWITCH
...

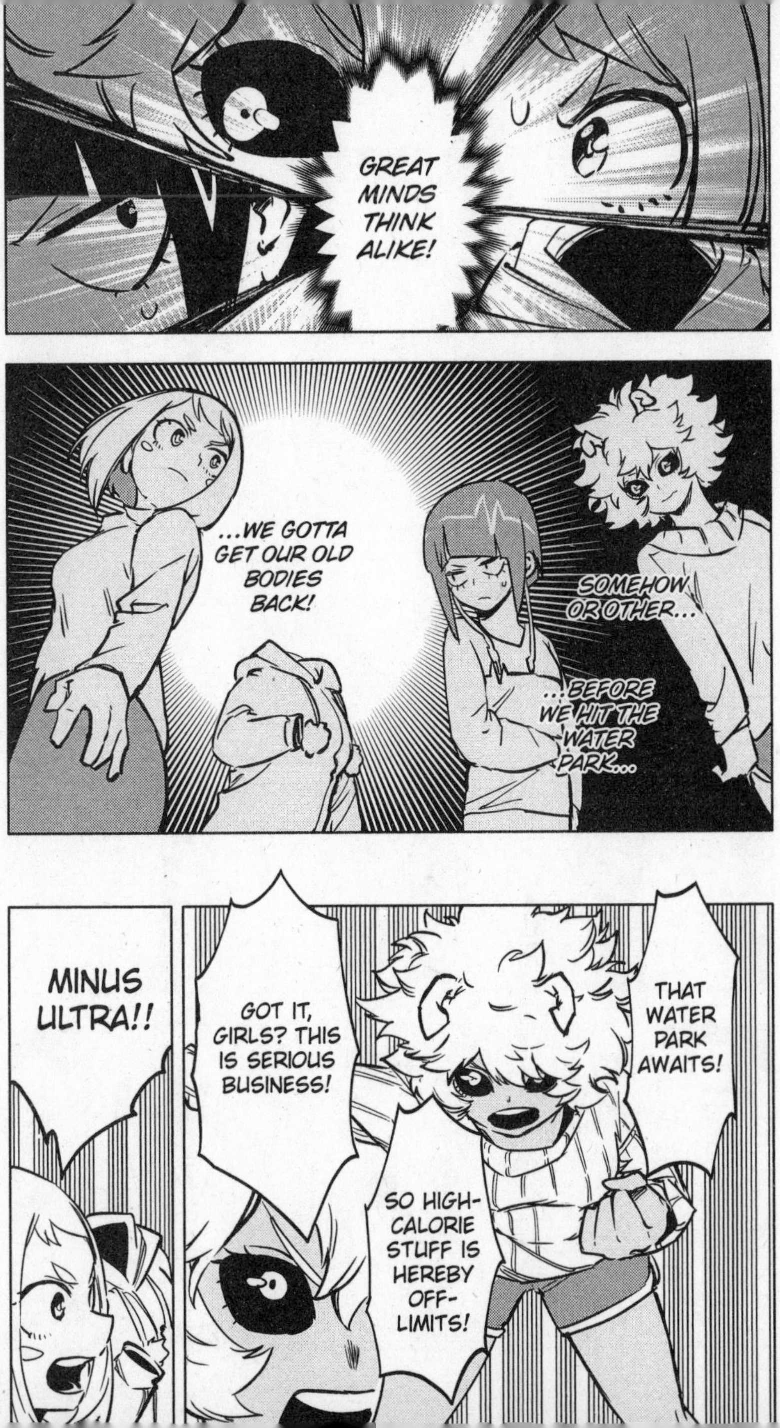
GREAT MINDS THINK ALIKE!
SOMEHOW OR OTHER...
...BEFORE WE HIT THE WATER PARK...
...WE GOTTA GET OUR OLD BODIES BACK!
THAT WATER PARK AWAITS!
GOT IT, GIRLS? THIS IS SERIOUS BUSINESS!
SO HIGH-CALORIE STUFF IS HEREBY OFF-LIMITS!
MINUS ULTRA!!

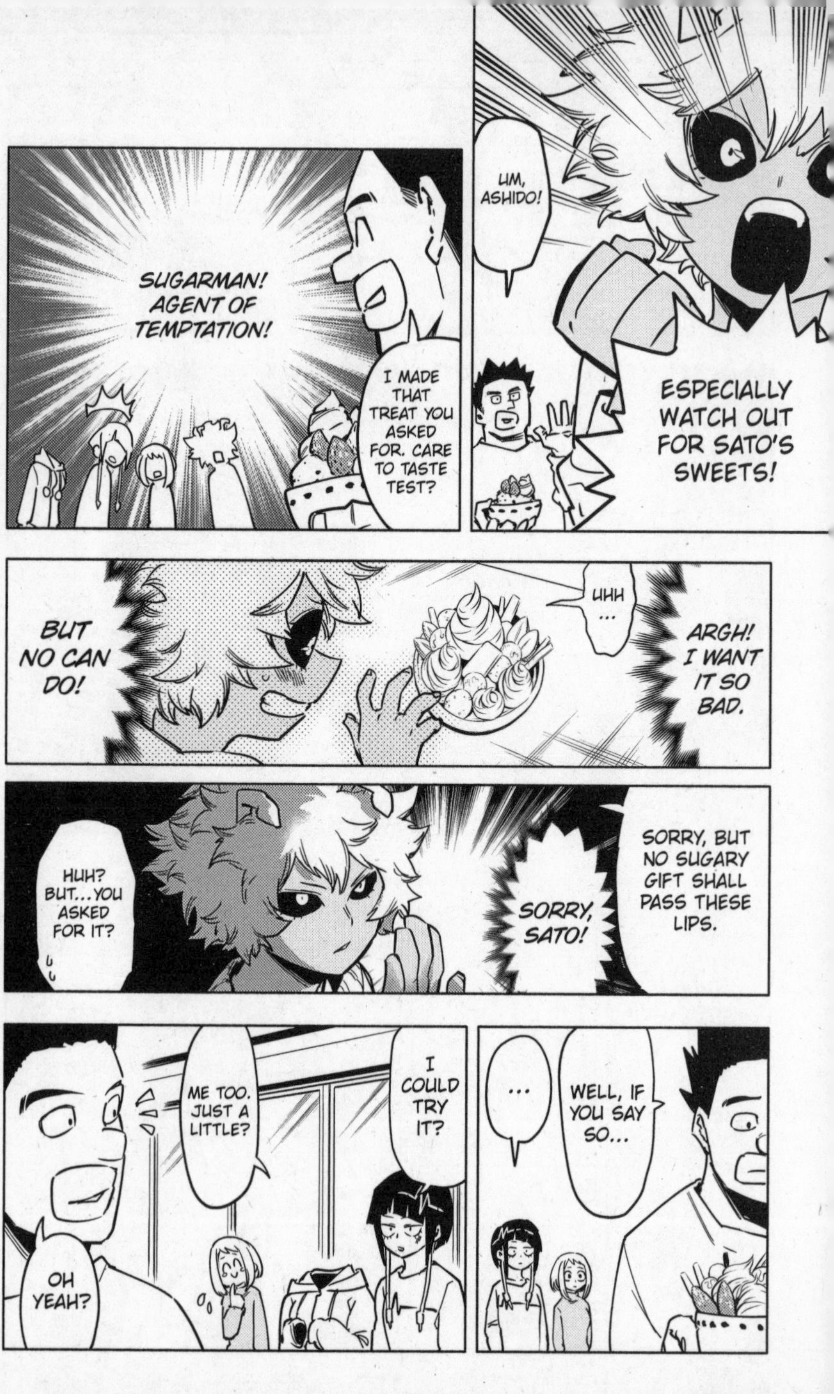
UM, ASHIDO!
ESPECIALLY WATCH OUT FOR SATO'S SWEETS!
I MADE THAT TREAT YOU ASKED FOR. CARE TO TASTE TEST?
SUGARMAN! AGENT OF TEMPTATION!
ARGH! I WANT IT SO BAD.
UHH...
BUT NO CAN DO!
SORRY, BUT NO SUGARY GIFT SHALL PASS THESE LIPS.
SORRY, SATO!
HUH? BUT...YOU ASKED FOR IT?
WELL, IF YOU SAY SO...
...
I COULD TRY IT?
ME TOO. JUST A LITTLE?
OH YEAH?

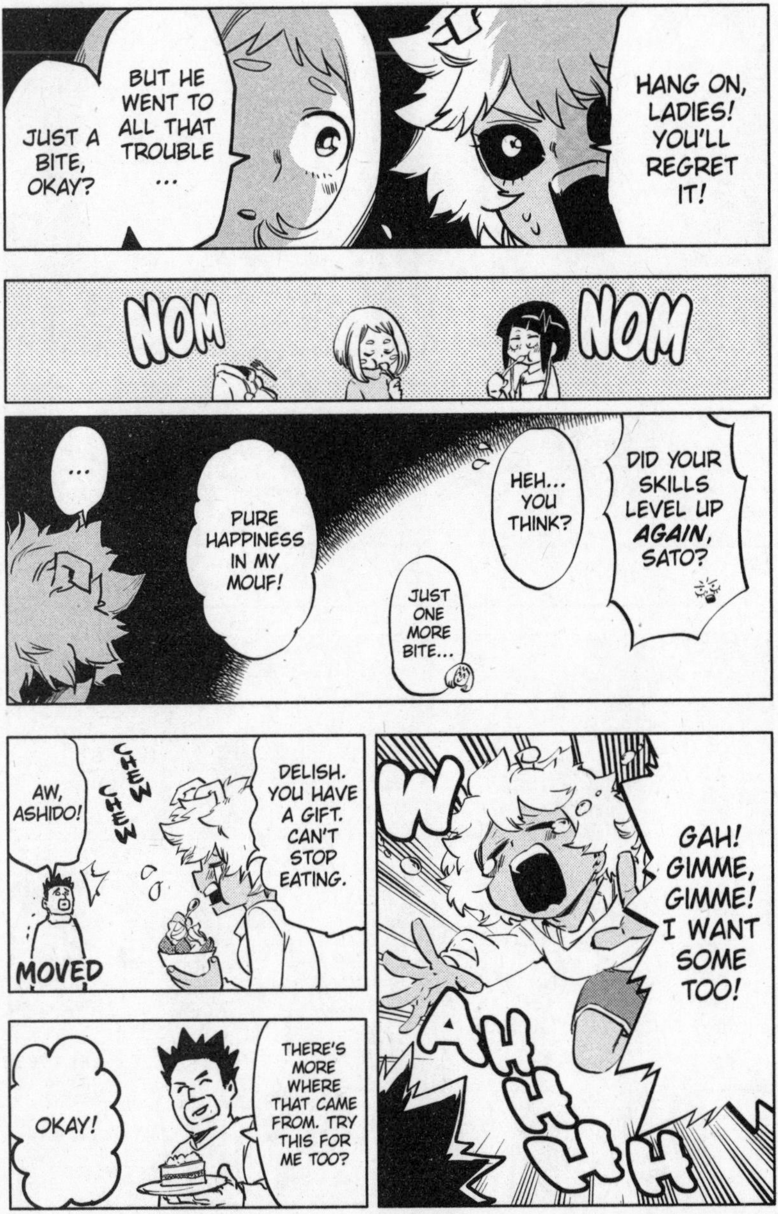
HANG ON, LADIES! YOU'LL REGRET IT!
BUT HE WENT TO ALL THAT TROUBLE...
JUST A BITE, OKAY?
NOM
NOM
DID YOUR SKILLS LEVEL UP AGAIN, SATO?
HEH... YOU THINK?
JUST ONE MORE BITE...
PURE HAPPINESS IN MY MOUF!
...
GAH! GIMME, GIMME! I WANT SOME TOO!
WAHHHHH
DELISH. YOU HAVE A GIFT. CAN'T STOP EATING.
CHEW CHEW
AW, ASHIDO!
MOVED
THERE'S MORE WHERE THAT CAME FROM. TRY THIS FOR ME TOO?
OKAY!

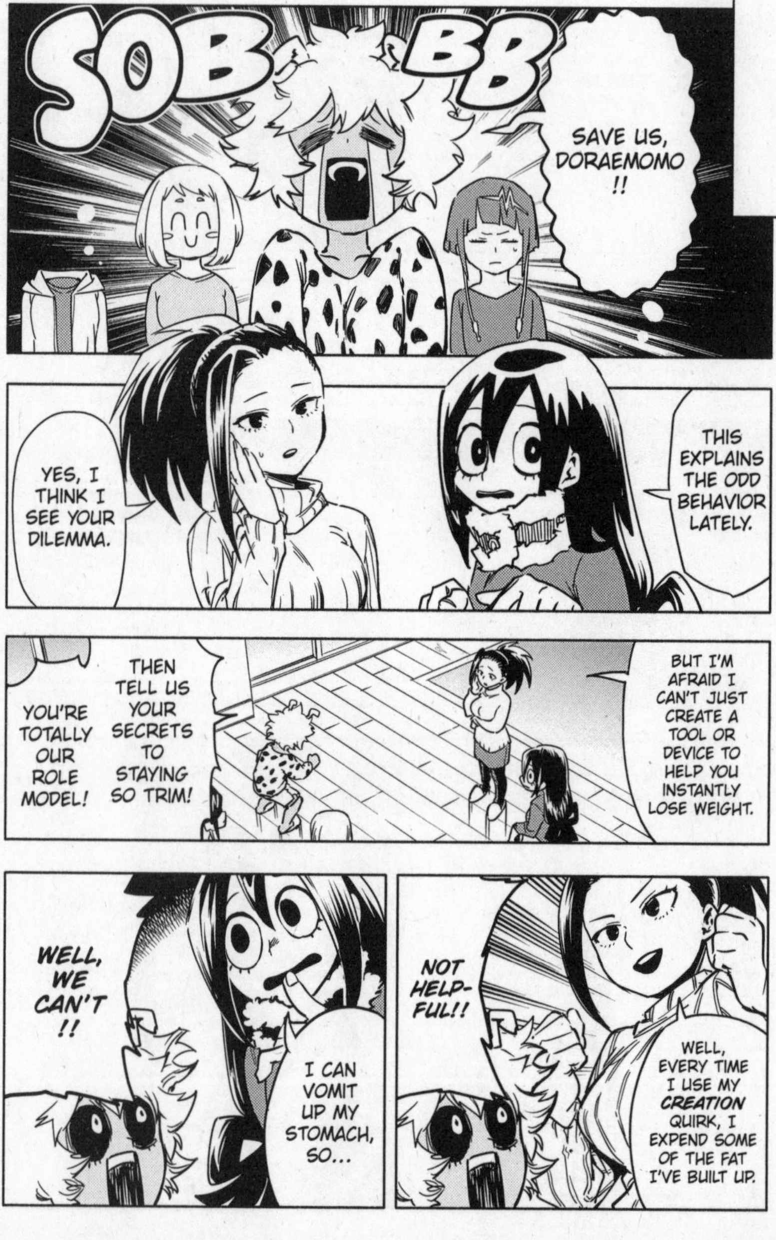
SOBBB
SAVE US, DORAEMOMO !!
THIS EXPLAINS THE ODD BEHAVIOR LATELY.
YES, I THINK I SEE YOUR DILEMMA.
BUT I'M AFRAID I CAN'T JUST CREATE A TOOL OR DEVICE TO HELP YOU INSTANTLY LOSE WEIGHT.
THEN TELL US YOUR SECRETS TO STAYING SO TRIM!
YOU'RE TOTALLY OUR ROLE MODEL!
WELL, EVERY TIME I USE MY CREATION QUIRK, I EXPEND SOME OF THE FAT I'VE BUILT UP.
NOT HELPFUL!!
I CAN VOMIT UP MY STOMACH, SO...
WELL, WE CAN'T !!

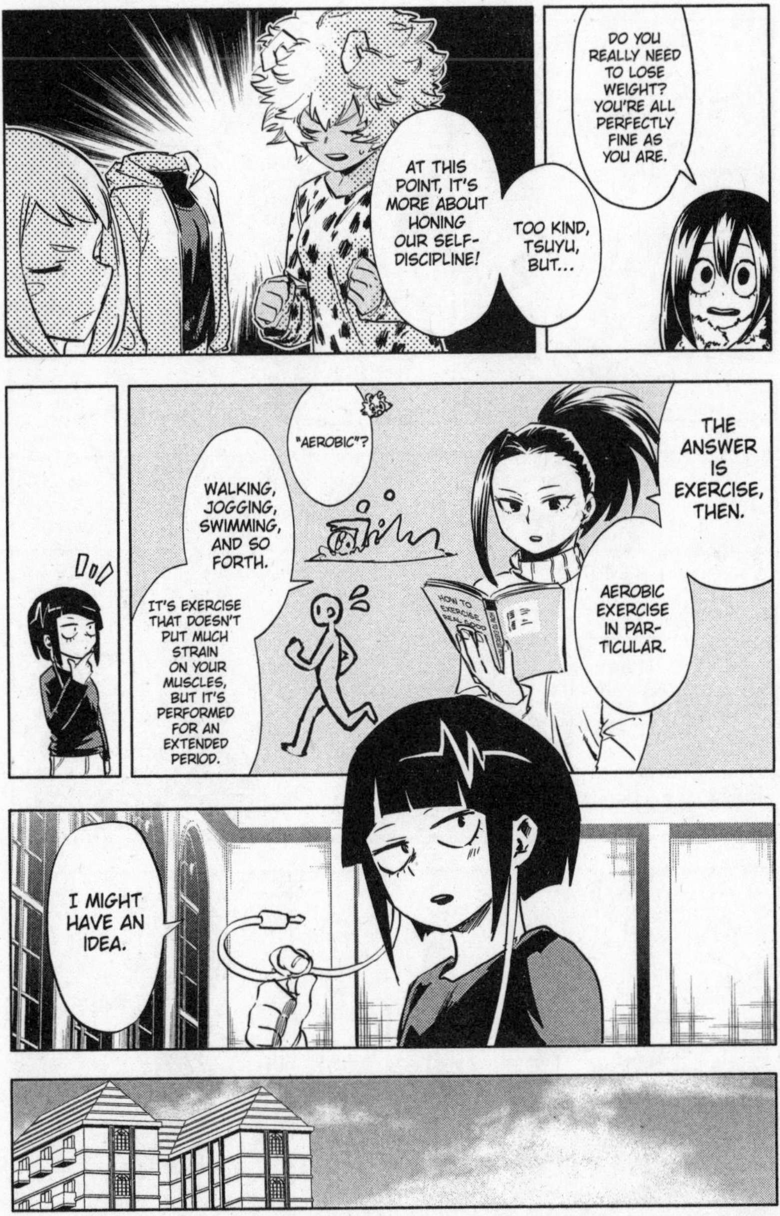
DO YOU REALLY NEED TO LOSE WEIGHT? YOU'RE ALL PERFECTLY FINE AS YOU ARE.
TOO KIND, TSUYU, BUT...
AT THIS POINT, IT'S MORE ABOUT HONING OUR SELF-DISCIPLINE!
THE ANSWER IS EXERCISE, THEN.
AEROBIC EXERCISE IN PARTICULAR.
"AEROBIC"?
WALKING, JOGGING, SWIMMING, AND SO FORTH.
IT'S EXERCISE THAT DOESN'T PUT MUCH STRAIN ON YOUR MUSCLES, BUT IT'S PERFORMED FOR AN EXTENDED PERIOD.
HOW TO EXERCISE REAL GOOD
I MIGHT HAVE AN IDEA.

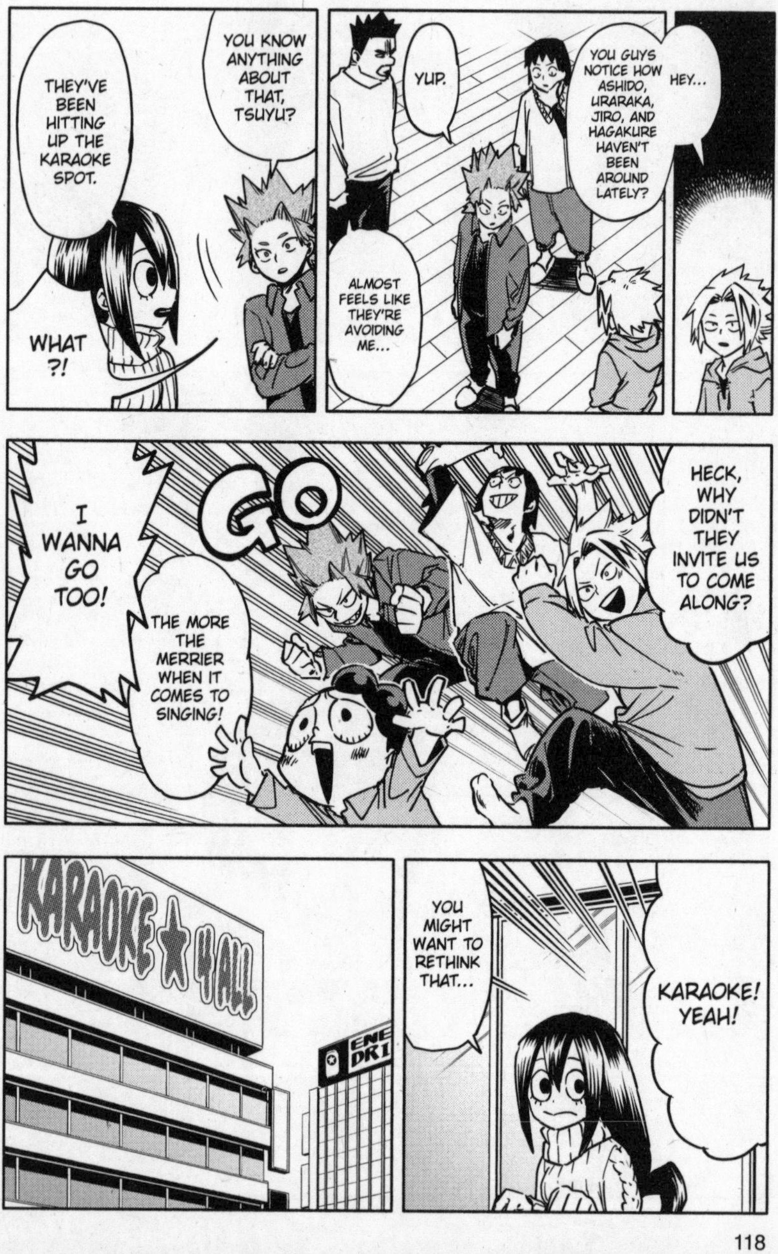
HEY...
YOU GUYS NOTICE HOW ASHIDO, URARAKA, JIRO, AND HAGAKURE HAVEN'T BEEN AROUND LATELY?
YUP.
ALMOST FEELS LIKE THEY'RE AVOIDING ME...
YOU KNOW ANYTHING ABOUT THAT, TSUYU?
THEY'VE BEEN HITTING UP THE KARAOKE SPOT.
WHAT ?!
HECK, WHY DIDN'T THEY INVITE US TO COME ALONG?
GO
I WANNA GO TOO!
THE MORE THE MERRIER WHEN IT COMES TO SINGING!
KARAOKE! YEAH!
YOU MIGHT WANT TO RETHINK THAT...
KARAOKE ★ 4 ALL

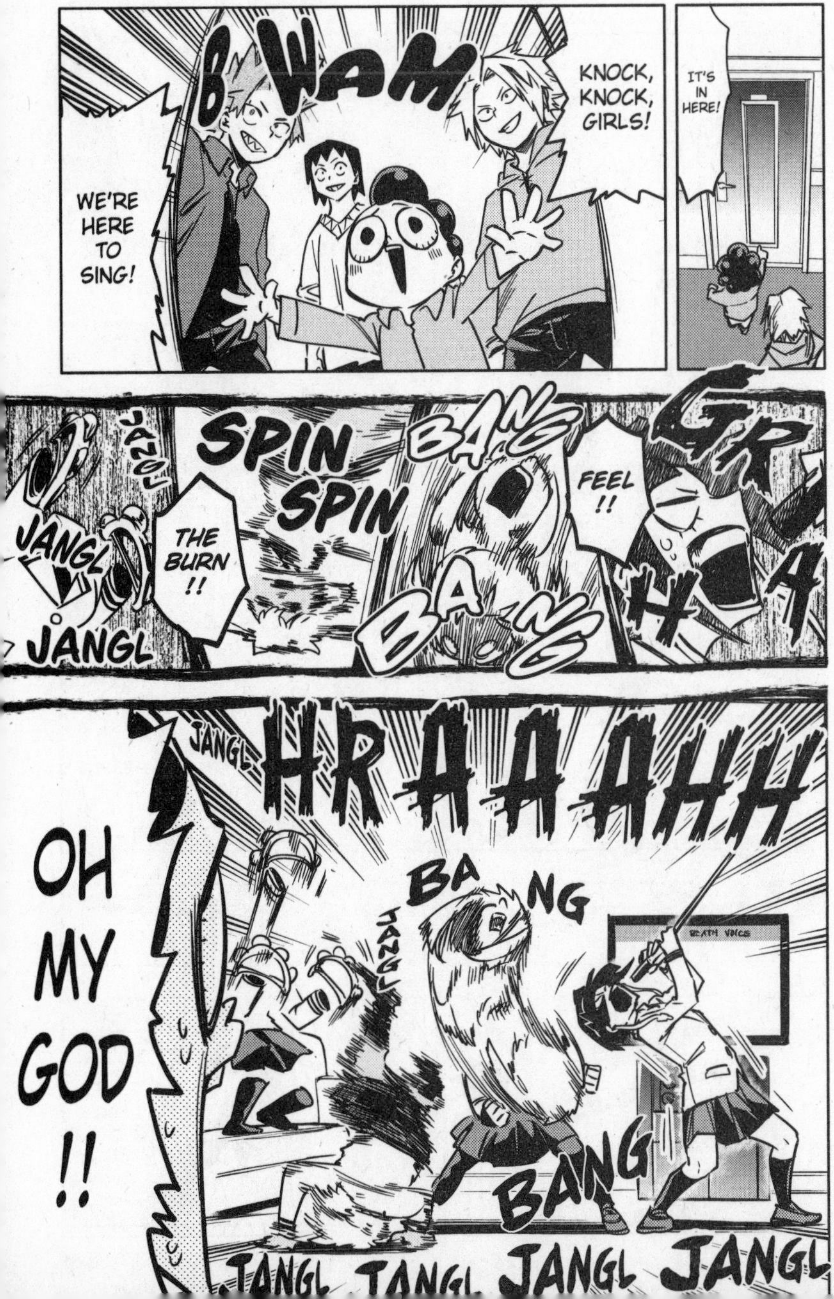

IT'S IN HERE!
KNOCK, KNOCK, GIRLS!
BWAM
WE'RE HERE TO SING!
GR
HA
FEEL !!
BANG
SPIN SPIN
BANG
THE BURN !!
JANGL
JANGL
JANGL
HRAAAHH
JANGL
BANG
JANGL
OH MY GOD !!
BANG
JANGL JANGL JANGL JANGL

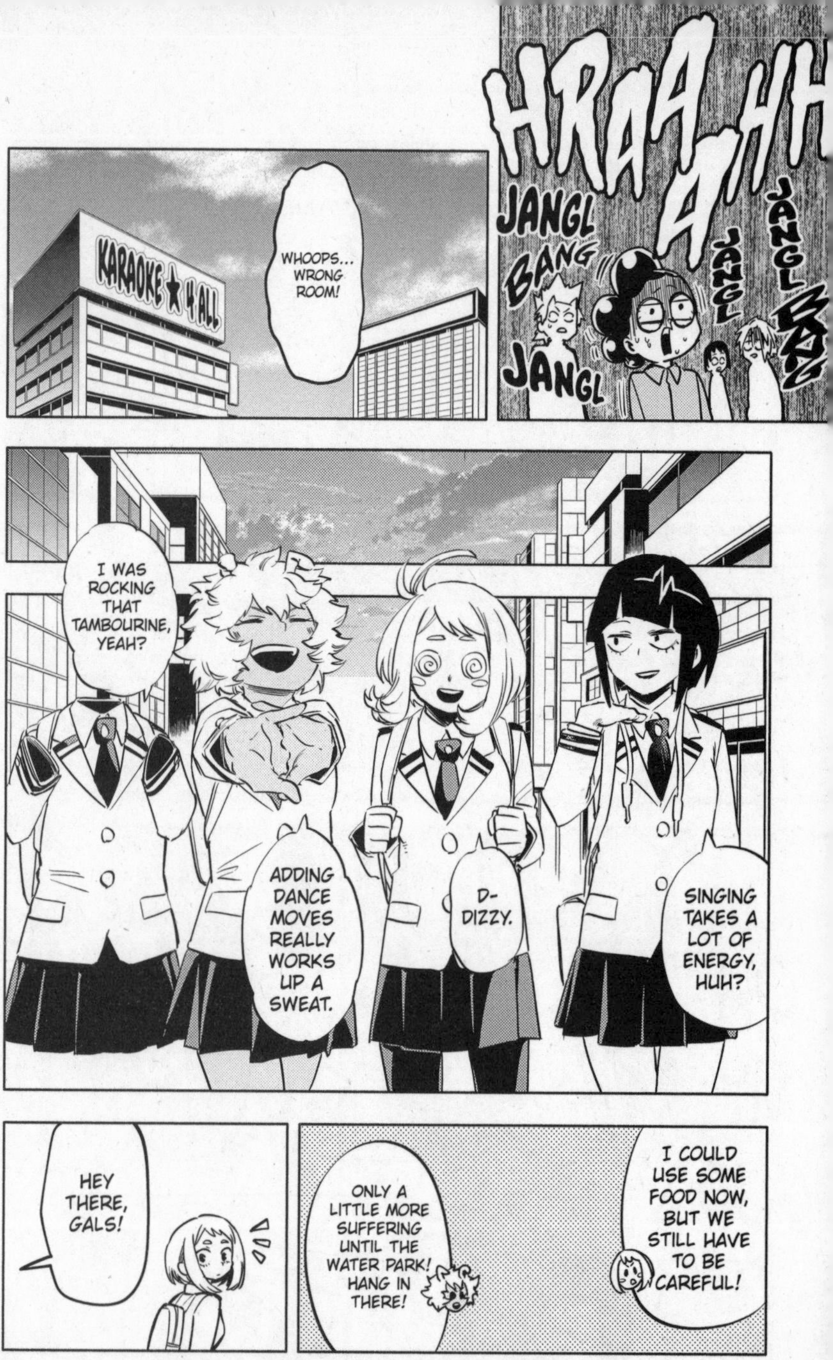
HRAAAAHH
JANGL
BANG
JANGL
JANGL
JANGL
BANG
WHOOPS... WRONG ROOM!
KARAOKE ★ 4 ALL
SINGING TAKES A LOT OF ENERGY, HUH?
D-DIZZY.
ADDING DANCE MOVES REALLY WORKS UP A SWEAT.
I WAS ROCKING THAT TAMBOURINE, YEAH?
I COULD USE SOME FOOD NOW, BUT WE STILL HAVE TO BE CAREFUL!
ONLY A LITTLE MORE SUFFERING UNTIL THE WATER PARK! HANG IN THERE!
HEY THERE, GALS!

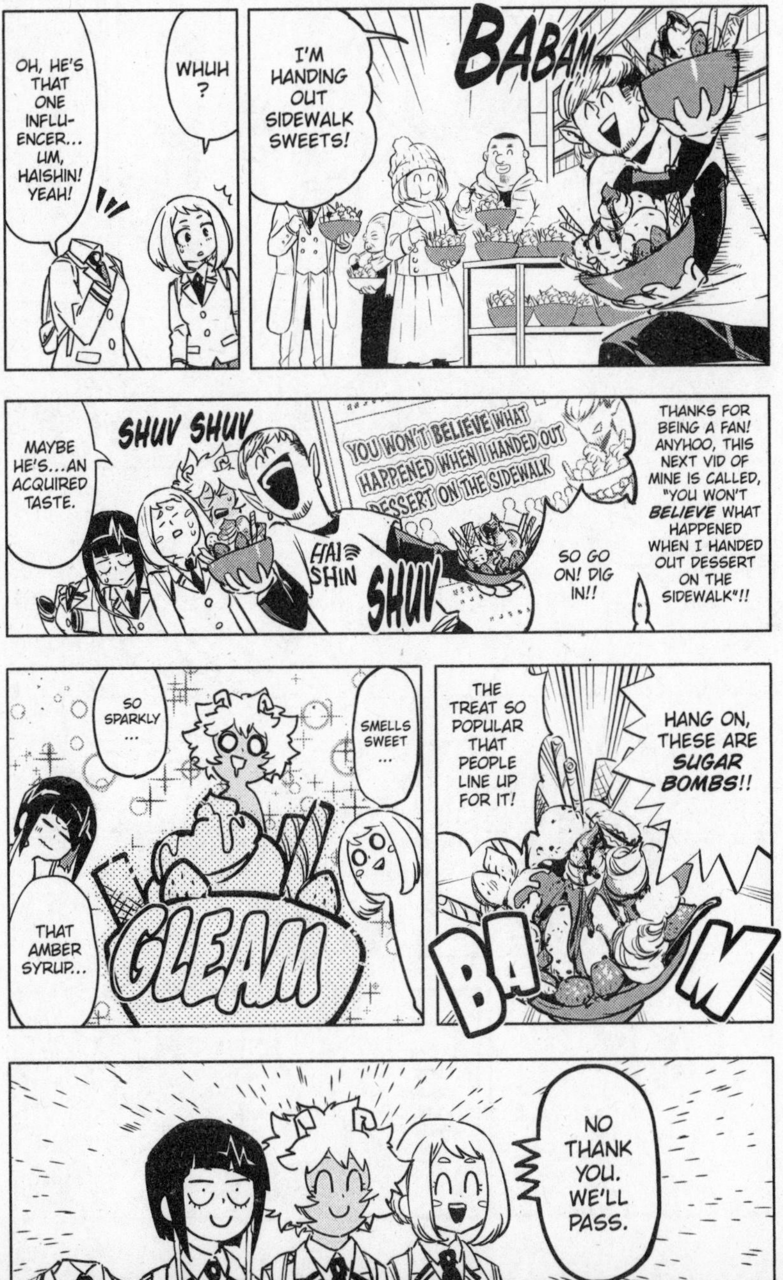
BABAM
I'M HANDING OUT SIDEWALK SWEETS!
WHUH ?
OH, HE'S THAT ONE INFLUENCER... UM, HAISHIN! YEAH!
THANKS FOR BEING A FAN! ANYHOO, THIS NEXT VID OF MINE IS CALLED, "YOU WON'T BELIEVE WHAT HAPPENED WHEN I HANDED OUT DESSERT ON THE SIDEWALK"!!
SO GO ON! DIG IN!!
YOU WON'T BELIEVE WHAT HAPPENED WHEN I HANDED OUT DESSERT ON THE SIDEWALK
SHUV SHUV
SHUV
HAI SHIN
MAYBE HE'S...AN ACQUIRED TASTE.
HANG ON, THESE ARE SUGAR BOMBS!!
THE TREAT SO POPULAR THAT PEOPLE LINE UP FOR IT!
BAM
SMELLS SWEET ...
SO SPARKLY ...
GLEAM
THAT AMBER SYRUP...
NO THANK YOU. WE'LL PASS.

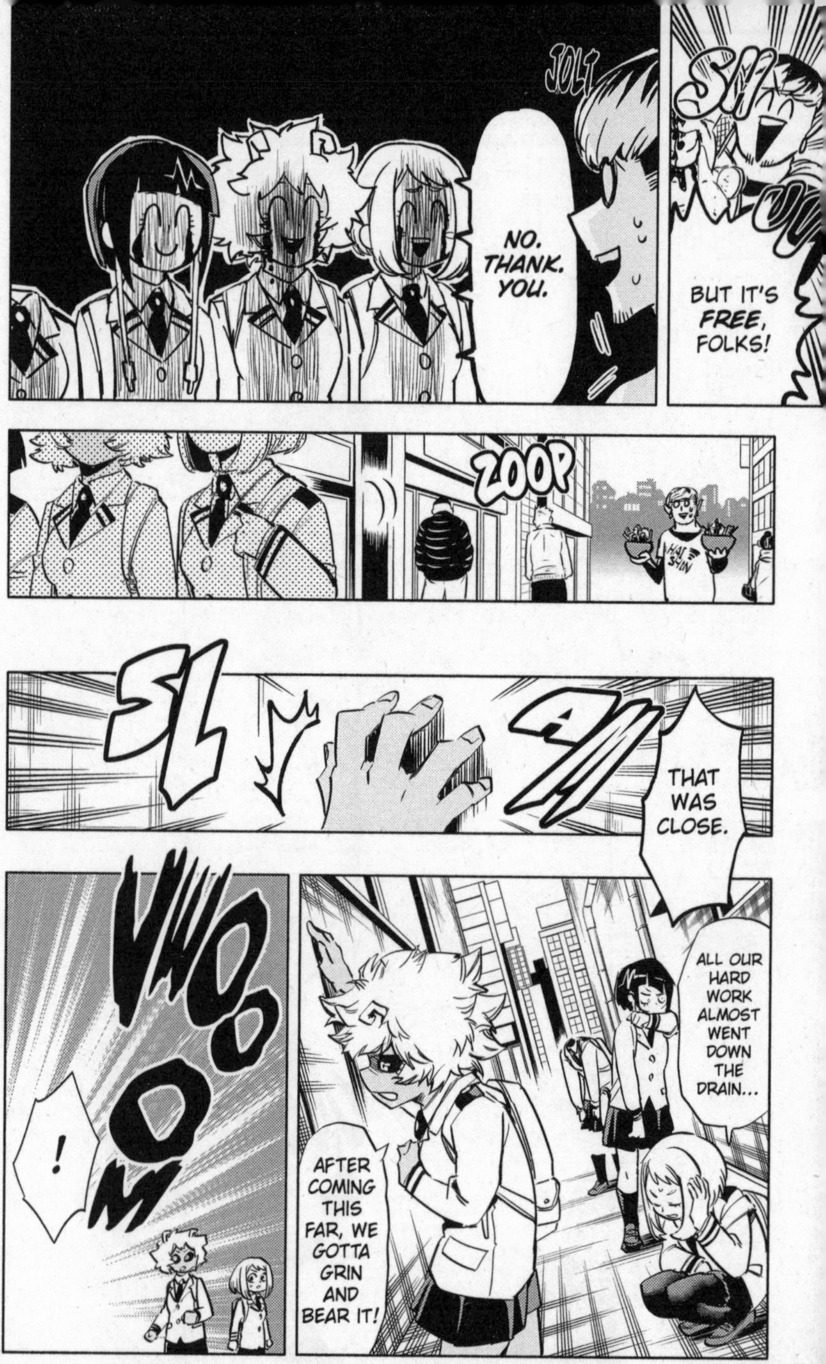
BUT IT'S FREE, FOLKS!
JOLT
NO. THANK. YOU.
ZOOP
THAT WAS CLOSE.
SLAM
ALL OUR HARD WORK ALMOST WENT DOWN THE DRAIN...
AFTER COMING THIS FAR, WE GOTTA GRIN AND BEAR IT!
!

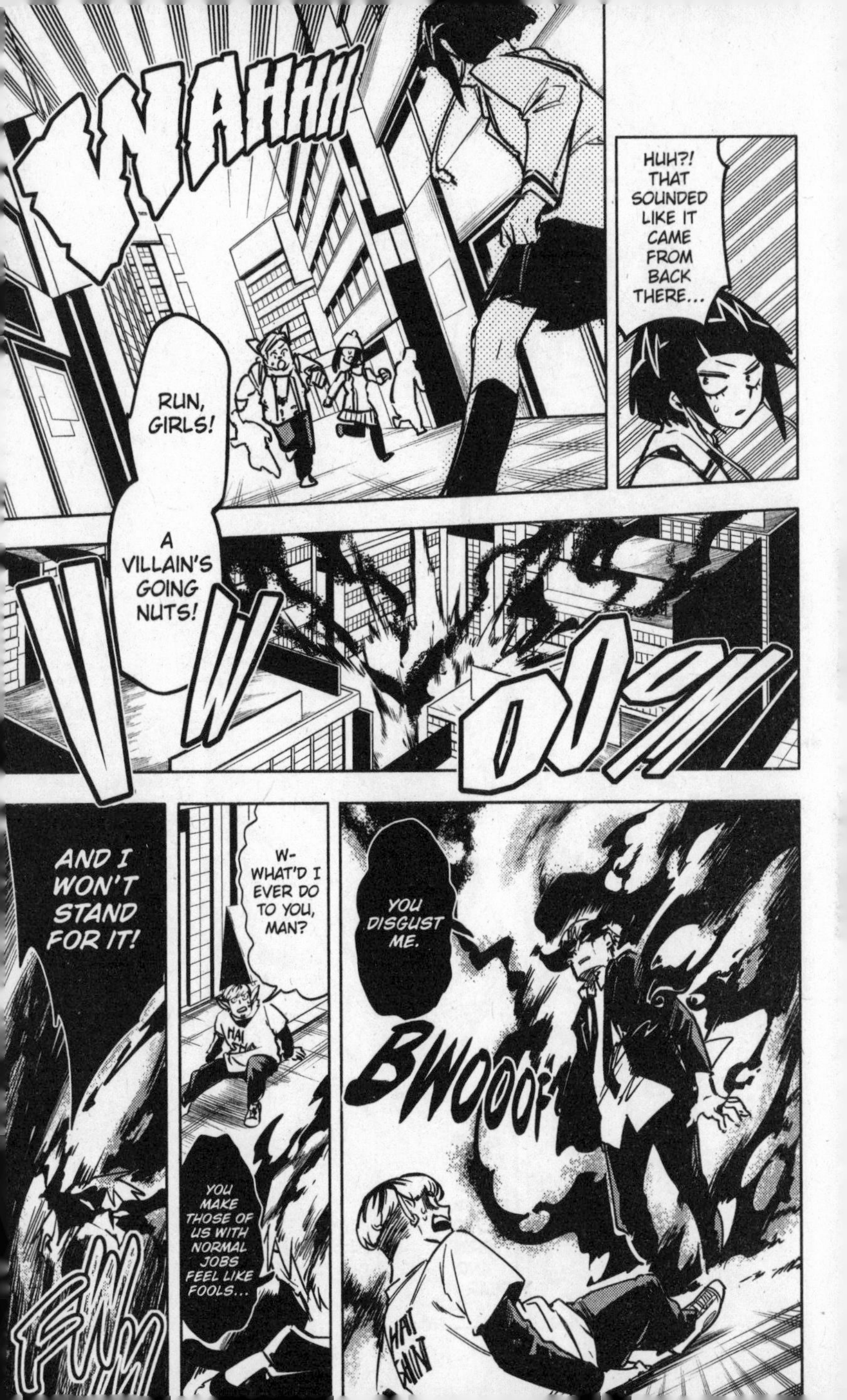

HUH?! THAT SOUNDED LIKE IT CAME FROM BACK THERE...
WAHHH
RUN, GIRLS!
A VILLAIN'S GOING NUTS!
YOU DISGUST ME.
BWOOOF
W- WHAT'D I EVER DO TO YOU, MAN?
YOU MAKE THOSE OF US WITH NORMAL JOBS FEEL LIKE FOOLS...
AND I WON'T STAND FOR IT!

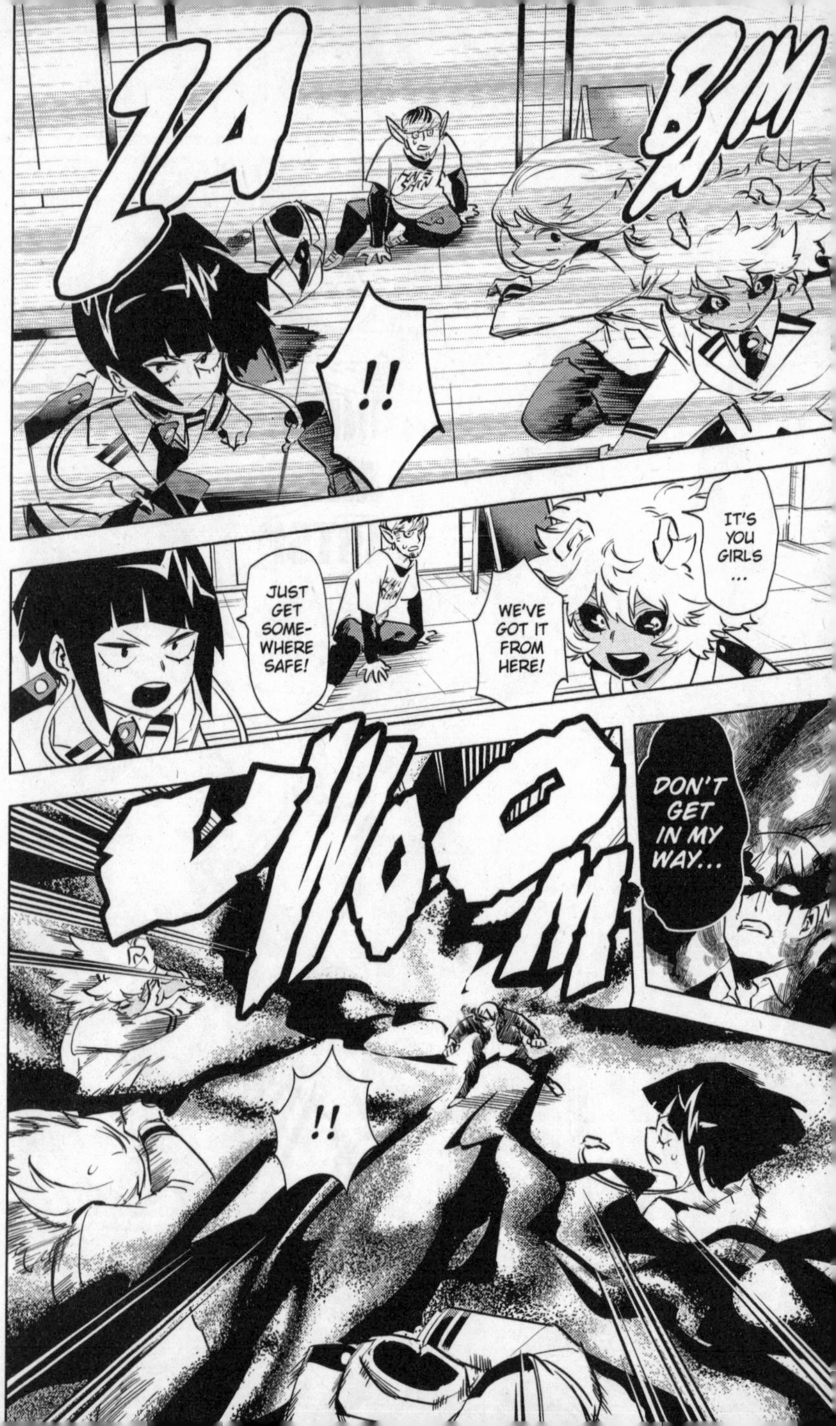
BAM
ZA
!!
IT'S YOU GIRLS ...
WE'VE GOT IT FROM HERE!
JUST GET SOME-WHERE SAFE!
DON'T GET IN MY WAY...
!!

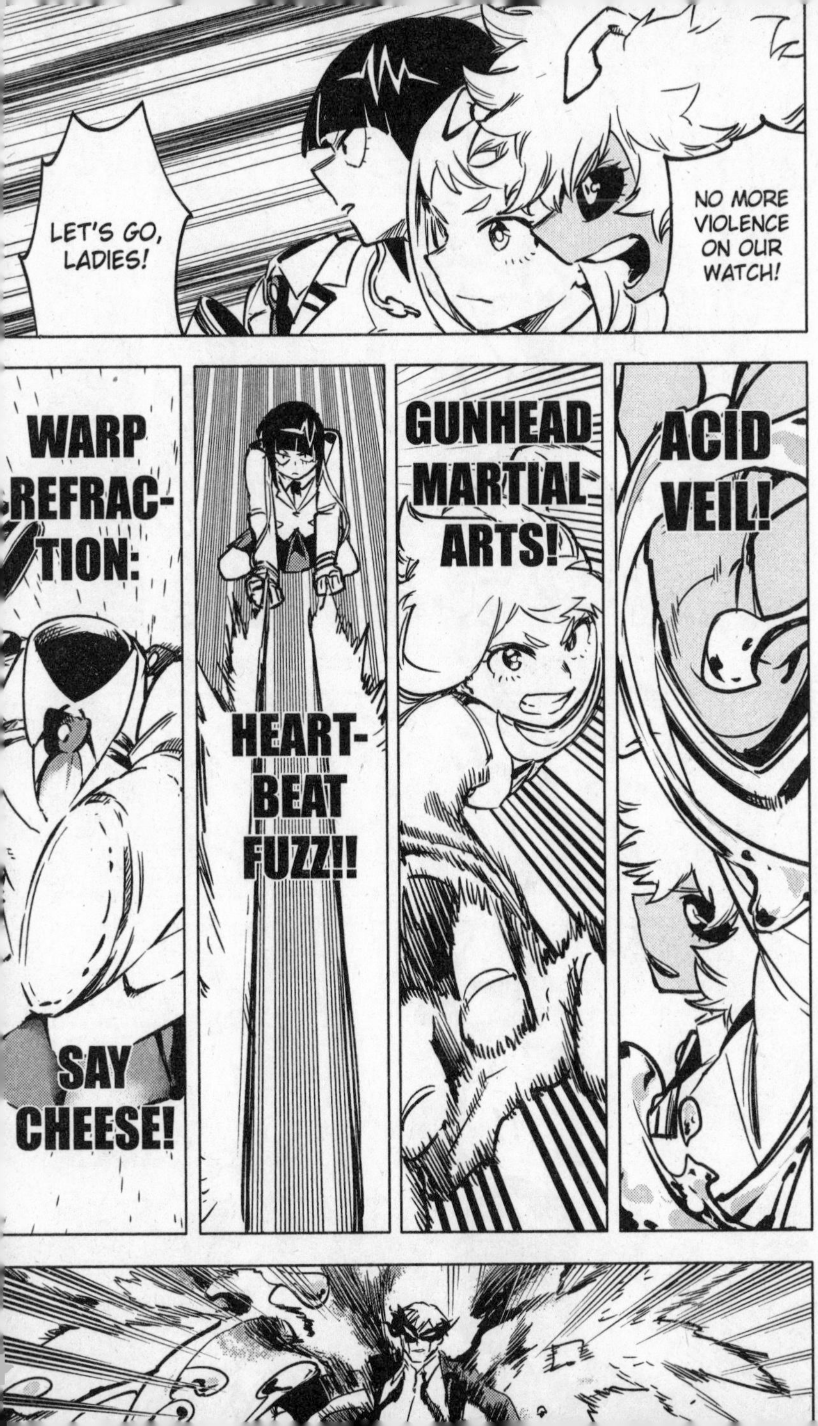
NO MORE VIOLENCE ON OUR WATCH!
LET'S GO, LADIES!
ACID VEIL!
GUNHEAD MARTIAL ARTS!
HEART-BEAT FUZZ!!
WARP REFRAC-TION:
SAY CHEESE!

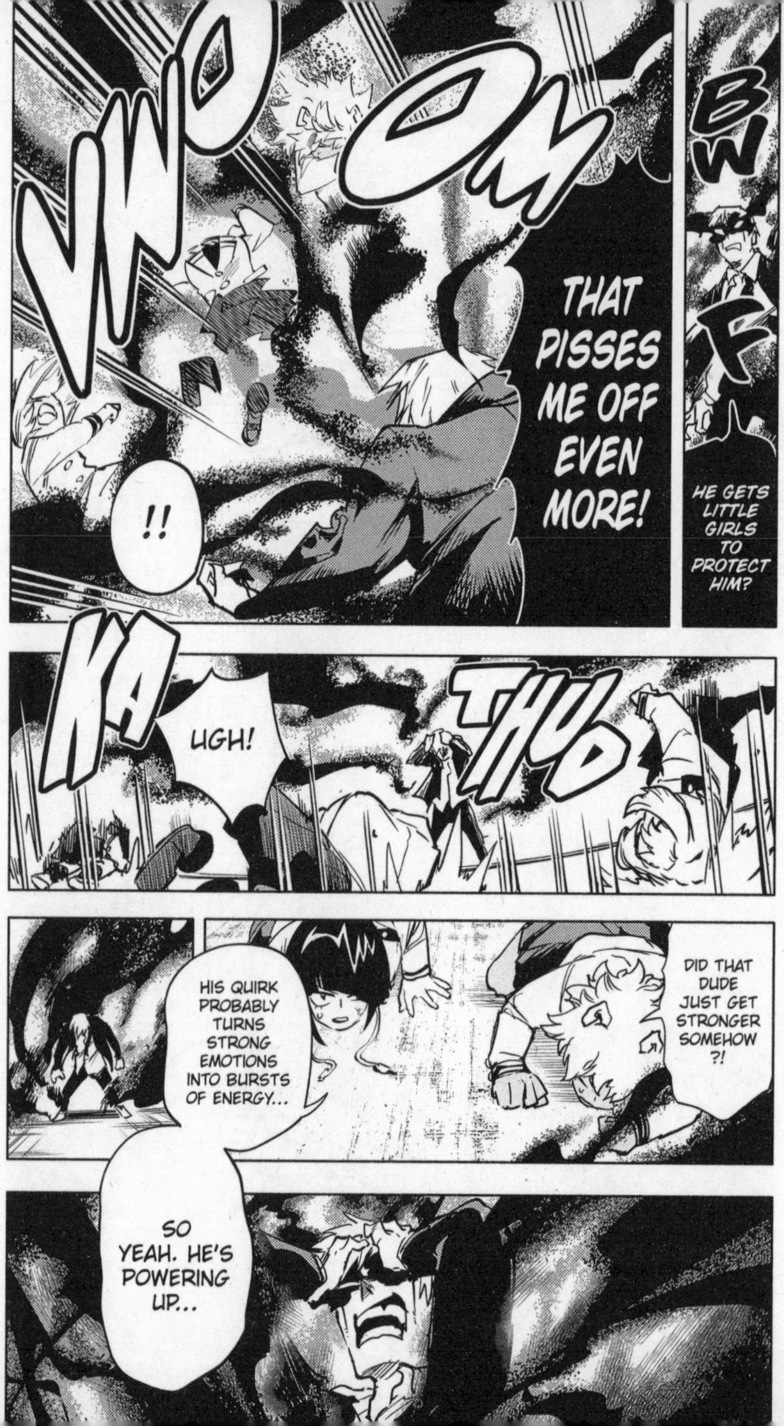
BWF
HE GETS LITTLE GIRLS TO PROTECT HIM?
VWOOM
THAT PISSES ME OFF EVEN MORE!
!!
THUD
UGH!
KA
DID THAT DUDE JUST GET STRONGER SOMEHOW?!
HIS QUIRK PROBABLY TURNS STRONG EMOTIONS INTO BURSTS OF ENERGY...
SO YEAH. HE'S POWERING UP...

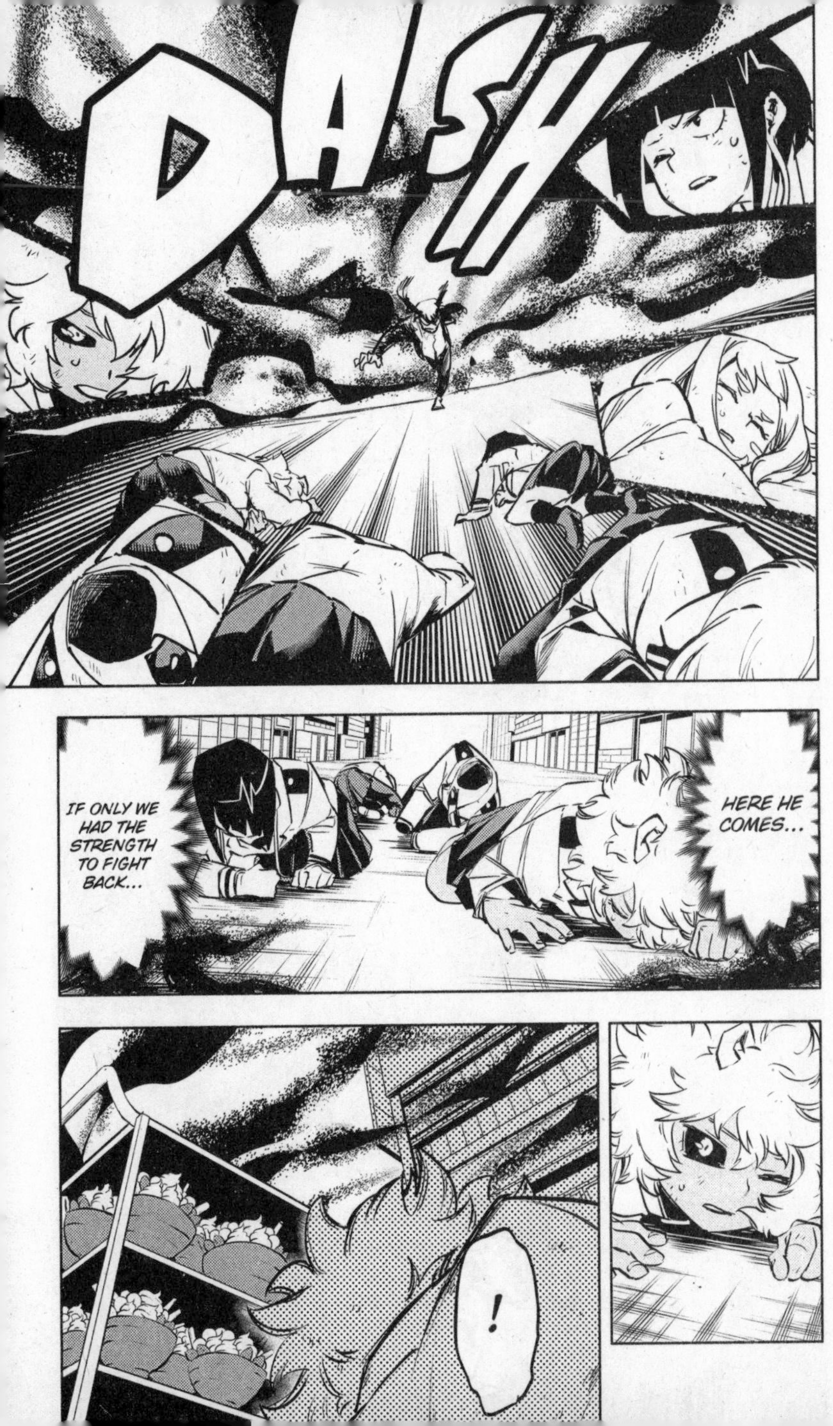
DASH
HERE HE COMES...
IF ONLY WE HAD THE STRENGTH TO FIGHT BACK...
!

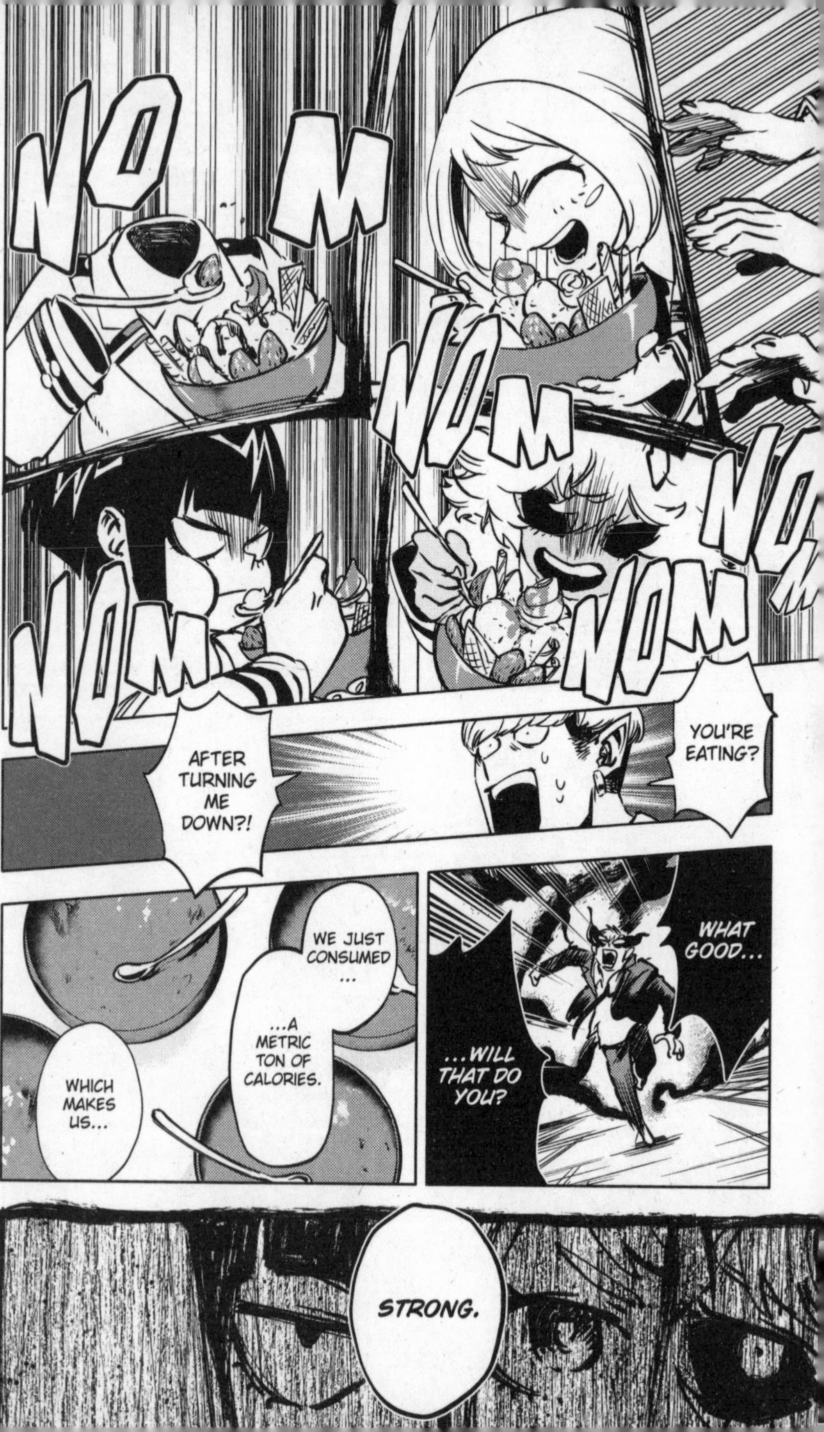
NOM
NOM
NOM
NOM
NOM
NOM
YOU'RE EATING?
AFTER TURNING ME DOWN?!
WHAT GOOD...
...WILL THAT DO YOU?
WE JUST CONSUMED ...
...A METRIC TON OF CALORIES.
WHICH MAKES US...
STRONG.

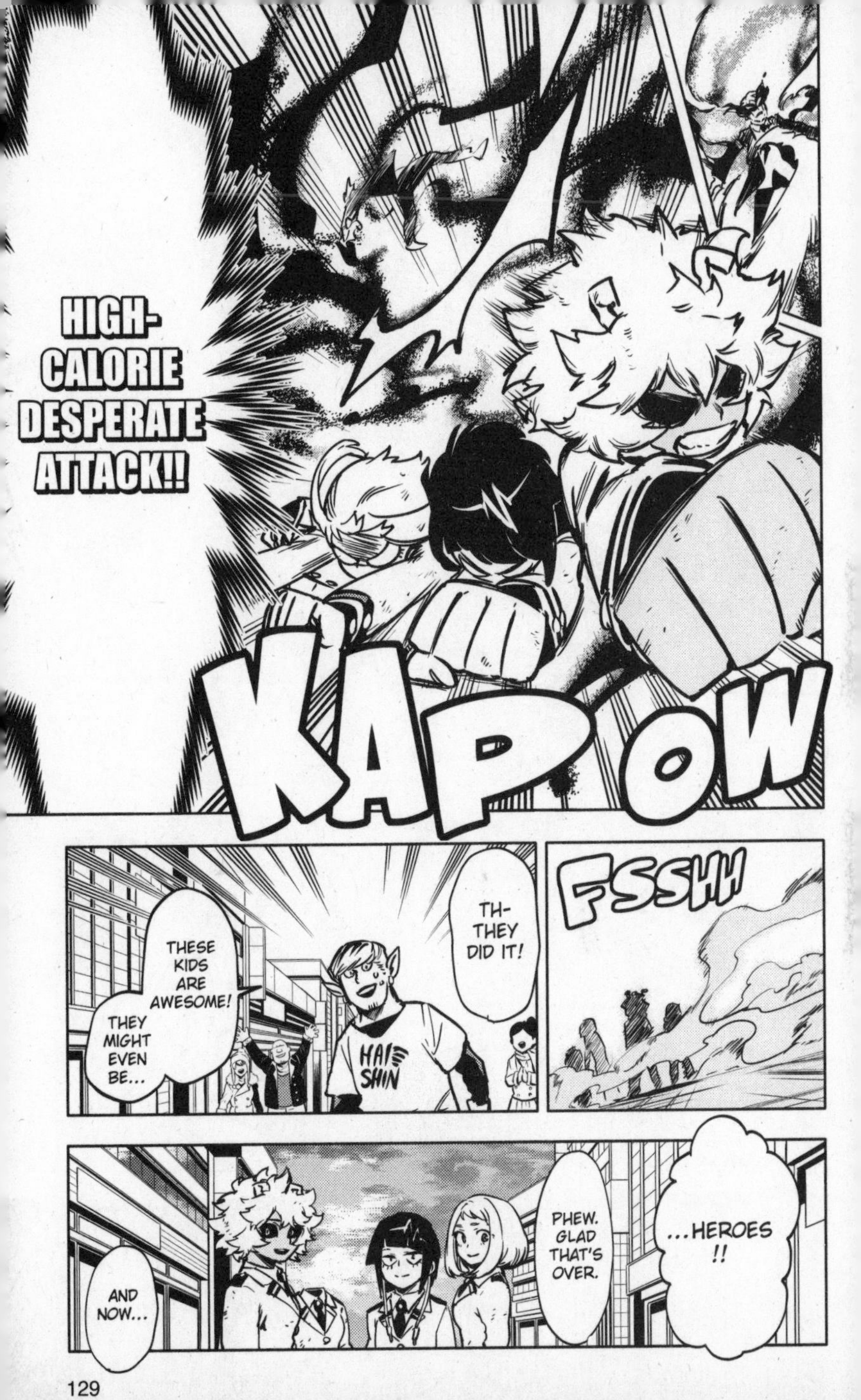
HIGH-CALORIE DESPERATE ATTACK!!
KAPOW
FSSHH
TH-THEY DID IT!
THESE KIDS ARE AWESOME!
THEY MIGHT EVEN BE...
...HEROES!!
PHEW. GLAD THAT'S OVER.
AND NOW...

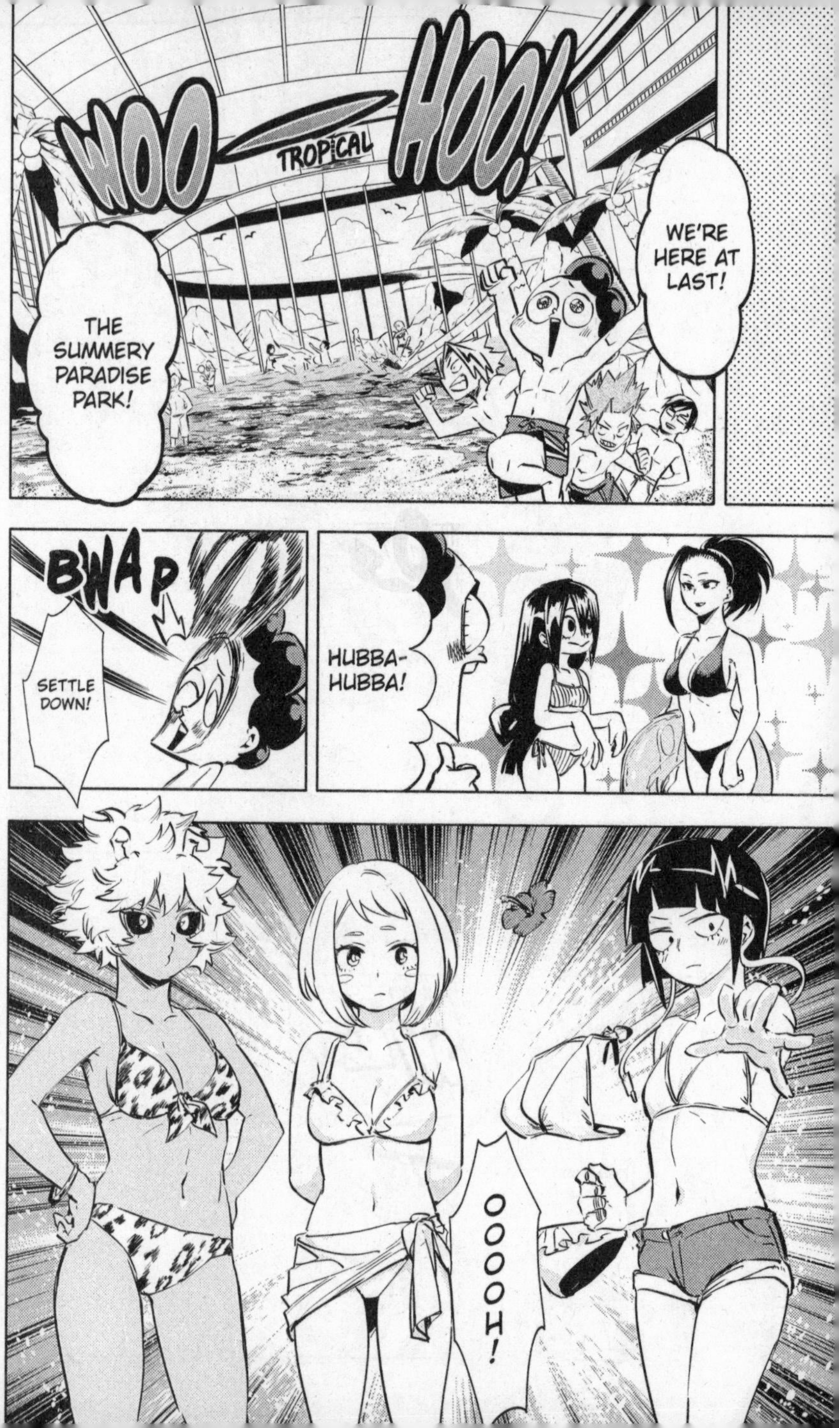
WOO—HOO!
TROPICAL
WE'RE HERE AT LAST!
THE SUMMERY PARADISE PARK!
HUBBA-HUBBA!
BWAP
SETTLE DOWN!
OOOOOH!

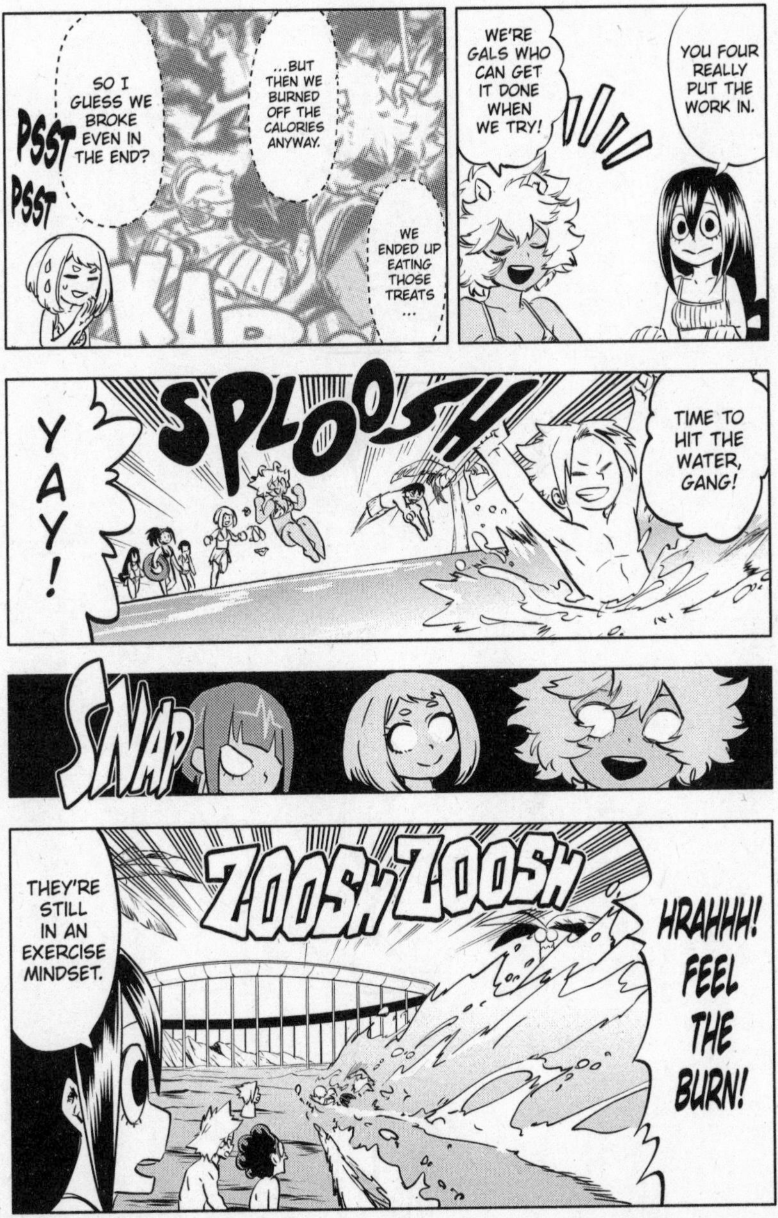
YOU FOUR REALLY PUT THE WORK IN.
WE'RE GALS WHO CAN GET IT DONE WHEN WE TRY!
WE ENDED UP EATING THOSE TREATS ...
...BUT THEN WE BURNED OFF THE CALORIES ANYWAY.
SO I GUESS WE BROKE EVEN IN THE END?
PSST
PSST
TIME TO HIT THE WATER, GANG!
SPLOOSH
YAY!
SNAP
HRAHHH! FEEL THE BURN!
ZOOSH ZOOSH
THEY'RE STILL IN AN EXERCISE MINDSET.

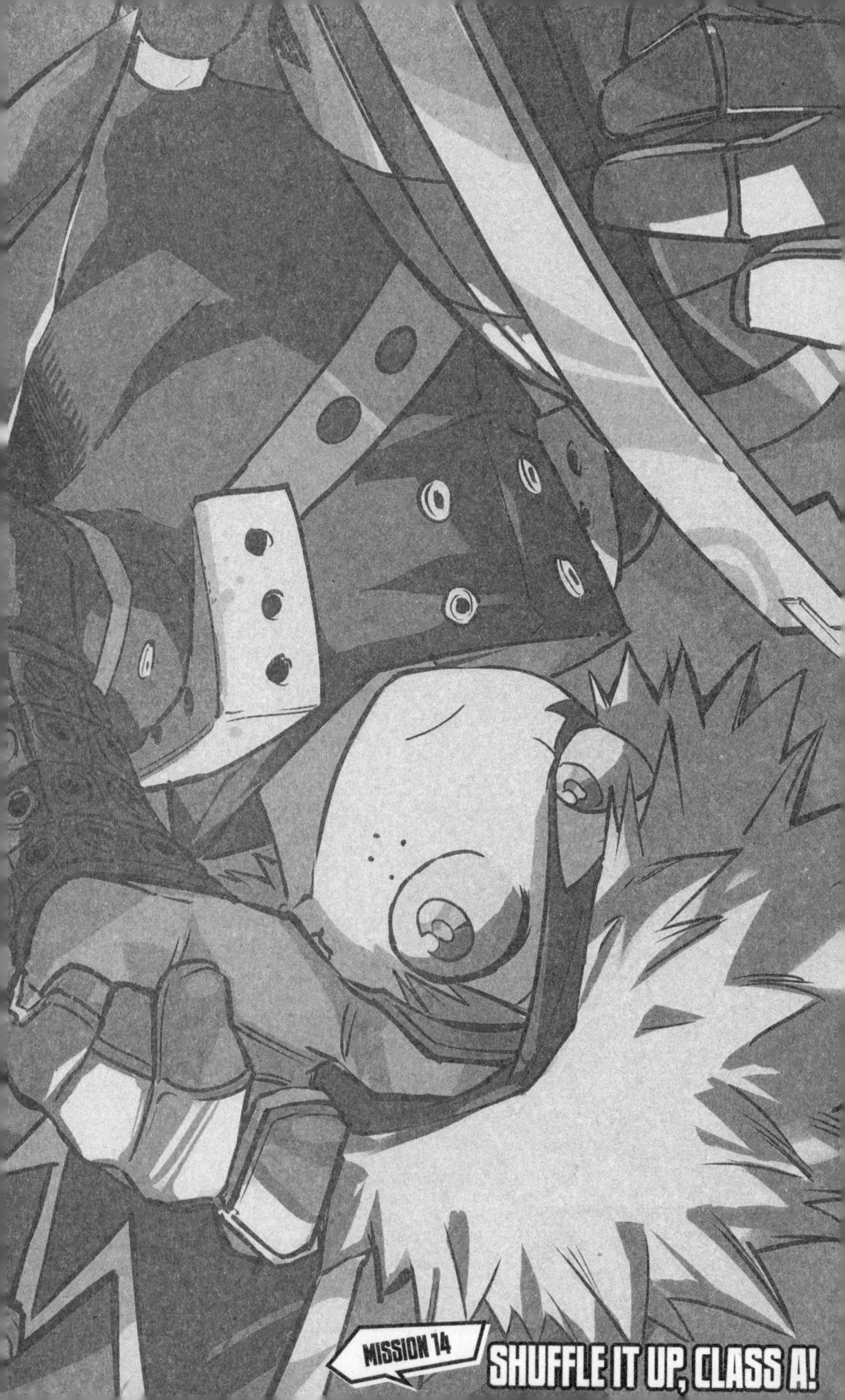
MISSION 14
SHUFFLE IT UP, CLASS A!

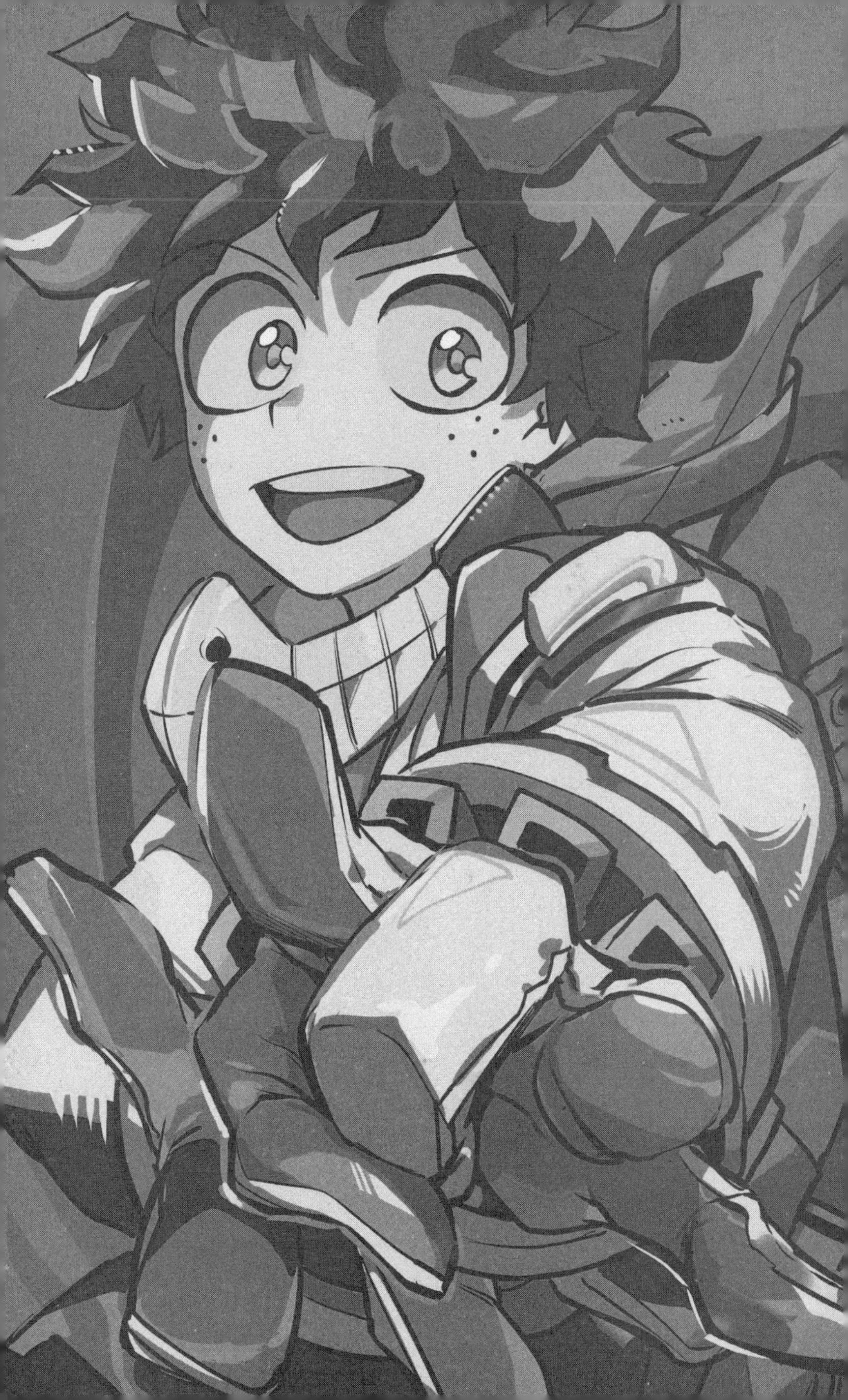

ABOUT CHAPTER 16

(This has to go here for layout reasons!)

Chapter 16 features Rody, the character from the movie *My Hero Academia: World Heroes' Mission.*

This little story is meant to take place after the events of the movie, so if you haven't seen it yet, I definitely recommend that you do! Mostly because it's a total blast! I'd love to gush about the movie, but that might amount to spoilers… Anyway, Rody is great! He moves my soul!

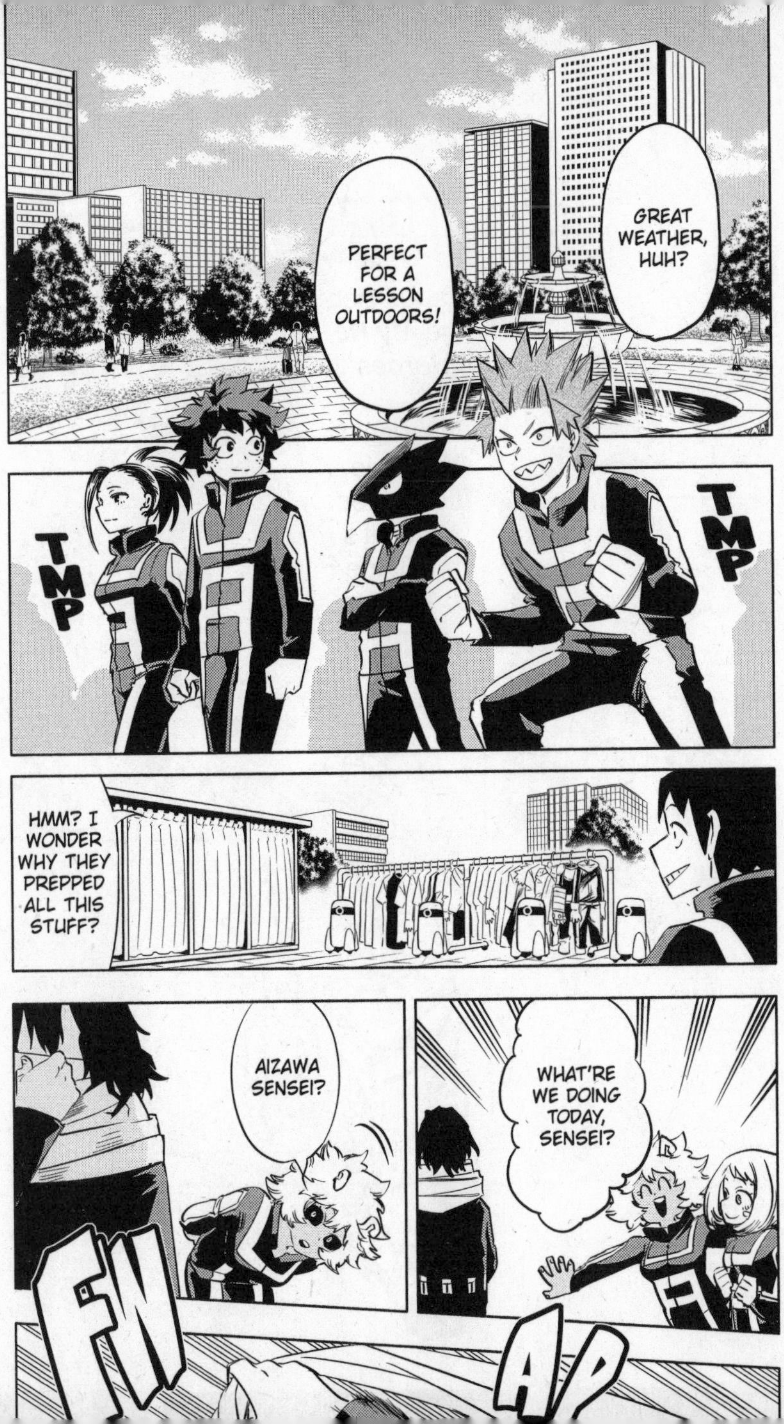
GREAT WEATHER, HUH?
PERFECT FOR A LESSON OUTDOORS!
TMP
TMP
HMM? I WONDER WHY THEY PREPPED ALL THIS STUFF?
WHAT'RE WE DOING TODAY, SENSEI?
AIZAWA SENSEI?

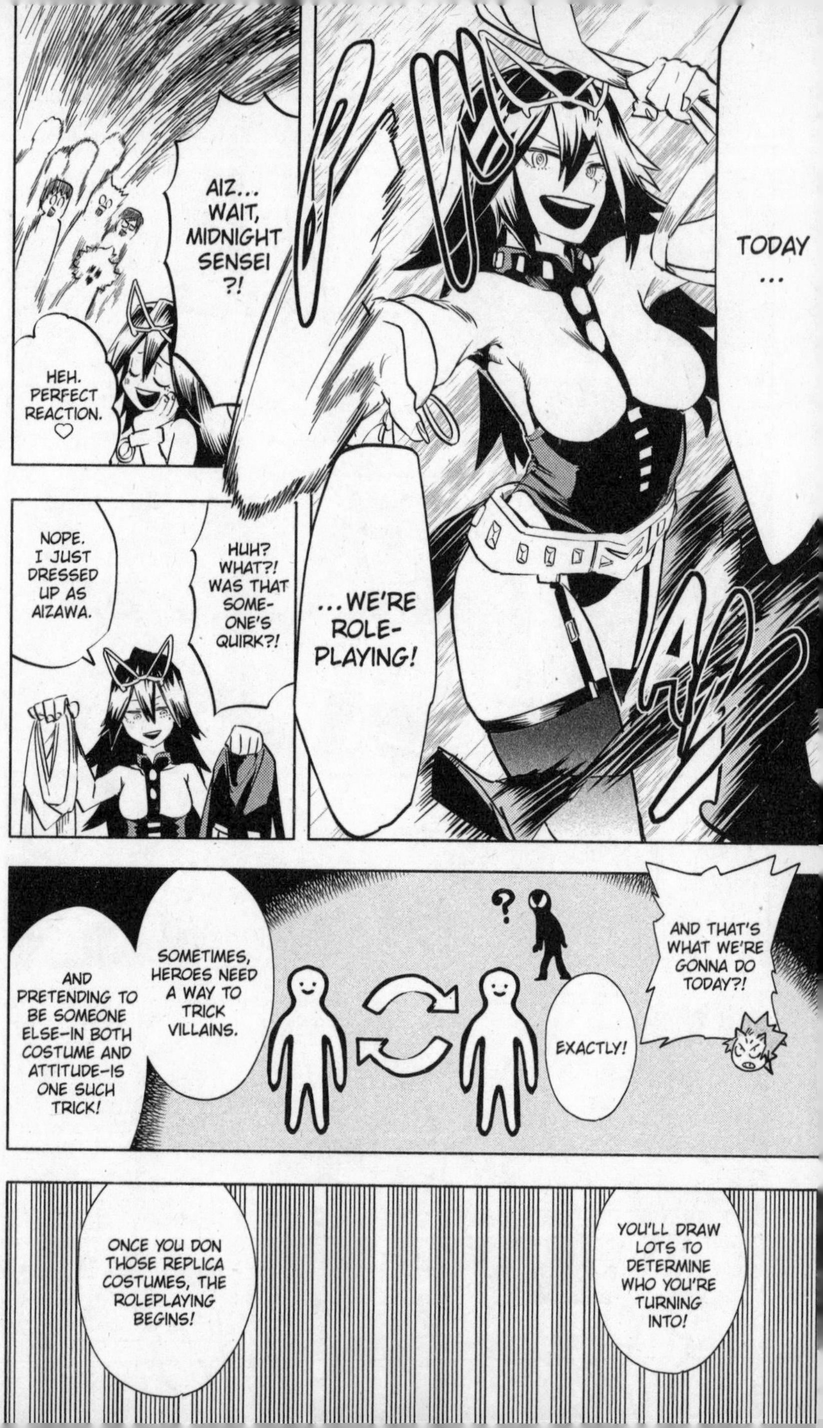
TODAY...
...WE'RE ROLE-PLAYING!
AIZ... WAIT, MIDNIGHT SENSEI?!
HEH. PERFECT REACTION. ♡
HUH? WHAT?! WAS THAT SOME-ONE'S QUIRK?!
NOPE. I JUST DRESSED UP AS AIZAWA.
AND THAT'S WHAT WE'RE GONNA DO TODAY?!
EXACTLY!
SOMETIMES, HEROES NEED A WAY TO TRICK VILLAINS.
AND PRETENDING TO BE SOMEONE ELSE–IN BOTH COSTUME AND ATTITUDE–IS ONE SUCH TRICK!
YOU'LL DRAW LOTS TO DETERMINE WHO YOU'RE TURNING INTO!
ONCE YOU DON THOSE REPLICA COSTUMES, THE ROLEPLAYING BEGINS!

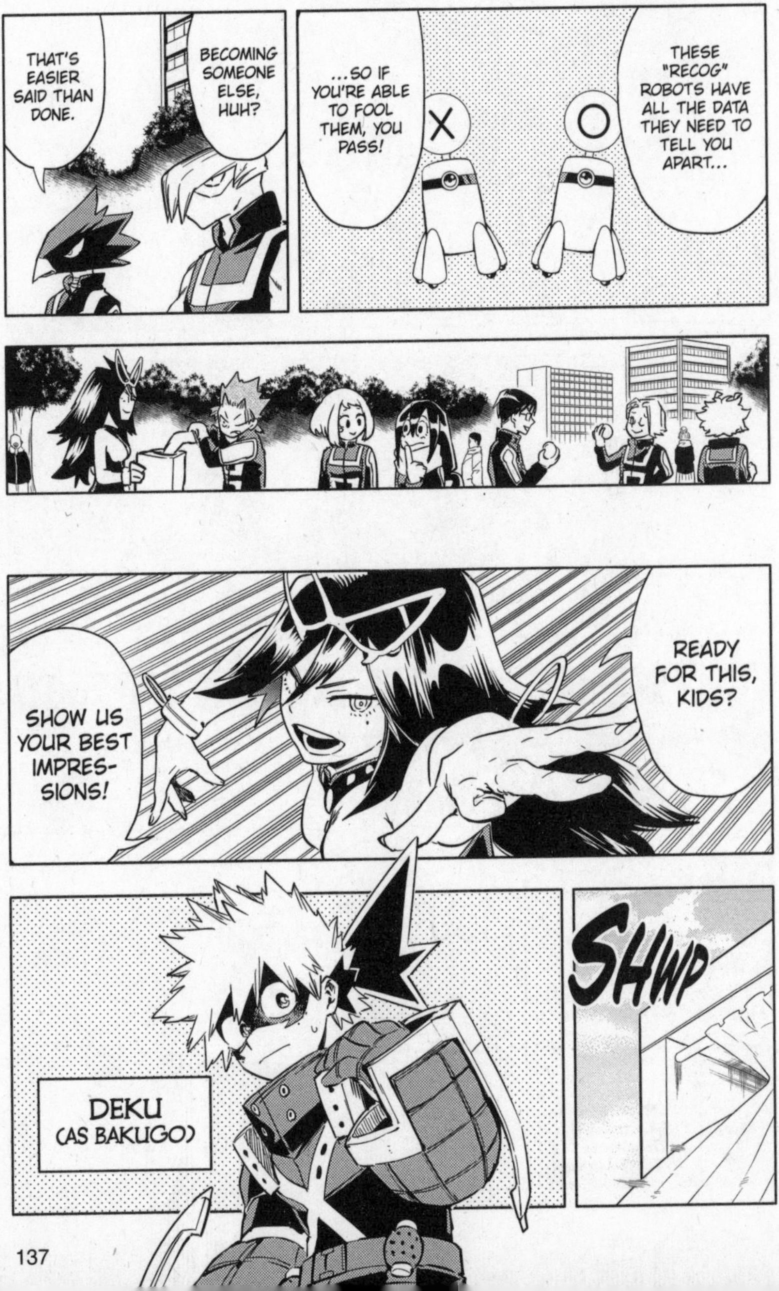
THESE "RECOG" ROBOTS HAVE ALL THE DATA THEY NEED TO TELL YOU APART...
...SO IF YOU'RE ABLE TO FOOL THEM, YOU PASS!
BECOMING SOMEONE ELSE, HUH?
THAT'S EASIER SAID THAN DONE.
READY FOR THIS, KIDS?
SHOW US YOUR BEST IMPRESSIONS!
SHWP
DEKU (AS BAKUGO)

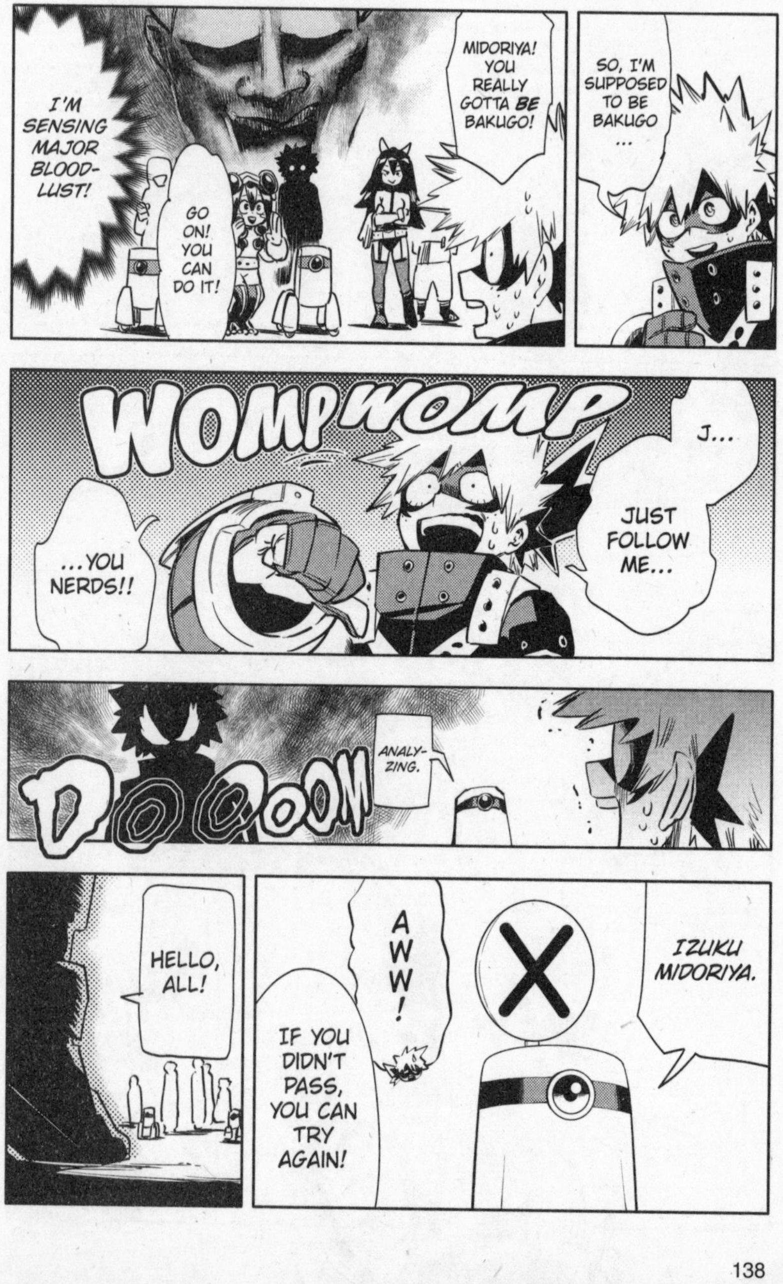
SO, I'M SUPPOSED TO BE BAKUGO ...
MIDORIYA! YOU REALLY GOTTA *BE* BAKUGO!
I'M SENSING MAJOR BLOOD-LUST!
GO ON! YOU CAN DO IT!
J...
JUST FOLLOW ME...
WOMP WOMP
...YOU NERDS!!
ANALY-ZING.
DOOOOM
IZUKU MIDORIYA.
AWW!
IF YOU DIDN'T PASS, YOU CAN TRY AGAIN!
HELLO, ALL!

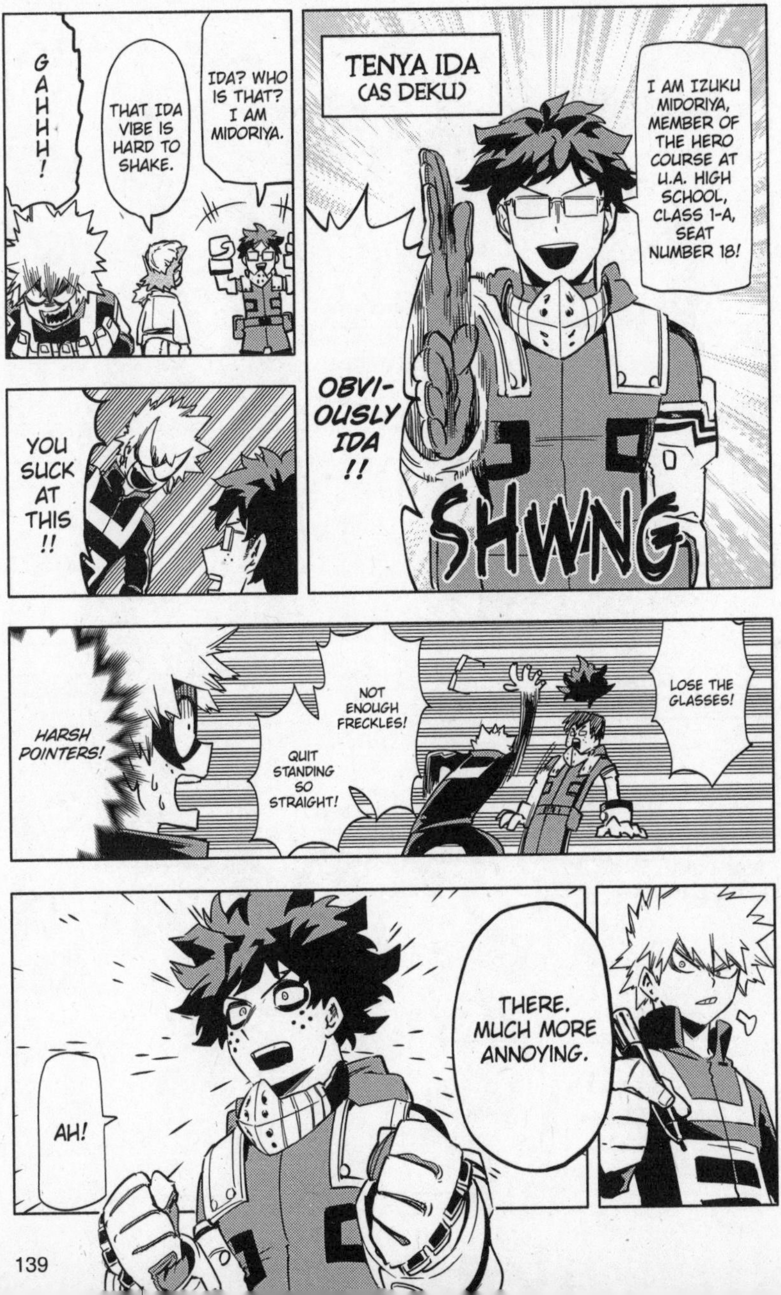
TENYA IDA (AS DEKU)
I AM IZUKU MIDORIYA, MEMBER OF THE HERO COURSE AT U.A. HIGH SCHOOL, CLASS 1-A, SEAT NUMBER 18!
OBVI-OUSLY IDA!!
SHWNG
IDA? WHO IS THAT? I AM MIDORIYA.
THAT IDA VIBE IS HARD TO SHAKE.
GAHHHH!
YOU SUCK AT THIS!!
LOSE THE GLASSES!
NOT ENOUGH FRECKLES!
QUIT STANDING SO STRAIGHT!
HARSH POINTERS!
THERE. MUCH MORE ANNOYING.
AH!

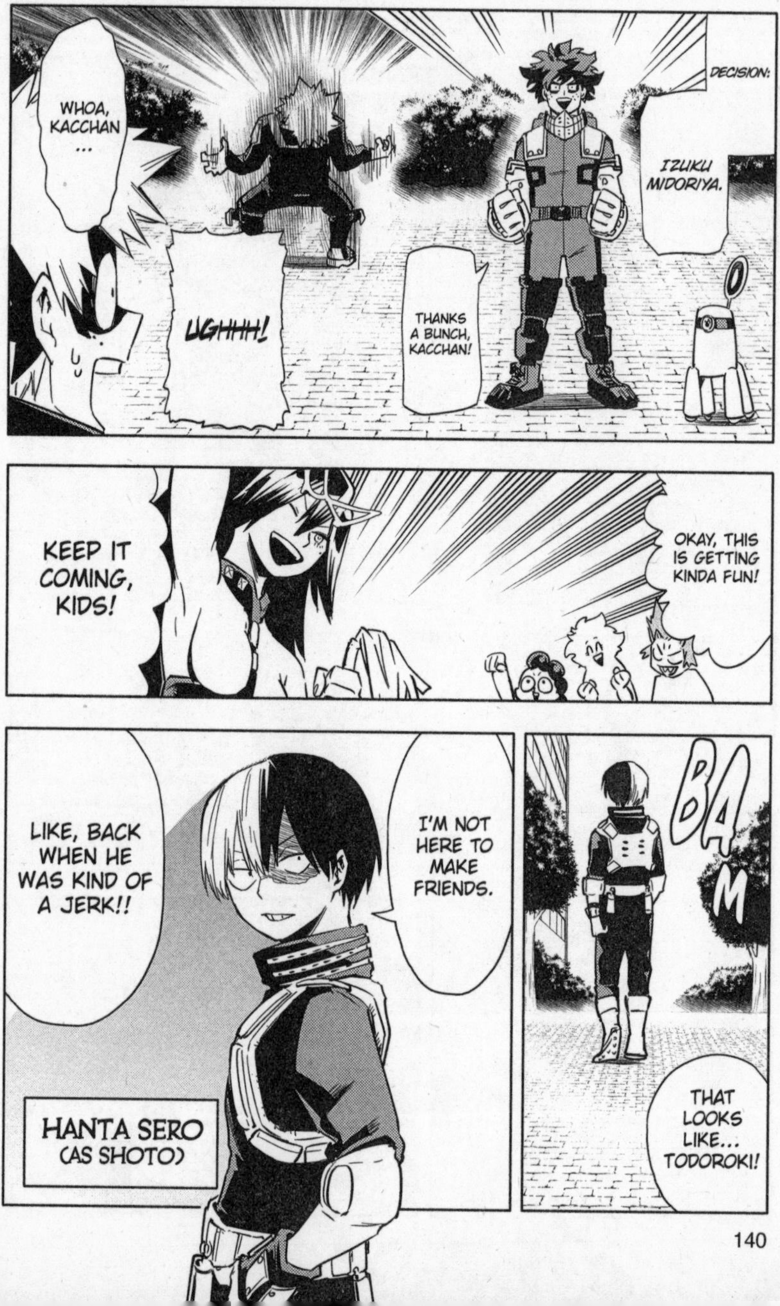
DECISION:
IZUKU MIDORIYA.
THANKS A BUNCH, KACCHAN!
UGHHH!
WHOA, KACCHAN...
OKAY, THIS IS GETTING KINDA FUN!
KEEP IT COMING, KIDS!
BAM
THAT LOOKS LIKE... TODOROKI!
I'M NOT HERE TO MAKE FRIENDS.
LIKE, BACK WHEN HE WAS KIND OF A JERK!!
HANTA SERO (AS SHOTO)

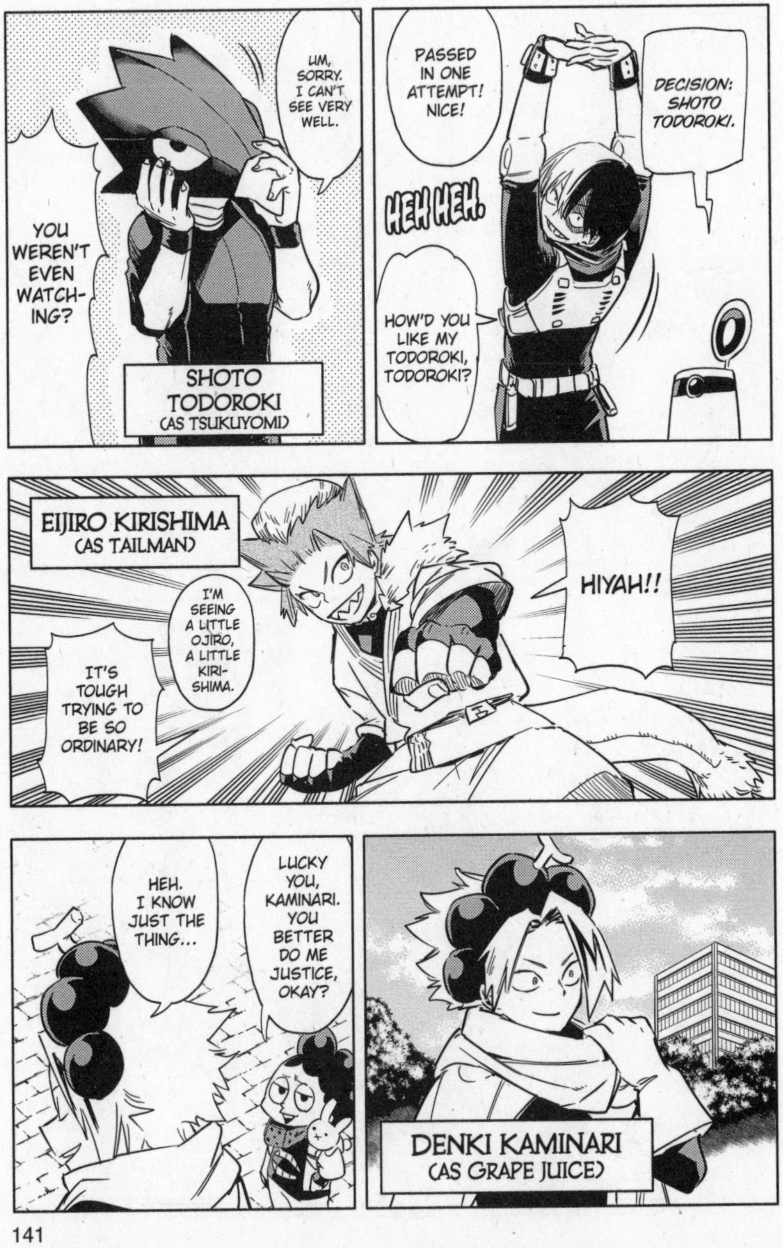
DECISION: SHOTO TODOROKI.
PASSED IN ONE ATTEMPT! NICE!
HEH HEH.
HOW'D YOU LIKE MY TODOROKI, TODOROKI?
UM, SORRY. I CAN'T SEE VERY WELL.
YOU WEREN'T EVEN WATCHING?
SHOTO TODOROKI (AS TSUKUYOMI)
HIYAH!!
EIJIRO KIRISHIMA (AS TAILMAN)
I'M SEEING A LITTLE OJIRO, A LITTLE KIRISHIMA.
IT'S TOUGH TRYING TO BE SO ORDINARY!
DENKI KAMINARI (AS GRAPE JUICE)
LUCKY YOU, KAMINARI. YOU BETTER DO ME JUSTICE, OKAY?
HEH. I KNOW JUST THE THING...

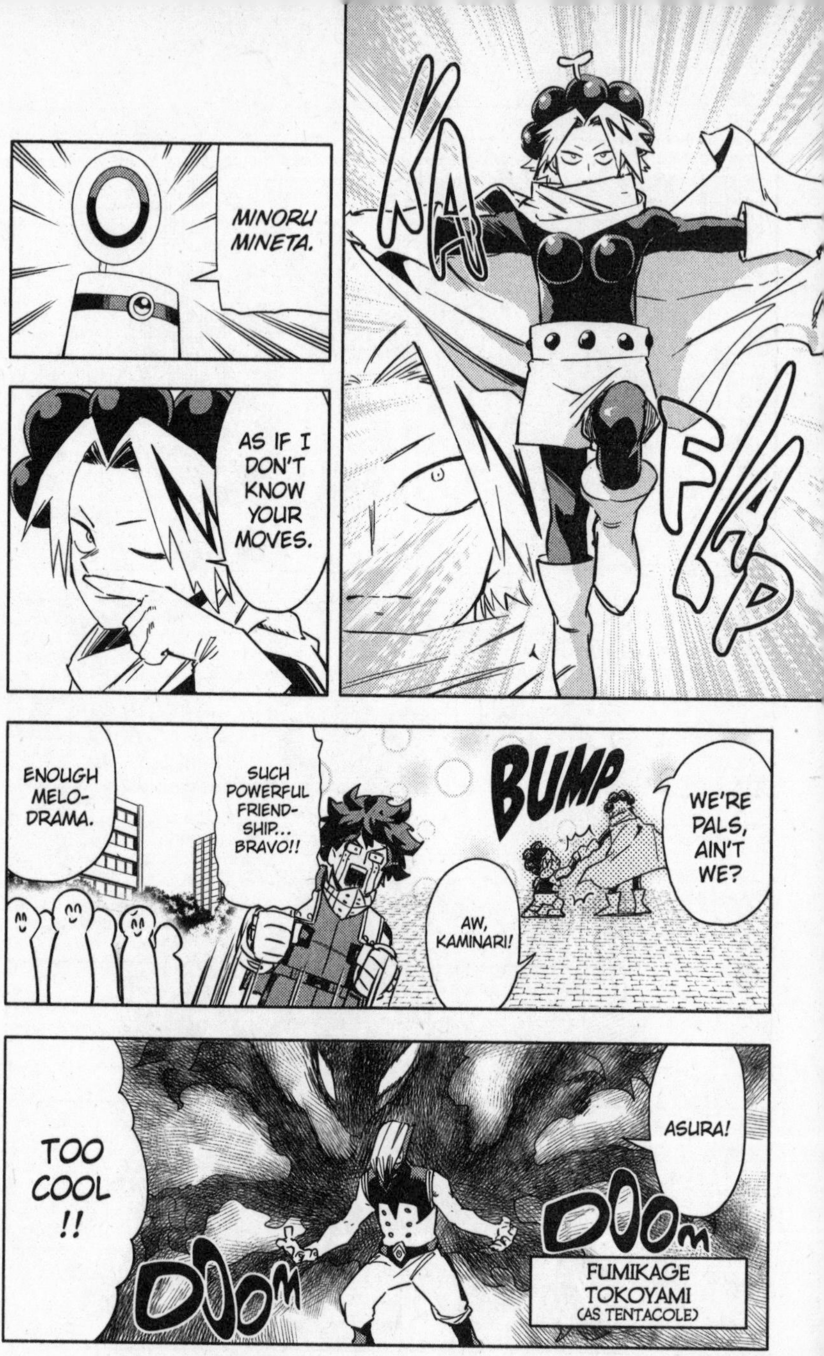
KA
FLAP
MINORU MINETA.
AS IF I DON'T KNOW YOUR MOVES.
WE'RE PALS, AIN'T WE?
BUMP
AW, KAMINARI!
SUCH POWERFUL FRIEND-SHIP... BRAVO!!
ENOUGH MELO-DRAMA.
ASURA!
DOOM
FUMIKAGE TOKOYAMI (AS TENTACOLE)
DOOM
TOO COOL !!

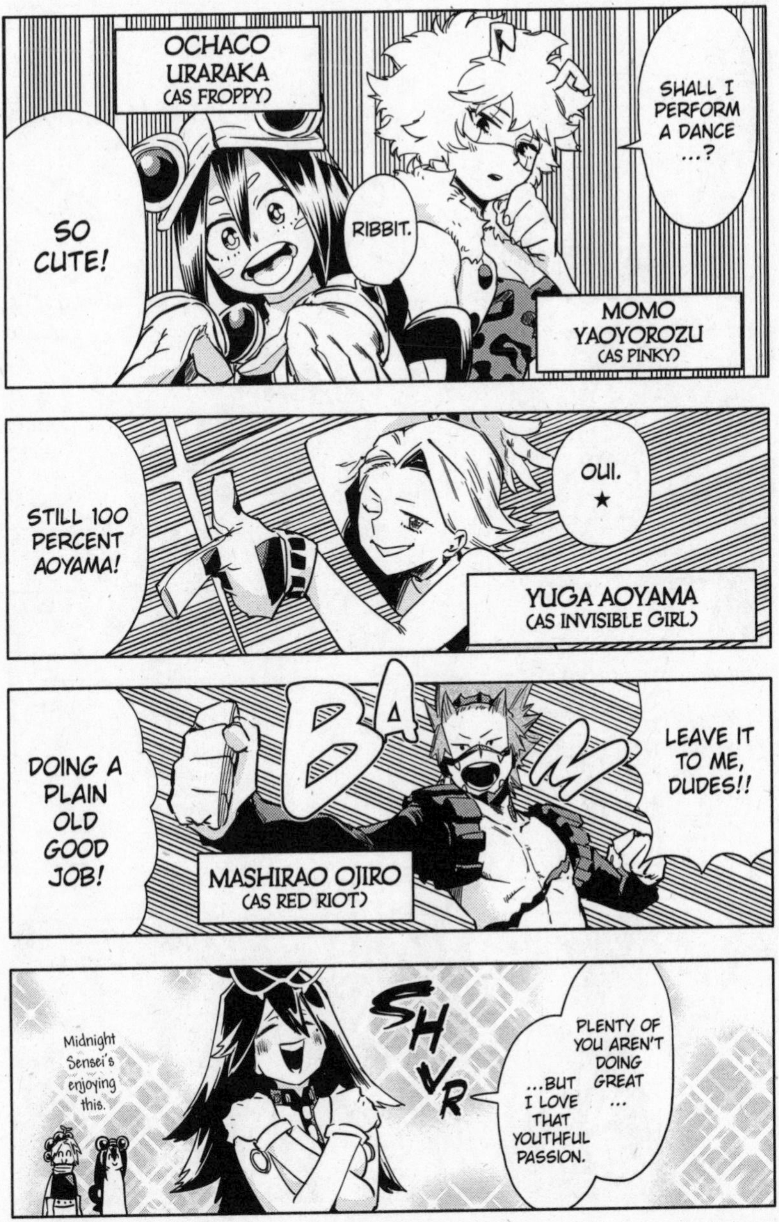
SHALL I PERFORM A DANCE ...?
OCHACO URARAKA (AS FROPPY)
RIBBIT.
MOMO YAOYOROZU (AS PINKY)
SO CUTE!
OUI. ★
YUGA AOYAMA (AS INVISIBLE GIRL)
STILL 100 PERCENT AOYAMA!
LEAVE IT TO ME, DUDES!!
BAM
MASHIRAO OJIRO (AS RED RIOT)
DOING A PLAIN OLD GOOD JOB!
PLENTY OF YOU AREN'T DOING GREAT ...
...BUT I LOVE THAT YOUTHFUL PASSION.
SHVR
Midnight Sensei's enjoying this.

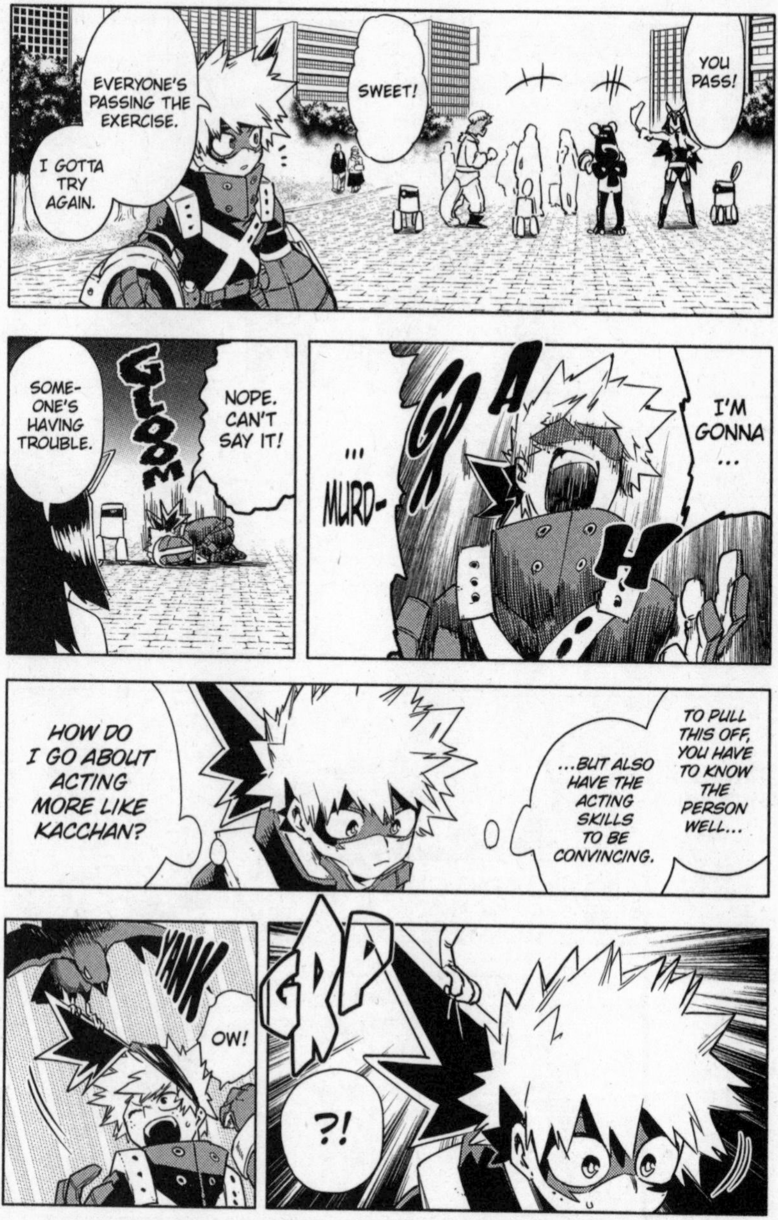
YOU PASS!
SWEET!
EVERYONE'S PASSING THE EXERCISE.
I GOTTA TRY AGAIN.
I'M GONNA ...
GRAH
MURD-
...
NOPE. CAN'T SAY IT!
GLOOM
SOME-ONE'S HAVING TROUBLE.
TO PULL THIS OFF, YOU HAVE TO KNOW THE PERSON WELL...
...BUT ALSO HAVE THE ACTING SKILLS TO BE CONVINCING.
HOW DO I GO ABOUT ACTING MORE LIKE KACCHAN?
GRP
?!
YANK
OW!

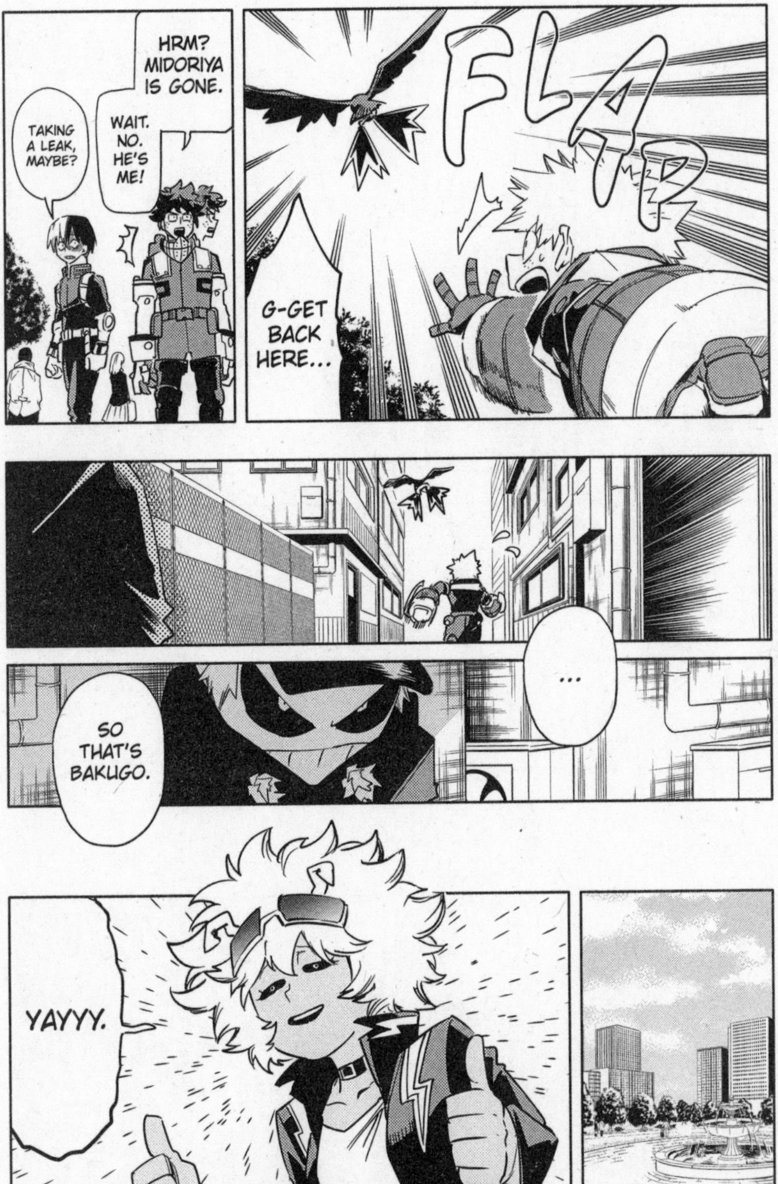
FLAP
G-GET BACK HERE...
HRM? MIDORIYA IS GONE.
WAIT. NO. HE'S ME!
TAKING A LEAK, MAYBE?
...
SO THAT'S BAKUGO.
YAYYY.

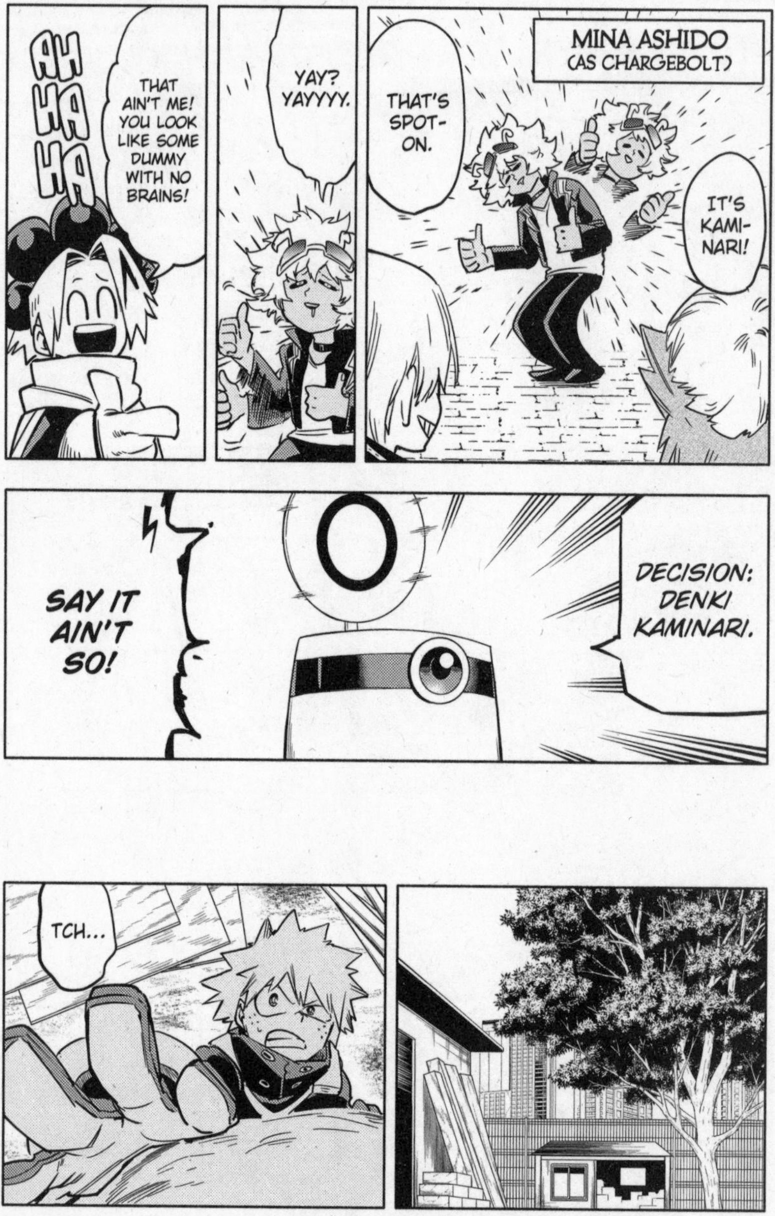
MINA ASHIDO (AS CHARGEBOLT)
IT'S KAMINARI!
THAT'S SPOT-ON.
YAY? YAYYYY.
THAT AIN'T ME! YOU LOOK LIKE SOME DUMMY WITH NO BRAINS!
AH HA HA HA
DECISION: DENKI KAMINARI.
SAY IT AIN'T SO!
TCH...

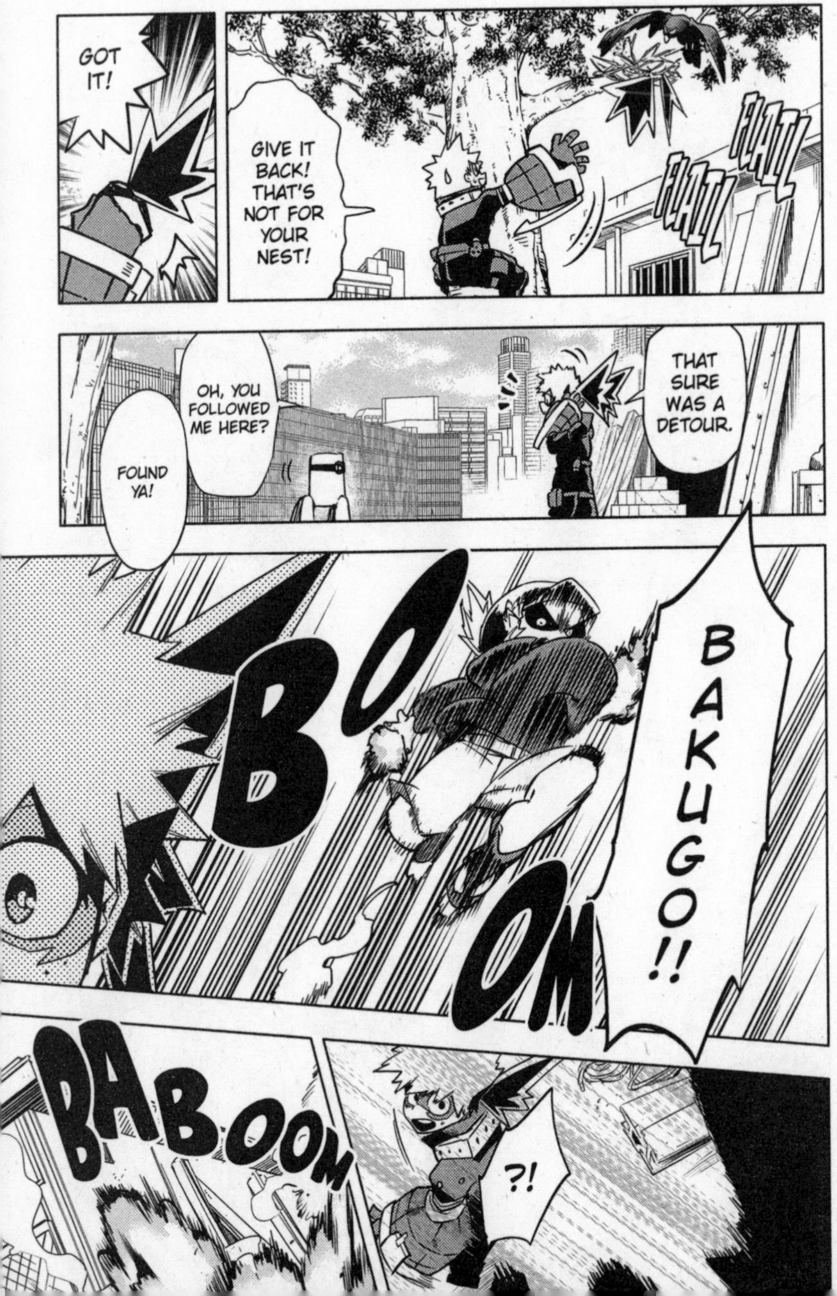
GIVE IT BACK! THAT'S NOT FOR YOUR NEST!
FLAIL FLAIL
GOT IT!
THAT SURE WAS A DETOUR.
OH, YOU FOLLOWED ME HERE?
FOUND YA!
BAKUGO!!
BOOM
?!
BABOOOM

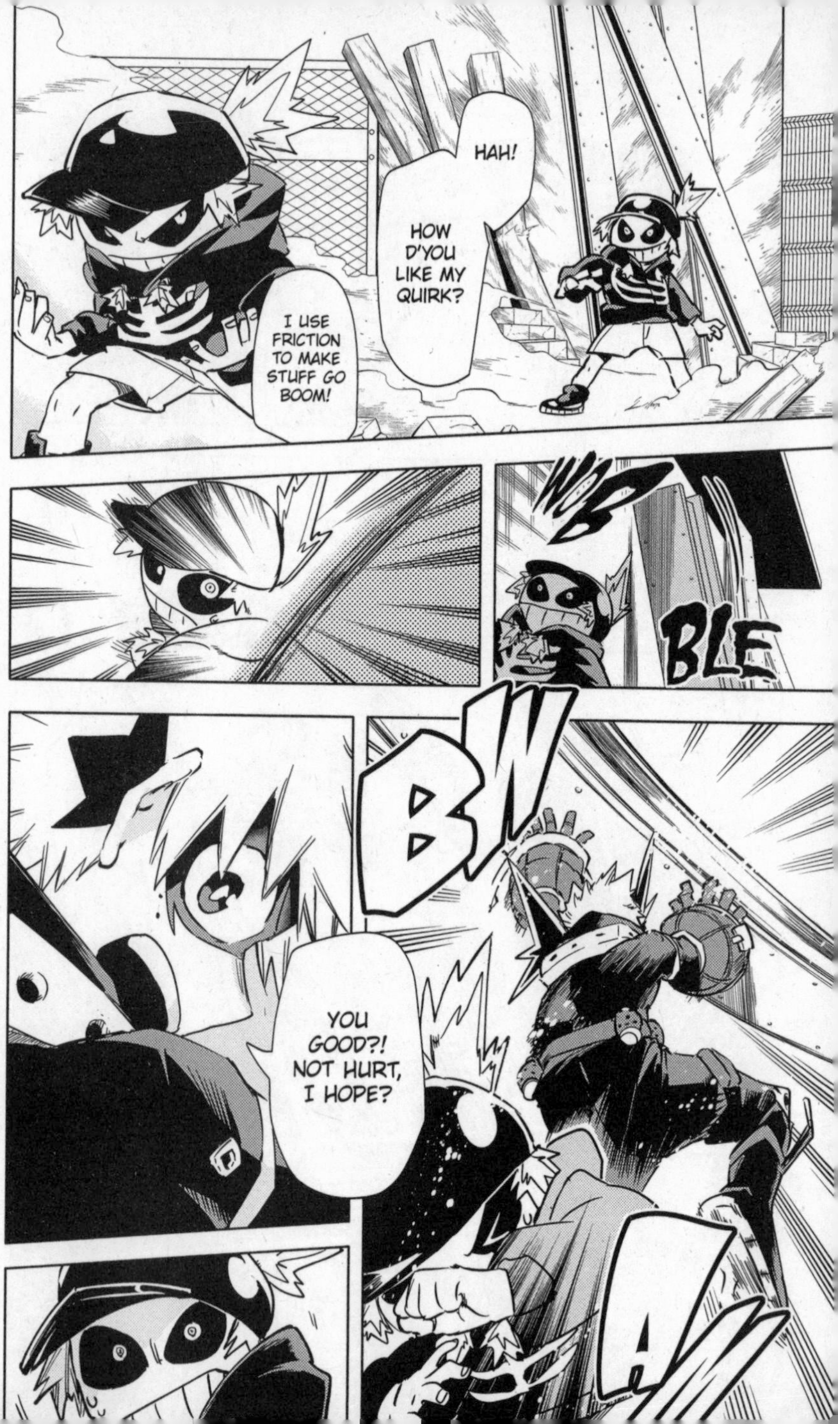
HAH!
HOW D'YOU LIKE MY QUIRK?
I USE FRICTION TO MAKE STUFF GO BOOM!
BLE
YOU GOOD?! NOT HURT, I HOPE?

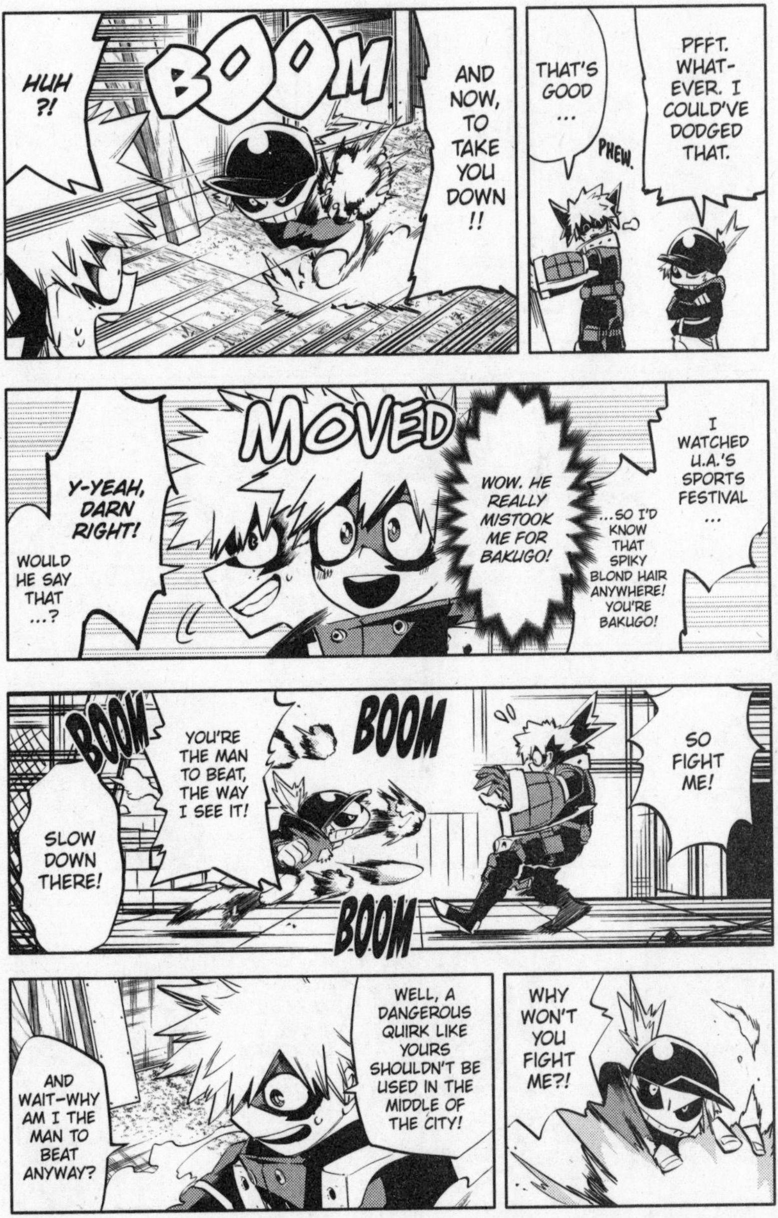
PFFT. WHATEVER. I COULD'VE DODGED THAT.
THAT'S GOOD...
PHEW.
AND NOW, TO TAKE YOU DOWN!!
BOOM
HUH?!
I WATCHED U.A.'S SPORTS FESTIVAL...
...SO I'D KNOW THAT SPIKY BLOND HAIR ANYWHERE! YOU'RE BAKUGO!
WOW. HE REALLY MISTOOK ME FOR BAKUGO!
MOVED
Y-YEAH, DARN RIGHT!
WOULD HE SAY THAT...?
SO FIGHT ME!
BOOM
YOU'RE THE MAN TO BEAT, THE WAY I SEE IT!
BOOM
SLOW DOWN THERE!
BOOM
WHY WON'T YOU FIGHT ME?!
WELL, A DANGEROUS QUIRK LIKE YOURS SHOULDN'T BE USED IN THE MIDDLE OF THE CITY!
AND WAIT—WHY AM I THE MAN TO BEAT ANYWAY?

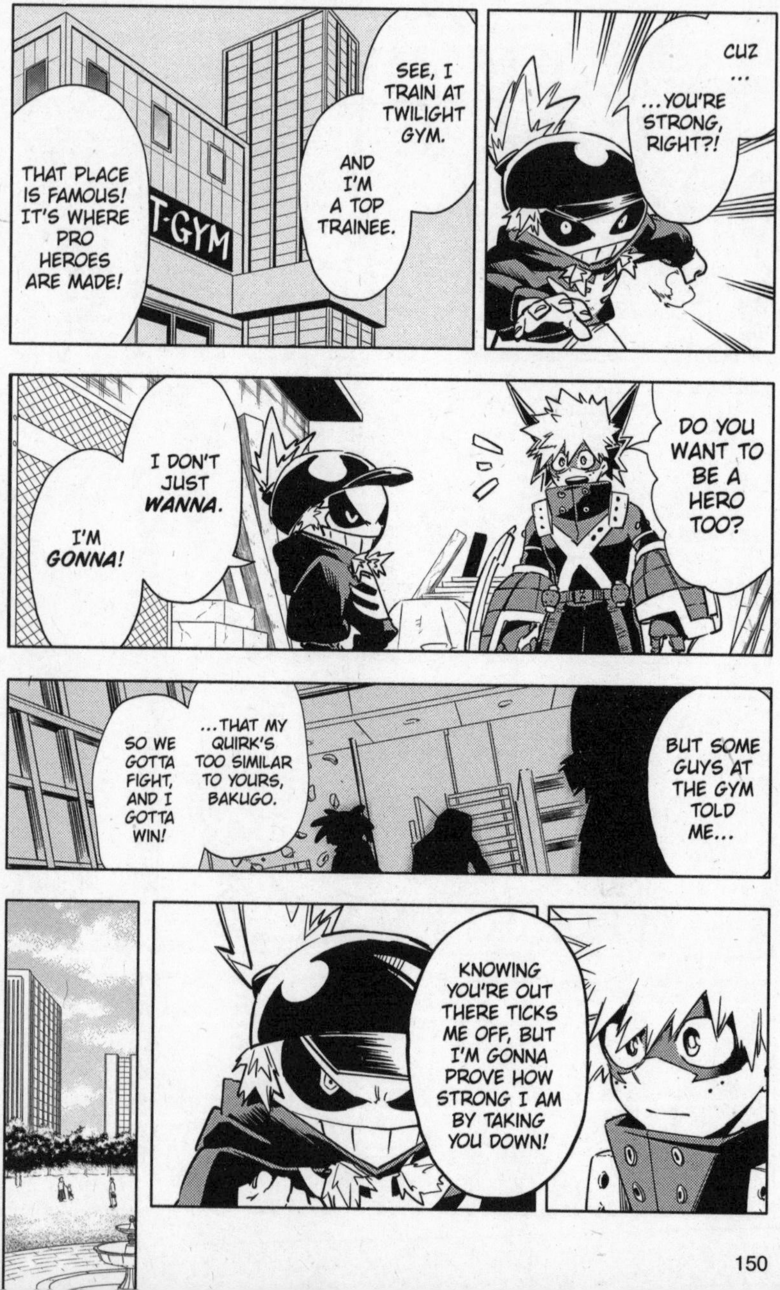
CUZ ...
...YOU'RE STRONG, RIGHT?!
SEE, I TRAIN AT TWILIGHT GYM.
AND I'M A TOP TRAINEE.
T-GYM
THAT PLACE IS FAMOUS! IT'S WHERE PRO HEROES ARE MADE!
DO YOU WANT TO BE A HERO TOO?
I DON'T JUST *WANNA*.
I'M *GONNA*!
BUT SOME GUYS AT THE GYM TOLD ME...
...THAT MY QUIRK'S TOO SIMILAR TO YOURS, BAKUGO.
SO WE GOTTA FIGHT, AND I GOTTA WIN!
KNOWING YOU'RE OUT THERE TICKS ME OFF, BUT I'M GONNA PROVE HOW STRONG I AM BY TAKING YOU DOWN!

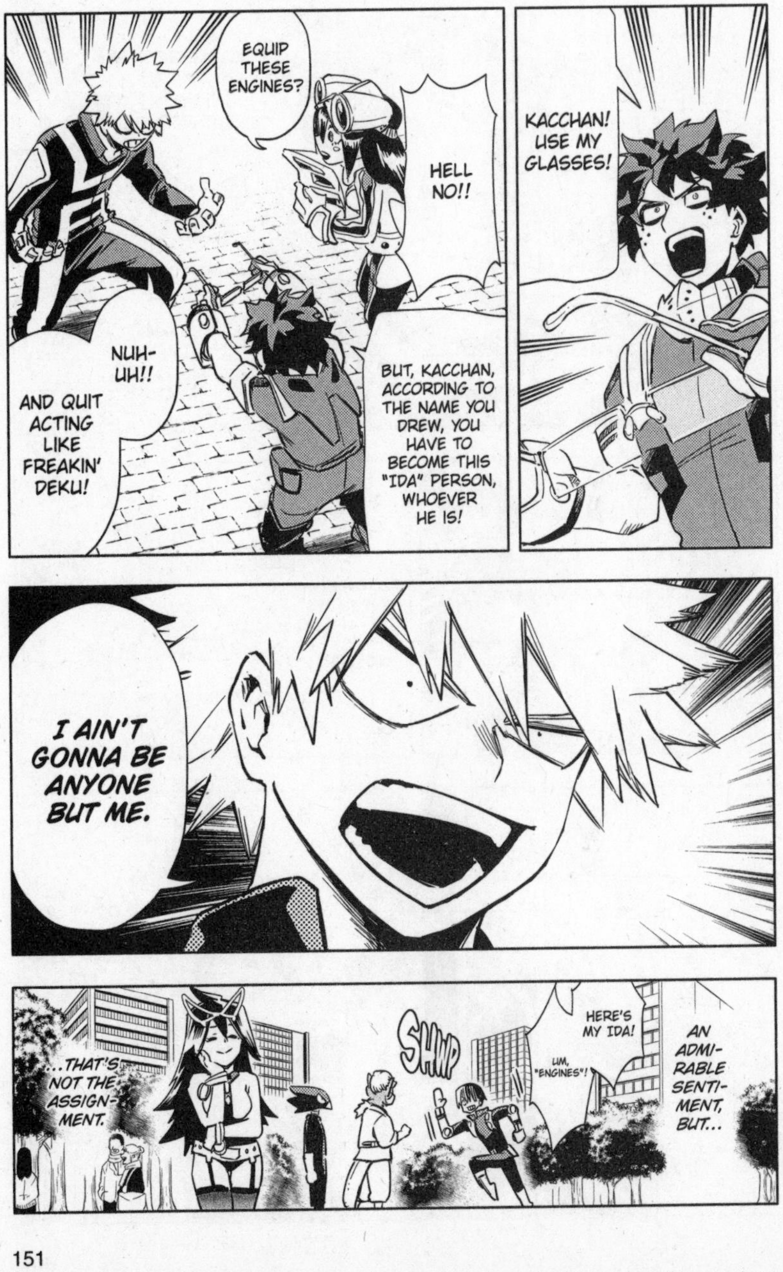
KACCHAN! USE MY GLASSES!
EQUIP THESE ENGINES?
HELL NO!!
BUT, KACCHAN, ACCORDING TO THE NAME YOU DREW, YOU HAVE TO BECOME THIS "IDA" PERSON, WHOEVER HE IS!
NUH-UH!!
AND QUIT ACTING LIKE FREAKIN' DEKU!
I AIN'T GONNA BE ANYONE BUT ME.
AN ADMIRABLE SENTIMENT, BUT...
HERE'S MY IDA!
UM, "ENGINES"!
SHWP
...THAT'S NOT THE ASSIGNMENT.

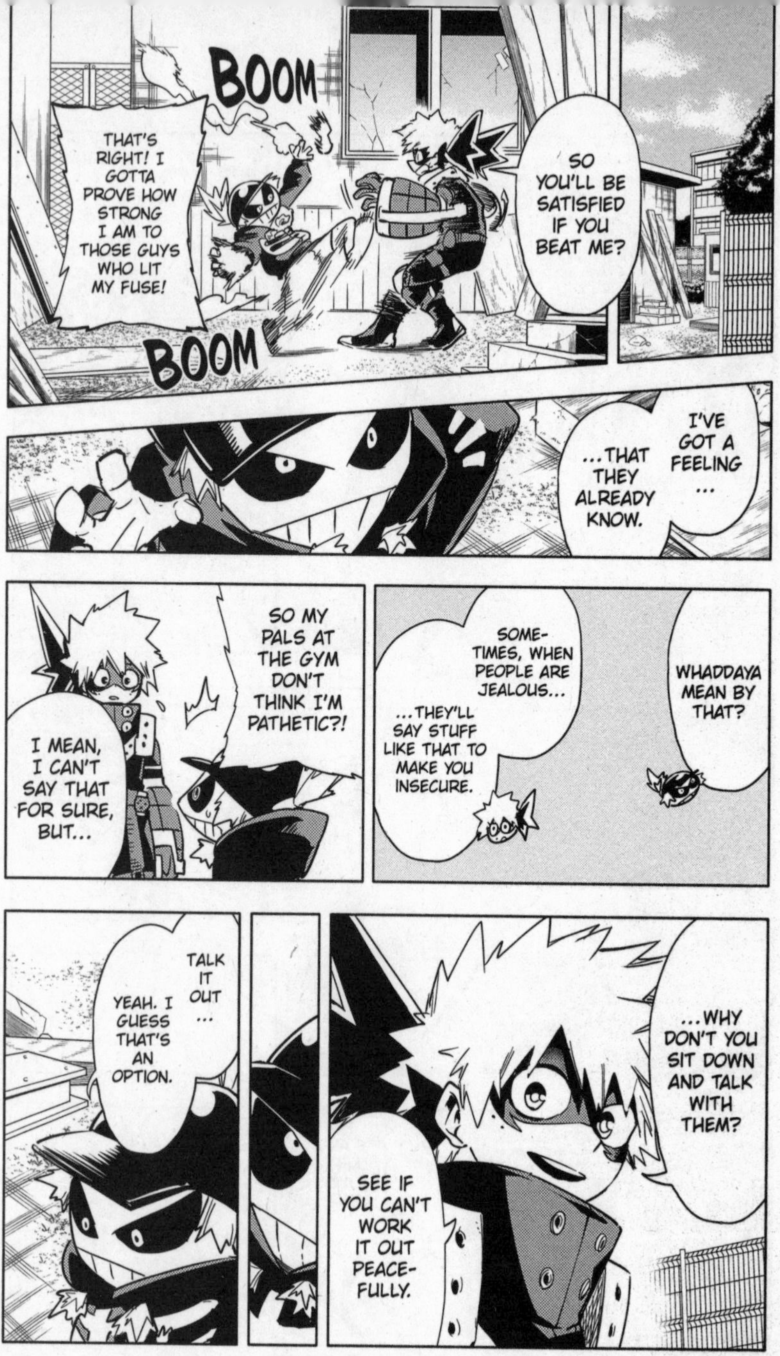
BOOM
SO YOU'LL BE SATISFIED IF YOU BEAT ME?
THAT'S RIGHT! I GOTTA PROVE HOW STRONG I AM TO THOSE GUYS WHO LIT MY FUSE!
BOOM
I'VE GOT A FEELING...
...THAT THEY ALREADY KNOW.
WHADDAYA MEAN BY THAT?
SOME-TIMES, WHEN PEOPLE ARE JEALOUS...
...THEY'LL SAY STUFF LIKE THAT TO MAKE YOU INSECURE.
SO MY PALS AT THE GYM DON'T THINK I'M PATHETIC?!
I MEAN, I CAN'T SAY THAT FOR SURE, BUT...
...WHY DON'T YOU SIT DOWN AND TALK WITH THEM?
SEE IF YOU CAN'T WORK IT OUT PEACE-FULLY.
TALK IT OUT...
YEAH. I GUESS THAT'S AN OPTION.

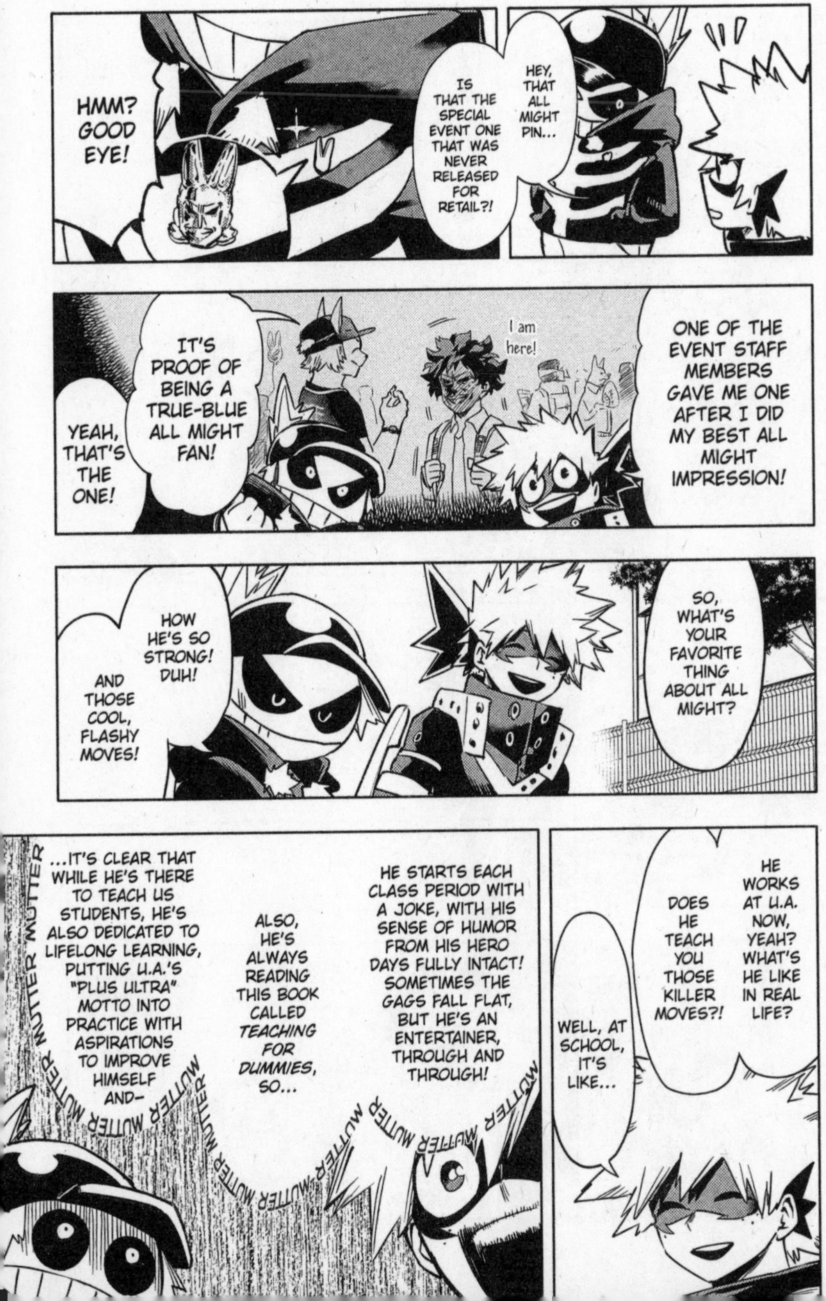
HEY, THAT ALL MIGHT PIN...
IS THAT THE SPECIAL EVENT ONE THAT WAS NEVER RELEASED FOR RETAIL?!
HMM? GOOD EYE!
ONE OF THE EVENT STAFF MEMBERS GAVE ME ONE AFTER I DID MY BEST ALL MIGHT IMPRESSION!
I am here!
IT'S PROOF OF BEING A TRUE-BLUE ALL MIGHT FAN!
YEAH, THAT'S THE ONE!
SO, WHAT'S YOUR FAVORITE THING ABOUT ALL MIGHT?
HOW HE'S SO STRONG! DUH!
AND THOSE COOL, FLASHY MOVES!
HE WORKS AT U.A. NOW, YEAH? WHAT'S HE LIKE IN REAL LIFE?
DOES HE TEACH YOU THOSE KILLER MOVES?!
WELL, AT SCHOOL, IT'S LIKE...
HE STARTS EACH CLASS PERIOD WITH A JOKE, WITH HIS SENSE OF HUMOR FROM HIS HERO DAYS FULLY INTACT! SOMETIMES THE GAGS FALL FLAT, BUT HE'S AN ENTERTAINER, THROUGH AND THROUGH!
ALSO, HE'S ALWAYS READING THIS BOOK CALLED *TEACHING FOR DUMMIES*, SO...
...IT'S CLEAR THAT WHILE HE'S THERE TO TEACH US STUDENTS, HE'S ALSO DEDICATED TO LIFELONG LEARNING, PUTTING U.A.'S "PLUS ULTRA" MOTTO INTO PRACTICE WITH ASPIRATIONS TO IMPROVE HIMSELF AND–
MUTTER MUTTER MUTTER MUTTER MUTTER MUTTER MUTTER MUTTER

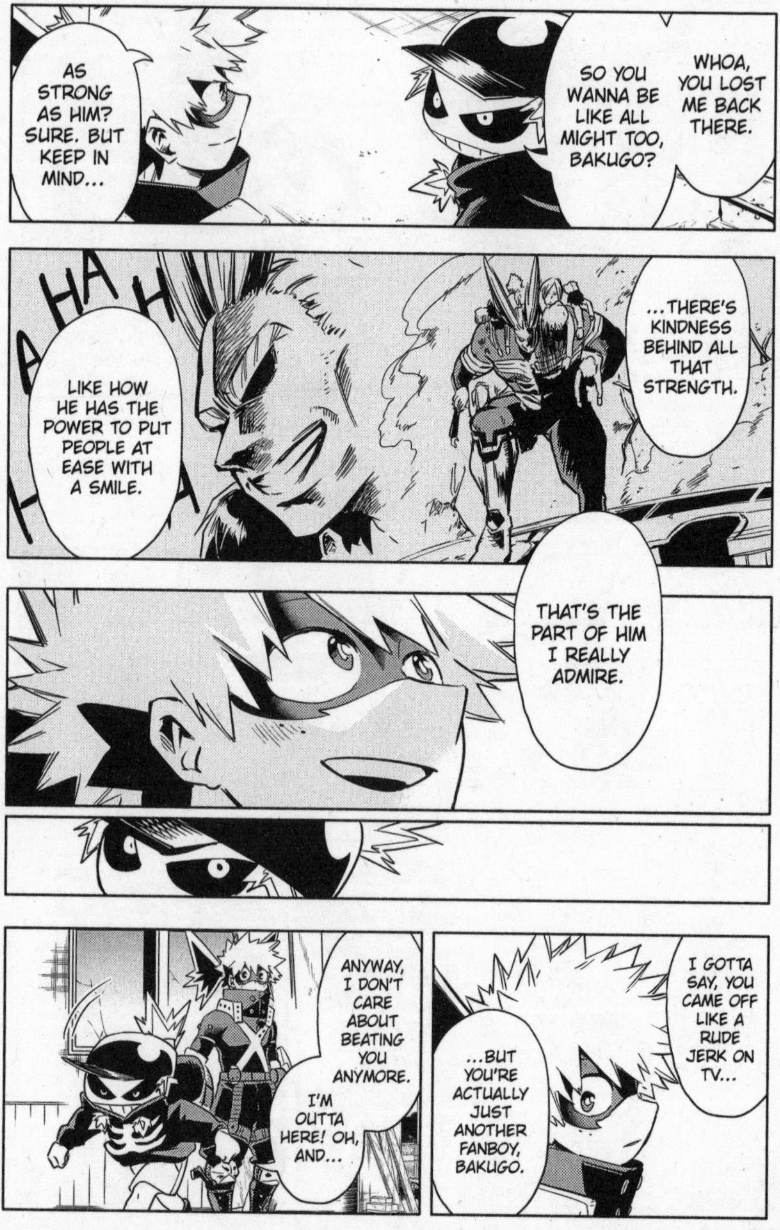
WHOA, YOU LOST ME BACK THERE.
SO YOU WANNA BE LIKE ALL MIGHT TOO, BAKUGO?
AS STRONG AS HIM? SURE. BUT KEEP IN MIND...
...THERE'S KINDNESS BEHIND ALL THAT STRENGTH.
HAHAHA
LIKE HOW HE HAS THE POWER TO PUT PEOPLE AT EASE WITH A SMILE.
THAT'S THE PART OF HIM I REALLY ADMIRE.
I GOTTA SAY, YOU CAME OFF LIKE A RUDE JERK ON TV...
...BUT YOU'RE ACTUALLY JUST ANOTHER FANBOY, BAKUGO.
ANYWAY, I DON'T CARE ABOUT BEATING YOU ANYMORE.
I'M OUTTA HERE! OH, AND...

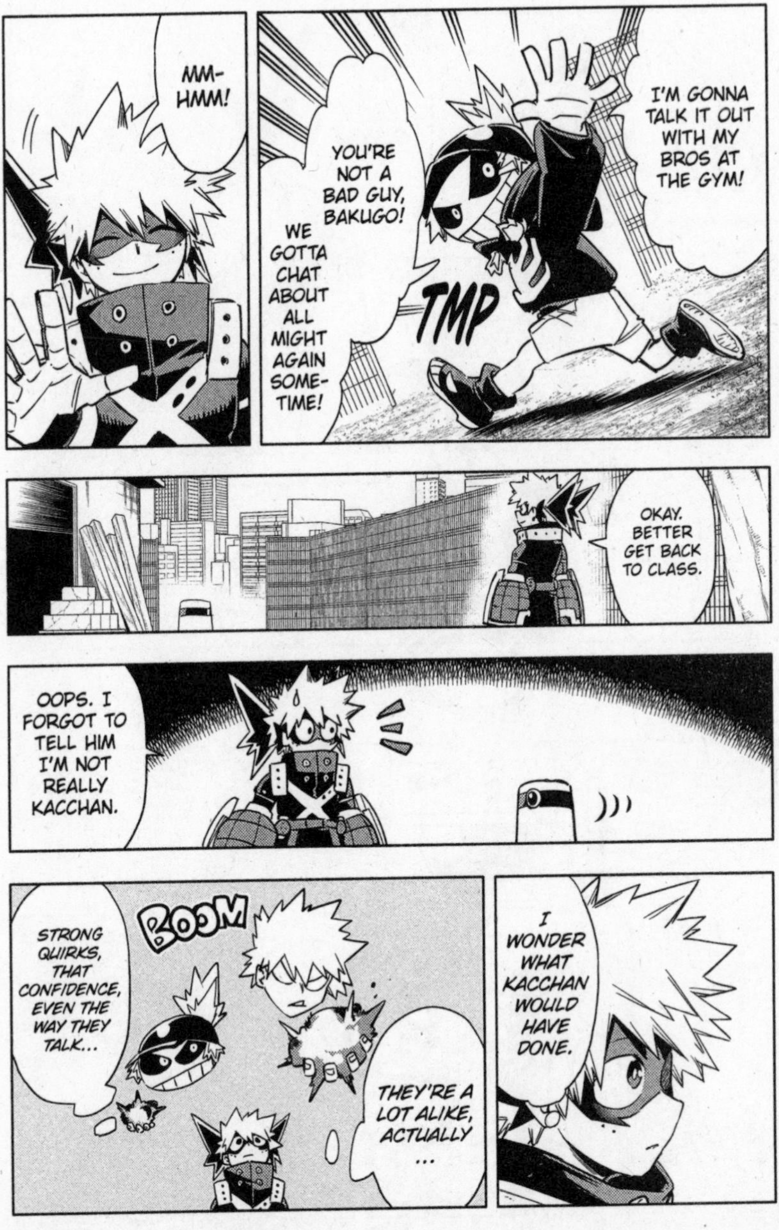
I'M GONNA TALK IT OUT WITH MY BROS AT THE GYM!
YOU'RE NOT A BAD GUY, BAKUGO!
WE GOTTA CHAT ABOUT ALL MIGHT AGAIN SOME-TIME!
TMP
MM-HMM!
OKAY. BETTER GET BACK TO CLASS.
OOPS. I FORGOT TO TELL HIM I'M NOT REALLY KACCHAN.
I WONDER WHAT KACCHAN WOULD HAVE DONE.
BOOM
STRONG QUIRKS, THAT CONFIDENCE, EVEN THE WAY THEY TALK...
THEY'RE A LOT ALIKE, ACTUALLY ...

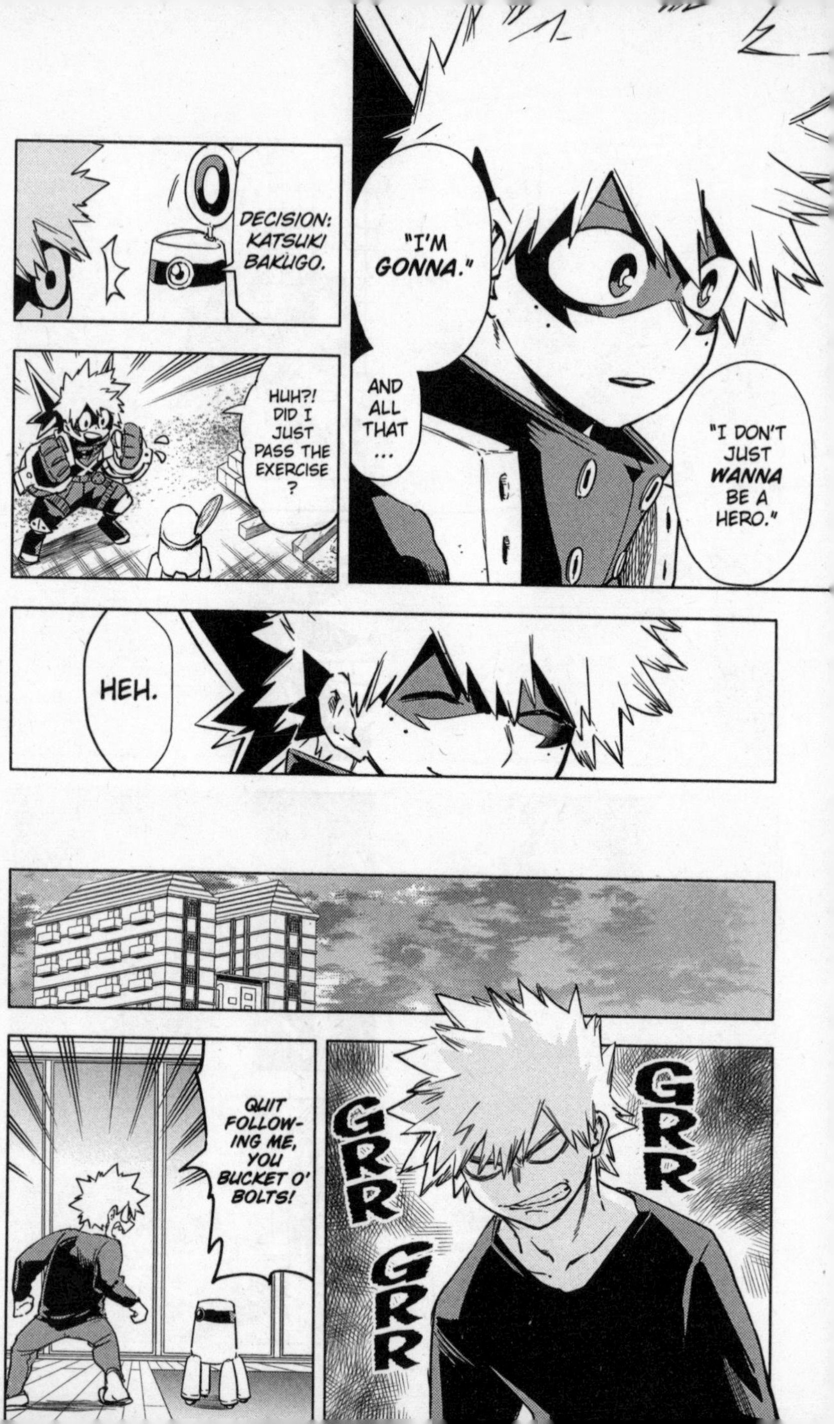
"I DON'T JUST WANNA BE A HERO."
"I'M GONNA."
AND ALL THAT...
DECISION: KATSUKI BAKUGO.
HUH?! DID I JUST PASS THE EXERCISE?
HEH.
GRR GRR
GRR GRR
QUIT FOLLOWING ME, YOU BUCKET O' BOLTS!

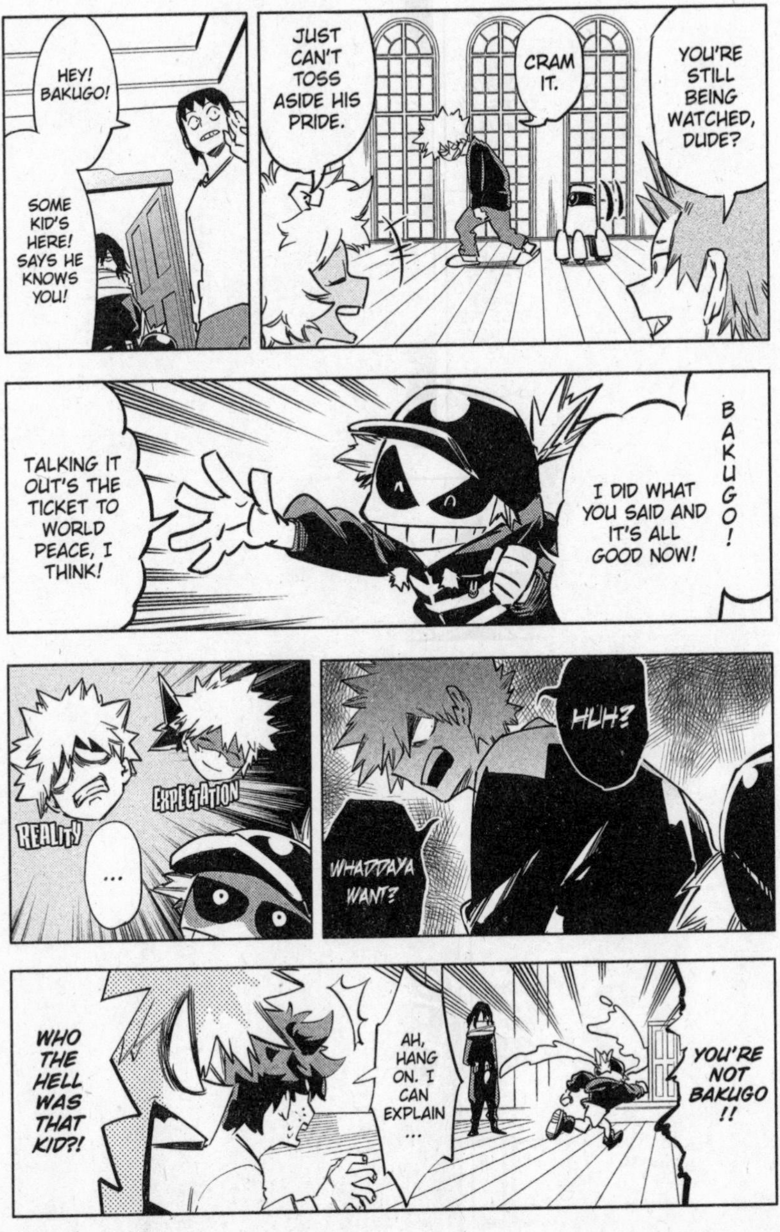
YOU'RE STILL BEING WATCHED, DUDE?
CRAM IT.
JUST CAN'T TOSS ASIDE HIS PRIDE.
HEY! BAKUGO!
SOME KID'S HERE! SAYS HE KNOWS YOU!
BAKUGO!
I DID WHAT YOU SAID AND IT'S ALL GOOD NOW!
TALKING IT OUT'S THE TICKET TO WORLD PEACE, I THINK!
HUH?
WHADDAYA WANT?
EXPECTATION
REALITY
...
YOU'RE NOT BAKUGO!!
AH, HANG ON. I CAN EXPLAIN...
WHO THE HELL WAS THAT KID?!

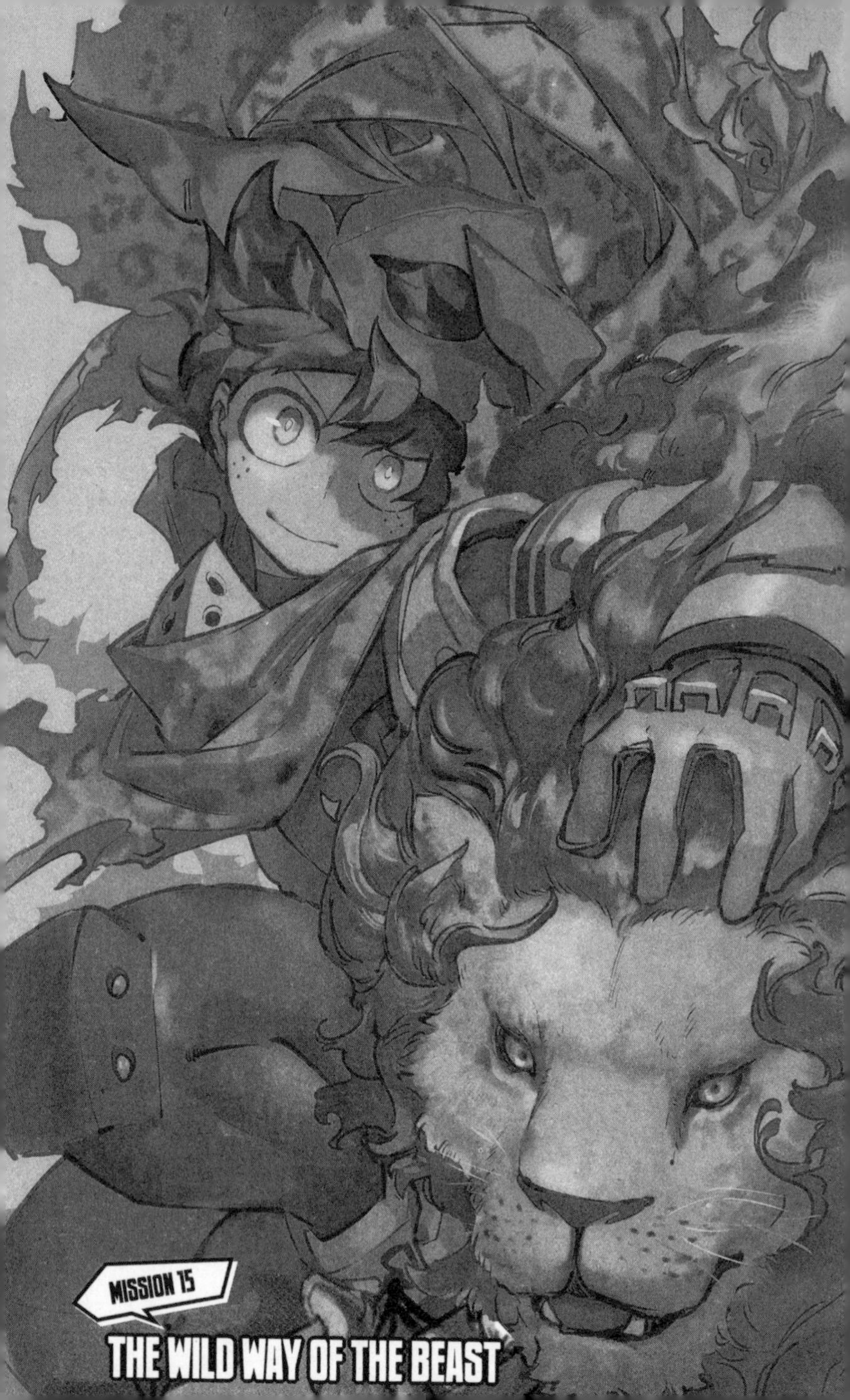
MISSION 15
THE WILD WAY OF THE BEAST

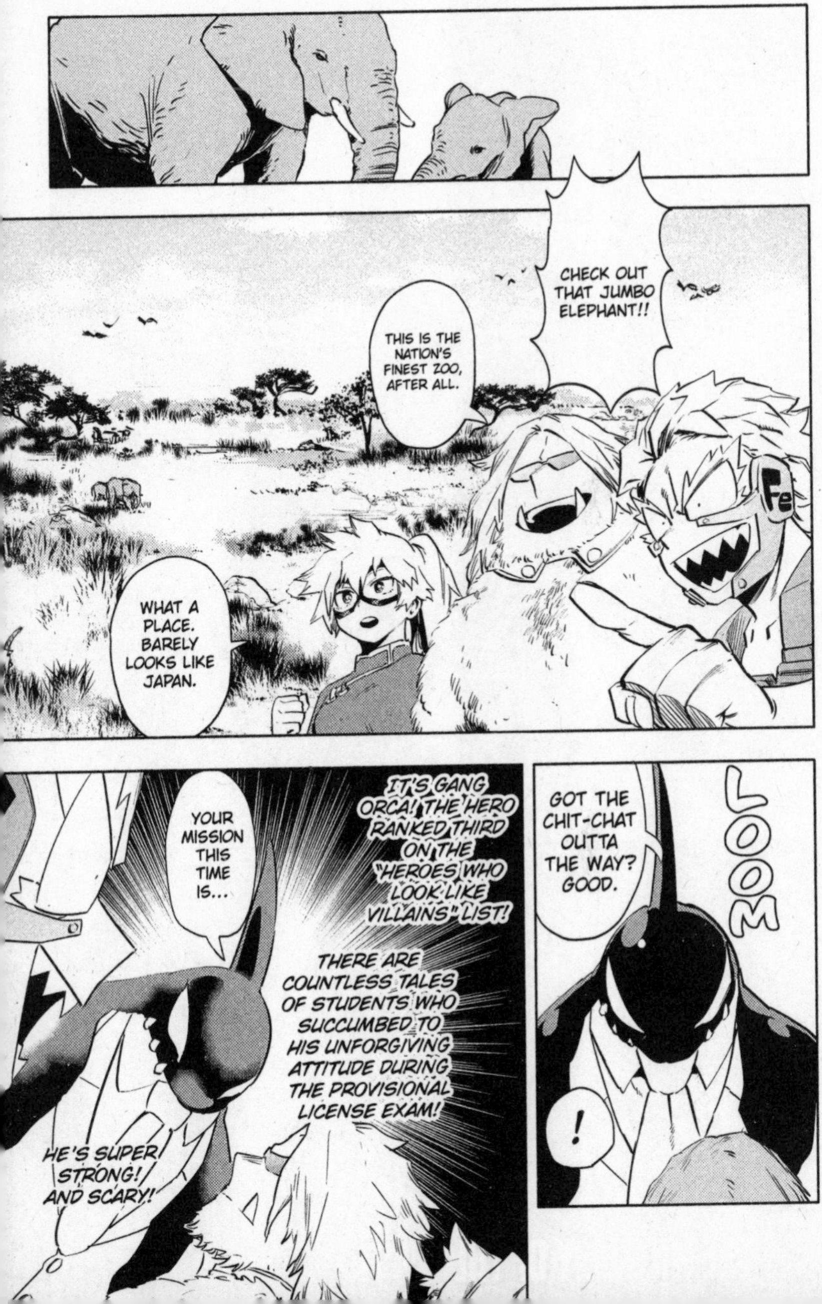
CHECK OUT THAT JUMBO ELEPHANT!!
THIS IS THE NATION'S FINEST ZOO, AFTER ALL.
WHAT A PLACE. BARELY LOOKS LIKE JAPAN.
LOOM
GOT THE CHIT-CHAT OUTTA THE WAY? GOOD.
!
IT'S GANG ORCA! THE HERO RANKED THIRD ON THE "HEROES WHO LOOK LIKE VILLAINS" LIST!
YOUR MISSION THIS TIME IS...
THERE ARE COUNTLESS TALES OF STUDENTS WHO SUCCUMBED TO HIS UNFORGIVING ATTITUDE DURING THE PROVISIONAL LICENSE EXAM!
HE'S SUPER STRONG! AND SCARY!

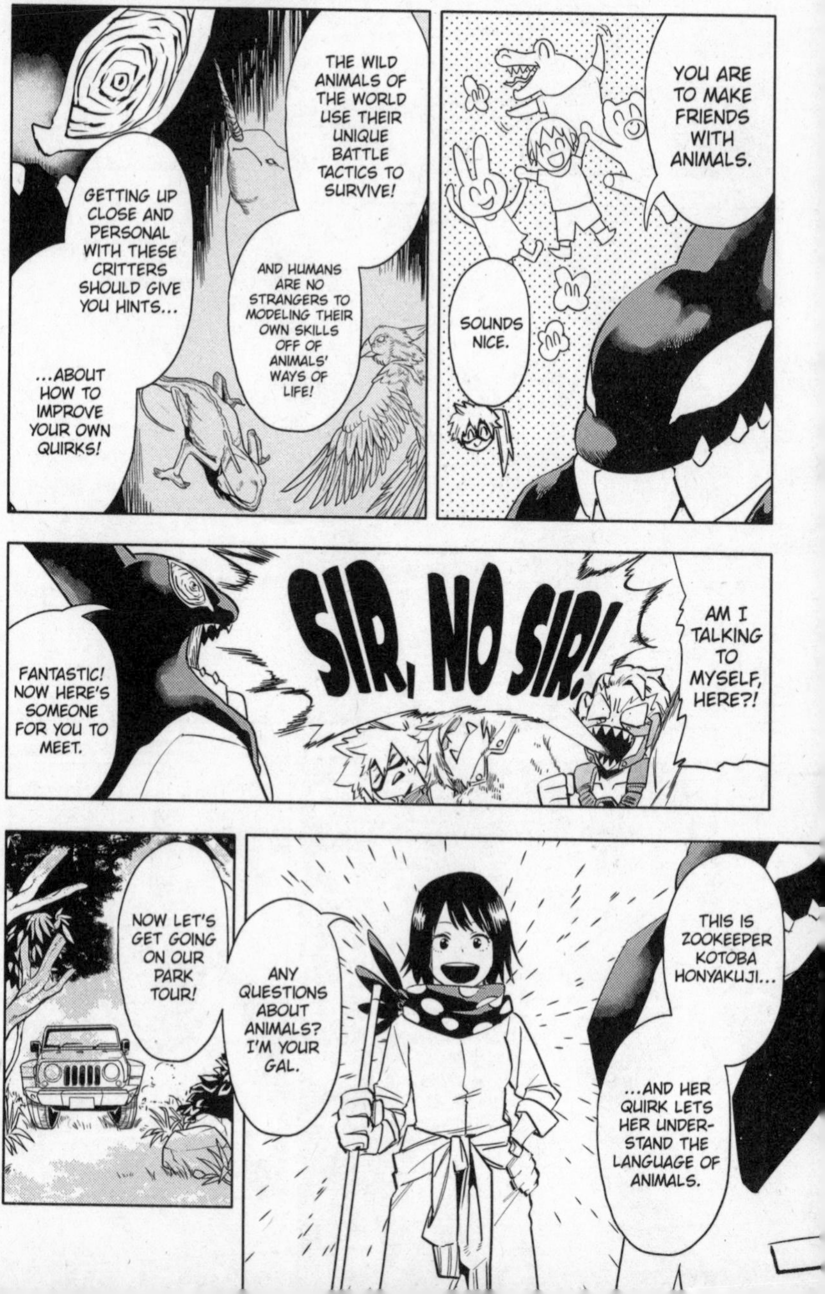
YOU ARE TO MAKE FRIENDS WITH ANIMALS.
SOUNDS NICE.
THE WILD ANIMALS OF THE WORLD USE THEIR UNIQUE BATTLE TACTICS TO SURVIVE!
AND HUMANS ARE NO STRANGERS TO MODELING THEIR OWN SKILLS OFF OF ANIMALS' WAYS OF LIFE!
GETTING UP CLOSE AND PERSONAL WITH THESE CRITTERS SHOULD GIVE YOU HINTS...
...ABOUT HOW TO IMPROVE YOUR OWN QUIRKS!
AM I TALKING TO MYSELF, HERE?!
SIR, NO SIR!
FANTASTIC! NOW HERE'S SOMEONE FOR YOU TO MEET.
THIS IS ZOOKEEPER KOTOBA HONYAKUJI...
...AND HER QUIRK LETS HER UNDER-STAND THE LANGUAGE OF ANIMALS.
ANY QUESTIONS ABOUT ANIMALS? I'M YOUR GAL.
NOW LET'S GET GOING ON OUR PARK TOUR!

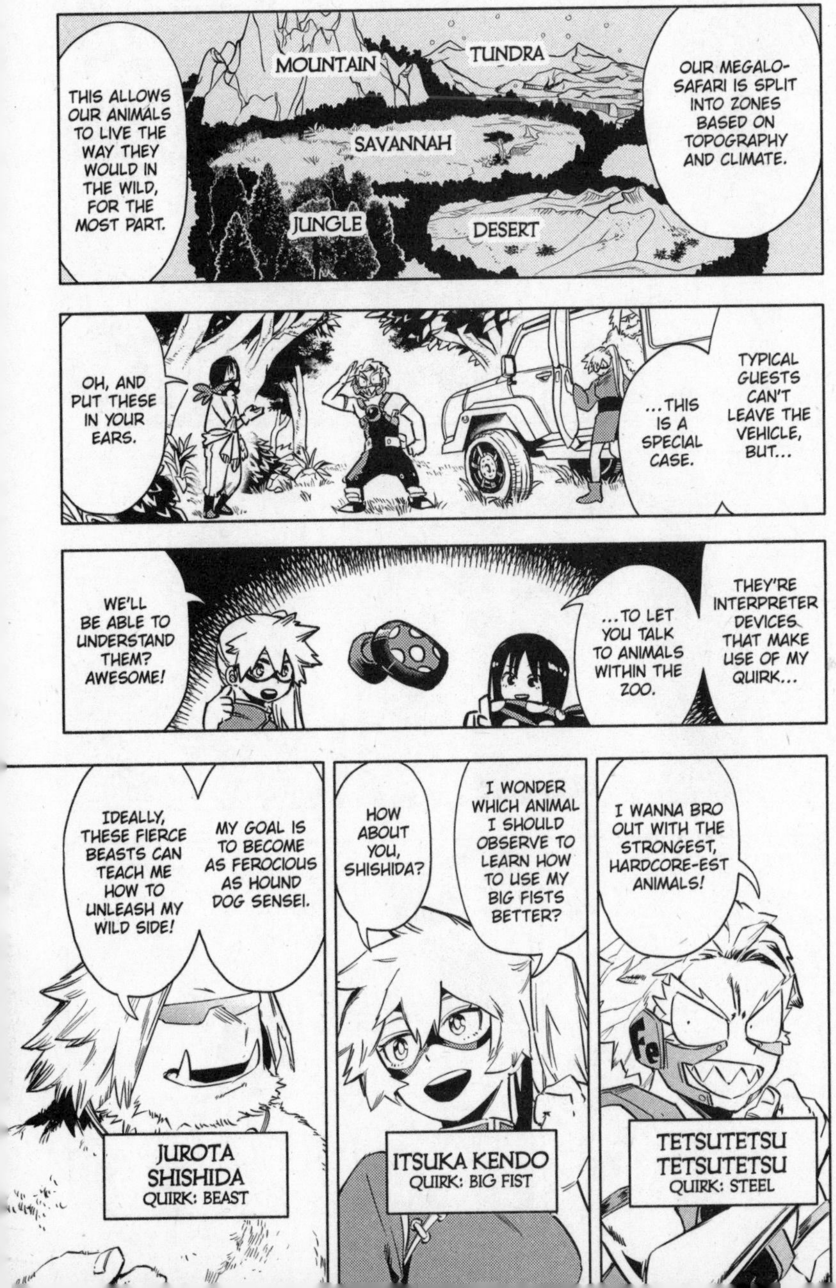
OUR MEGALO-SAFARI IS SPLIT INTO ZONES BASED ON TOPOGRAPHY AND CLIMATE.
TUNDRA
MOUNTAIN
SAVANNAH
DESERT
JUNGLE
THIS ALLOWS OUR ANIMALS TO LIVE THE WAY THEY WOULD IN THE WILD, FOR THE MOST PART.
TYPICAL GUESTS CAN'T LEAVE THE VEHICLE, BUT...
...THIS IS A SPECIAL CASE.
OH, AND PUT THESE IN YOUR EARS.
THEY'RE INTERPRETER DEVICES THAT MAKE USE OF MY QUIRK...
...TO LET YOU TALK TO ANIMALS WITHIN THE ZOO.
WE'LL BE ABLE TO UNDERSTAND THEM? AWESOME!
I WANNA BRO OUT WITH THE STRONGEST, HARDCORE-EST ANIMALS!
TETSUTETSU TETSUTETSU
QUIRK: STEEL
I WONDER WHICH ANIMAL I SHOULD OBSERVE TO LEARN HOW TO USE MY BIG FISTS BETTER?
HOW ABOUT YOU, SHISHIDA?
ITSUKA KENDO
QUIRK: BIG FIST
MY GOAL IS TO BECOME AS FEROCIOUS AS HOUND DOG SENSEI.
IDEALLY, THESE FIERCE BEASTS CAN TEACH ME HOW TO UNLEASH MY WILD SIDE!
JUROTA SHISHIDA
QUIRK: BEAST

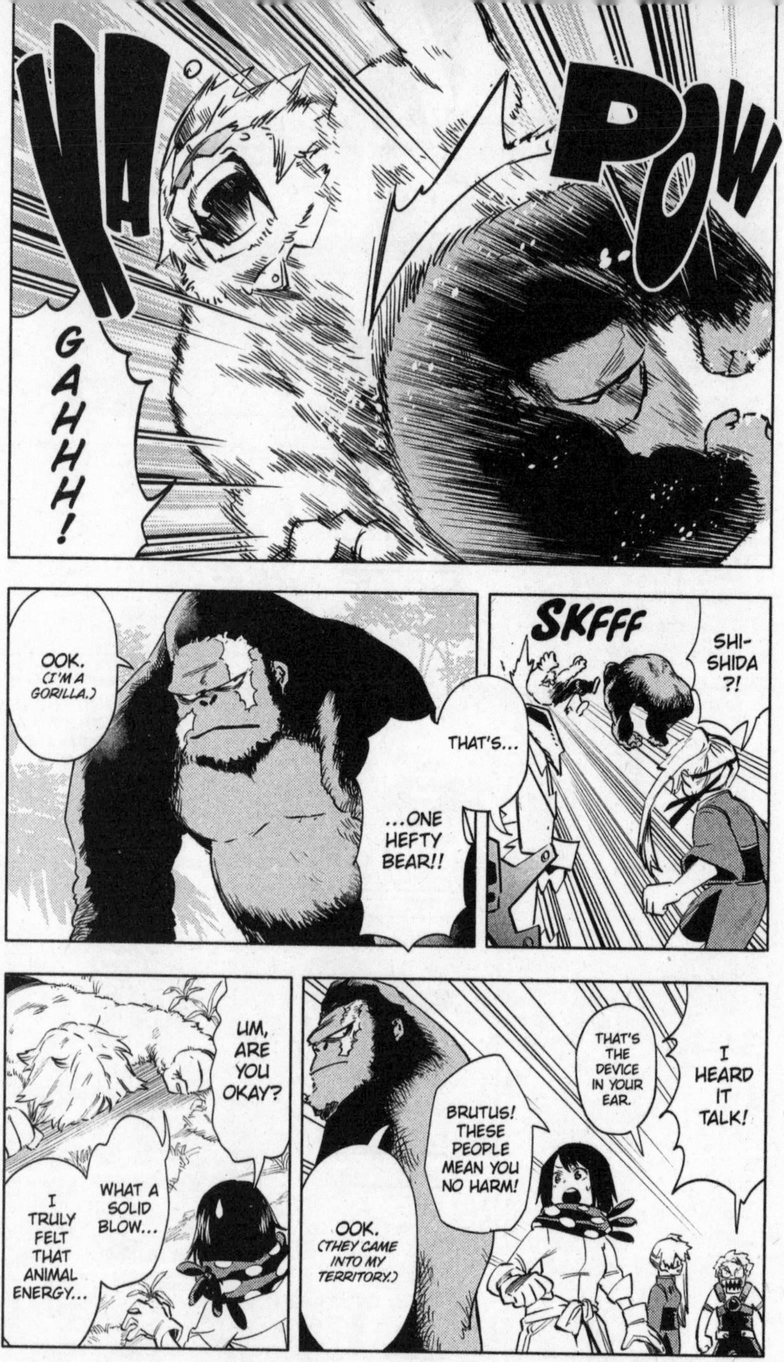
POW
WHA
GAHHHH!
SKFFF
SHI-SHIDA?!
THAT'S...
...ONE HEFTY BEAR!!
OOK. (I'M A GORILLA.)
I HEARD IT TALK!
THAT'S THE DEVICE IN YOUR EAR.
BRUTUS! THESE PEOPLE MEAN YOU NO HARM!
OOK. (THEY CAME INTO MY TERRITORY.)
UM, ARE YOU OKAY?
WHAT A SOLID BLOW...
I TRULY FELT THAT ANIMAL ENERGY...

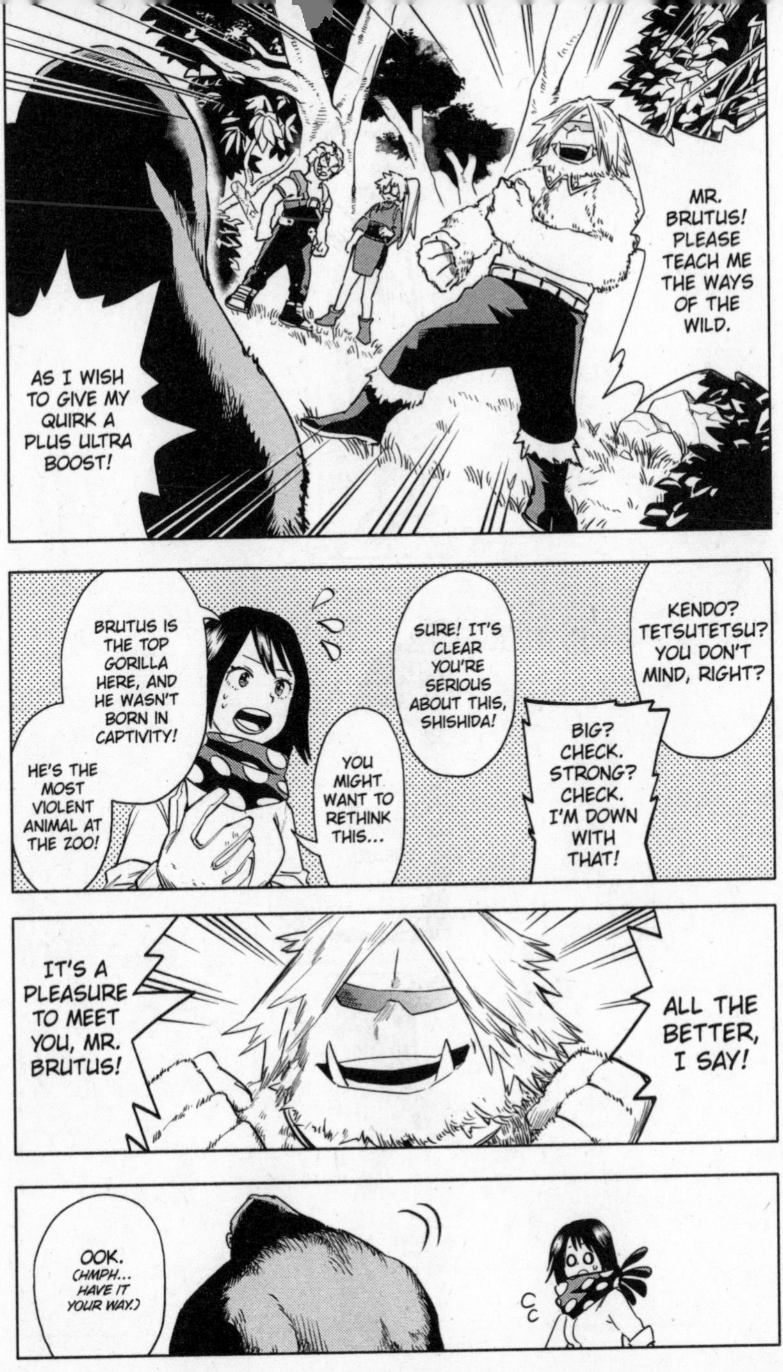
MR. BRUTUS! PLEASE TEACH ME THE WAYS OF THE WILD.
AS I WISH TO GIVE MY QUIRK A PLUS ULTRA BOOST!
KENDO? TETSUTETSU? YOU DON'T MIND, RIGHT?
BIG? CHECK. STRONG? CHECK. I'M DOWN WITH THAT!
SURE! IT'S CLEAR YOU'RE SERIOUS ABOUT THIS, SHISHIDA!
YOU MIGHT WANT TO RETHINK THIS...
BRUTUS IS THE TOP GORILLA HERE, AND HE WASN'T BORN IN CAPTIVITY!
HE'S THE MOST VIOLENT ANIMAL AT THE ZOO!
ALL THE BETTER, I SAY!
IT'S A PLEASURE TO MEET YOU, MR. BRUTUS!
OOK. (HMPH... HAVE IT YOUR WAY.)

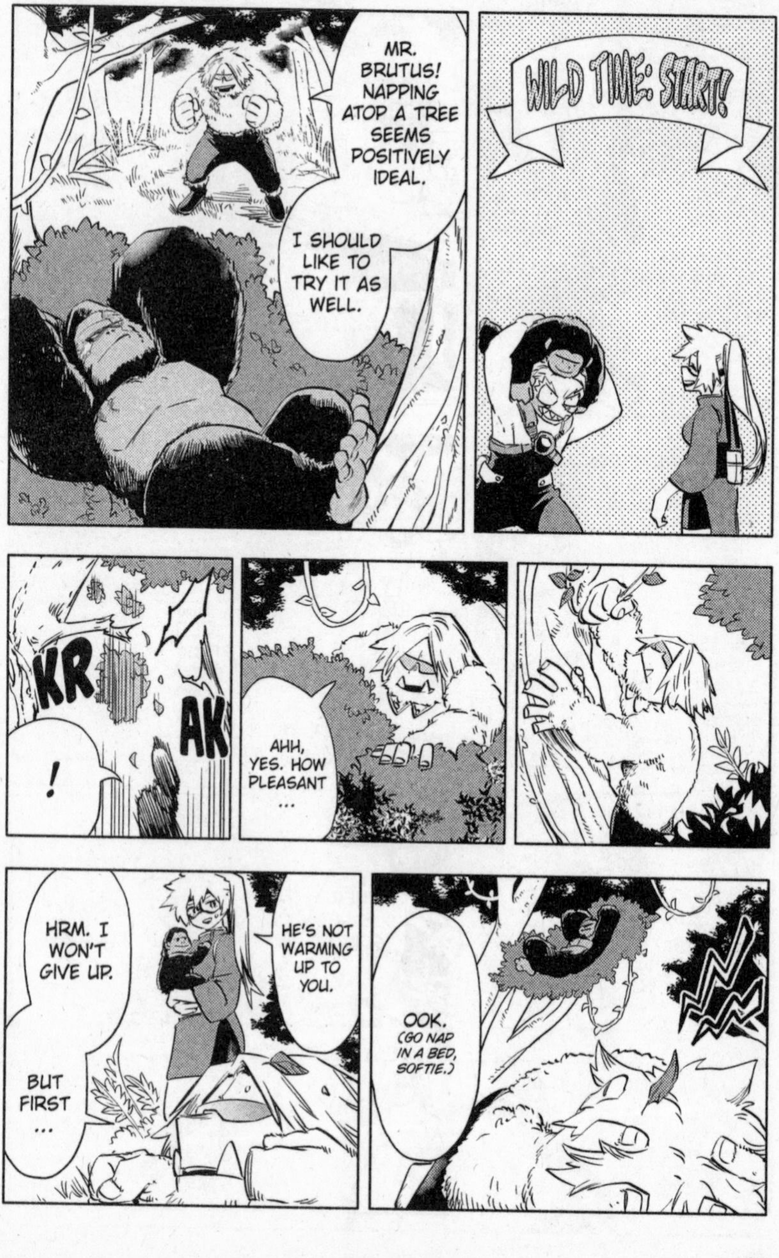
WILD TIME: START!
MR. BRUTUS! NAPPING ATOP A TREE SEEMS POSITIVELY IDEAL.
I SHOULD LIKE TO TRY IT AS WELL.
AHH, YES. HOW PLEASANT ...
KR AK
!
OOK. (GO NAP IN A BED, SOFTIE.)
HE'S NOT WARMING UP TO YOU.
HRM. I WON'T GIVE UP.
BUT FIRST ...

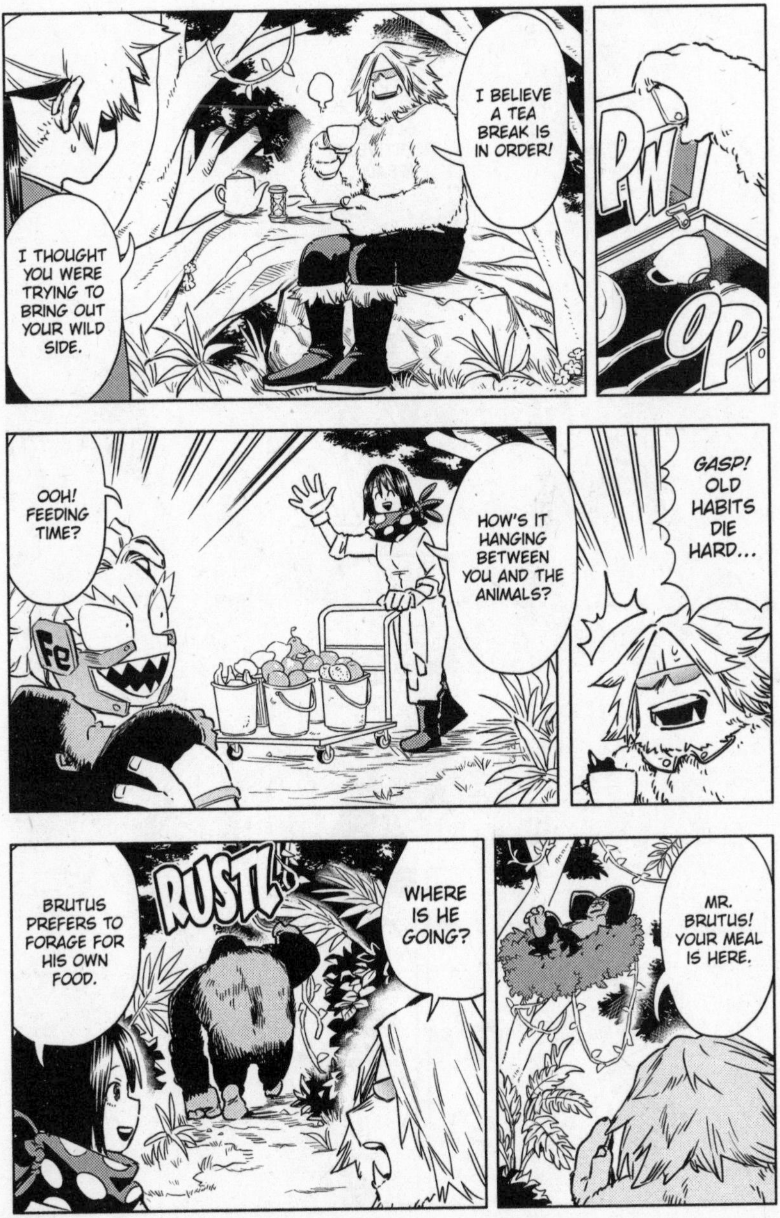
PW
OP
I BELIEVE A TEA BREAK IS IN ORDER!
I THOUGHT YOU WERE TRYING TO BRING OUT YOUR WILD SIDE.
GASP! OLD HABITS DIE HARD...
HOW'S IT HANGING BETWEEN YOU AND THE ANIMALS?
OOH! FEEDING TIME?
MR. BRUTUS! YOUR MEAL IS HERE.
WHERE IS HE GOING?
RUSTL
BRUTUS PREFERS TO FORAGE FOR HIS OWN FOOD.

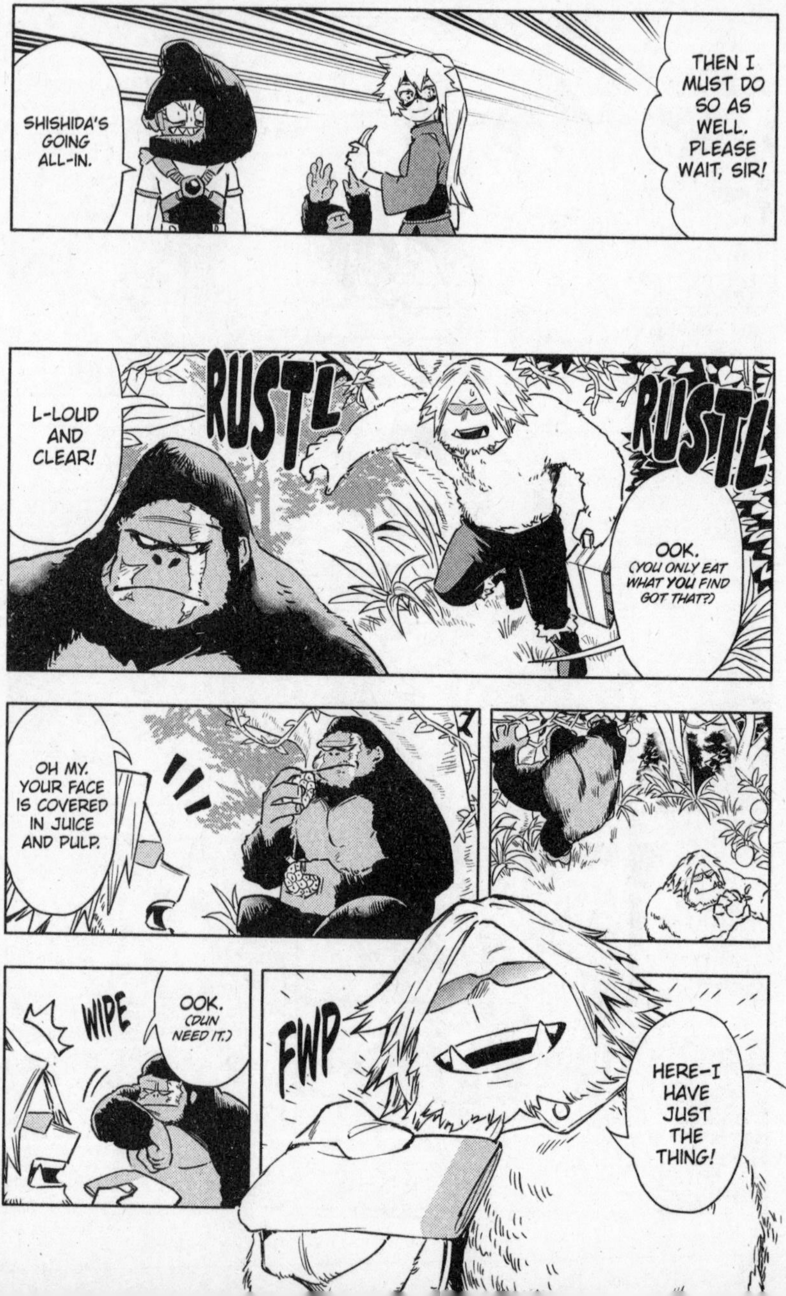
THEN I MUST DO SO AS WELL. PLEASE WAIT, SIR!
SHISHIDA'S GOING ALL-IN.
RUSTL
RUSTL
OOK. (YOU ONLY EAT WHAT YOU FIND GOT THAT?)
L-LOUD AND CLEAR!
OH MY. YOUR FACE IS COVERED IN JUICE AND PULP.
FWP
HERE–I HAVE JUST THE THING!
OOK. (DUN NEED IT.)
WIPE

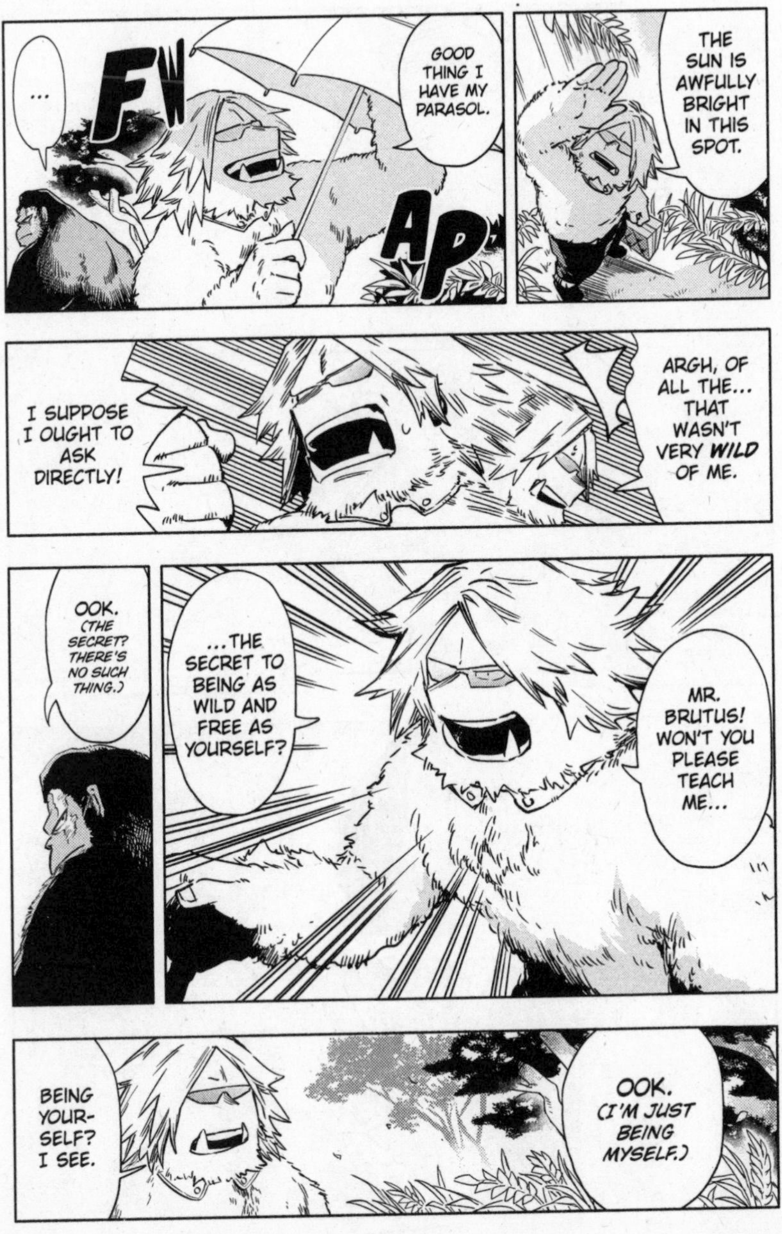
THE SUN IS AWFULLY BRIGHT IN THIS SPOT.
GOOD THING I HAVE MY PARASOL.
FWAP
...
ARGH, OF ALL THE... THAT WASN'T VERY *WILD* OF ME.
I SUPPOSE I OUGHT TO ASK DIRECTLY!
MR. BRUTUS! WON'T YOU PLEASE TEACH ME...
...THE SECRET TO BEING AS WILD AND FREE AS YOURSELF?
OOK. (THE SECRET? THERE'S NO SUCH THING.)
OOK. (I'M JUST BEING MYSELF.)
BEING YOUR-SELF? I SEE.

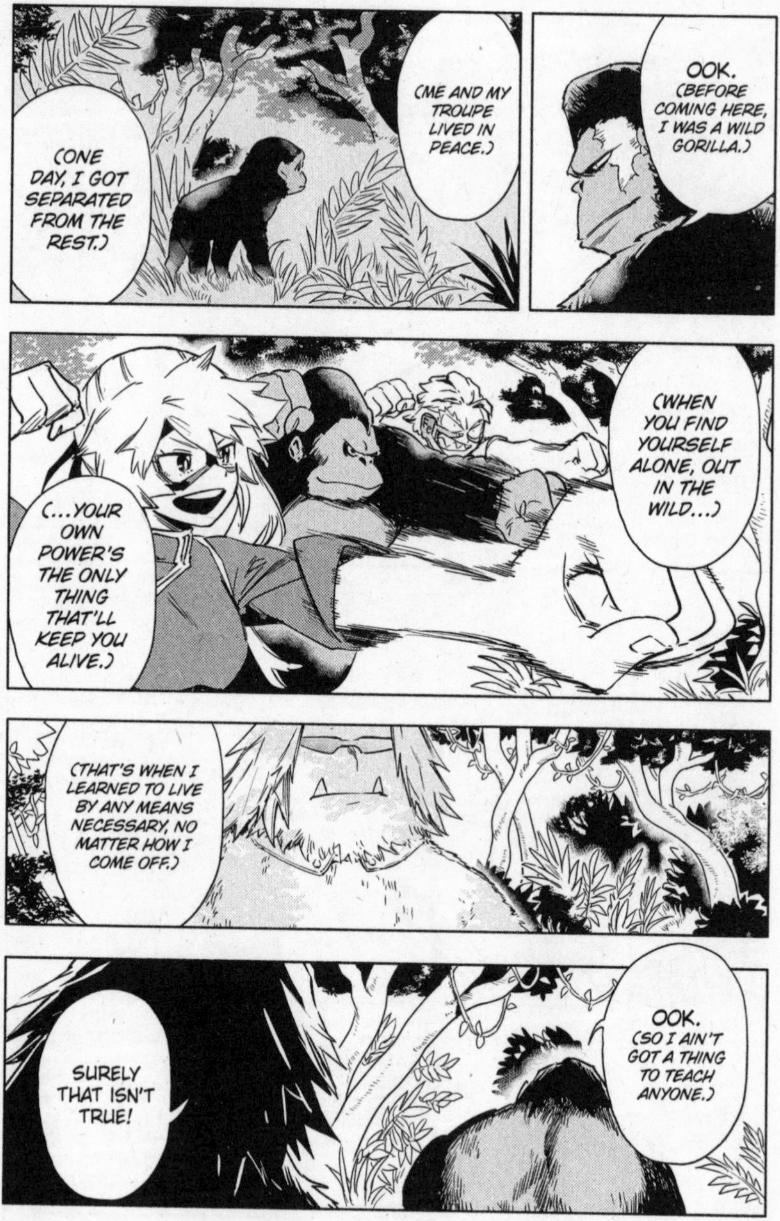
OOK. (BEFORE COMING HERE, I WAS A WILD GORILLA.)
(ME AND MY TROUPE LIVED IN PEACE.)
(ONE DAY, I GOT SEPARATED FROM THE REST.)
(WHEN YOU FIND YOURSELF ALONE, OUT IN THE WILD...)
(...YOUR OWN POWER'S THE ONLY THING THAT'LL KEEP YOU ALIVE.)
(THAT'S WHEN I LEARNED TO LIVE BY ANY MEANS NECESSARY, NO MATTER HOW I COME OFF.)
OOK. (SO I AIN'T GOT A THING TO TEACH ANYONE.)
SURELY THAT ISN'T TRUE!

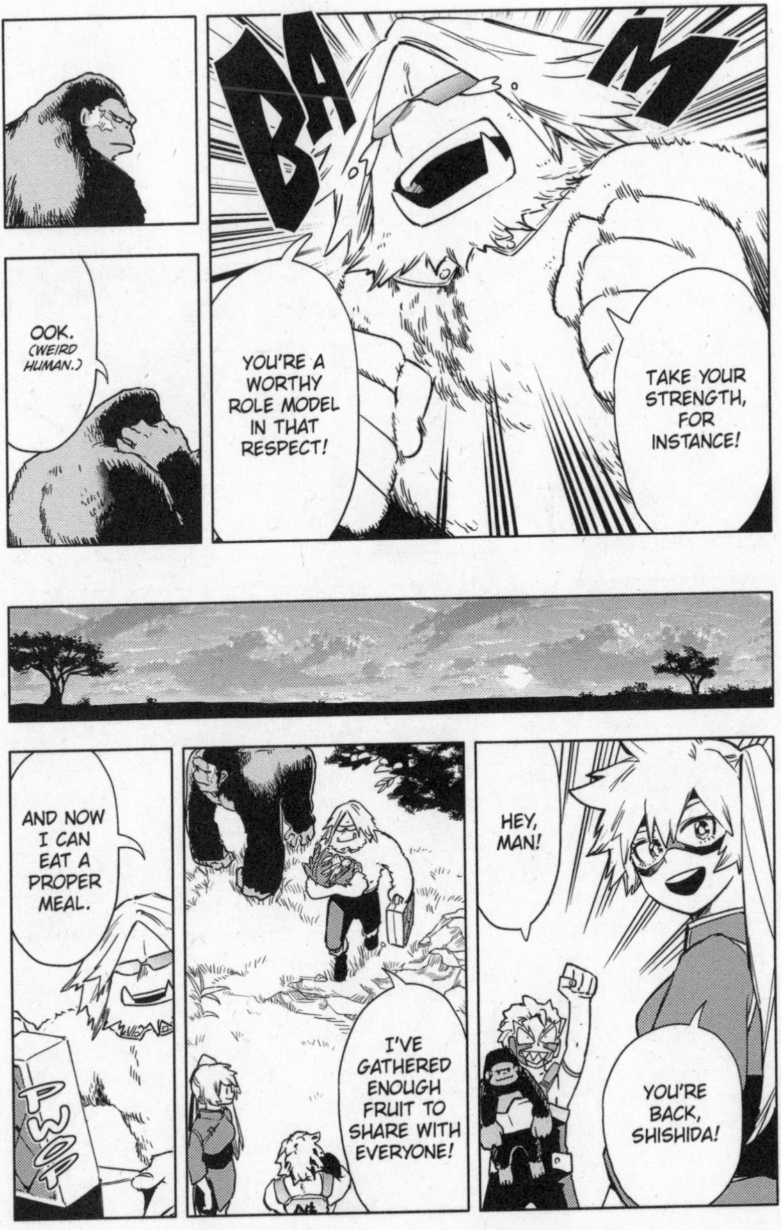
BAM
TAKE YOUR STRENGTH, FOR INSTANCE!
YOU'RE A WORTHY ROLE MODEL IN THAT RESPECT!
OOK. (WEIRD HUMAN.)
HEY, MAN!
YOU'RE BACK, SHISHIDA!
I'VE GATHERED ENOUGH FRUIT TO SHARE WITH EVERYONE!
AND NOW I CAN EAT A PROPER MEAL.
PWOP

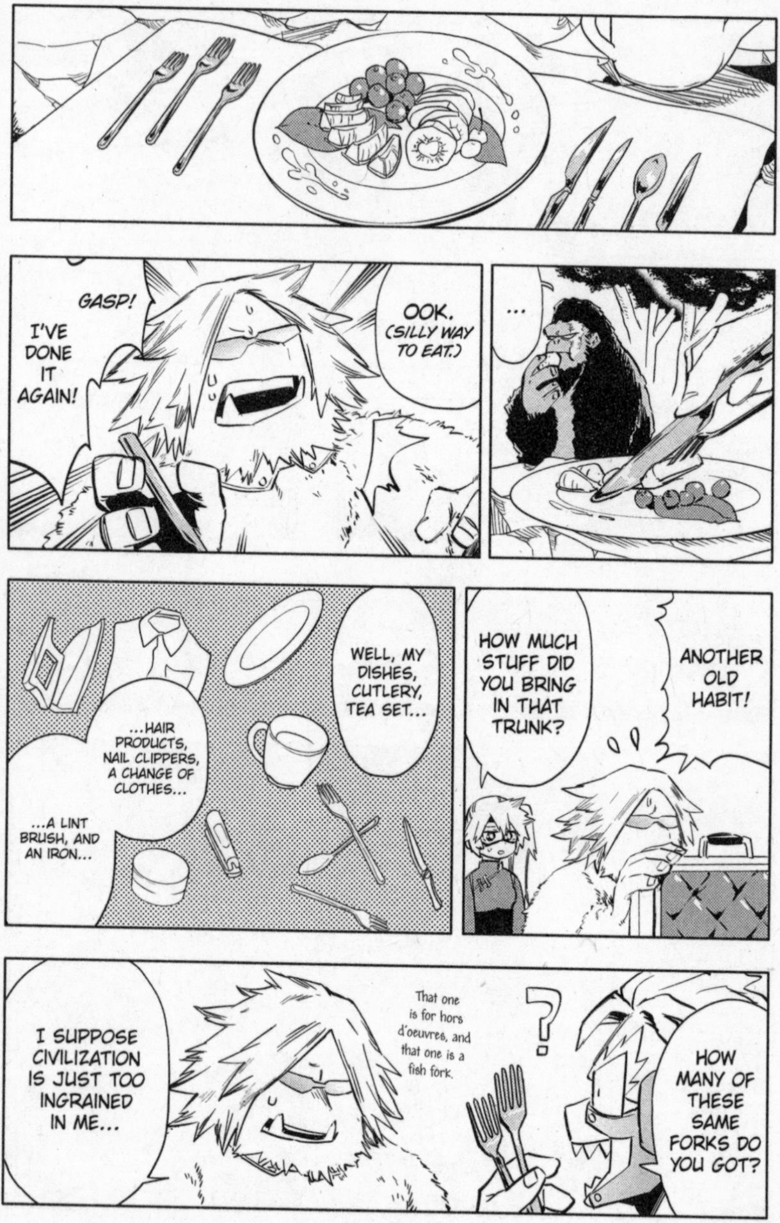
...
OOK. (SILLY WAY TO EAT.)
GASP!
I'VE DONE IT AGAIN!
ANOTHER OLD HABIT!
HOW MUCH STUFF DID YOU BRING IN THAT TRUNK?
WELL, MY DISHES, CUTLERY, TEA SET...
...HAIR PRODUCTS, NAIL CLIPPERS, A CHANGE OF CLOTHES...
...A LINT BRUSH, AND AN IRON...
HOW MANY OF THESE SAME FORKS DO YOU GOT?
?
That one is for hors d'oeuvres, and that one is a fish fork.
I SUPPOSE CIVILIZATION IS JUST TOO INGRAINED IN ME...

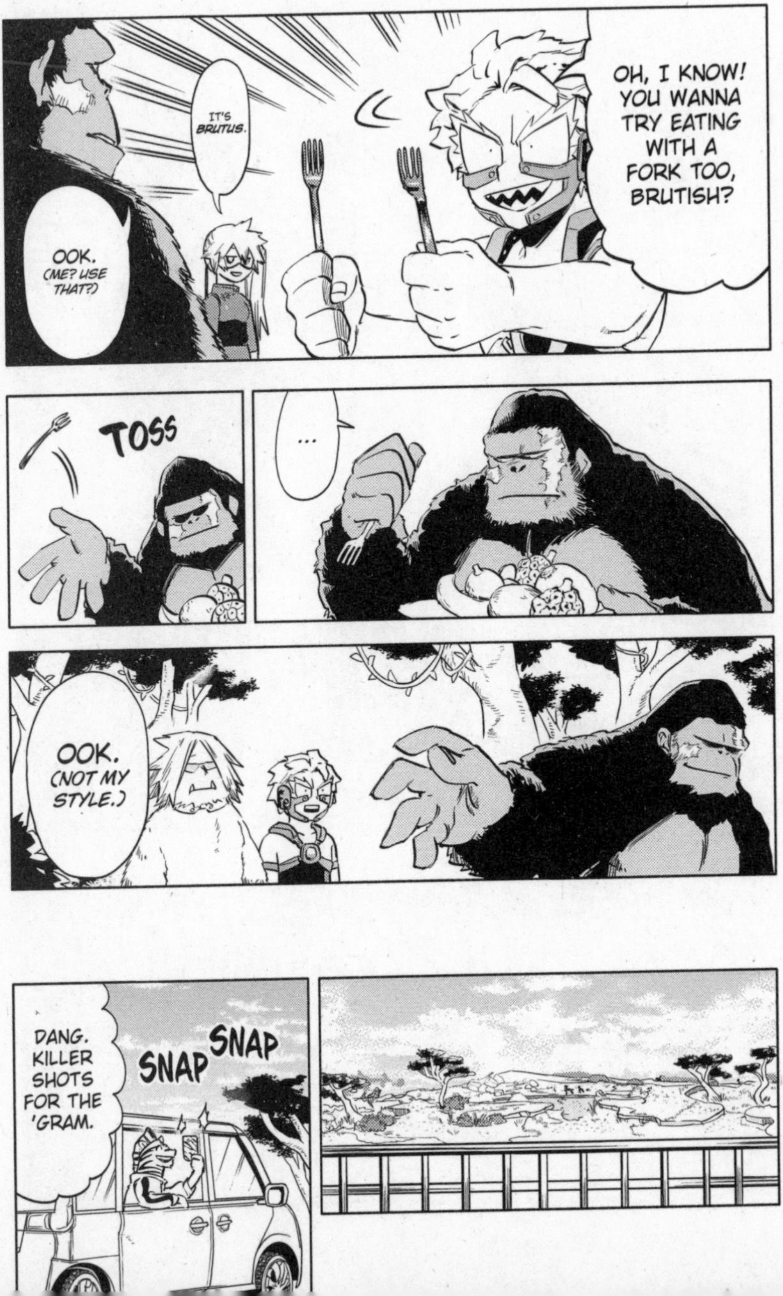
OH, I KNOW! YOU WANNA TRY EATING WITH A FORK TOO, BRUTISH?
IT'S BRUTUS.
OOK. (ME? USE THAT?)
...
TOSS
OOK. (NOT MY STYLE.)
SNAP
SNAP
DANG. KILLER SHOTS FOR THE 'GRAM.

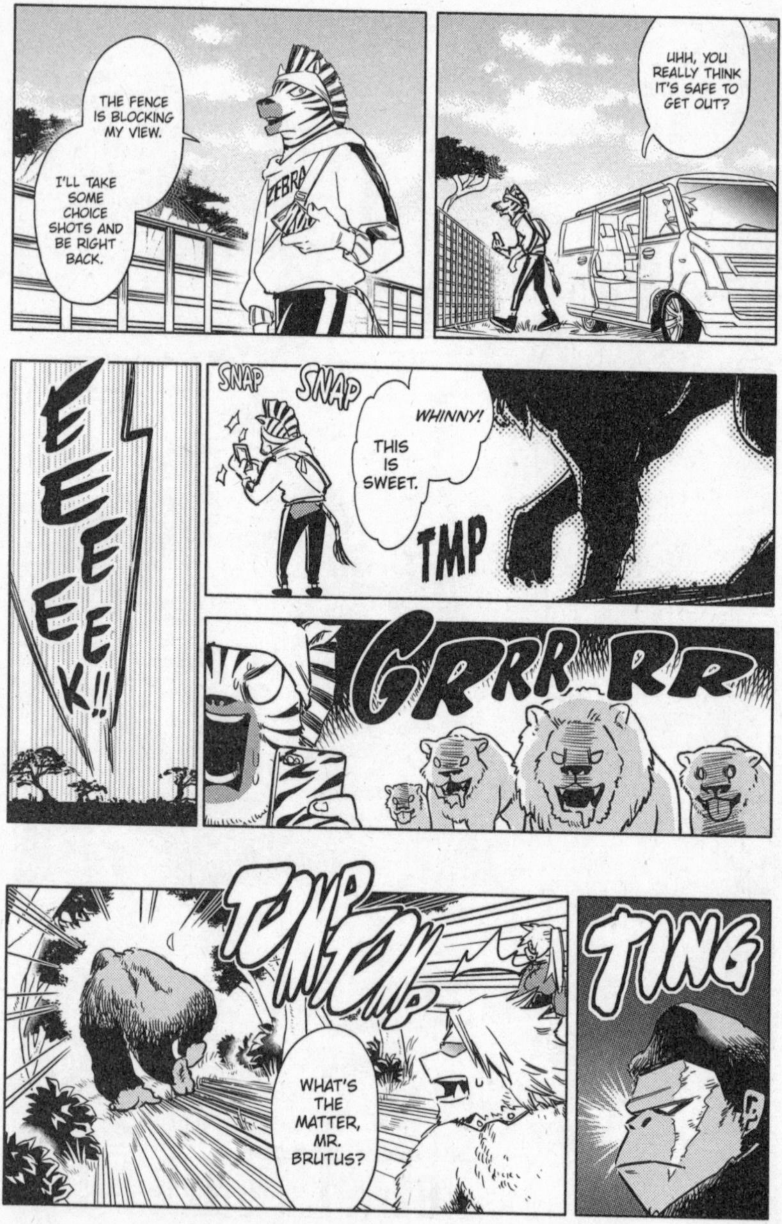
UHH, YOU REALLY THINK IT'S SAFE TO GET OUT?
THE FENCE IS BLOCKING MY VIEW.
I'LL TAKE SOME CHOICE SHOTS AND BE RIGHT BACK.
SNAP
SNAP
WHINNY!
THIS IS SWEET.
TMP
GRRR RR
EEEEEEK!!
TING
TMP TMP
WHAT'S THE MATTER, MR. BRUTUS?

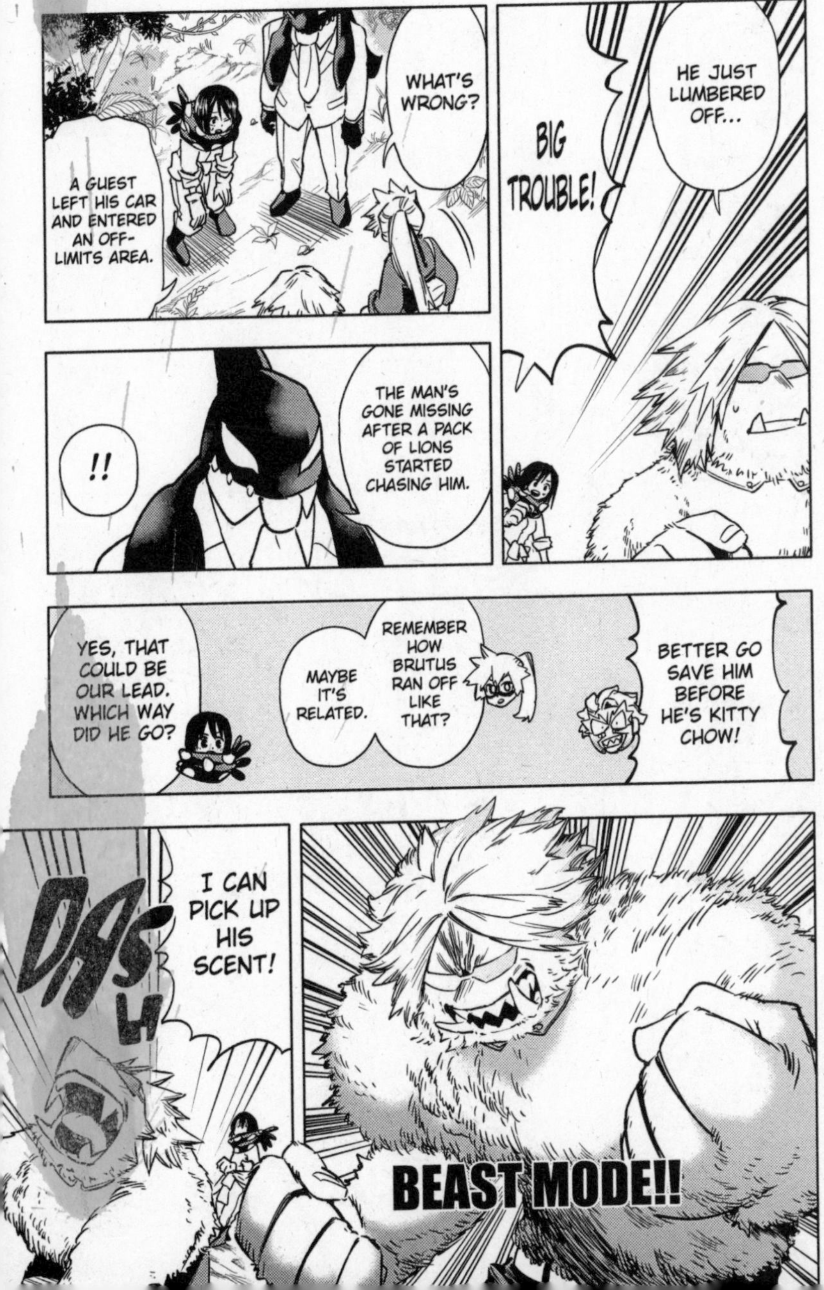
HE JUST LUMBERED OFF...
BIG TROUBLE!
WHAT'S WRONG?
A GUEST LEFT HIS CAR AND ENTERED AN OFF-LIMITS AREA.
THE MAN'S GONE MISSING AFTER A PACK OF LIONS STARTED CHASING HIM.
!!
BETTER GO SAVE HIM BEFORE HE'S KITTY CHOW!
REMEMBER HOW BRUTUS RAN OFF LIKE THAT?
MAYBE IT'S RELATED.
YES, THAT COULD BE OUR LEAD. WHICH WAY DID HE GO?
BEAST MODE!!
I CAN PICK UP HIS SCENT!
DASH

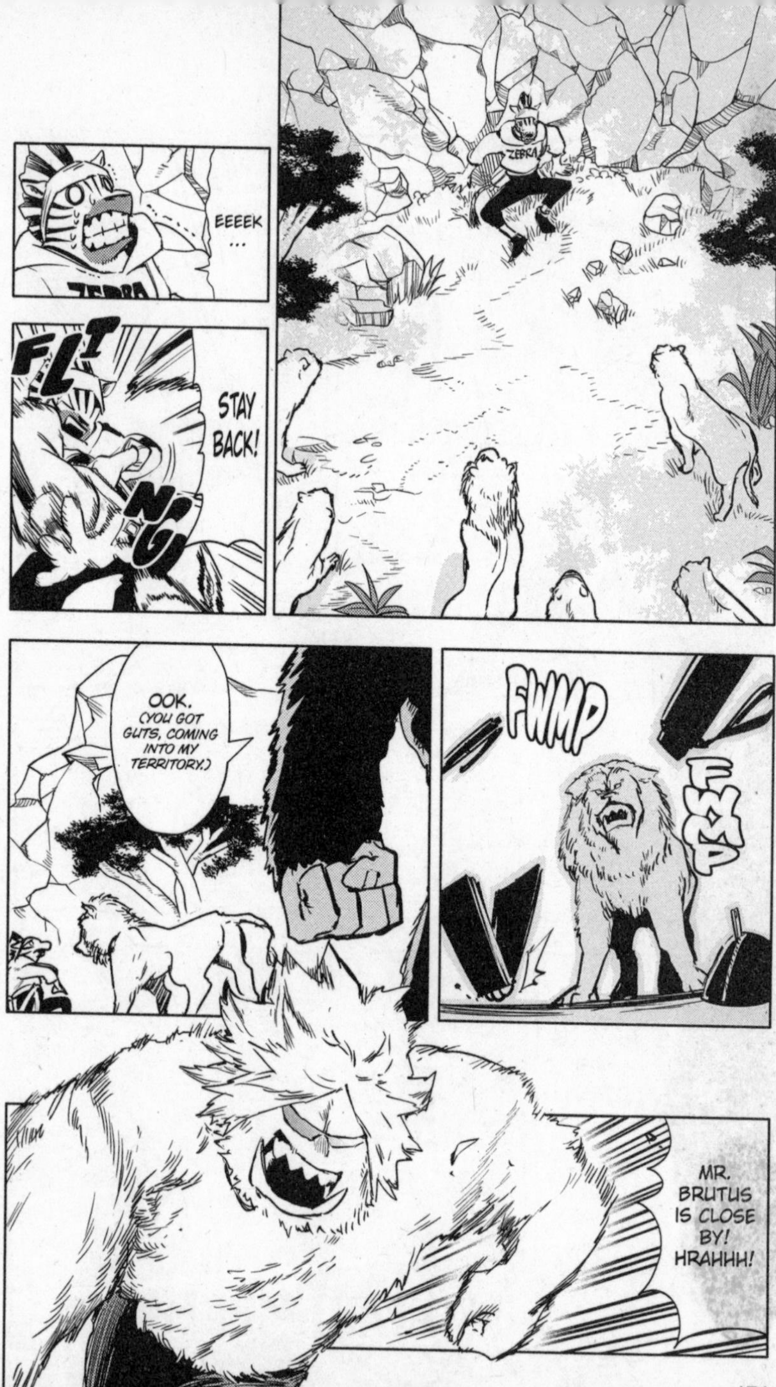
EEEEK ...
STAY BACK!
FLING
FWMP
FWMP
OOK.
(YOU GOT GUTS, COMING INTO MY TERRITORY.)
MR. BRUTUS IS CLOSE BY! HRAHHH!

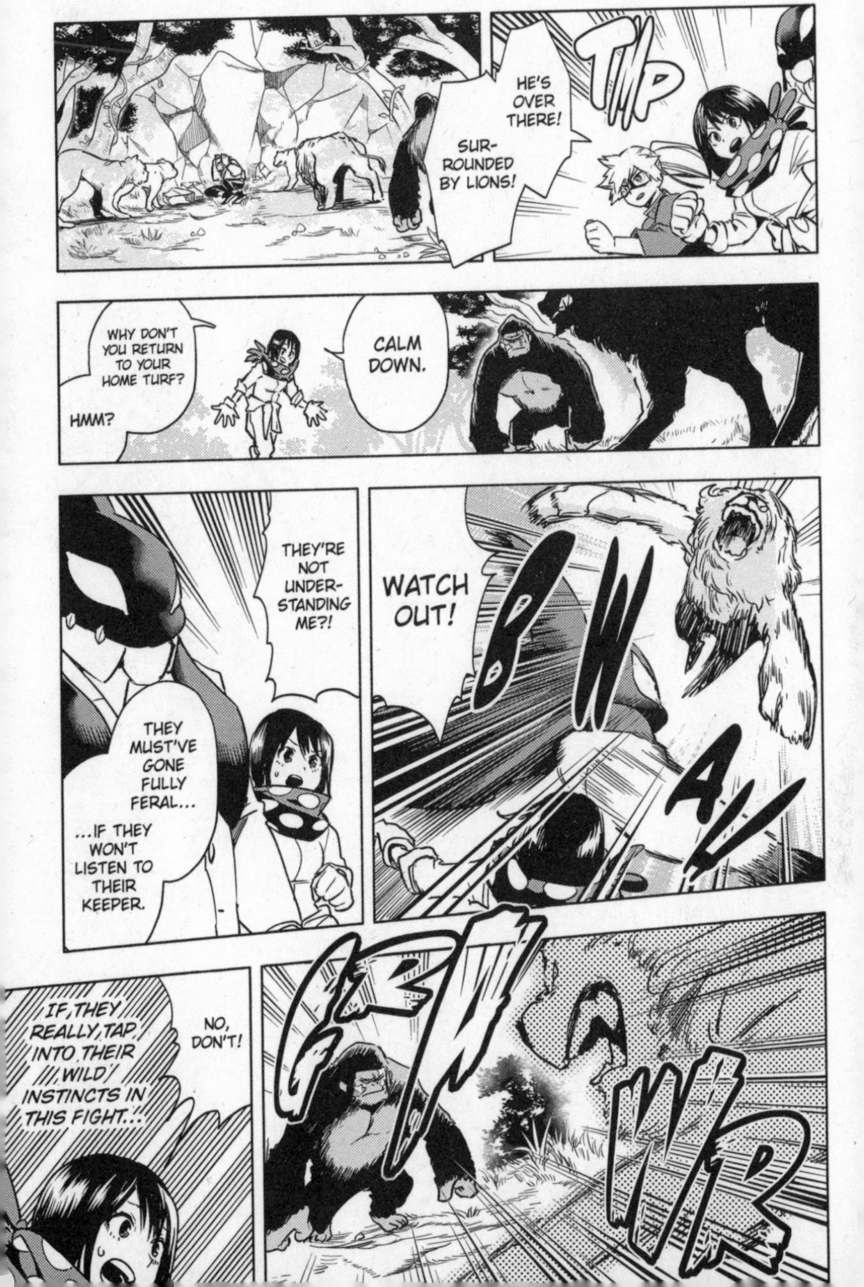
TMP
HE'S OVER THERE!
SUR-ROUNDED BY LIONS!
CALM DOWN.
WHY DON'T YOU RETURN TO YOUR HOME TURF?
HMM?
WATCH OUT!
THEY'RE NOT UNDER-STANDING ME?!
THEY MUST'VE GONE FULLY FERAL...
...IF THEY WON'T LISTEN TO THEIR KEEPER.
NO, DON'T!
IF THEY REALLY TAP INTO THEIR WILD INSTINCTS IN THIS FIGHT...

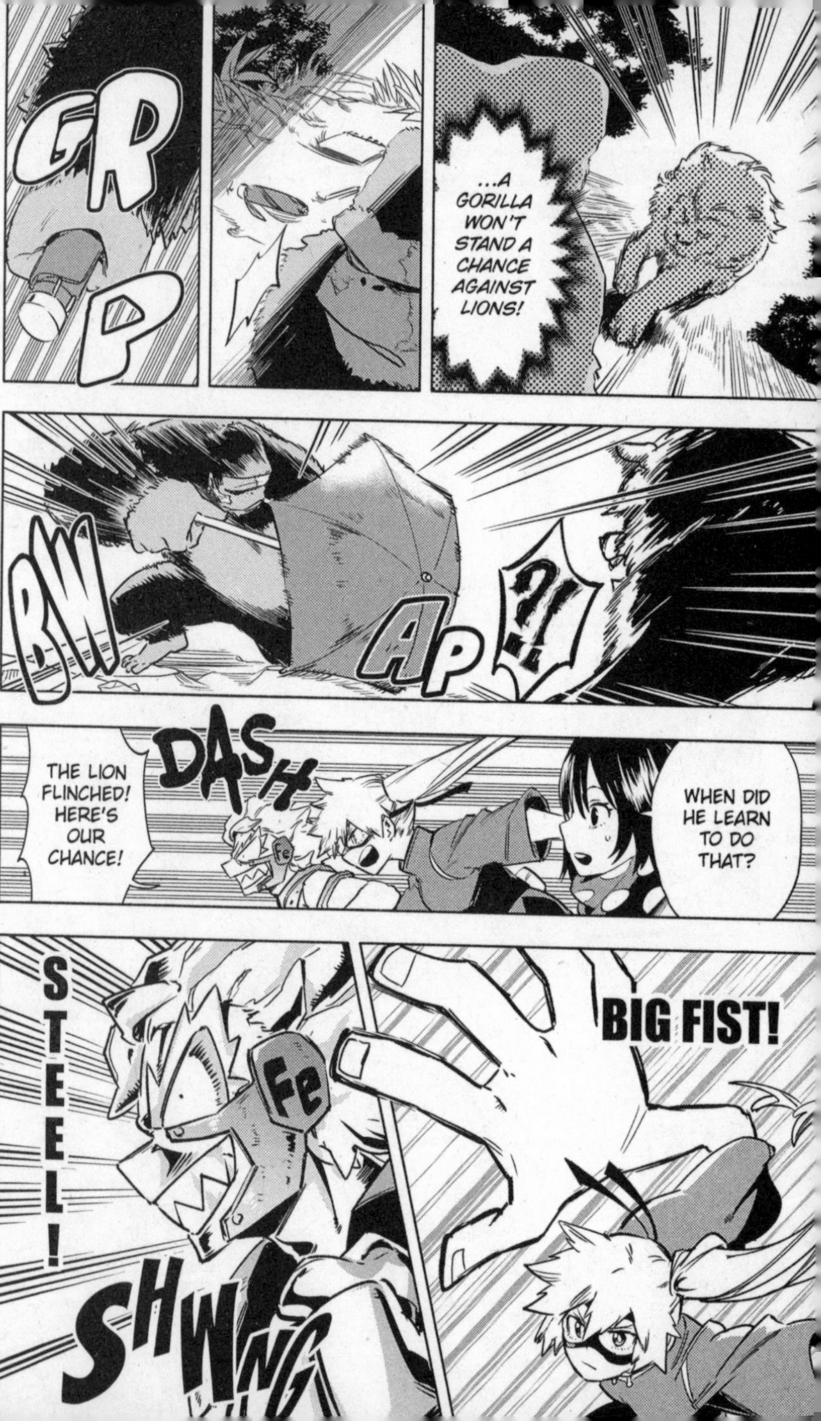
...A GORILLA WON'T STAND A CHANCE AGAINST LIONS!
GRP
?!
BWAP
WHEN DID HE LEARN TO DO THAT?
DASH
THE LION FLINCHED! HERE'S OUR CHANCE!
BIG FIST!
STEEL!
SHWNG

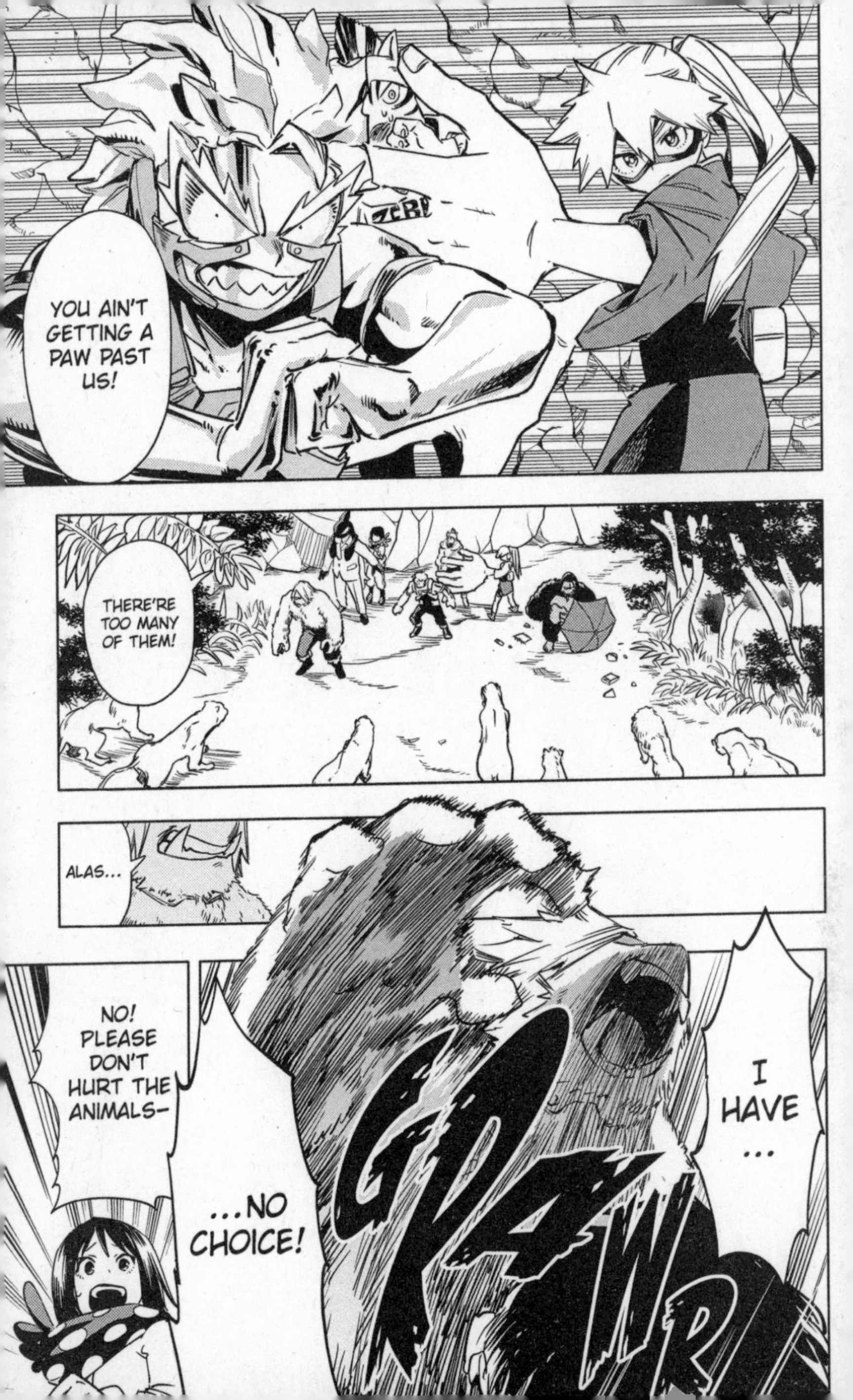
YOU AIN'T GETTING A PAW PAST US!
THERE'RE TOO MANY OF THEM!
ALAS...
I HAVE...
...NO CHOICE!
NO! PLEASE DON'T HURT THE ANIMALS-

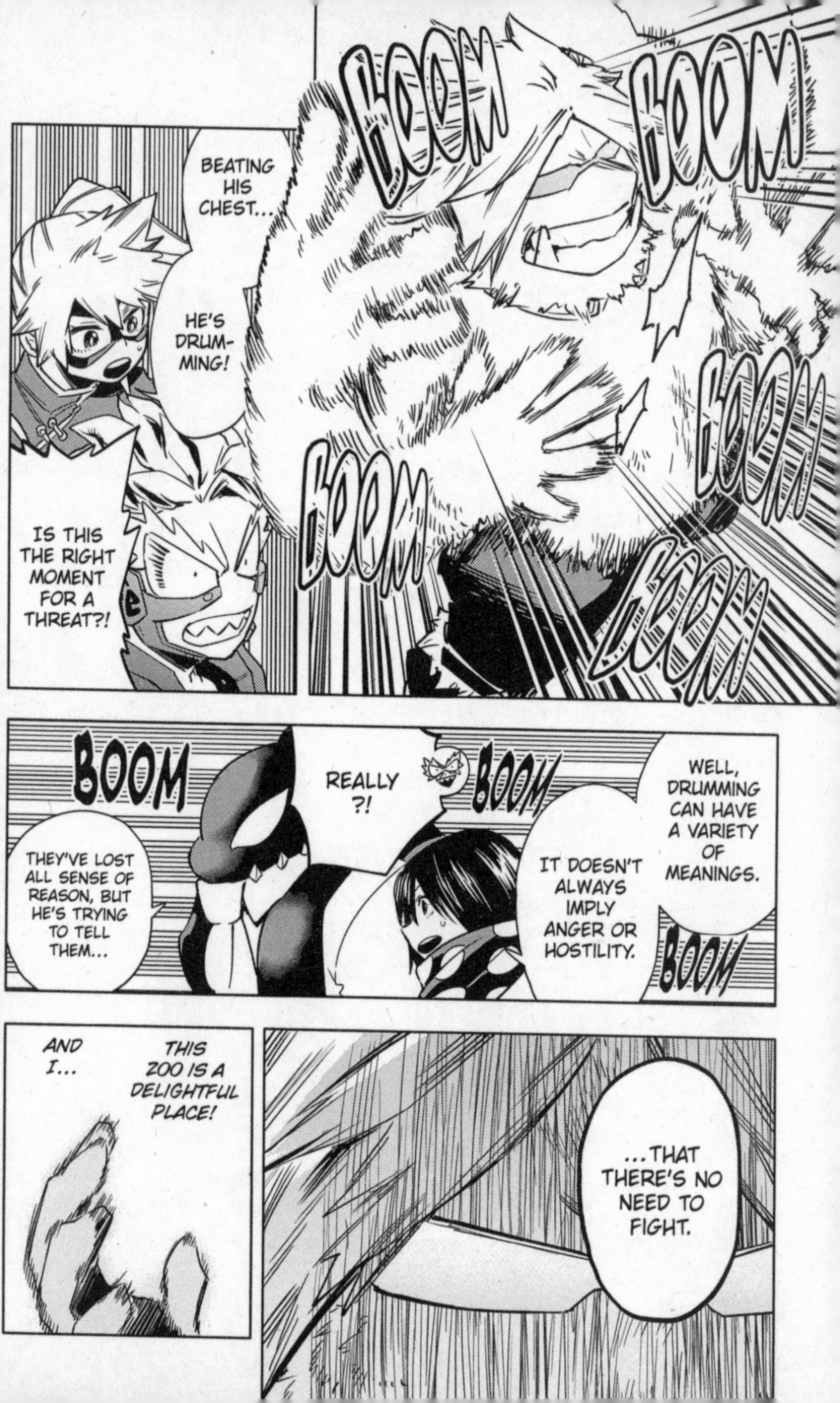
BOOM
BOOM
BOOM
BOOM
BOOM
BEATING HIS CHEST...
HE'S DRUMMING!
IS THIS THE RIGHT MOMENT FOR A THREAT?!
WELL, DRUMMING CAN HAVE A VARIETY OF MEANINGS.
BOOM
IT DOESN'T ALWAYS IMPLY ANGER OR HOSTILITY.
BOOM
REALLY ?!
BOOM
THEY'VE LOST ALL SENSE OF REASON, BUT HE'S TRYING TO TELL THEM...
...THAT THERE'S NO NEED TO FIGHT.
THIS ZOO IS A DELIGHTFUL PLACE!
AND I...

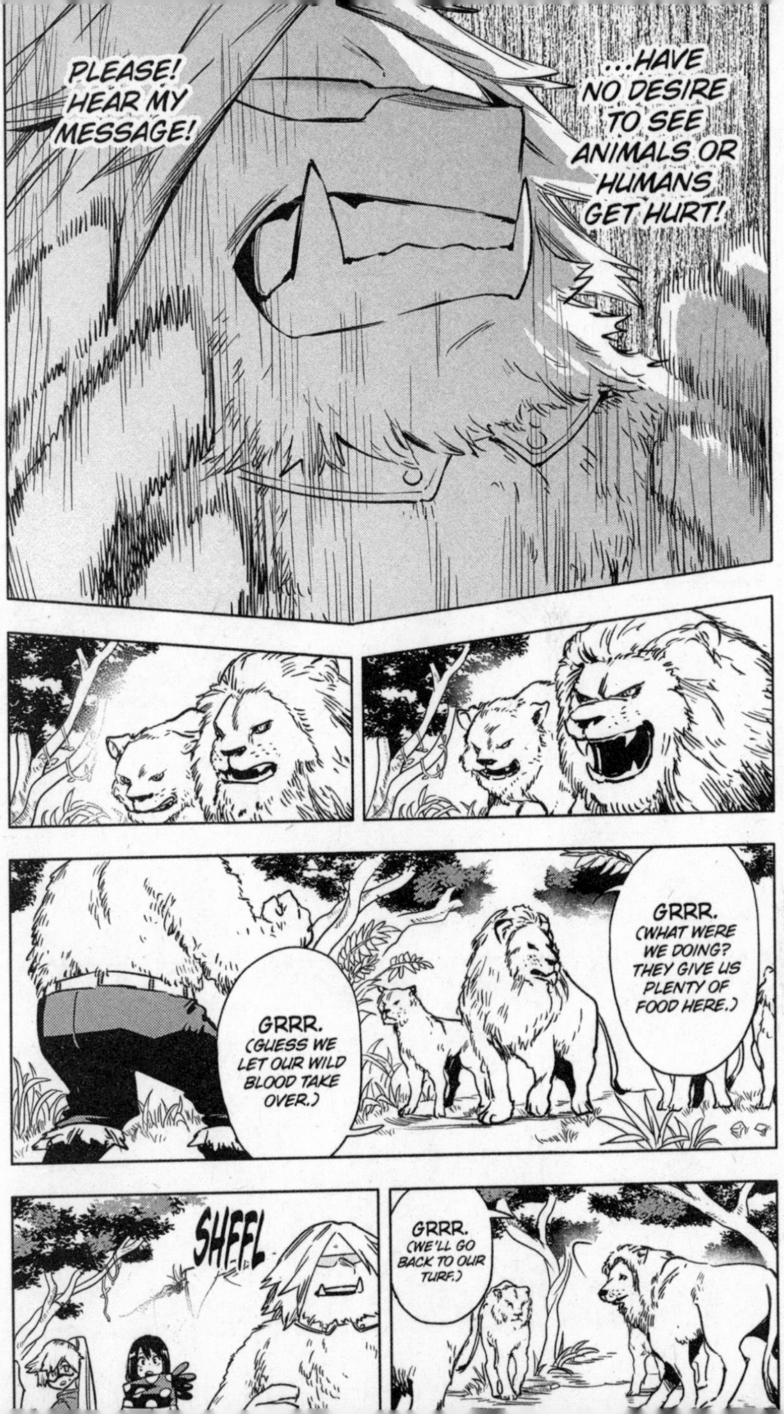
...HAVE NO DESIRE TO SEE ANIMALS OR HUMANS GET HURT!
PLEASE! HEAR MY MESSAGE!
GRRR. (WHAT WERE WE DOING? THEY GIVE US PLENTY OF FOOD HERE.)
GRRR. (GUESS WE LET OUR WILD BLOOD TAKE OVER.)
GRRR. (WE'LL GO BACK TO OUR TURF.)
SHFFL

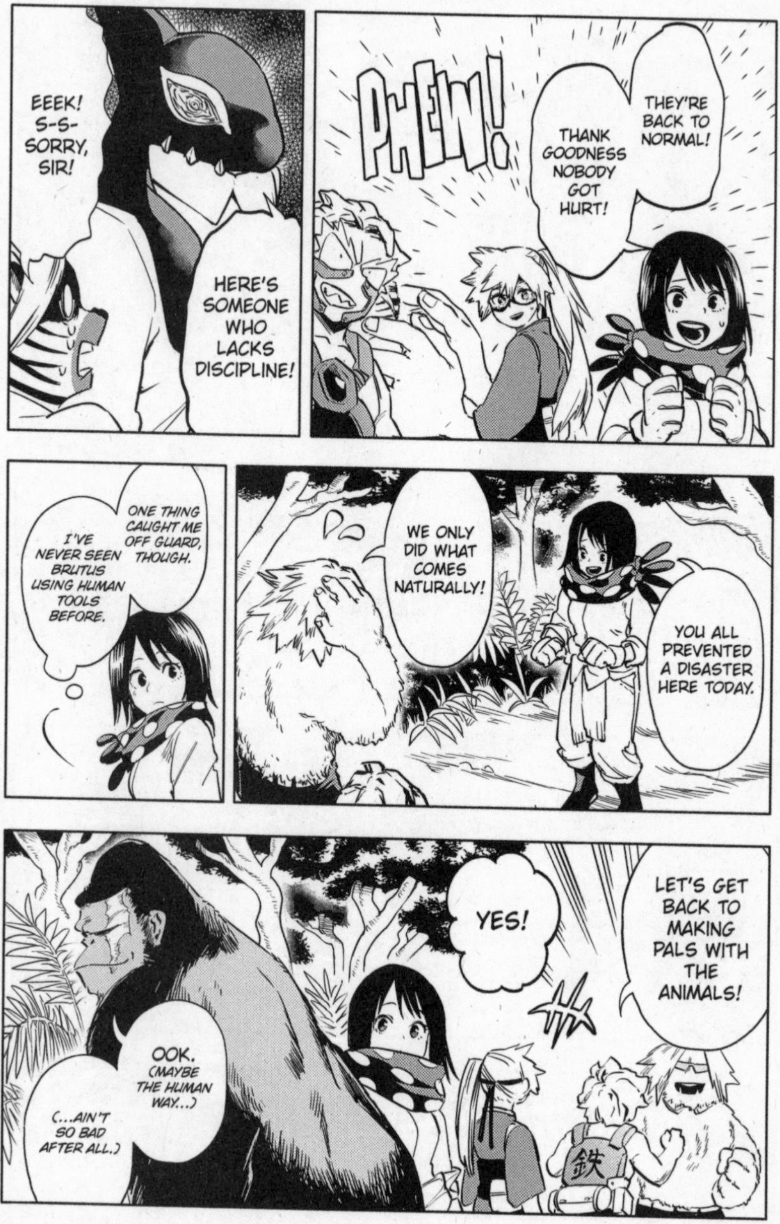
PHEW!
THEY'RE BACK TO NORMAL!
THANK GOODNESS NOBODY GOT HURT!
EEEK! S-S-SORRY, SIR!
HERE'S SOMEONE WHO LACKS DISCIPLINE!
YOU ALL PREVENTED A DISASTER HERE TODAY.
WE ONLY DID WHAT COMES NATURALLY!
ONE THING CAUGHT ME OFF GUARD, THOUGH.
I'VE NEVER SEEN BRUTUS USING HUMAN TOOLS BEFORE.
LET'S GET BACK TO MAKING PALS WITH THE ANIMALS!
YES!
OOK. (MAYBE THE HUMAN WAY...)
(...AIN'T SO BAD AFTER ALL.)
鉄

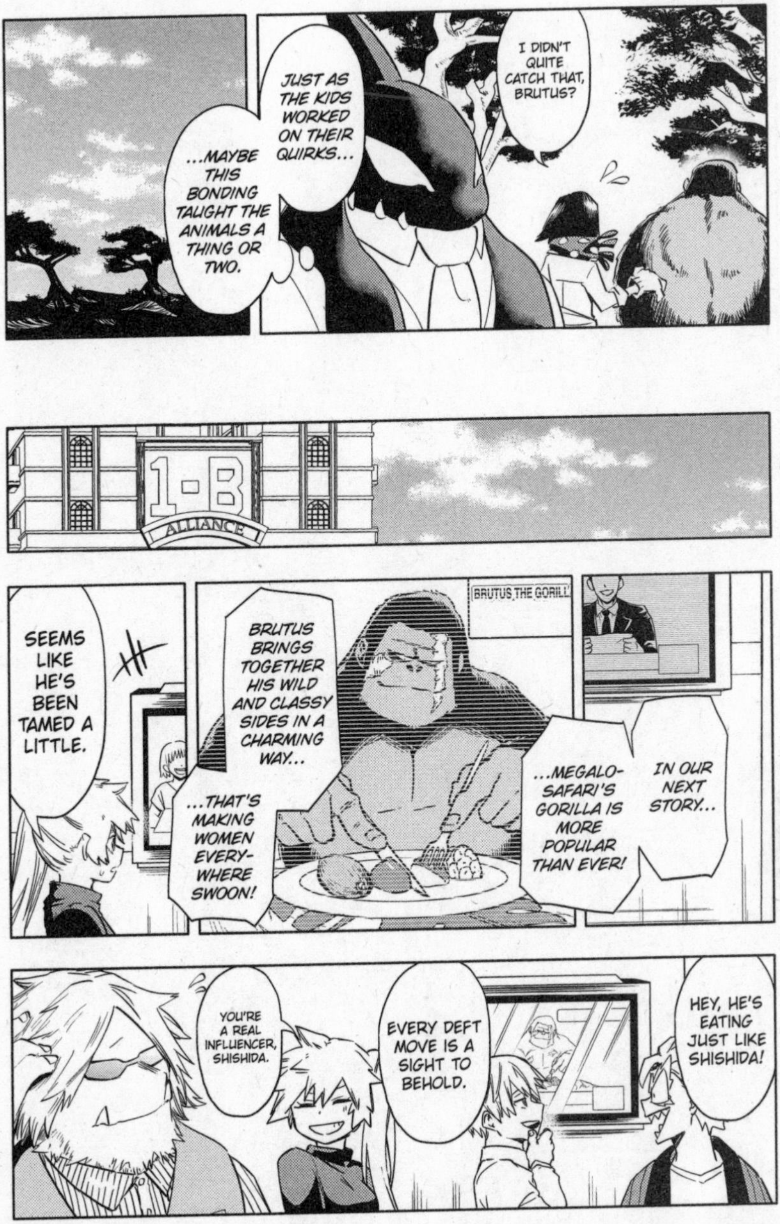
I DIDN'T QUITE CATCH THAT, BRUTUS?
JUST AS THE KIDS WORKED ON THEIR QUIRKS...
...MAYBE THIS BONDING TAUGHT THE ANIMALS A THING OR TWO.
1-B
ALLIANCE
IN OUR NEXT STORY...
...MEGALO-SAFARI'S GORILLA IS MORE POPULAR THAN EVER!
BRUTUS THE GORILL
BRUTUS BRINGS TOGETHER HIS WILD AND CLASSY SIDES IN A CHARMING WAY...
...THAT'S MAKING WOMEN EVERY-WHERE SWOON!
SEEMS LIKE HE'S BEEN TAMED A LITTLE.
HEY, HE'S EATING JUST LIKE SHISHIDA!
EVERY DEFT MOVE IS A SIGHT TO BEHOLD.
YOU'RE A REAL INFLUENCER, SHISHIDA.

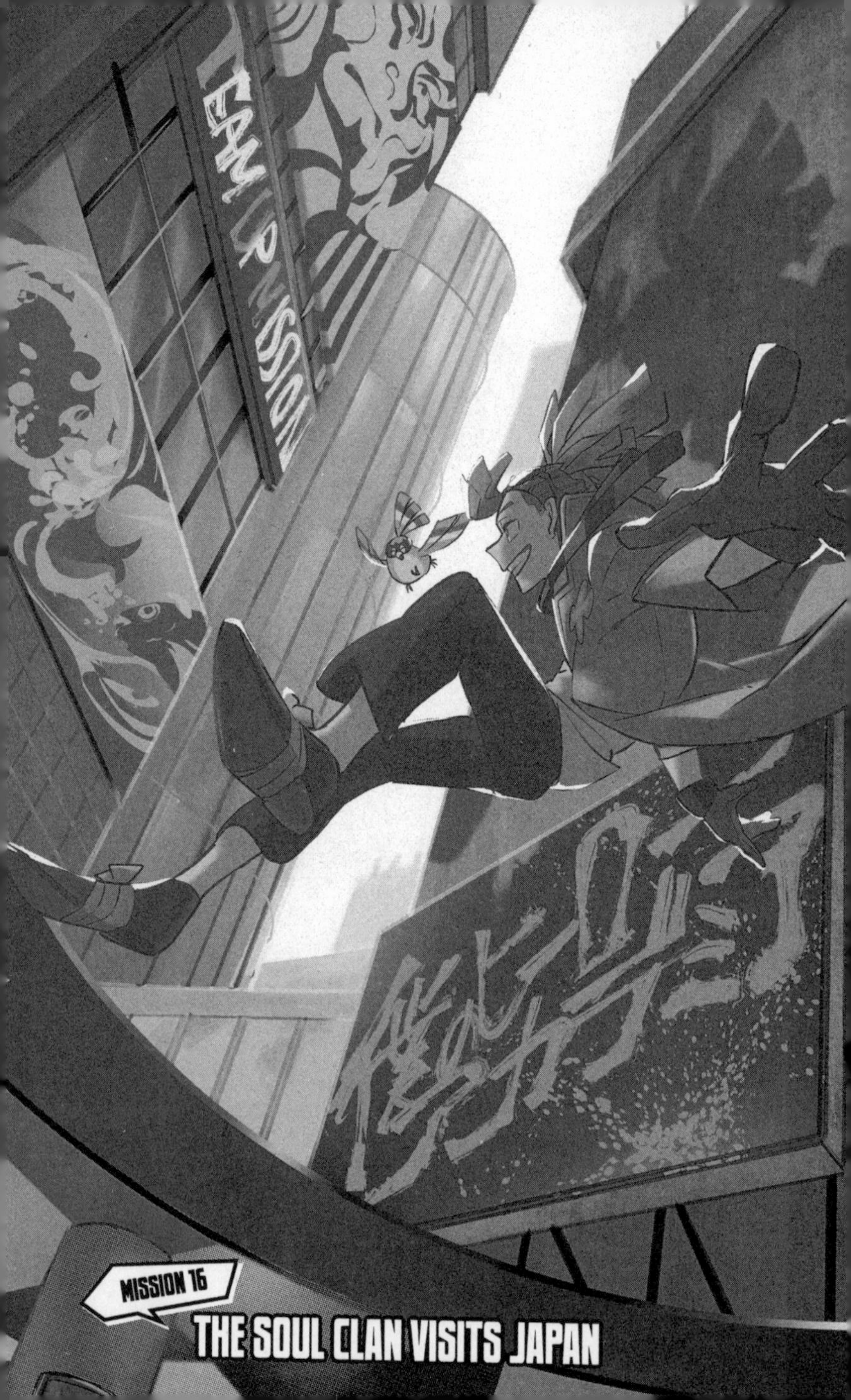
MISSION 16
THE SOUL CLAN VISITS JAPAN

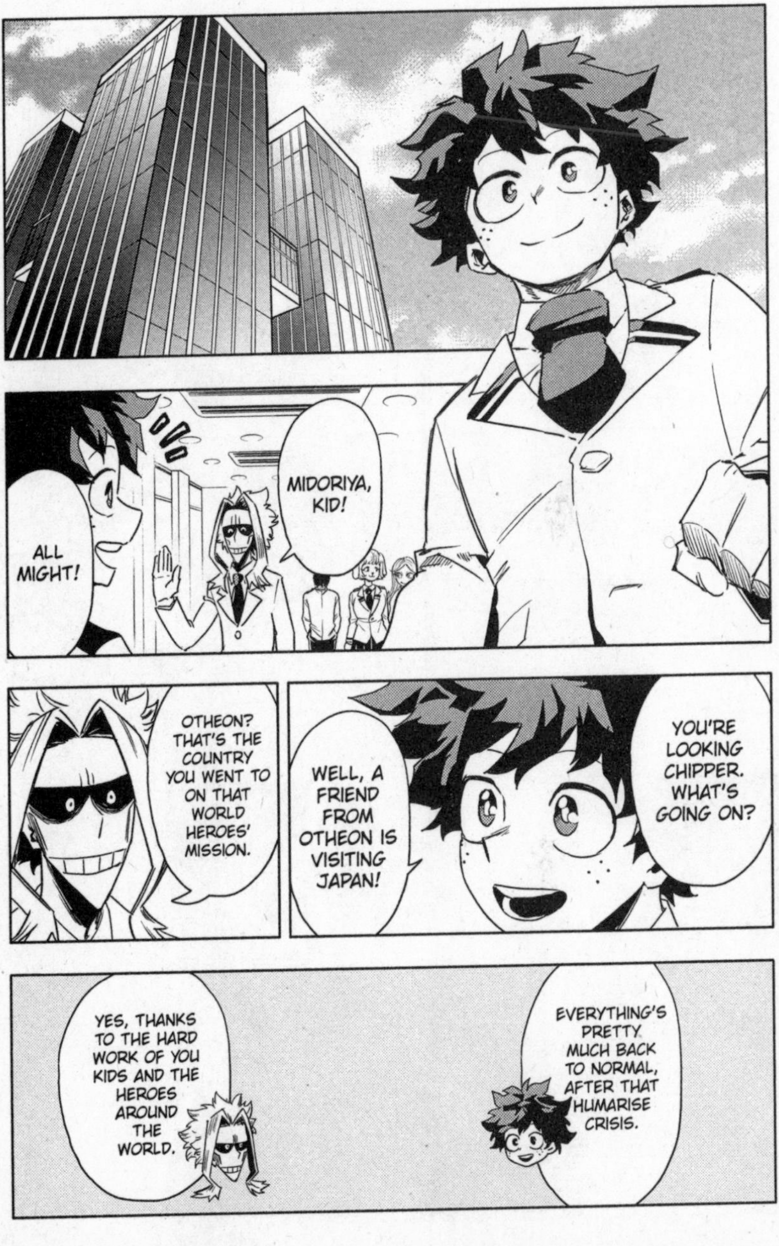
MIDORIYA, KID!
ALL MIGHT!
YOU'RE LOOKING CHIPPER. WHAT'S GOING ON?
WELL, A FRIEND FROM OTHEON IS VISITING JAPAN!
OTHEON? THAT'S THE COUNTRY YOU WENT TO ON THAT WORLD HEROES' MISSION.
EVERYTHING'S PRETTY MUCH BACK TO NORMAL, AFTER THAT HUMARISE CRISIS.
YES, THANKS TO THE HARD WORK OF YOU KIDS AND THE HEROES AROUND THE WORLD.

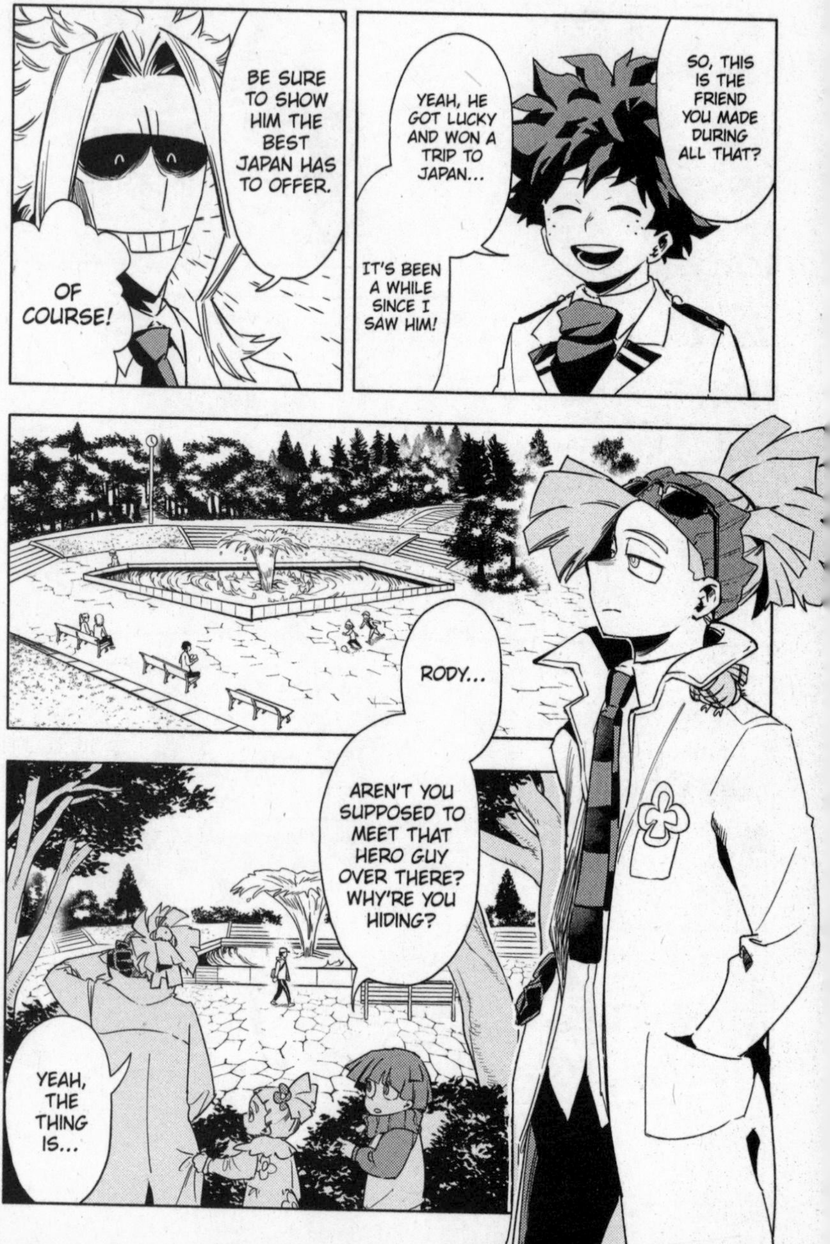
SO, THIS IS THE FRIEND YOU MADE DURING ALL THAT?
YEAH, HE GOT LUCKY AND WON A TRIP TO JAPAN...
IT'S BEEN A WHILE SINCE I SAW HIM!
BE SURE TO SHOW HIM THE BEST JAPAN HAS TO OFFER.
OF COURSE!
RODY...
AREN'T YOU SUPPOSED TO MEET THAT HERO GUY OVER THERE? WHY'RE YOU HIDING?
YEAH, THE THING IS...

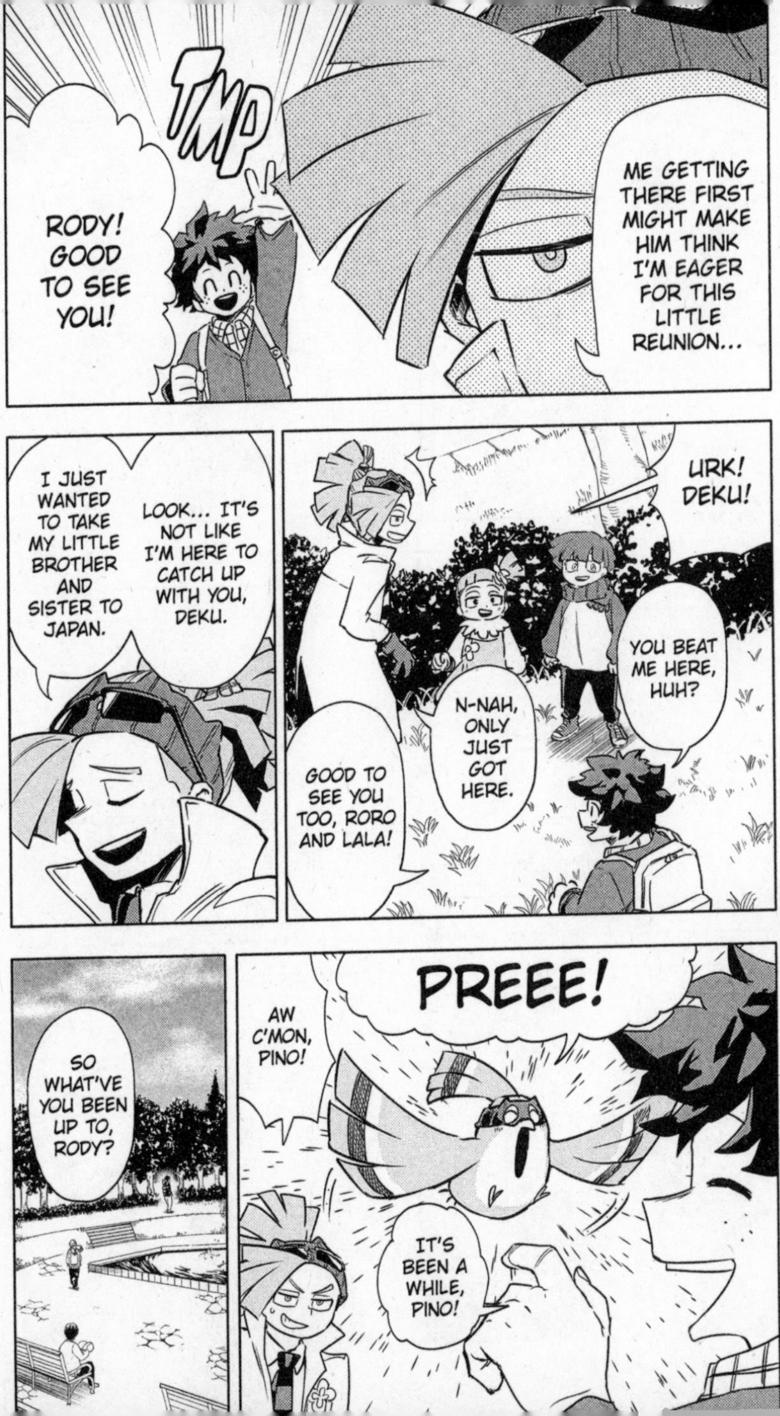
ME GETTING THERE FIRST MIGHT MAKE HIM THINK I'M EAGER FOR THIS LITTLE REUNION...
TMP
RODY! GOOD TO SEE YOU!
URK! DEKU!
YOU BEAT ME HERE, HUH?
N-NAH, ONLY JUST GOT HERE.
GOOD TO SEE YOU TOO, RORO AND LALA!
LOOK... IT'S NOT LIKE I'M HERE TO CATCH UP WITH YOU, DEKU.
I JUST WANTED TO TAKE MY LITTLE BROTHER AND SISTER TO JAPAN.
PREEE!
AW C'MON, PINO!
IT'S BEEN A WHILE, PINO!
SO WHAT'VE YOU BEEN UP TO, RODY?

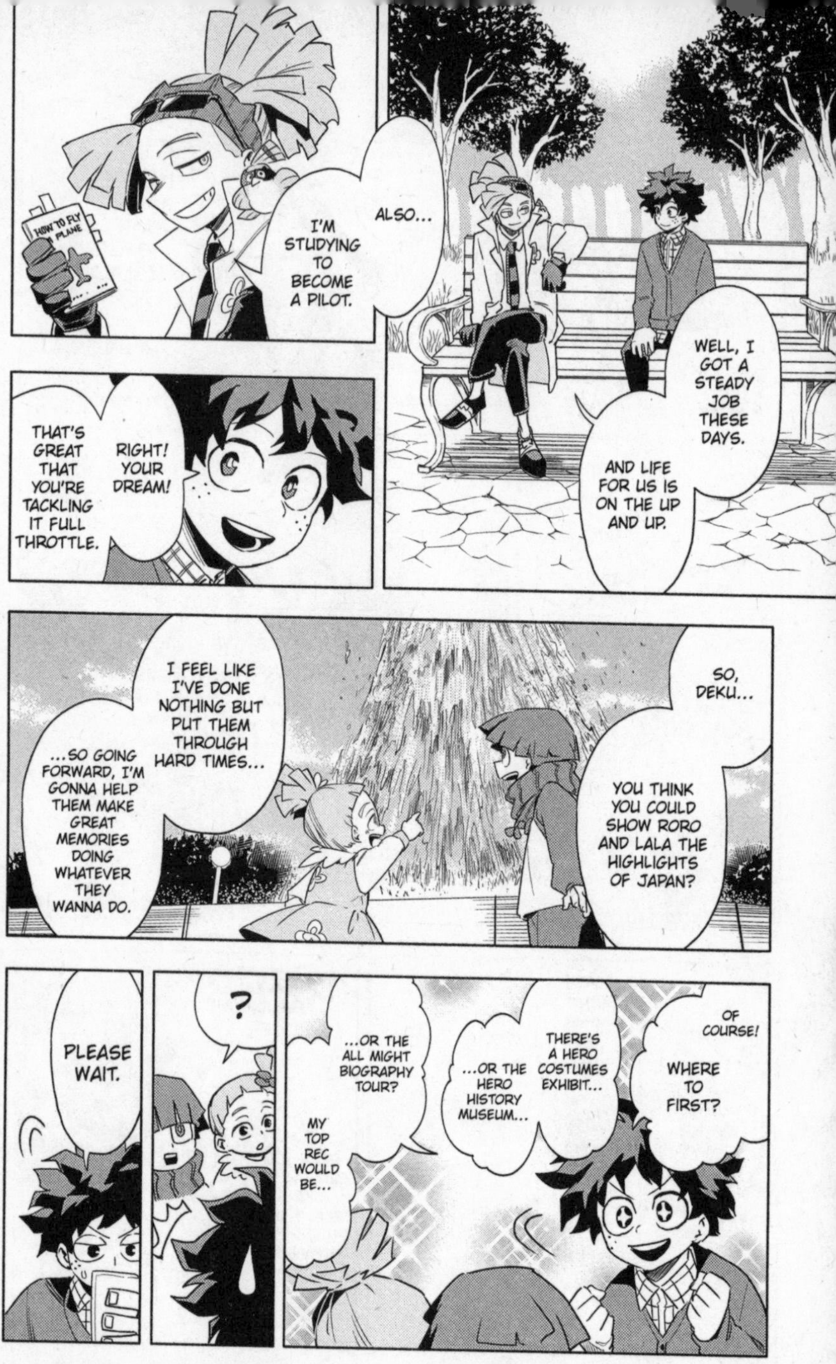
WELL, I GOT A STEADY JOB THESE DAYS.
AND LIFE FOR US IS ON THE UP AND UP.
ALSO...
I'M STUDYING TO BECOME A PILOT.
HOW TO FLY
PLANE
RIGHT! YOUR DREAM!
THAT'S GREAT THAT YOU'RE TACKLING IT FULL THROTTLE.
SO, DEKU...
YOU THINK YOU COULD SHOW RORO AND LALA THE HIGHLIGHTS OF JAPAN?
I FEEL LIKE I'VE DONE NOTHING BUT PUT THEM THROUGH HARD TIMES...
...SO GOING FORWARD, I'M GONNA HELP THEM MAKE GREAT MEMORIES DOING WHATEVER THEY WANNA DO.
OF COURSE!
WHERE TO FIRST?
THERE'S A HERO COSTUMES EXHIBIT...
...OR THE HERO HISTORY MUSEUM...
...OR THE ALL MIGHT BIOGRAPHY TOUR?
MY TOP REC WOULD BE...
?
PLEASE WAIT.

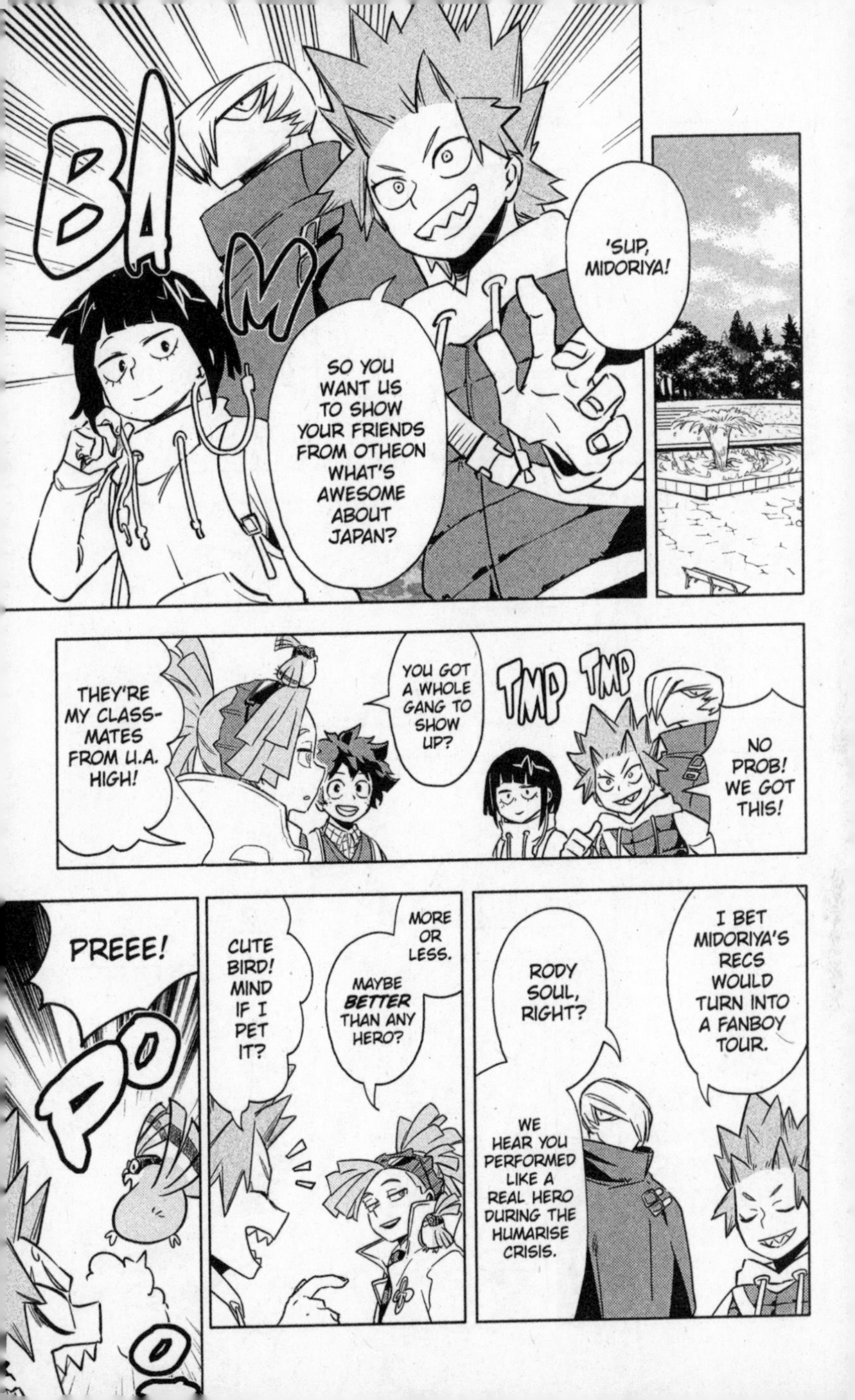
'SUP, MIDORIYA!
BAM
SO YOU WANT US TO SHOW YOUR FRIENDS FROM OTHEON WHAT'S AWESOME ABOUT JAPAN?
NO PROB! WE GOT THIS!
TMP TMP
YOU GOT A WHOLE GANG TO SHOW UP?
THEY'RE MY CLASSMATES FROM U.A. HIGH!
I BET MIDORIYA'S RECS WOULD TURN INTO A FANBOY TOUR.
RODY SOUL, RIGHT?
WE HEAR YOU PERFORMED LIKE A REAL HERO DURING THE HUMARISE CRISIS.
MORE OR LESS.
MAYBE *BETTER* THAN ANY HERO?
CUTE BIRD! MIND IF I PET IT?
PREEE!
POO

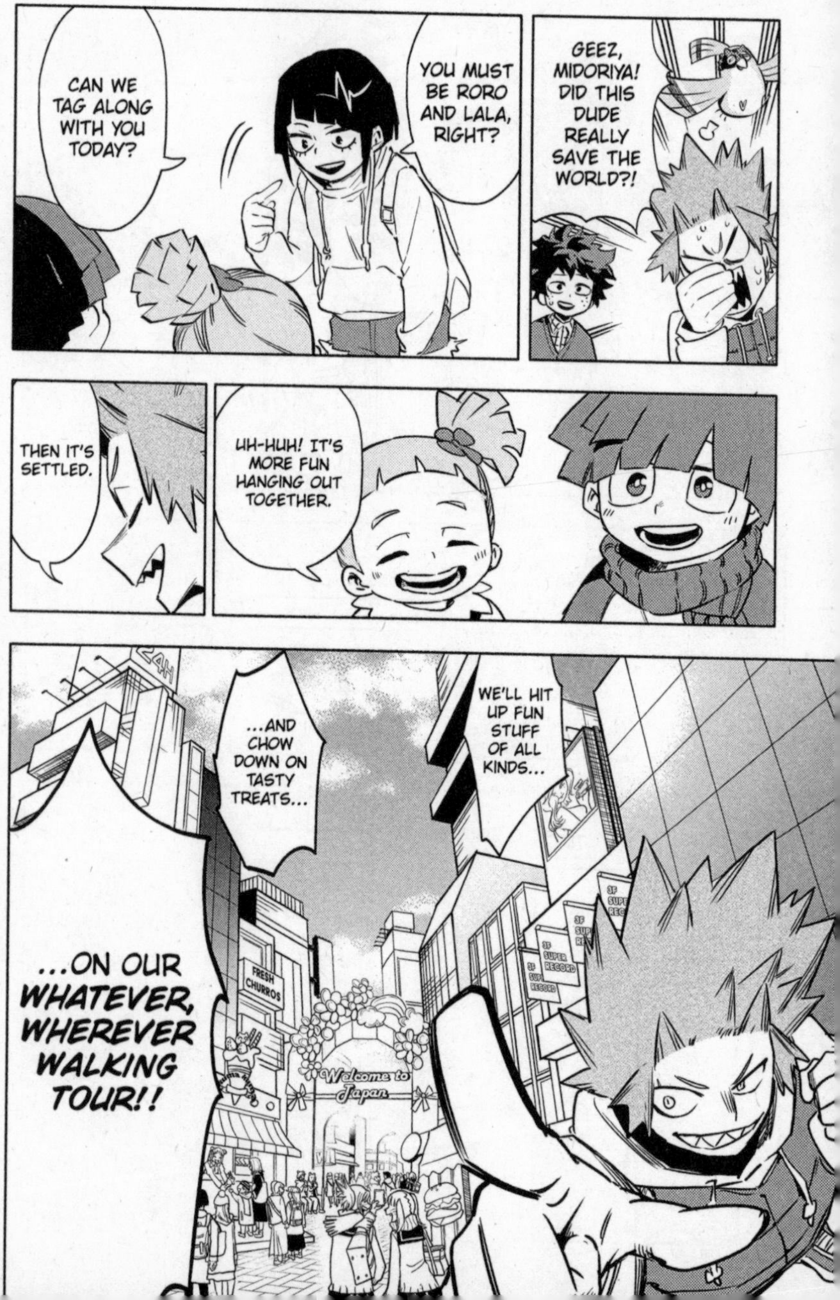
GEEZ, MIDORIYA! DID THIS DUDE REALLY SAVE THE WORLD?!
YOU MUST BE RORO AND LALA, RIGHT?
CAN WE TAG ALONG WITH YOU TODAY?
UH-HUH! IT'S MORE FUN HANGING OUT TOGETHER.
THEN IT'S SETTLED.
24H
WE'LL HIT UP FUN STUFF OF ALL KINDS...
...AND CHOW DOWN ON TASTY TREATS...
3F SUPER RECORD
FRESH CHURROS
Welcome to Japan
...ON OUR WHATEVER, WHEREVER WALKING TOUR!!

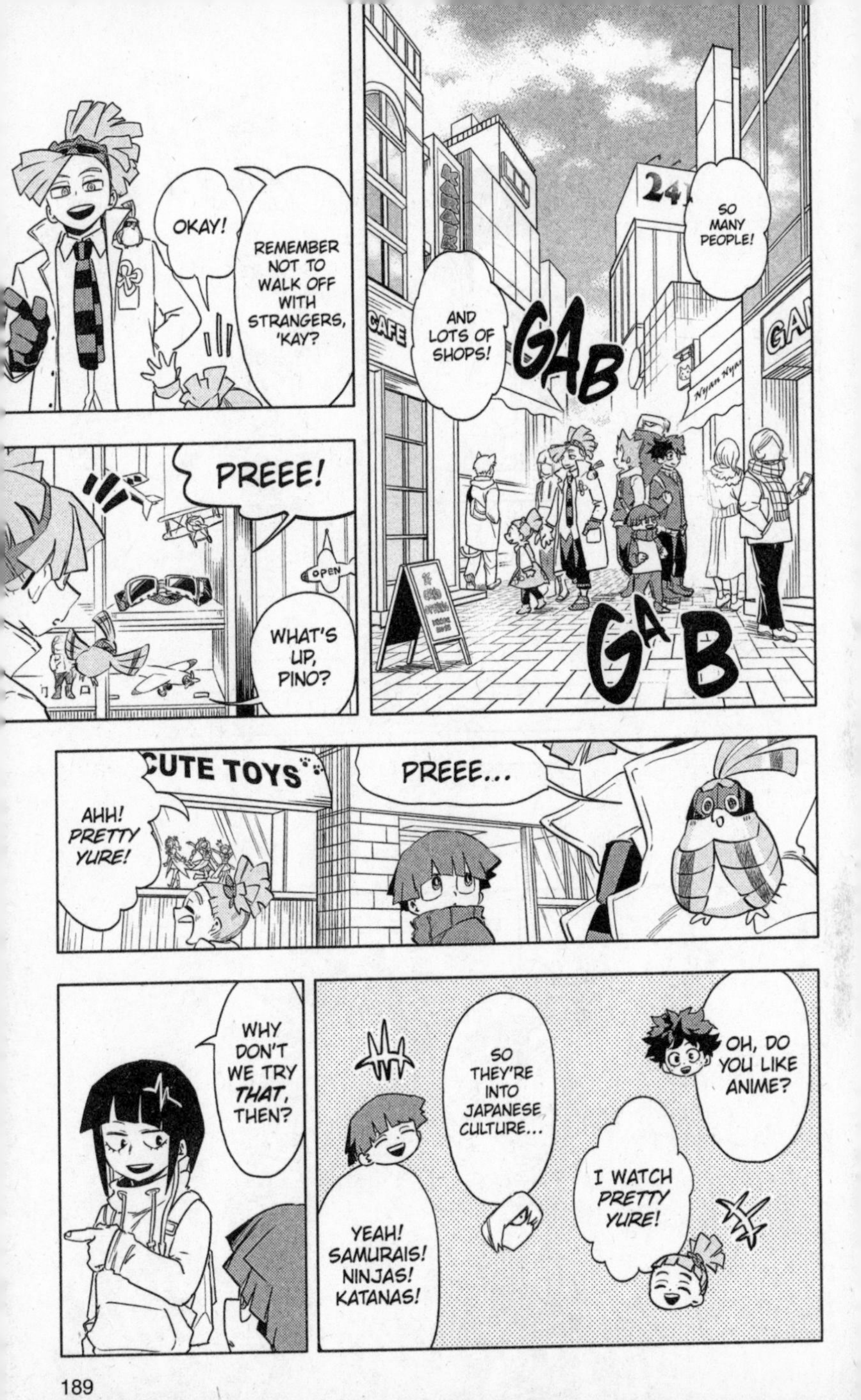
SO MANY PEOPLE!
AND LOTS OF SHOPS!
GAB
GAB
CAFE
OPEN
Nyan Nyan
REMEMBER NOT TO WALK OFF WITH STRANGERS, 'KAY?
OKAY!
PREEE!
WHAT'S UP, PINO?
PREEE...
CUTE TOYS
AHH! *PRETTY YURE!*
OH, DO YOU LIKE ANIME?
I WATCH *PRETTY YURE!*
SO THEY'RE INTO JAPANESE CULTURE...
YEAH! SAMURAIS! NINJAS! KATANAS!
WHY DON'T WE TRY *THAT*, THEN?

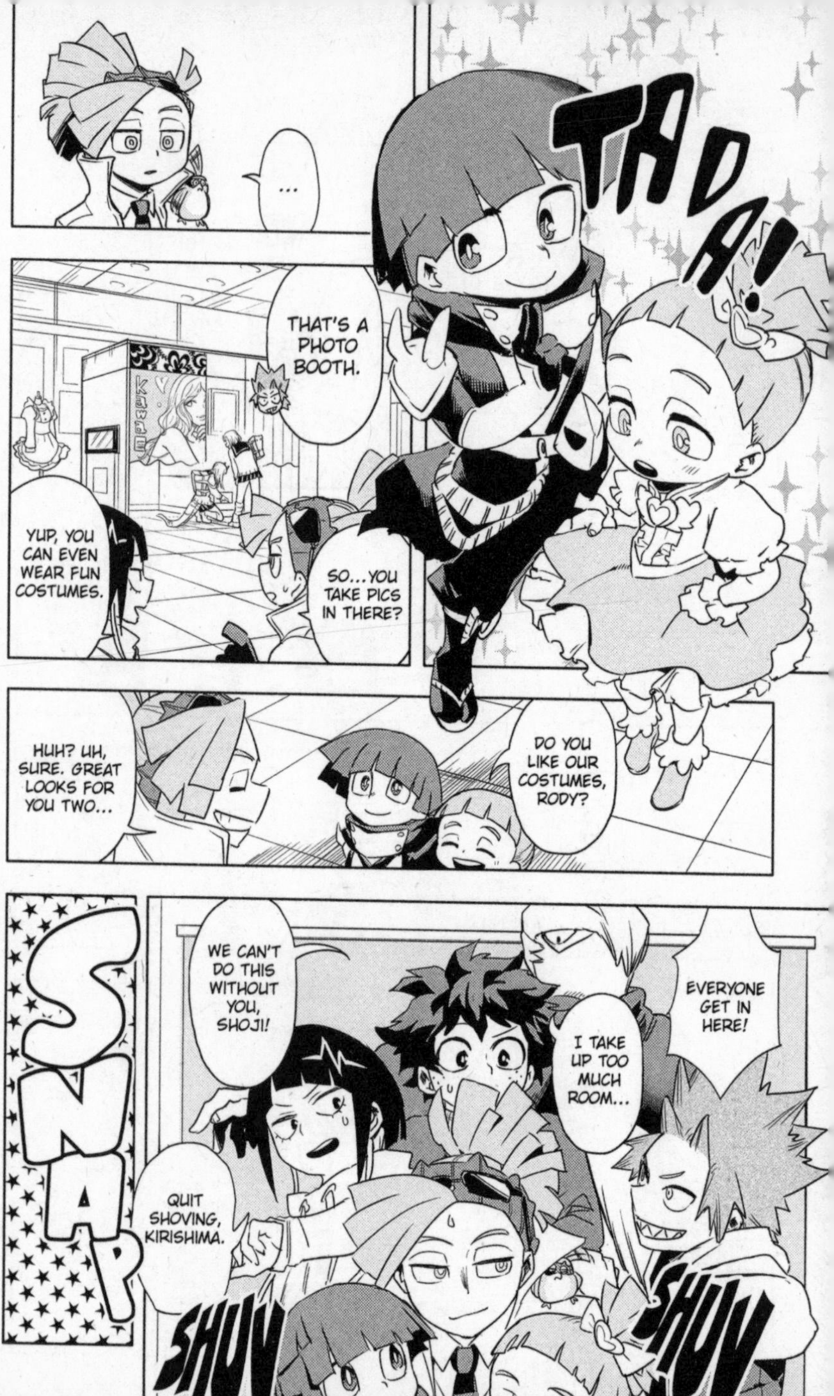

TA DA!
...
THAT'S A PHOTO BOOTH.
SO...YOU TAKE PICS IN THERE?
YUP, YOU CAN EVEN WEAR FUN COSTUMES.
DO YOU LIKE OUR COSTUMES, RODY?
HUH? UH, SURE. GREAT LOOKS FOR YOU TWO...
EVERYONE GET IN HERE!
I TAKE UP TOO MUCH ROOM...
WE CAN'T DO THIS WITHOUT YOU, SHOJI!
SHUV
QUIT SHOVING, KIRISHIMA.
SHUV
SNAP

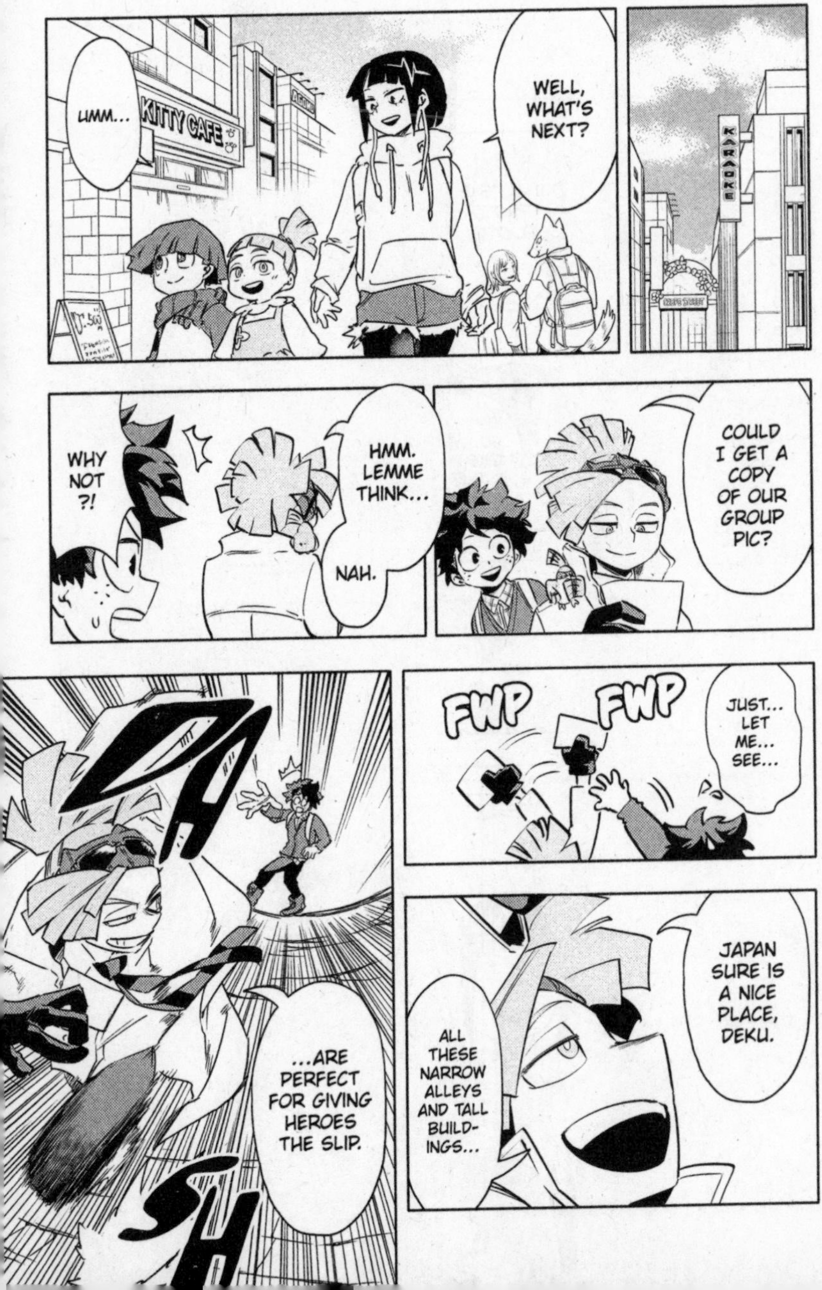
KARAOKE
WELL, WHAT'S NEXT?
UMM...
KITTY CAFE
COULD I GET A COPY OF OUR GROUP PIC?
HMM. LEMME THINK...
NAH.
WHY NOT ?!
JUST... LET ME... SEE...
FWP FWP
JAPAN SURE IS A NICE PLACE, DEKU.
ALL THESE NARROW ALLEYS AND TALL BUILD-INGS...
...ARE PERFECT FOR GIVING HEROES THE SLIP.
DASH

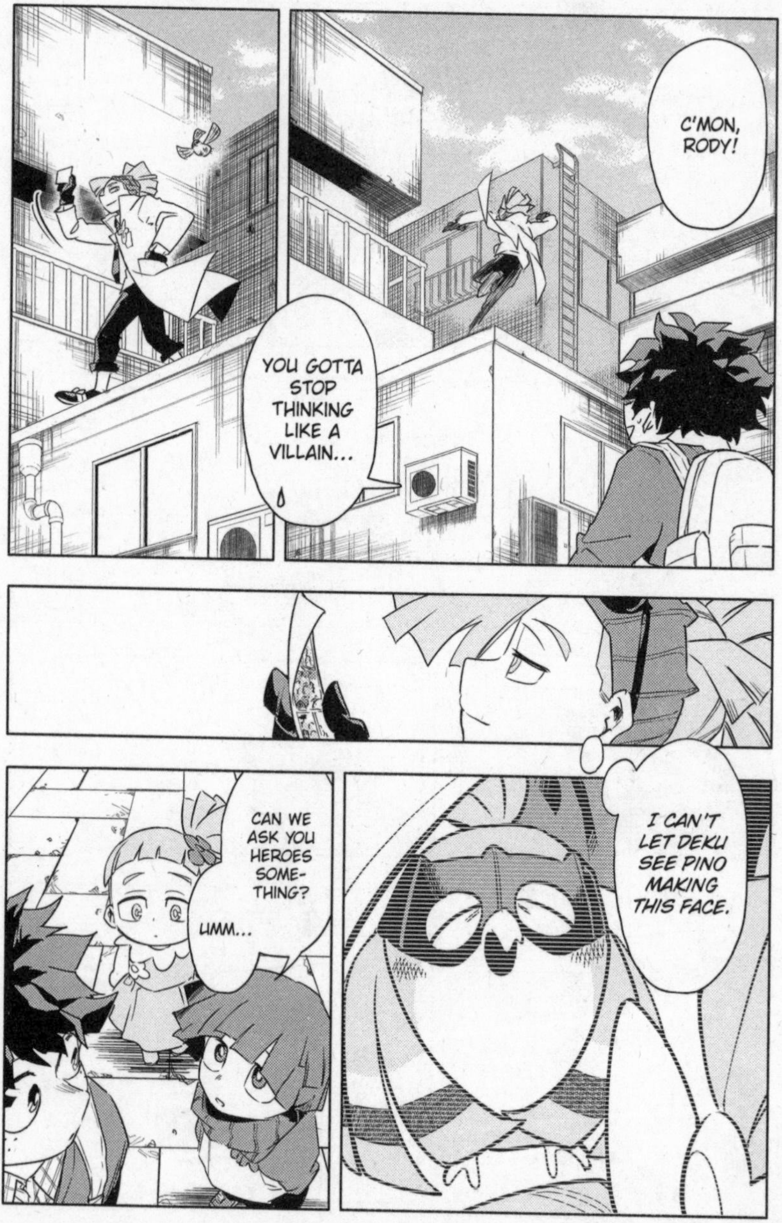
C'MON, RODY!
YOU GOTTA STOP THINKING LIKE A VILLAIN...
I CAN'T LET DEKU SEE PINO MAKING THIS FACE.
CAN WE ASK YOU HEROES SOME-THING?
UMM...

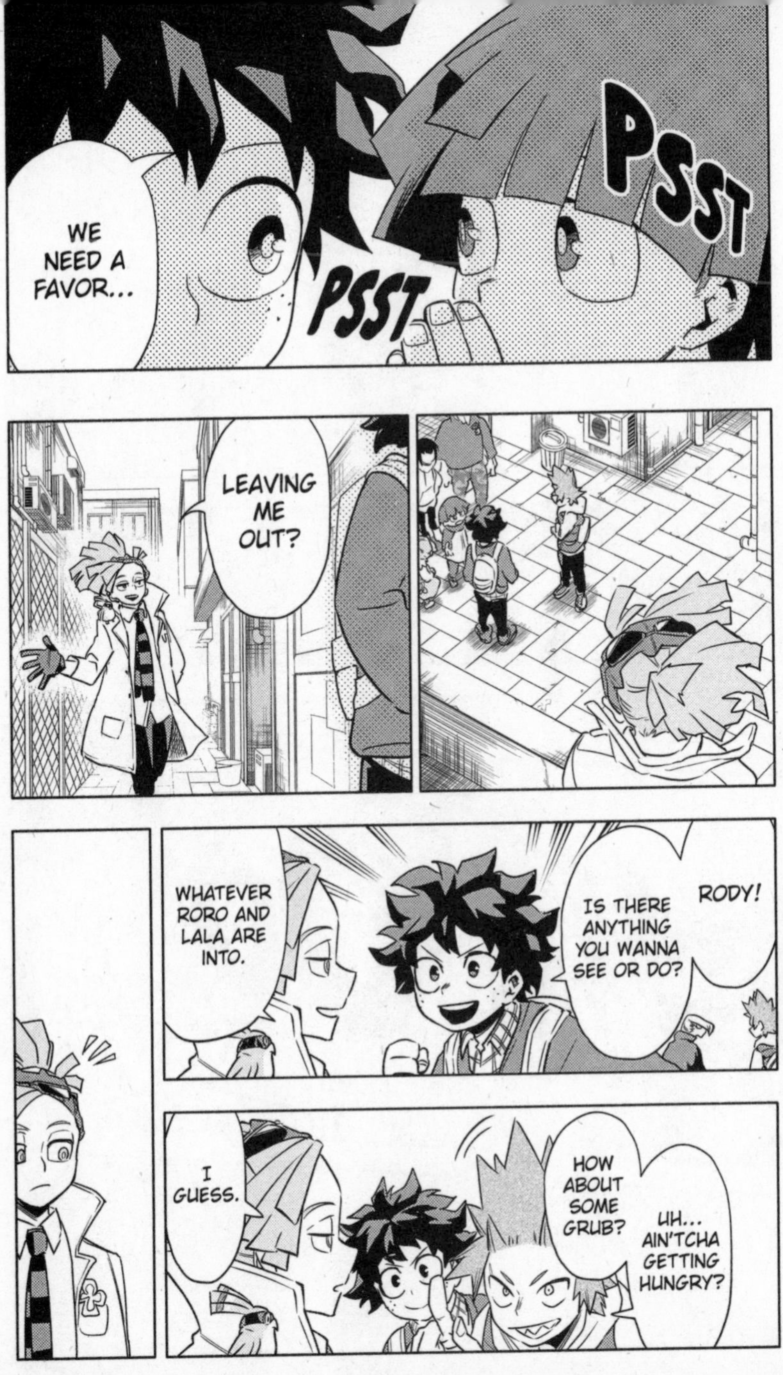
PSST
PSST
WE NEED A FAVOR...
LEAVING ME OUT?
RODY!
IS THERE ANYTHING YOU WANNA SEE OR DO?
WHATEVER RORO AND LALA ARE INTO.
UH... AIN'TCHA GETTING HUNGRY?
HOW ABOUT SOME GRUB?
I GUESS.

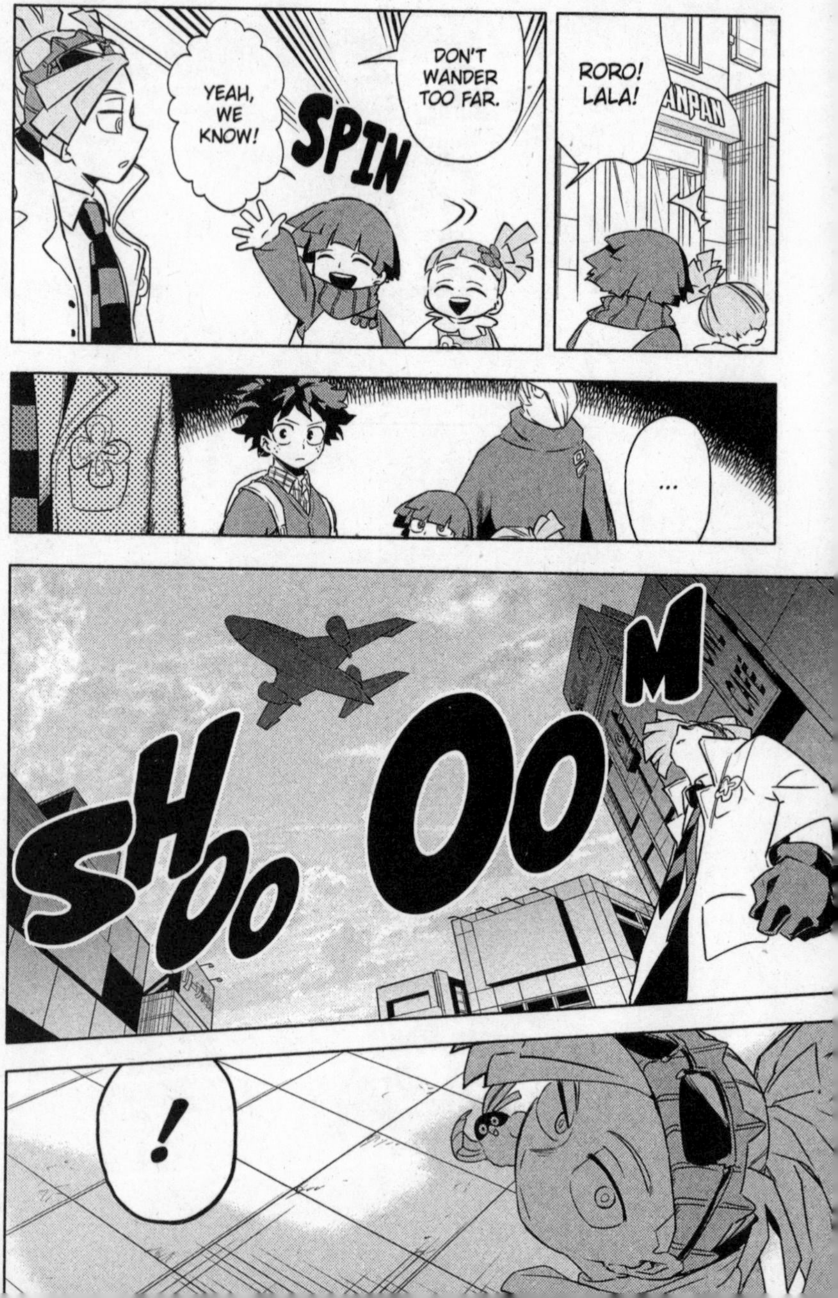
RORO! LALA!
DON'T WANDER TOO FAR.
YEAH, WE KNOW!
SPIN
...
SHOOOOM
!

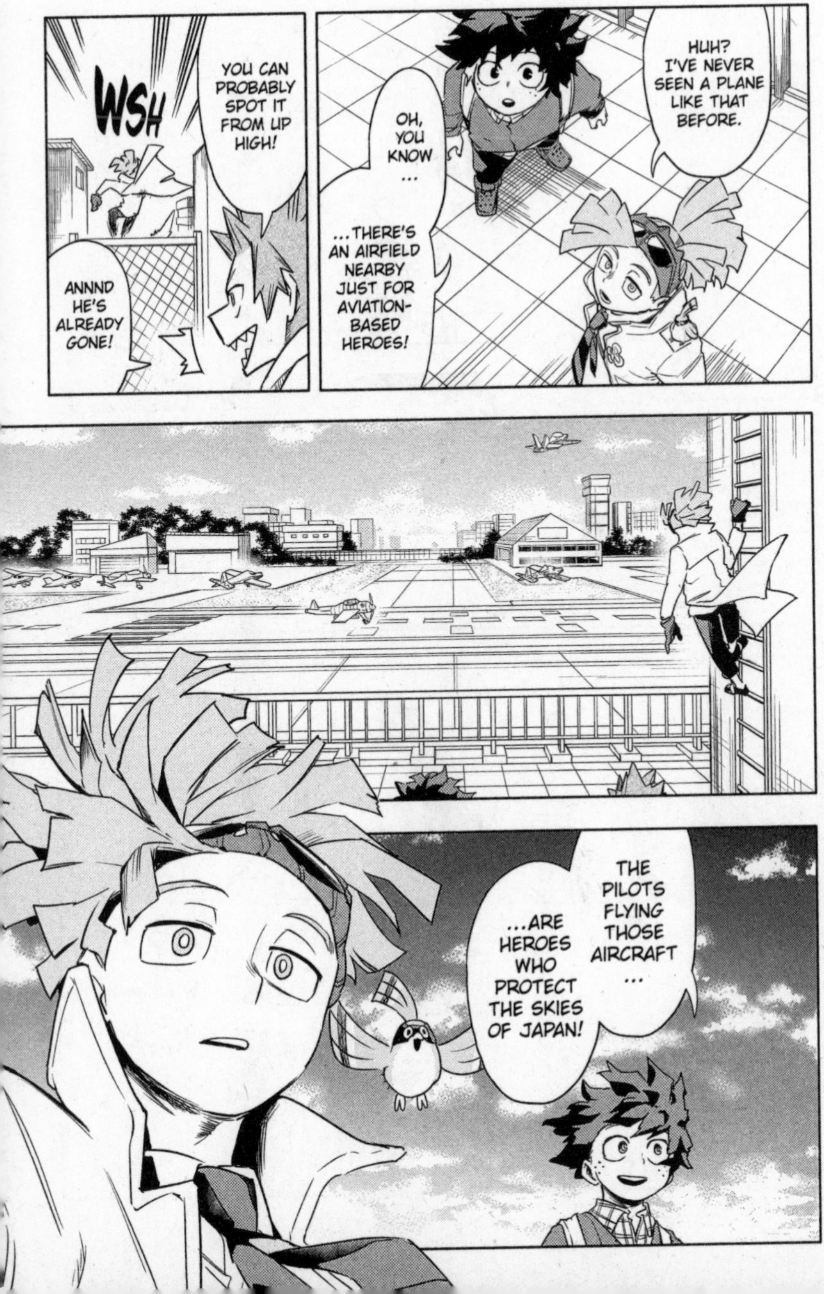
HUH? I'VE NEVER SEEN A PLANE LIKE THAT BEFORE.
OH, YOU KNOW ...
...THERE'S AN AIRFIELD NEARBY JUST FOR AVIATION-BASED HEROES!
YOU CAN PROBABLY SPOT IT FROM UP HIGH!
WSH
ANNND HE'S ALREADY GONE!
THE PILOTS FLYING THOSE AIRCRAFT ...
...ARE HEROES WHO PROTECT THE SKIES OF JAPAN!

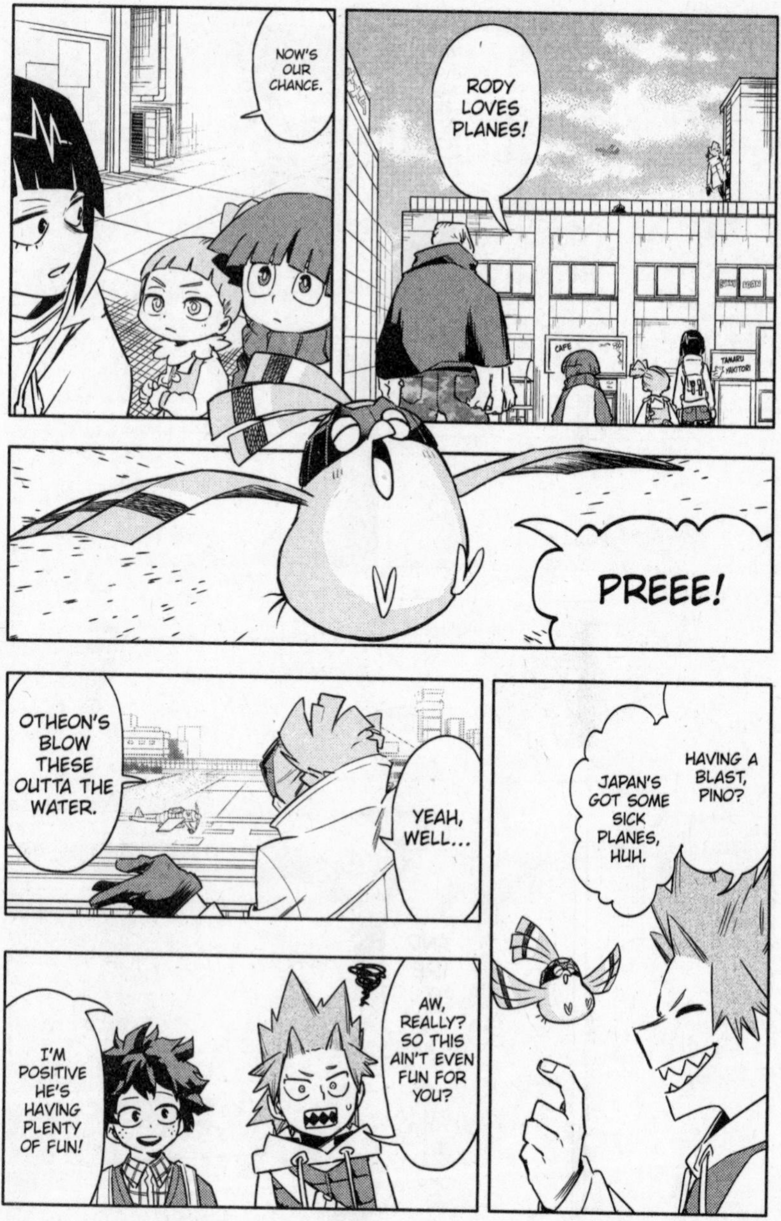
RODY LOVES PLANES!
CAFE
TAMARU YAKITORI
NOW'S OUR CHANCE.
PREEE!
HAVING A BLAST, PINO?
JAPAN'S GOT SOME SICK PLANES, HUH.
YEAH, WELL...
OTHEON'S BLOW THESE OUTTA THE WATER.
AW, REALLY? SO THIS AIN'T EVEN FUN FOR YOU?
I'M POSITIVE HE'S HAVING PLENTY OF FUN!

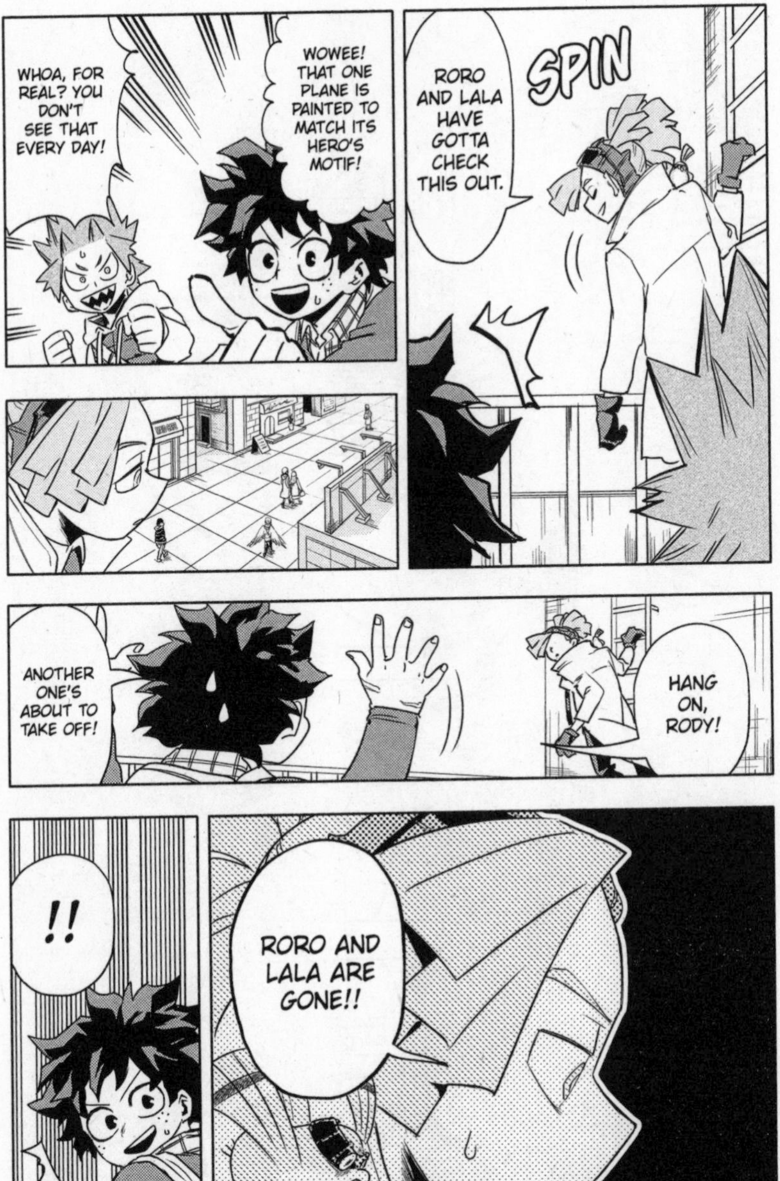
SPIN
RORO AND LALA HAVE GOTTA CHECK THIS OUT.
WOWEE! THAT ONE PLANE IS PAINTED TO MATCH ITS HERO'S MOTIF!
WHOA, FOR REAL? YOU DON'T SEE THAT EVERY DAY!
HANG ON, RODY!
ANOTHER ONE'S ABOUT TO TAKE OFF!
RORO AND LALA ARE GONE!!
!!

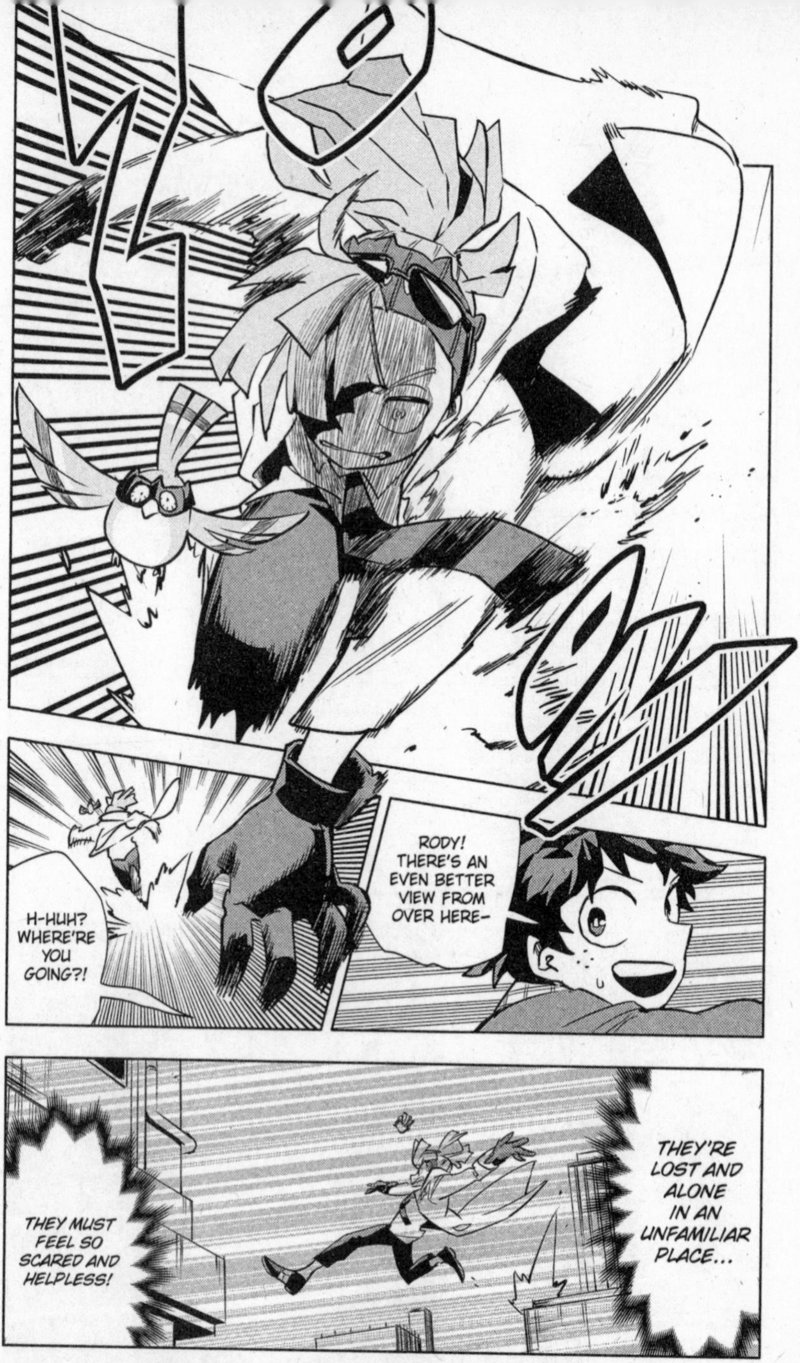
RODY! THERE'S AN EVEN BETTER VIEW FROM OVER HERE-
H-HUH? WHERE'RE YOU GOING?!
THEY'RE LOST AND ALONE IN AN UNFAMILIAR PLACE...
THEY MUST FEEL SO SCARED AND HELPLESS!

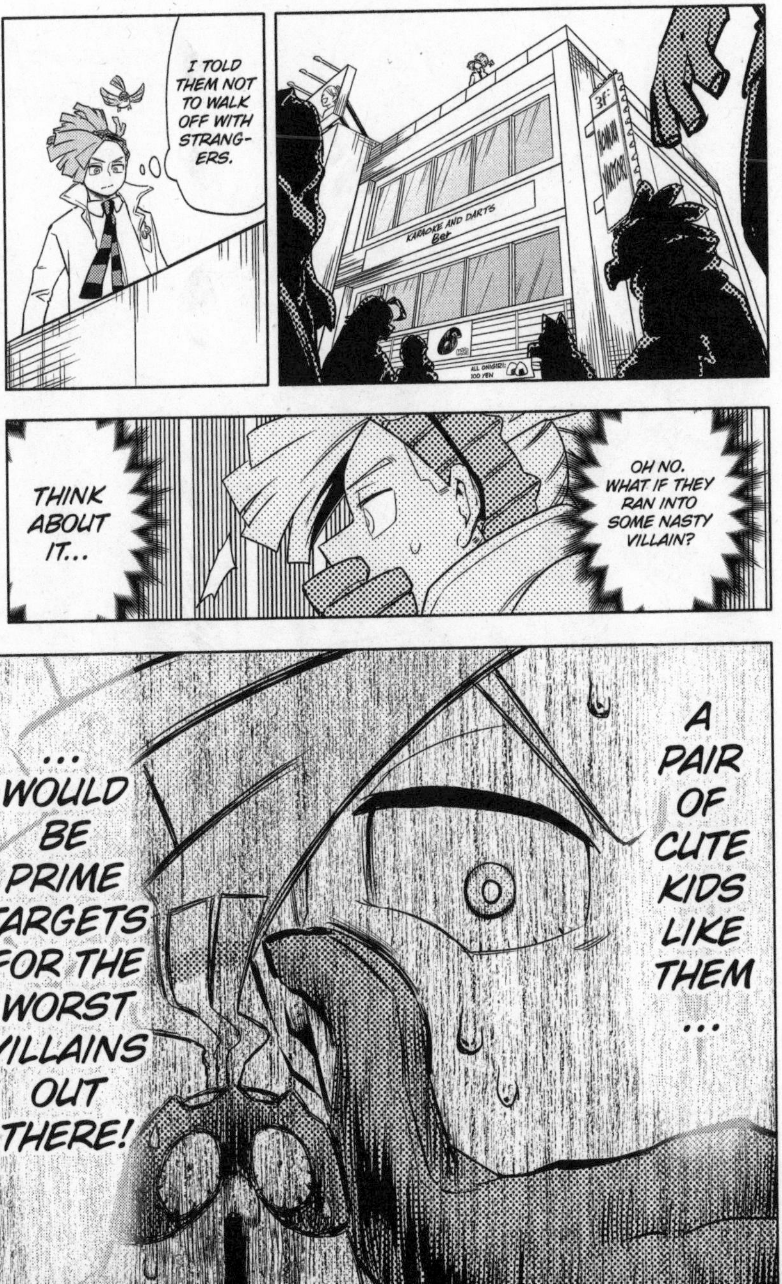
KARAOKE AND DARTS Bar
ALL ONIGIRI: 100 YEN
I TOLD THEM NOT TO WALK OFF WITH STRANGERS.
OH NO. WHAT IF THEY RAN INTO SOME NASTY VILLAIN?
THINK ABOUT IT...
A PAIR OF CUTE KIDS LIKE THEM...
...WOULD BE PRIME TARGETS FOR THE WORST VILLAINS OUT THERE!

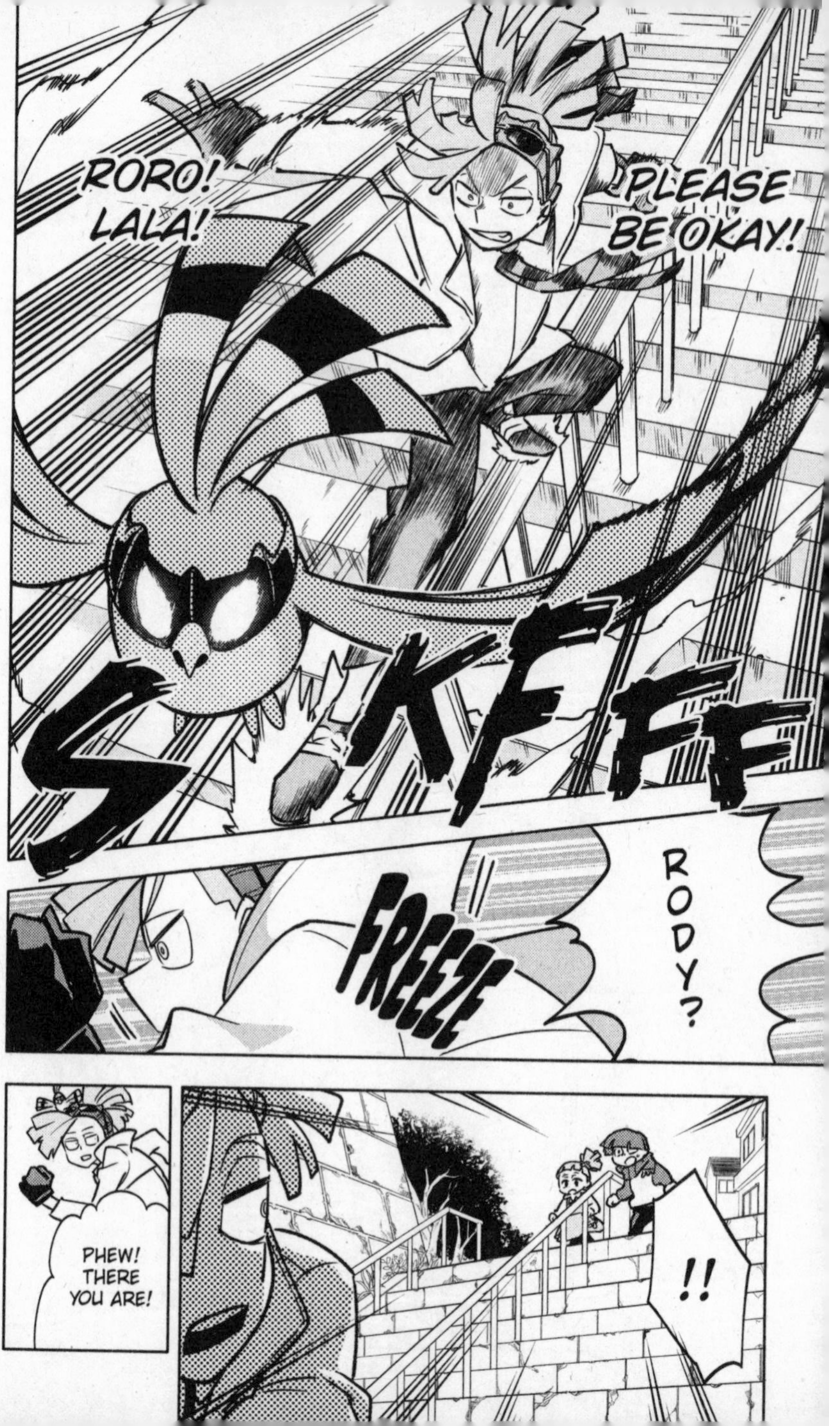
PLEASE BE OKAY!
RORO! LALA!
SKFFF
RODY?
FREEZE
!!
PHEW! THERE YOU ARE!

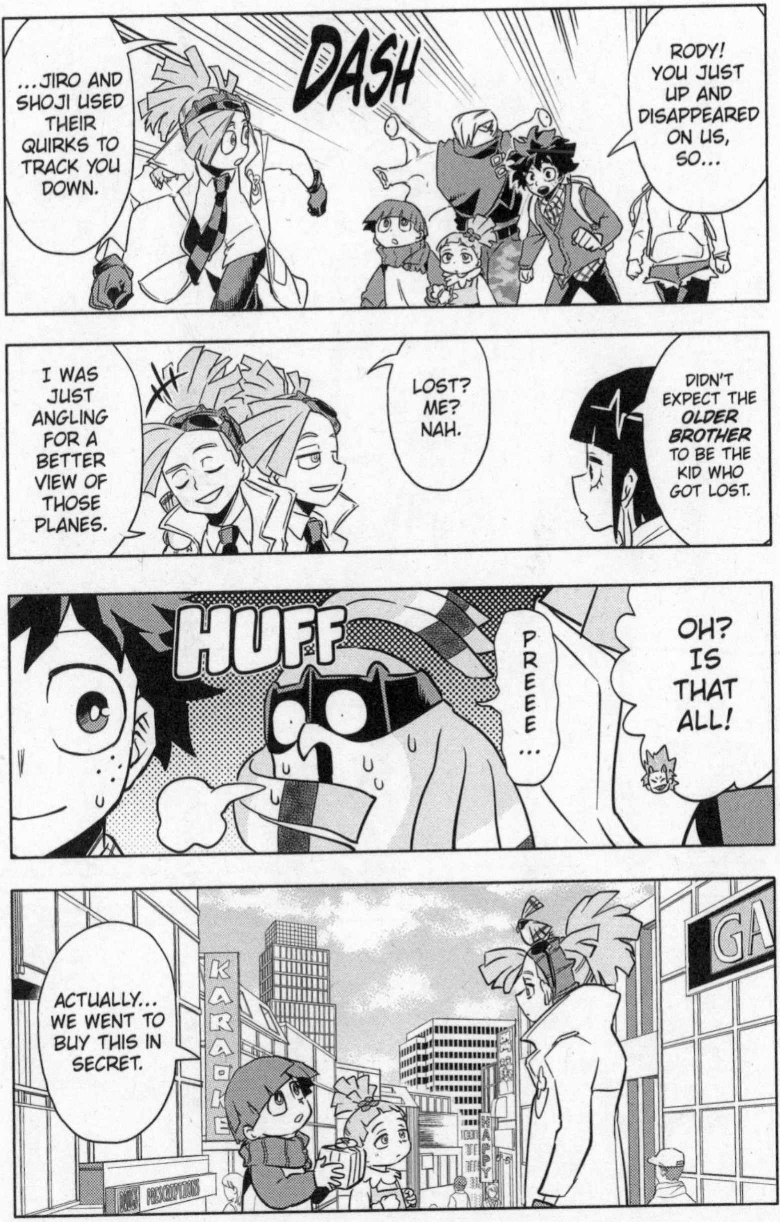
RODY! YOU JUST UP AND DISAPPEARED ON US, SO...
DASH
...JIRO AND SHOJI USED THEIR QUIRKS TO TRACK YOU DOWN.
DIDN'T EXPECT THE *OLDER BROTHER* TO BE THE KID WHO GOT LOST.
LOST? ME? NAH.
I WAS JUST ANGLING FOR A BETTER VIEW OF THOSE PLANES.
OH? IS THAT ALL!
PREEE...
HUFF
GA
KARAOKE
HAPPY
ACTUALLY... WE WENT TO BUY THIS IN SECRET.
DRUGS
PRESCRIPTIONS

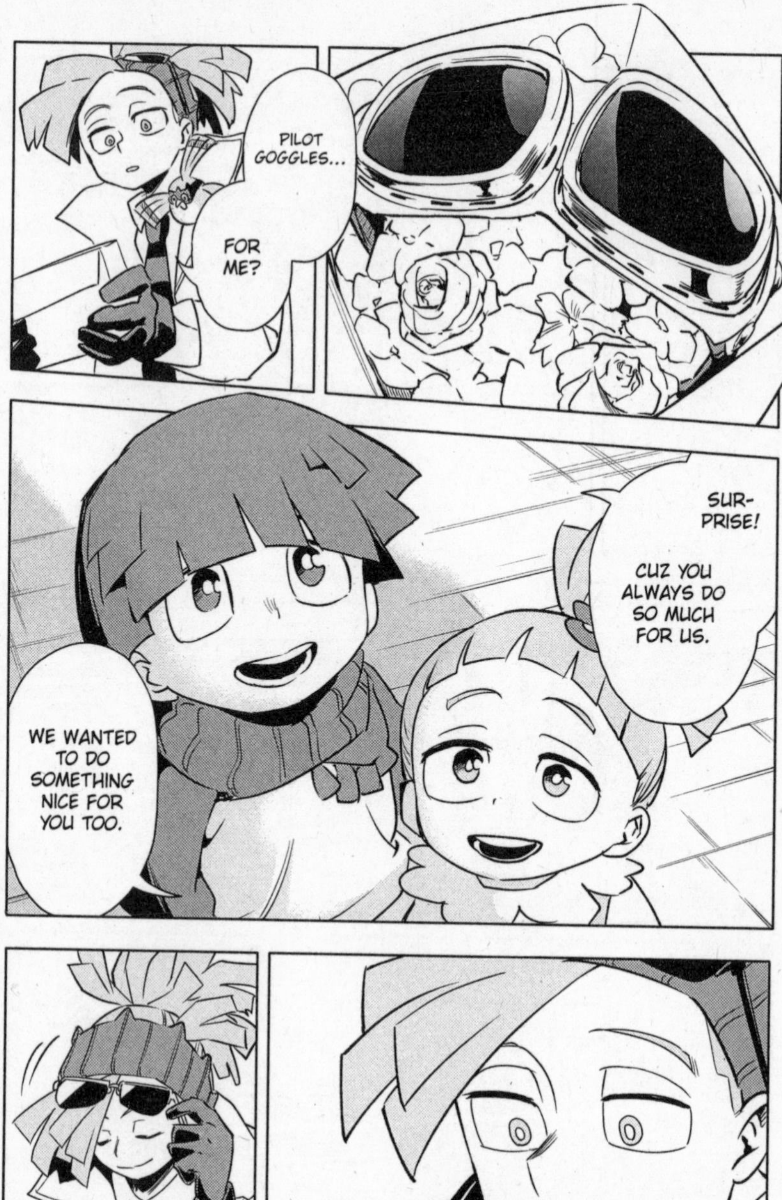
PILOT GOGGLES...
FOR ME?
SUR-PRISE!
CUZ YOU ALWAYS DO SO MUCH FOR US.
WE WANTED TO DO SOMETHING NICE FOR YOU TOO.

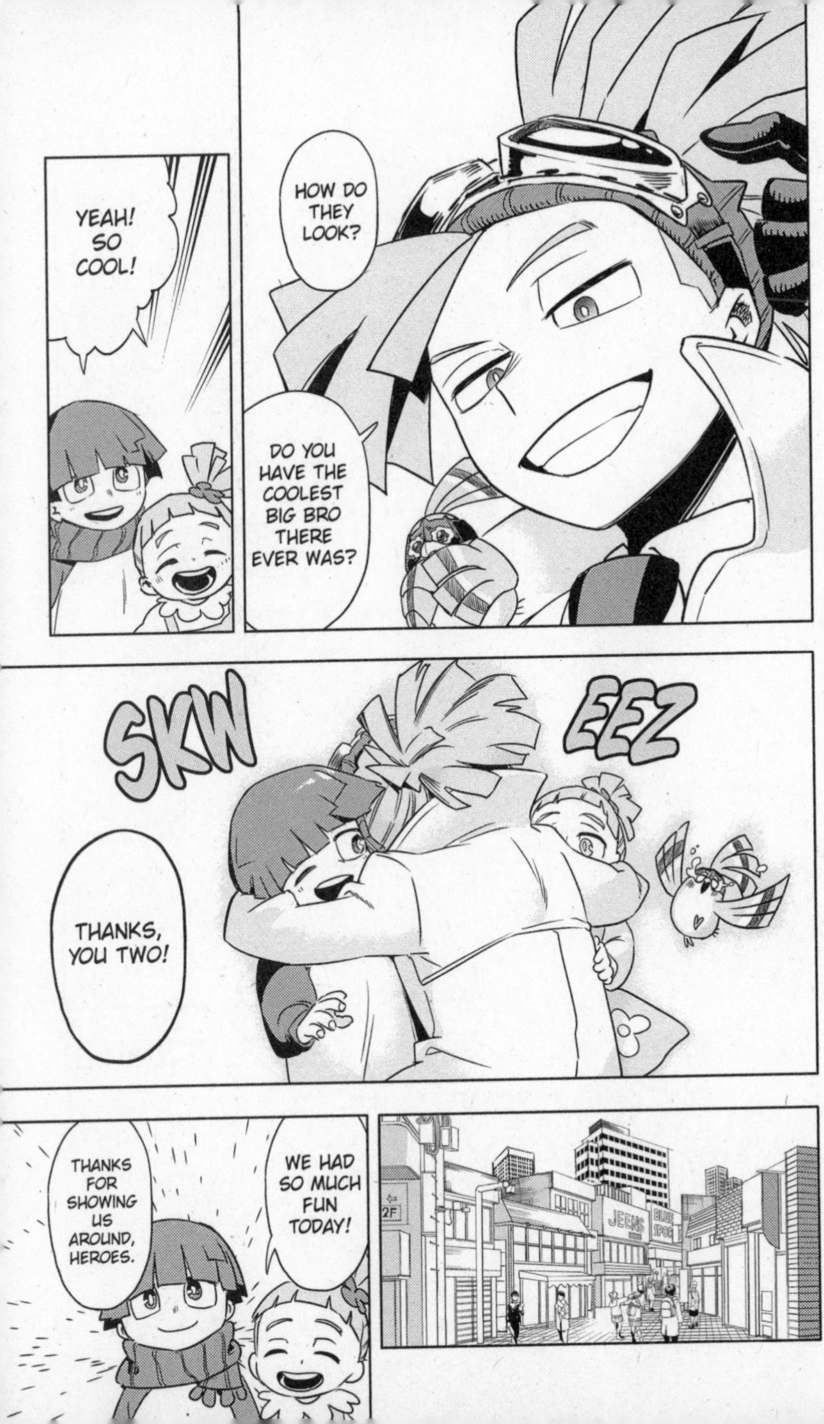
HOW DO THEY LOOK?
DO YOU HAVE THE COOLEST BIG BRO THERE EVER WAS?
YEAH! SO COOL!
SKW
EEZ
THANKS, YOU TWO!
2F
JEENS
BLUE
WE HAD SO MUCH FUN TODAY!
THANKS FOR SHOWING US AROUND, HEROES.

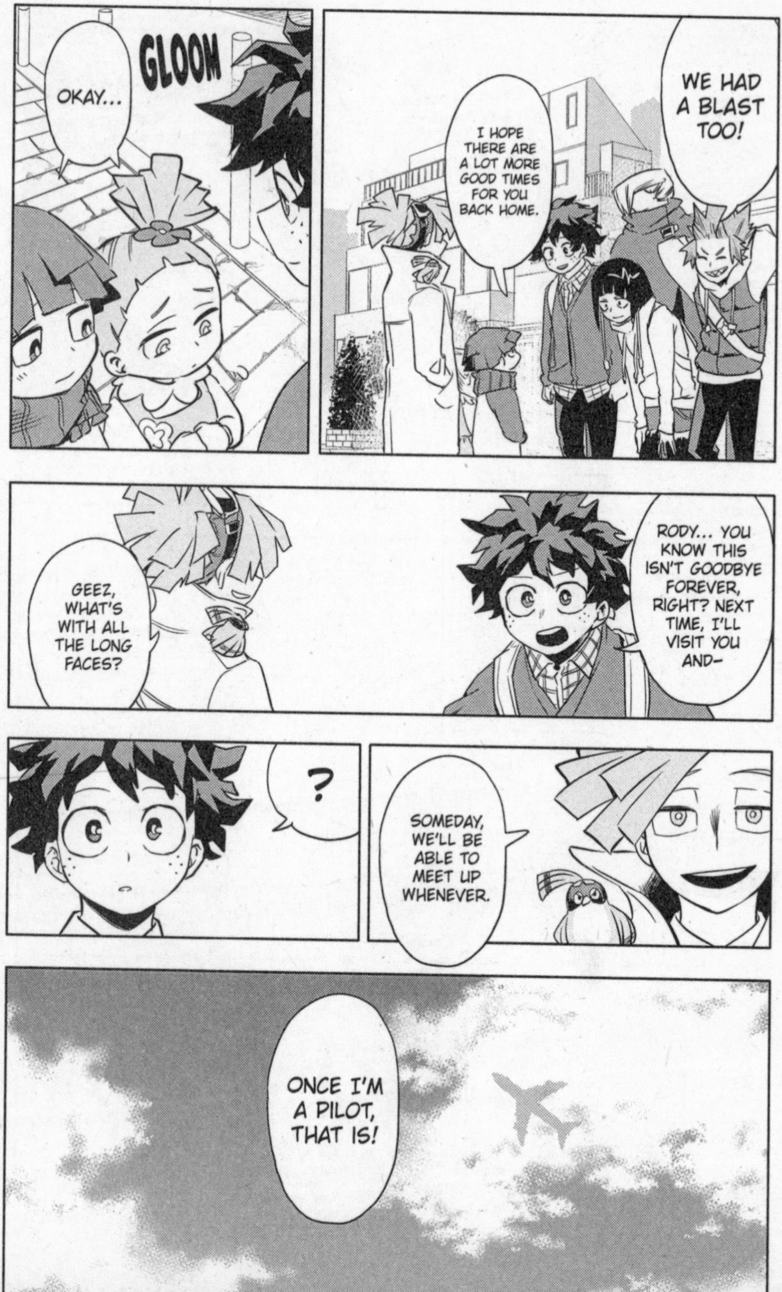
WE HAD A BLAST TOO!
I HOPE THERE ARE A LOT MORE GOOD TIMES FOR YOU BACK HOME.
GLOOM
OKAY...
RODY... YOU KNOW THIS ISN'T GOODBYE FOREVER, RIGHT? NEXT TIME, I'LL VISIT YOU AND—
GEEZ, WHAT'S WITH ALL THE LONG FACES?
SOMEDAY, WE'LL BE ABLE TO MEET UP WHENEVER.
?
ONCE I'M A PILOT, THAT IS!

YOU'RE READING THE WRONG WAY!

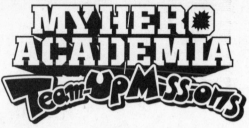

MY HERO ACADEMIA
Team-Up Missions

My Hero Academia: Team-Up Missions reads from right to left, starting in the upper-right corner. Japanese is read from right to left, meaning that action, sound effects, and word-balloon order are completely reversed from English order.

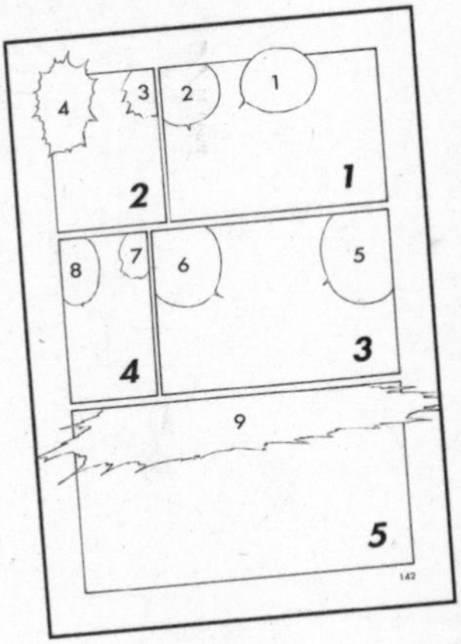

1
2
3
4
1
2
5
6
7
8
3
4
9
5
142

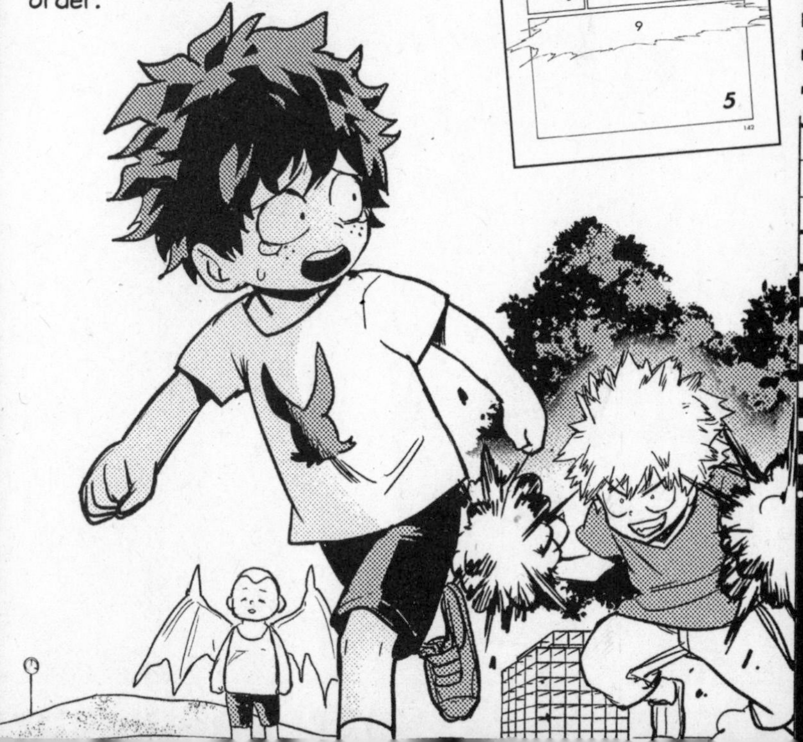

WHAT IF MISSION 14

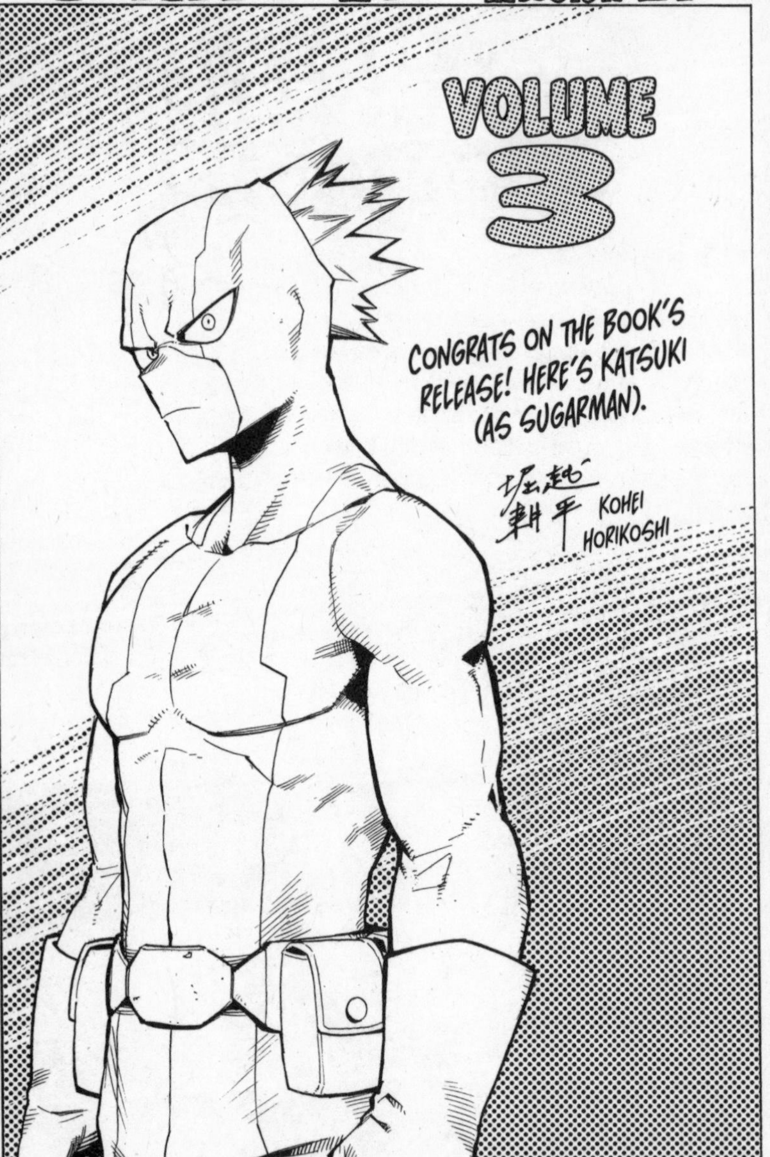
VOLUME 3
CONGRATS ON THE BOOK'S RELEASE! HERE'S KATSUKI (AS SUGARMAN).
堀越耕平
KOHEI HORIKOSHI

MESSAGE from KOHEI HORIKOSHI

AFTERWORD

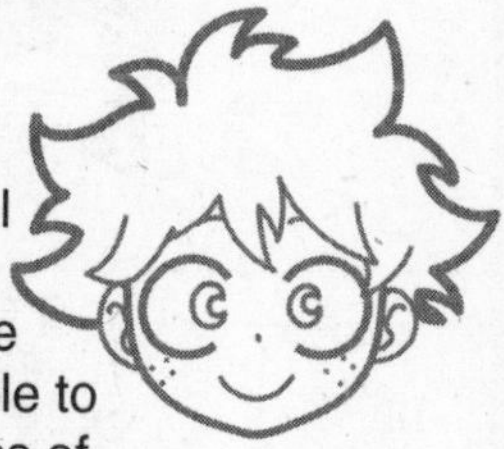

This has been volume 3. A book of low-key, peaceful stories that contrast with the grim material over in the main series. I have many people to thank for the continued success of this spin-off, including everyone involved in its production, Horikoshi Sensei himself (who takes time out of his busy schedule to supervise), and all you readers out there.

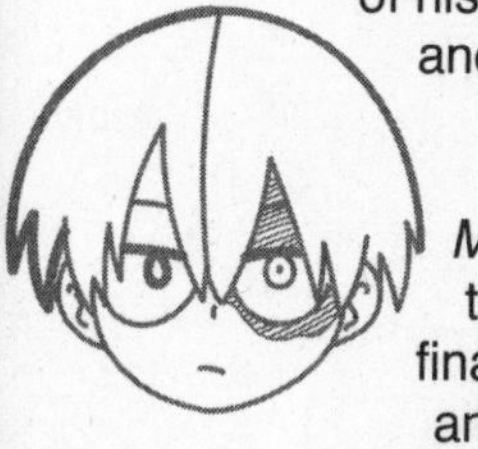

Over in the main *My Hero Academia* series, the story has entered the final act, with explosive twists and turns all over the place! Meanwhile, I'm working hard to make *Team-Up Missions* an exciting, worthy member of the *My Hero Academia* expanded universe!

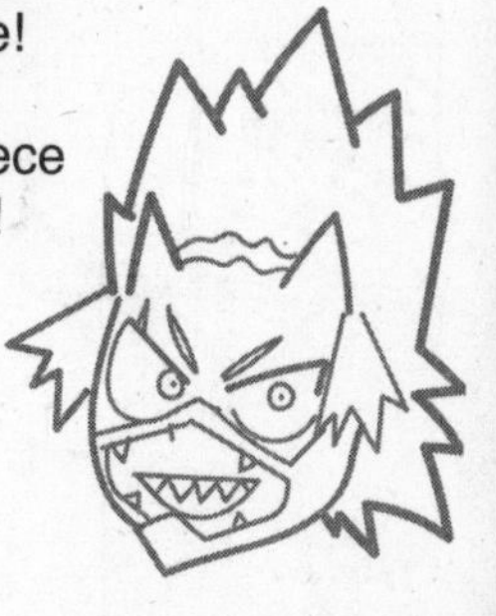

To end this book, we have a piece of art from Horikoshi Sensei! Thank you for that!

And I'll see all of you in volume 4!

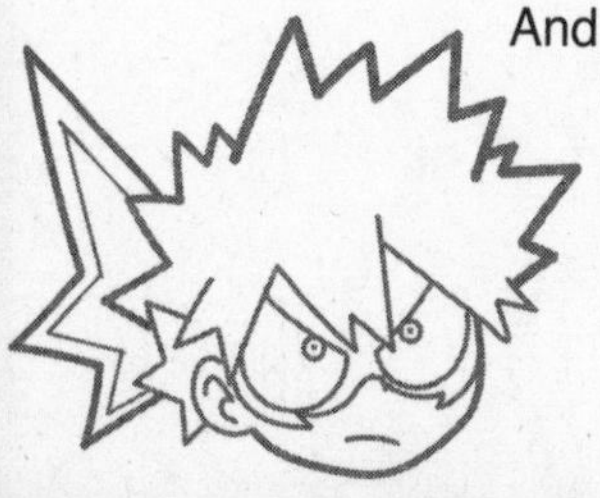

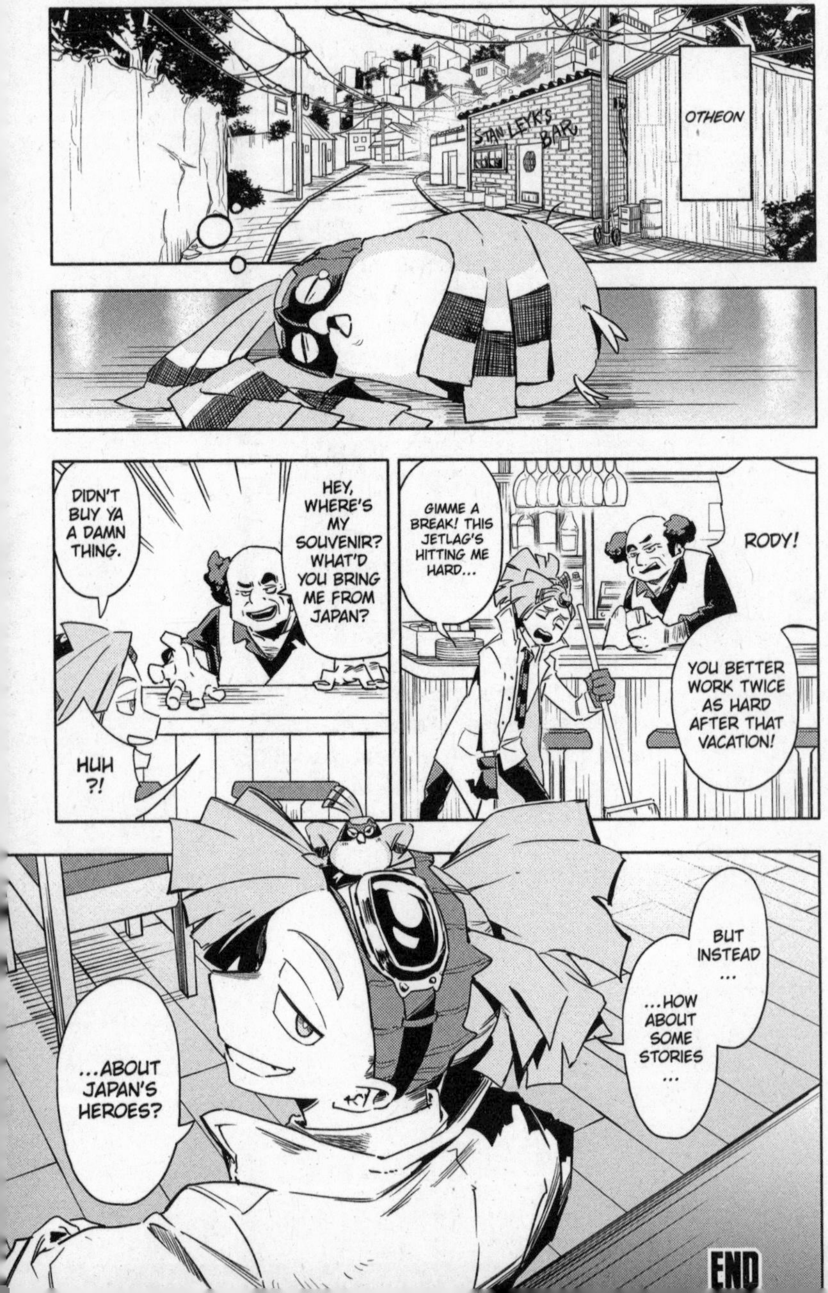
OTHEON
STANLEYK'S BAR
RODY!
GIMME A BREAK! THIS JETLAG'S HITTING ME HARD...
YOU BETTER WORK TWICE AS HARD AFTER THAT VACATION!
HEY, WHERE'S MY SOUVENIR? WHAT'D YOU BRING ME FROM JAPAN?
DIDN'T BUY YA A DAMN THING.
HUH ?!
BUT INSTEAD ...
...HOW ABOUT SOME STORIES ...
...ABOUT JAPAN'S HEROES?
END